D1608293

ITALIAN MOVIE
GODDESSES

STEFANO MASI   ENRICO LANCIA

ITALIAN MOVIE
GODDESSES

Over 80 of the Greatest Women
in Italian Cinema

GREMESE

Acknowledgements:
The Authors and Publisher sincerely thank Armando Giuffrida for the precious photographs and film-bills lent from his personal archives. Also special thanks to Marina Calviello and Cesare Frioni of the Centro Studi Cinematografico, and Luigi Morra for some of the photos. Many thanks also for the photographs courtesy of Angelo Frontoni, Vittorio Martinelli and Evelina Nazzari lent from their personal archives.

On the cover:
Sophia Loren, Ornella Muti *(left)*, and Gina Lollobrigida *(right)*

Cover:
Photos by Angelo Frontoni

Jacket design:
Fabrizio Patucchi

Layout:
Fortunato Romani

Photocomposition and photolithography:
Graphic Art 6 s.r.l. – Rome – Italy

Printed and bound by:
Atena s.r.l. – Rome – Italy

English translation:
Lucia Alma Braconi, Charles Nopar, Lenore Rosenberg

Edited by:
Sandra Tokunaga

First edition published in English translation by:
© 1997 GREMESE INTERNATIONAL s.r.l.
P.O. Box 14335 – 00149 Rome

ISBN 88-7301-071-7

CONTENTS

PALE STARS OF THE DAWN

1930: pictures can finally talk. They even talk in Fascist Italy where up on the silver screen Mussolini grows in stature declaiming great military feats and imperial destinies.

The movie *La canzone dell'amore* [Love song] (1930) starring two twittering damsels, Dria Paola and Isa Pola, breaks box office records. A miracle! The lengthy crisis afflicting the Italian movie industry finally seems to be easing. The cure-all is sound, the chirping of words of love. Italy's ambition is to become an operetta: it yearns for melodies, carefree voices, sweetness…

The princesses of this new realm were certainly not the stars of silent pictures, ladened with glory, money, and years. The fragrance of the *fleurs du mal* was too strong, the passions too lacerating and literary. That style of stardom was now out of date.

According to the newspapers of the early thirties, even the expression "diva" had a shabby ring to it. No one was interested in seeing such improbable women, clad in long veils, lost in sighs and leaning against door frames. Enough of these women who trembled as if they had Parkinson's disease and buried their faces in bouquets of flowers as if to eat them. In Italy, as abroad, the advent of talking pictures cut the ground from under the stars of the previous generation.

The tune had changed and so had the names. Sometimes the voice did not prove to be as charming as the face. And during the first years of talking pictures, recording technology was so primitive and complicated that dubbing was out of the question. So, most of the stars of silent pictures retired. Some were forced out early as a result of the crisis in the Italian motion picture industry during the second half of the twenties. Others bowed out gracefully crowning their careers with fabulous marriages, like star Francesca Bertini who married Count Paul Cartier in 1921. Three years earlier, femme fatale Lyda Borelli (whom the then socialist Antonio Gramsci referred to as "a piece of primordial prehistoric humanity") had snared

herself the enormously wealthy Count Cini. By that time she was living in a princely residence in Venice on the Grand Canal.

The same fate awaited the extremely sexy Sicilian star, Pina Menichelli. She bid the movie world adieu at the beginning of the twenties after her marriage to Carlo Amato. Soava Gallone was yet another silent-film star to end her career prematurely. Of noble blood and Polish origin, she had been famous for tresses that fell to her ankles. Gallone became the wife of director Carmine Gallone and soon abandoned the set in 1930 to dedicate herself to raising a family.

Just a year earlier, Leda Gys, the Mary Pickford of Italian cinema, also deserted the screen. In 1919 she married the resourceful Gustavo Lombardo, founder of the distribution company Titanus. Her son, Goffredo Lombardo, would eventually become one of Italy's most powerful tycoons of the postwar years and producer of *Il Gattopardo* (1963) (*The Leopard*).

Many other stars of the period were lost in the mists of time, including Diana Karenne, of Ukrainian origin, considered the Asta Nielson of Italian silent movies. The destiny of others was fairly dull, like Mary Cléo Tarlarini, whom the talkies transformed into an obscure character actress (she appeared in *La donna perduta* [The lost woman] in 1940, and then in a few other rare pictures).

Queen of the silent movies, Francesca Bertini.

Francesca Bertini

Lyda Borelli's adieu to the cinema was final. Bertini's wasn't. "The Countess Cartier Is Once Again Francesca Bertini" announced the authoritative magazine, *Cinema Illustrazione*, in the fall of 1930. The body was still in good shape, though the engine was slowing down.

Italian moviegoers could finally hear her tiny voice, a little high-pitched yet passable. The former diva shot *La femme d'une nuit* [Woman for a night] (1931) in a double version: the French version, directed by the former master of the avant garde Marcel L'Herbier, and the Italian version by the promising Amleto Palermi.

The era of silent pictures was over, but Francesca Bertini was still living in a state of self-adoration. She tried to foster a cult that no longer had any foundation: she was forty-two and still a femme fatale. And more than anything else, she was a leading lady. Unfortunately, however, she was having a hard time finding roles that satisfied her ego. In 1944 she joined the cast of *Dora o le spie* [Dora or the spies] that director Raffaello Matarazzo shot in Spain. She was over fifty at the time and still a beautiful, alluring woman.

Later on, Elena Vitiello, alias Francesca Bertini, allowed herself other sporadic appearances in the Italian cinema. In 1976, over eighty and reduced to a shadow of her former self, she played the role of a nun-aunt in Bernardo Bertolucci's colossal *Novecento* (1976) *(1900),* a film that, in many respects, recalls the extravagant productions of the century's first decades.

Maria Jacobini

Along with Letizia Quaranta, another bright star of the silent pictures was the female lead in the cast of *La scala* [The stairs] (1931), Maria Jacobini. Here she plays the role of a lawyer's wife, distraught with emotional problems and overcome by the death of her daughter. During the thirties and forties she had played a series of intensely passionate roles (Lucrezia Borgia, Beatrice Cenci, and others). Talking pictures made their appearance when she was already forty, after which she would have to be satisfied playing the role of mother. She, however, was one of the very few silent picture stars who was able to continue appearing in starring roles. Moreover, the lovely Jacobini, niece of a cardinal who was the Minister of State for Pope Leo XIII, was also the lifelong companion of Gennaro Righelli, who directed the first Italian talking picture, *La canzone dell'amore*. Righelli gave her the role of the mature leading lady in the 1931

Maria Jacobini, from leading lady of the silent movies to obscure character actress in the 1930s.

comedy *Patatrac* where she plays the role of Mara Di Faggio, an attractive married woman, conquered by the wooing of an incorrigible dandy, the Count Aragosta, played by Armando Falconi.

Righelli only directed his wife Maria in two or three movies during the thirties, although the decade as a whole was a successful one for Jacobini. Her acting style, entirely lacking in frills and histrionics, was fitting for the era of talking pictures. Her voice, trained during her years of theater, was good. But after 1931, Jacobini had a difficult time finding roles of any standing and was one of the few stars of silent pictures who managed to make the transition from leading lady to supporting roles. Before this metamorphosis, however, she still starred in a few films that made full use of her charms, such as Napoleon's wife in *Le educande di Saint-Cyr* [The schoolgirls of Saint-Cyr] (1939) a delightful nineteenth-century fresco directed by Righelli. In the comedy *Gli uomini non sono ingrati* [Men are not ungrateful] (1937) she plays the first of her mother roles, with a tough-looking Isa Pola, more a young woman than a little girl, as her daughter.

Twice, Maria Jacobini plays the mother of a great composer: in *Melodie eterne* [Eternal melodies] (1940) she is Anna Maria Mozart, mother of the sublime Amadeus, and in *Giuseppe Verdi* (1938), the cautious mother of the great Italian musician. But aside from small roles in movies by established directors such as Gallone, Birgnone, Neufeld, Chiarini, Zampa, and Castellani, Maria Jacobini also trained an entire generation of actresses. From 1938 to 1943 she taught at the Centro Sperimentale di Cinematografia, the experimental center of filmmaking set up by Mussolini to train the artistic and technical personnel of the emergent Italian movie industry.

EVERYBODY'S LADY

Isa Miranda

What was it that everyone said about Isa Miranda during the thirties? That she was the only actress in Italy with the right to physical defects. And that was simply because she had none. Her talents as an actress, the determination with which she poured her enigmatic charm into her characters, made her a sort of Marlene Dietrich, generated by Fascist Cinecittà.

More than any other Italian actress, Isa was the exemplar of what it meant to be photogenic. At first glance, hers was a transparent everyday beauty but one which exploded into a fourth dimension on the motion picture screen. Miranda had the

ability to endow her characters with a capacity of expression unknown to other actresses of the Fascist years. She filled the screen as only the stars of Hollywood could do.

She was not the most pleasing of them. Maria Denis, Irasema Dilian, and Mariella Lotti had likeability to spare and based their success on a twittering, birdlike charm. Isa on the other hand came from more aristocratic stock; she was one of those creatures who appeared to glide above the ground.

Ines Isabella Sampietro was born on July 5, 1909 to a family of farmers from the Lomellina region of Lombardy in northern Italy. When she was only twelve she left school to work in a factory. She later worked

Isa Miranda is "everybody's lady" in **La signora di tutti** *(1934).*

Isa Miranda as Velia, a Roman patrician woman, in the Fascist spectacular The Defeat of Hannibal *(1937).*

as a salesgirl, a model and a secretary. At the same time, she studied acting at the Accademia dei Filodrammatici (the Acting Academy), making her debut at Milan's Arcimboldi Theater in a comedy entitled *Le tre ragazze poco vestite* [The three scantily clad girls]. Legend has it that Isa's first success occurred the night she forgot to wear panties under her tutu... but make no mistake about it, Isa Miranda was a very serious young woman.

Her leap to stardom was the movie *La signora di tutti* (1934) where she plays the "everybody's lady" of the title and which also marked publisher Angelo Rizzoli's entry into the world of moviemaking. The circulation of his weekly *Novella* rose from 180,000 to 250,000 copies, thanks to *La signora di tutti* by Salvator Gotta, a novel it had serialized. The novel inevitably had to become a film.

At the beginning of 1934, *Novella* ran a contest to find a leading lady. The story goes that Angelo Rizzoli himself chose Isa Miranda from thousands of candidates.

She plays the role of the movie star Gaby Doriot, the "everybody's lady" who is found lifeless in a pool of blood in her luxury apartment. Why did she kill herself? In a lengthy flashback, director Max Ophüls leads us into this woman's past, to the time when Gaby was called simply Gabriella Murge. At school, one of her teachers kills himself for love of her. An excellent beginning. Later she goes to work for a respectable bourgeois family where her appeal only sows death and destruction. The head of the family goes mad over her, neglecting the family's factory, plunging into bankruptcy, and ending up in prison. His paralyzed wife hurls herself down the stairs in her wheelchair. Their son Roberto also falls in love with Gabriella but despises her for her affair with his father. Released from prison, the industrialist goes to see a film starring Gabriella, now Gaby, a famous movie star. Leaving the movie theater distraught, he is hit by a car. When Gaby tries to win back Roberto's love, she discovers that the young man has married her sister Anna. Desperate, she kills herself.

Put a popular novel into the hands of a director as fine as Max Ophüls and you have

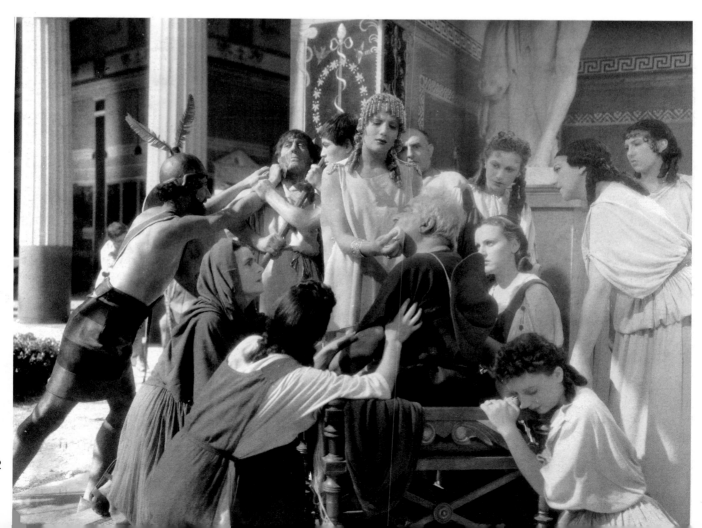

a great drama that will go down in film history. The theme song by Ruggero Lerchi and Daniele Amphitheatrof accompanies the credits of a movie destined to become one of the mainstays of the new Italian cinema. Isa is a revelation. Her acting style, and slightly monotonous voice, are reminiscent of the great actresses of the silver screen, from Greta Garbo to Marlene Dietrich.

Isa was at ease in any narrative situation. In a panorama of actresses who continued to display some of the histrionics of silent pictures, Miranda never overacted. Elegant, fatale, desperate, winking, painful, anguished: to express three lines of adjectives in a page of screenplay, all she needed was the simplest of glances. She was a modern actress, aware of the expressive amplification produced by close-ups and sound.

The second proof of her versatility came with *Come le foglie* [As the leaves] (1934) by director Mario Camerini based on the play of the same name by Giacosa. She explained, "In the film by Max Ophüls, *La signora di tutti*, I was an elegant blond. A femme fatale. But Camerini wanted me dark, modest, simple, to make me forget that first character completely. He felt that it was the only way for me to portray the candid character of Nennele."

Miranda (Nennele) plays the daughter of a wealthy industrialist overwhelmed by a financial crisis, the greed of his spendthrift wife, and the pettiness of his eldest son who is a card shark. Nennele is the angel of that house. Miranda's piercing eyes stare out of the well-scrubbed face of the girl with the short hair. The former "everybody's lady" is unrecognizable in this role. There is a great deal of dignity in this young, upper middle-class woman who makes the best of a bad situation. Nennele gives up the privileges of her class and resigns herself to a life of hard work. But in her new working-class life she maintains bearing and elegance.

Isa owed her success primarily to her own talent, but part of the credit was also due to young producer Alfredo Guarini, her husband, who carefully directed her career, just as Carlo Ponti would do for Sophia Loren and Dino De Laurentis for Silvana Mangano after the war. Miranda first acted in a motion picture produced by Guarini in 1935, *Passaporto rosso* [Red passport]. It is quite possible, however, that he was in the background even before that.

Passaporto rosso added a new page to the album of Miranda's great heroines. Here she plays the role of an emigrant left alone after her father's death. An unscrupulous character coerces her into performing as a singer in a sinister South American dive.

After the success of this movie, Guarini worked to make Miranda an international

Before going to Hollywood, Isa Miranda was offered the leading role in Pierre Chenal's Il fu Mattia Pascal *(1937). From left to right Olga Solbelli, Isa Miranda, Enrico Glori and Cesare Zoppetti.*

star. It was an ambitious project. The Italian cinema had just emerged from a long crisis and none of its new actresses seemed capable of crossing the national borders. Guarini's first target was the German market, relatively accessible given the ideological affinity between Mussolini's Italy and the Third Reich. The second was Hollywood.

Between 1936 and 1938, Isa became Italy's greatest star and appeared almost exclusively in important productions aimed at foreign markets. Placed under directors such as Karl Heinz Martin, Pierre Chenal, and Viktor Tourjansky, Miranda was speeding her way towards the international public.

But she was also in the cast of the colossal film, being produced by the Fascist regime to give new polish to the myth of ancient Rome, *Scipione L'Africano* (1937) *(The Defeat of Hannibal)*. She plays the role of Velia, a Roman patrician, the fiancée of the young soldier Arunte. Hers was an inevitably decorative role in the universe of this male-dominated movie. In this historical picture-postcard movie, Velia shows off an already Hollywood-style glamour, with an improbable coiffure of blonde banana curls.

Her participation in *The Defeat of Hannibal* was merely the price she had to pay to the Fascist regime to receive her permit for the States. In an interview given just a few weeks before her departure, Isa defended herself, "I adore Italy. I'll never become Americanized: I'll take a little bit of Italy with me at all costs, in spite of everyone, even Roosevelt and Ford. I could never become American! I don't think I could ever adapt to Taylorism..."

Isa left Italy on August 26, 1937 aboard the oceanliner Rex, a couple of days after the gala premier of *The Defeat of Hannibal* at the Fifth Exhibition of Cinematographic Art in Venice, where the movie won the Mussolini Cup.

As Miranda cruised the Atlantic, Paramount's promotional machinery was already grinding into gear to build the image of the newly imported star. They were going to sell Isa by underlining her resemblance to the divine Marlene Dietrich. She went to live in a house in pure Mediterranean style at 7277 Hillside Avenue, in a then remote area of Hollywood. She brought an Italian maid with her, but the strategic role in the household was played by Mrs. Morris, her English teacher.

Robert Florey directed her in a melodrama set during World War I, *Hotel Imperial* (1939). Outfitted by the great costume designer Edith Head, her features softened by makeup and the camera, Miranda looks like the twin sister of Marlene Dietrich in *Shanghai Express*.

Once off the set she kept away from society, and did not participate in the *dolce vita* of Beverley Hills or Malibu. "She's not fond of parties or receptions." In the language of Hollywood diplomacy, this expression underlined the fact that the actress from abroad did not belong and she wasn't putting down roots.

After passing the test of melodrama with neither glory nor disgrace, Paramount tried her out in comedy in *Adventure in Diamonds* (1940). Here she played the part of a diamond smuggler in South Africa. With George Brent at her side, Miranda has charm, allure, elegance and sex-appeal. But the philosophy of the studio system kept her from showing her talent: forced to be no more than the imitation of American stars, Miranda was unconvincing.

She ended her two-year stay in the States on December 14, 1939.

The Rex carried Miranda back to an Italy more isolated and self-absorbed than ever. It was inevitable that the Regime did not welcome their prodigal daughter with open arms, that it was suspicious of a product "Made in the U.S.A." Even Hollywood's motion pictures were forbidden on Italian screens: Isa's two American films did not escape the bans of the severe law.

"In Italy," said Miranda, "a sad surprise was awaiting me. My government considered me a reprobate. A letter from the Fascist Minister of Culture ordered newspapers not to write about me and the Minister of the Interior ordered that my passport was not to be renewed."

In addition, rumor was that she had grown up in a family with socialist leanings. From the heights to the depths. It was almost like starting all over again. She managed it thanks to Guarini who, for her

Malombra (1942) and its eerie protagonist.

sake, cast himself in the unusual role of director. He directed her in three movies, the most infelicitous of which was probably *Senza cielo* [Skyless] (1940) where Miranda played the role of a female Tarzan, among pasteboard palm tress and Italians with blacked faces.

The star that Alfredo Guarini patiently rebuilt was still a splendid actress. But now everything was hard for her. It was almost dangerous to include her in the cast of a movie. During those years of nationalism and xenophobia, she had to pay for the non-Italian nature of her image. She often played characters who were French, German, and even Polish. Not even Hollywood, where subtlety concerning national stereotypes was never a primary concern, had given her Italian characters to play. Moreover, her much vaunted resemblance to Dietrich was proof that Miranda did not look Mediterranean.

She had never really been a politically aligned actress, not even in the days of *The Defeat of Hannibal.* But during the war she was openly boycotted by the Fascist regime. In spite of this, she managed to obtain starring roles in two very important movies, *Malombra* and *Zazà* (1942), masterpieces of the so-called *realismo calligrafico*, or formal realism.

Wrapped in the gloomy robes designed by Maria De Matteis, Marina di Malombra, the mad marquise, is one of the loveliest creatures of the cinema of the forties. Obsessed by a book she has read on metempsychosis, she is convinced she is the reincarnation of an ancestor. Ecstatic, pale and exquisite, Isa is a magnificent angel of death. Her elegance takes on the colors of insanity.

The singer Zazà, the radiant heroine of the movie of the same name directed by Renato Castellani, is far removed from the ectoplasmic grace of the marquise of Malombra. Once again, Isa is cast in the role of a non-Italian, the famous smoldering star of the Alhambra cabaret, as aggressive as Lili Marlene. She is transformed, however, when she falls in love with the young, goodlooking, well-to-do Parisian Albert Dufresne. Zazà is unaware of the fact that her lover already has a wife: the discovery is terrible, but she bears the pain with dignity. With tones of intense truthfulness, Miranda restores moral standing to a strong, fervent woman who is suddenly made vulnerable by a man's betrayal. A genuine metamorphosis. The feminine arrogance of the singer and performer is shattered by love. Zazà, capricious, unreliable, self-important, becomes docile and anxious. And destiny strikes without pity.

As in *Malombra*, in *Zazà* too, the talented costume designer Maria De Matteis dresses

Miranda, who here wears spectacular gowns made up of trains, veils, ostrich feathers, gewgaws and voluminous skirts. The final touch is a crowning star that Zazà shows off in her rebellious curls.

A stage of Miranda's career ends with this fragile Zazà, reminiscent of the Belle Epoque. After the end of the war she is one of the few actresses who still has credibility as a star. The modern style of her acting and an appeal that was never based on youth, allow her to experience a new, stirring season as an actress.

But Isa remains essentially the great romantic actress of the Fascist era. It is said that she was the only actress capable of weeping without glycerine. All she had to do was concentrate. With her sophisticated style, Miranda never had the unconditional support of her Italian audience who seemed to prefer the fresh-faced image of the girl-next-door.

Isa Miranda in the title role of Zazà *(1942) as a sentimental and fragile cabaret singer.*

[see also p. 144]

THE THREE MUSKETEERS OF THE REGIME

Elsa Merlini

The biggest novelty that 1931 gave Italian moviegoers was a girl from Trieste with the face of a little rascal and a contagious smile. Elsa Tscheliessnig, Elsa Merlini's original name, had the innocent air of a clown and the charm of a shy little girl. Her first movie, *La segretaria privata (Sunshine Susie)*, swept Italian cinema clean of the stereotyped femininity of its stars.

Sophisticated comedy in the midst of Mussolini's gray Italy: it was as if someone had suddenly opened a window. The morning air felt fresh and sweet. It was a new day for Italian cinema.

Elsa was born in Trieste on July 26, 1904 and studied acting with Luigi Rasi in Florence. From the middle of the twenties the young actress was a member of Annibale Ninchi's theatrical company. In Naples she played the part of Scilla in *Glauco* by Morselli and earned her first acclaim acting in *Il giorno* [The day] by Matilde Serao. Then she was engaged by Alfredo De Sanctis, and eventually became leading lady in the company of Renato Cialente. Elsa was also Cialente's wife for many years.

The perfect couple of 1930s cinema: Elsa Merlini and Nino Besozzi.

In 1929, when Vera Vergani abandoned the stage, Dario Niccodemi invited Elsa Merlini to replace her, alongside actors such as Stefano Tofano, Luigi Cimara and Nino Besozzi.

In those years of crisis for the Italian theater, Niccodemi had a marvelous idea: a variety show with great theatrical actors. This was the beginning of the musical fantasy *Triangoli* [Triangles] starring Besozzi, Cimara, and a sparkling Elsa Merlini who also revealed her talent as a singer. The success of the review paved the way for a series of lighthearted performances. *Fanny e i suoi domestici* [Fanny and her servants], *La buona fata* [The good fairy], and *La maestrina* [The schoolteacher] all consolidated Merlini's popularity as a comic actress.

Elsa came to motion pictures in 1931, carried on the wave of fame. Italy's silver screens had only started talking a few months earlier, and now variety and motion pictures could intermingle. Just as in Hollywood, Italy too hoped that a new form of comedy could pull the movie industry out of its slump. Moreover, *La canzone dell'amore* [Love song] (1930), Italy's first talking picture, full of shrill little voices and cheery melodies, had been greeted enthusiastically.

But with *Sunshine Susie* (1931) director Goffredo Alessandrini wanted to do something else: he tried to bring the captivating narrative rhythms of a variety show to the screen. Elsa Merlini was the key to this project. Miss Elsa Lorenzi is Merlini's first movie character. Once the opening credits are over, she gets off the train that has brought her into the city and absent-mindedly makes her way through a railway station that smacks heavily of art deco and pasteboard. Like all good girls from the sticks, she settles into a boarding house populated by staunch young women with only two desires in life: a good office job and a nice young man with (as the song went) "a thousand lire a month," a tidy sum for the times. Elsa too needs a job. She goes knocking on the doors of dozens of companies. Otello, an errand boy at the International Bank, has a word with his demanding boss and Elsa finds herself recruited in the vast army of typists behind their

barrage of chattering typewriters. Tap tip tap. Music!

What could be more wonderful for a small-town girl in 1931 than a job as a typist? As she steps out onto the street, Elsa is bursting with joy. Suddenly the movie is a musical with whirling rhythms; the sidewalk turns into a stage and Merlini warbles: "*Oh! Come son felice, felice, felice!*" (Oh! How happy, happy I am...)

1929 was only a couple of years behind and the spectre of the Great Depression still hovered over the country. You needed to get busy. Work was precious, and hard to find.

This was a time when everyone was looking for a job to make ends meet. Young women of marriageable age put aside their embroidery and piano lessons to take up the typewriter. Typist, stenographer and bookkeeper became the conventional jobs of Italian working girls, the maidens of a new regime: bureaucracy. And while their fingers glided busily over the keys, their heads were free for romantic daydreams: a young manager, handsome, courteous and ready for love – with honorable intentions, it goes without saying... Cinderella and Prince Charming, this time in offices... including the office where Elsa Lorenzi (Elsa Merlini) was working.

Her boss, Berri, is charmed by Elsa's glib tongue, when she mistakes him for a simple employee. A comedy of errors with the inevitable happy ending on the horizon. Glasses of champagne, swirling skirts and Elsa's winning smile are the recipe for this Italian version of the sophisticated comedy.

Alongside Merlini in *Sunshine Susie* are two great actors of the Niccodemi Theatrical Company: Nino Besozzi, the banker Berri, and Sergio Tofano, the errand boy Otello, constantly entangled in Elsa's antics. All the while she chirps like a canary, wrinkles up her nose, squints in a nearsighted stare and pushes rebellious curls off her forehead.

Merlini brought those winning smiles, those sudden impulsive outbursts and lively spirit, that were the basis of her theatrical success, to the movies. She still needed to learn how to modulate her gestures in front of a camera. She sometimes seemed to go too far, forgetting how close-ups magnified an actor's mannerisms and movements.

The thirties began in triumph for Elsa Merlini but they ended quietly. She decided she was better off in the theater to which she ultimately returned, leaving motion pictures behind her. Moreover, the word was that she had become capricious and demanding, insisting on playing roles unsuitable for her image.

The next time she would join the cast of a film was in 1951 when the Italian motion picture industry was spurred by no less a political power than Giulio Andreotti, then undersecretary to the Presidency of the Council of Ministers for the Performing Arts.

The idea was to produce a movie that would give Elsa Merlini the chance to make a comeback in a starring role. And that, apparently, is how *Cameriera bella presenza offresi* [Maid available excellent appearance] (1951) all began.

Elsa Merlini in the double role of mother and daughter in the brilliant "Hungarian" comedy L'ultimo ballo *(1941).*

Elisa Cegani

From the *Contessa di Parma* (1937) *(The Countess of Parma)* onwards, the muse of Alessandro Blasetti's filmmaking was Elisa Cegani, an actress from Turin with a stiff, disconcerting beauty. The movements of her slim body were nervous. Even her thin lips, so often curved in a sardonic smile, were tense. Any feeling at all could have been hidden behind that smile: treachery or reticence, a sense of superiority or acquiescence.

Born on June 10, 1911, Elisa belonged to the generation of actresses who had to wait until the second half of the thirties to earn their success. By then it was too late to make their mark on a decade hurtling towards war. Her film debut was supposed to have taken place in 1934. There were plans to have her star in a movie that Carl Theodor Dreyer was planning to shoot in Africa. But madness drove Dreyer from the set and Cegani, calling herself Elisa Sandri, appeared for the first time on the screen in Blasetti's *Aldebaran* (1935). In the female supporting role, with an excellent Evi Maltagliati in the starring role, Cegani plays Nora, the plain wife of a Navy officer.

Cegani proves to be much more suitable for epic rather than comedy films. On the other hand, from that moment on, Alessandro Blasetti turns her into his muse. After 1935, Blasetti makes few films without a role for her, just as there are few movies in which Elisa has other directors.

Cegani is bound to Blasetti with a common artistic destiny as well as a sentimental bond that can be sensed in the attention that the "director in boots" (so-called for his penchant for wearing boots on the set) pays her. Moreover, Elisa's beauty, defined as "solemn" by the journalists of the period, seems to fit the epic taste of Blasetti's motion pictures. Elisa is not fond of hearing herself described as "solemn"; she considers it a kind of insult.

Why was Blasetti with his boots so entranced by Elisa's beauty? Most certainly because she was anti-bourgeois, and abstract. She was far removed from the bright chirpy style found in the drawing rooms of the "white telephone" films, a key genre of the cinema of the Fascist era, characterized by make-believe situations, ostentatious settings and unbelievable romantic entanglements. Cegani is instead the ideal captain's woman in *Ettore Fieramosca*, where she plays Giovanna, duchess of Morreale.

The asexual noblewoman, dressed as high priestess of war, dreams of a husband-soldier able to crush the Spanish and French forces that besiege the sacred Italian soil. The wicked duke of Asti marries her through trickery but Giovanna finally finds in Fieramosca the Latin male she longs for. The bureaucrats of the Ministry of Popular Culture modelled the Italian vision of the motion picture industry along the lines of the Soviet approach. With her martial bearing, Cegani in *Ettore Fieramosca* reveals the synthetic beauty reminiscent of Soviet stars. It takes little effort to imagine her in the cast of *Alexander Nevsky* (1938), here shot from below according to the rhetoric of social realism with a flashing sky in the background, sword in hand, eyes gazing into the distance, warriorlike. If that isn't solemn…

Another role typical of Cegani is the one

Elisa Cegani's classic image: draped in quasi-religious costumes that revealed almost nothing of her body, as in Ettore Fieramosca *(1938).*

Blasetti gives her in *La corona di ferro* (1941) *(The Iron Crown)*, Cinecittà's symbolic fable of the thirties, a sort of fascist *Gone With the Wind* (1939). Here Elisa plays the role of the much-loved daughter of King Sedemondo. Once again Blasetti creates a female character to fit Cegani: Elisa, the pouting princess, is very unhappy. To bring her joy (and a husband), her father Sedemondo organizes a tournament, promising that the winner will have Elisa's hand and half of his kingdom.

Elisa Cegani is magnificent in the splendid costumes Marina Arcangeli designs for her, particularly in a close-up that shows her covered in jewels and her face hidden by a thin veil. A shower of pearls circles her neck, her gown is quilted with silver, her cloak decorated with arabesques, and on her head she wears a golden crown.

Nothing of her slim body is visible: all that can be seen are her eyes, her forehead and part of her face. Elisa adores clothing that shrouds her body almost completely. No other Italian actress had fewer décolletés. She continually wears garments that make her look like a nun, even when she isn't playing one. It is a harbinger of the role Alessandro Blasetti gives her at the end of the war in *Un giorno nella vita* (1946) *(A Day of Life)*. In *The Iron Crown*, Elisa's abstract beauty has an oriental flavor: she looks as if she has stepped right out of *A Thousand and One Nights*. She is beautiful but still glacial, particularly when she acts alongside the fiery Tundra, played by Luisa Ferida, a veritable tigress.

For Elisa, on the other hand, sensuality is quite foreign to her nature; had there been an Italian Hammer Films during the thirties, Cegani would have been an excellent lady vampire!

Elisa has few moments of on-screen laughter. She is a dramatic actress par excellence. She had a serious, mature and resigned air about her, and she seemed old even when she was young. And yet this sober anti-diva was an important model of fascist femininity: hers was the beauty of austerity. She had beauty matched with sobriety, and the ability to repress any impulse she might feel in the name of the right cause.

[see also p. 149]

Paola Barbara

Admired for her elegance, Paola Barbara was the Italian actress who could wear any costume, contemporary or period, with the greatest ease.

It was natural for her to give out fashion tips on the pages of current magazines. Here is what she suggested to her readers for a rainy day: "Shop windows are full of hundreds of raincoats of all styles and colors. Try to choose one that is good for the rain but suitable for

the sun, too. If you already have a rain coat that you don't really like very much, try adding accessories to liven it up. But for heaven's sake, keep out of the way of those oil skins that one sees around so much and that make you look like a North Sea fisherman. And be careful about hoods! They are at the height of fashion but risky. While they can make you look as charming as Red Riding Hood, there are also a number of witches around..."

With her round face, full cheeks, dark red hair, large sensuous mouth, and the lazy walk of a house pet, Paola Barbara on the screen is maternal femininity incarnate.

Massimo Girotti and Elisa Cegani in **The Iron Crown** *(1941).*

Paola Barbara

hide their victims. Behind locked doors and walled up windows, it is a claustrophobic setting that nevertheless retains something of the luxury of a Grand Hotel. The poor heroine is utterly tormented at times, giving Paola Barbara the chance to show her talent in highly effective dramatic scenes.

Paola treats her disagreeable, resigned imprisoned comrades with firmness. She compels them to rebel against their jailers rather than to live a life of dread and she has the chance to act a remarkable scene resounding in political rebellion. *L'albergo degli assenti* is ostensibly set in England but it is easy to glimpse something of the Italian situation. The year is 1939 and discontent is growing in Fascist Italy.

Three years after her debut, Barbara was to be offered the most important character of her career: Maria Ferrante in *La peccatrice* [The sinner]. The most famous scriptwriters of the times: Luigi Chiarini, Umberto Barbaro, Francesco Pasinetti were engaged to create an intense character with a thousand twists to her personality. Thus was born a role redolent of realist literature, from Dostoevsky to Zola, from Verga to Mastriani.

Poor Maria Ferrante! A woman who has sunk into the moral abyss of a brothel, selling body and soul to the demon of debauchery. Paola Barbara's sensuality is transformed into suffering. We see her at the deathbed of an unfortunate companion, consumed by tuberculosis and fated to die behind the scenes of a sordid world of sex. Then Amleto Palermi tells us her story: seduced and abandoned by a dandy, she leaves her mother's house and is afraid to return.

The child born of her affair dies and Maria drifts aimlessly. She becomes a prostitute. She struggles to free herself from the shackles of transgression but is inescapably dragged back. She tries to lead a good life by seeking refuge with a family of farmers – but men lust after her. According to the ethics of the Fascist era, a fallen woman could never rise again.

Slightly heavy, with full lips and moist, sad eyes, high cheekbones and provocative curves, she resembles the women directed by Giuseppe De Santis during the neorealistic period. Paola Barbara was perfectly cast. In a number of scenes she appears without any makeup, a very rare occurrence for a time when screen beauty obeyed strict aesthetic rules.

Paola Barbara in *La peccatrice* is a forerunner of neorealism. But it is almost impossible not to think of Clara Calamai in *Ossessione* (1943) [Obsession]. Paola Barbara recalled that Luchino Visconti initially offered *her* the role of Massino Girotti's diabolic mistress in the film. "Unfortunately, my husband and I were leaving for Spain."

Ossessione was not the only big opportunity Barbara missed; her destiny seemed to have always run parallel to that of the languid

Born in Rome on July 22, 1912 of a Roman mother and Sicilian father, her real name was Paolina Prato. She lived alone with her mother who moved first to Florence and then to Prato. As a child she liked to cut out photos of Francesca Bertini from the newspaper. From the time she was little she had only one ambition: to be an actress.

After studying acting in Florence at the school of Edi Picello, she headed right for motion pictures. In 1936 she starred in *Amazzoni bianche* [White Amazons], a movie financed by her family and directed by Gennaro Righelli. In the cast, along with Barbara, there were some other lovely young girls, all of them more or less newcomers like her. Two of them, Doris Duranti and Luisa Ferida, would have meteoric careers.

Barbara plays her first real dramatic role in *L'albergo degli assenti* [The hotel of the missing]. In the film she is a young jobless woman who becomes the paid companion of a British heiress. The girl falls into the clutches of a gang that specializes in kidnappings on commission. The "hotel of the missing" of the title is an abandoned hotel where the criminals

Clara Calamai. In fact she was even initially offered the role of Ginevra in *La cena delle beffe* [The dinner of derision] (1941).

By now she is a big star. She receives a large number of offers to join the cast of historical movies, biographies and costume movies, from *Rossini* (1942), where she plays the part of Isabella Colbran, to *Il ponte dei sospiri* [The bridge of sighs] (1940) and from *Il bravo di Venezia* [The good man of Venice] (1941) to *Il re si diverte* (1941) *(The King's Jester)*. They are all roles of courtesans, based on a decorative model of feminine beauty and behavior.

A more important moment comes in the film *Confessione* [Confession] (1941) directed by Calzavara. Paola plays Luisa Tolnay, the mistress of Mayer, who runs a booth in an amusement park. Luisa is another doomed character who invests Paola Barbara with an air of French realism à la Marcel Carné.

On the set of *Confessione*, Barbara met the thirty-eight-year-old assistant director, Primo Zeglio, whom she soon married. They fled Italy together for Spain, thus avoiding the torment of the war and the temptation to join the Cinecittà of the Republic of Salò.

Luck was not with Paola Barbara. She came

into vogue at the end of the thirties and took a couple of years to prove what she could do. Then she missed two chances that would have set her on the path to stardom *(La cena delle beffe* and *Ossessione)*. And then, she never had time to enjoy the best years of her career.

In Spain, apart from the terrible *Accadde a Damasco* [It happened in Damascus] she made some good movies. But the Italian motion picture industry after the war considered her a mere revival, to be used accordingly.

[see also p. 146]

Paola Barbara, considered the "sinful woman" of Italian cinema, here with Aldo Silvani in La danza del fuoco *(1943).*

Paola Barbara and Aldo Silvani in Confessione *(1942).*

Four of the most popular sweethearts of Italy: Maria Denis, Assia Noris, Alida Valli and Mariella Lotti.

SWEETHEARTS OF ITALY

In Fascist culture, a woman was wife and mother. The companion of the warrior or of the laborious worker. She nursed the child who was tomorrow's male. Women who were not yet wives or mothers were young girls with no social status. Or they were sweethearts.

In the Italian imagination of the thirties, a sweetheart lived in a sort of limbo: she was no longer a schoolgirl but she was not yet a mother. She was awaiting a strategic mission, to swell the ranks of Italian citizens. She was supposed to bear, wean and educate – in full respect for Fascist doctrine – the little *Balilla* (the paramilitary organization of Fascist youth), who marched in rank and file in military parades. Il Duce wanted large numbers of them to conquer a few more slices of the world.

The sweethearts of Fascist movies rarely had the gaiety of the postwar heroines who were poor, but beautiful and dreamy. The sweethearts of the Fascist period lived in a military, macho society that forced women to walk with their eyes downcast. Shame was always looming ahead. Consider Maria Denis in *Sissignora* [Yes Ma'am] (1941) with a veil of resignation shading her face.

Like colts with blinders, the sweethearts of the Fascist years pulled the plow of their youth: for the love of a son or a husband, they rolled up their sleeves and turned themselves into strong draughthorses.

In *Noi vivi* (1942) *(We the Living)*, Kira, played by Alida Valli, hears talk of female emancipation but the woman speaking is an unpleasant Communist, an unkempt slut, the essence of anti-femininity. Alida turns up her nose. Sweethearts like her wanted a man to tremble for, to suffer for, to cry over. Love meant suffering.

The sweethearts of Fascist cinema were really lower middle-class women. But like Cinderella they wanted to go to the ball, to mix with high society at least once in their lives. When they finally get the chance, they realize that the joys of life come from other things; from a young, honest laborer, a modest home in the outskirts, a quiet serene destiny protected from the excesses and extravagances of the rich. In *Il Signor Max* (1937) the young governess played by Assia Noris is disgusted with the vanity of her mistress, Lady Paola, and her aristocratic friends. Noris flees into the arms of newspaper vendor Vittorio De Sica without realizing that the very same young man dressed up as a snob is Signor Max. Italy's honest sweethearts did not like men like Signor Max: they were only dreams. And however lovely, a dream was not going to lead you to the altar.

Maria Denis

She looked like a porcelain statue. Small-boned and dainty, with full cheeks, an apple-round face, be-ribboned hair in braids or a bun, an upturned nose and large eyes, good-natured and expressive – Maria Denis was the perfect little doll. This was a girl who didn't lay traps and had no knowledge of treachery.

Her birth certificate read Maria Ester Belmonte. Both parents were Italian but she was born in San Lorenzo, near Buenos Aires, Argentina, on November 22, 1916. Her father, originally from the region of Apulia, was an army officer. Her mother, with Tuscan blood running in her veins, had left youthful aspirations of an acting career behind, but not without some regret. In 1919 the family moved to Rome, to a proper middle-class building on Via Piave.

Seconda B [Twelfth grade], directed by Goffredo Alessandrini was the movie that first brought her into the public eye.

"Am I really so bad, sir?" says mischievous Maria Denis to Sergio Tofano, her teacher, in the school movie **Seconda B** *(1934).*

Academic year 1911-1912: at the turn of the century the ladies of the best middle-class families study at the Women's International Institute. The girls sit at their desks with a sporting air. They learn a few facts here and there and play tricks. They do gym in uniforms, with black skirts below their knees, dark stockings and a black belt snug around their waists. Maria Denis plays the sassiest of the well-off bunch. Her teacher, played by Stefano Tofano, wants to punish the girl who sneaked a mouse into the classroom. But how can he? She's the daughter of a member of parliament. To make up for it, the mischievous girl helps Tofano tidy the school's science lab, which incites the jealousy of Dina Perbellini, a spinster teacher patiently courting her colleague.

An absent-minded tomboy at school, in her demure high-school uniform, Denis turned herself into an elegant young lady as soon as she was old enough, with bows on her dress and a Sunday hat.

Towards the end of the decade, Maria lost her tomboy look once and for all and became an extremely sentimental actress who, when she wept, brought tears to the eyes of her public. Poggioli, Italy's director of the most heart-rending Fascist melodramas, directed her in two important movies, *Addio giovinezza!* [Good-bye youth!] (1940) and *Sissignora* (1941). In both productions, Maria was placed in the hands of great costume designers: Gino C. Sensani for *Addio giovinezza!* and Maria De Matteis for *Sissignora*.

In *Addio giovinezza!* Denis plays the role of Dorina, a dressmaker from a modest family in Turin, who is engaged to Adriano Rimoldi, a wealthy young man from the provinces who moves to Turin to study medicine. Gentle and patient, sentimental and good-as-gold, Dorina spends her time sewing while the rascal Rimoldi succumbs to the charms of Clara Calamai, being her usual self. After repeatedly betraying Maria's trust, Rimoldi abandons her. The sugar-sweet Dorina, who has already embroidered a mountainous trousseau, is left alone with her dreams.

Maria Denis' Dorina is delightful as she wrinkles her nose – an infantile sign of joy. But she is equally charming when she daydreams with needle and thread. A whole generation of dressmakers could see themselves in her.

Maria becomes the muse of the tearful genre of movies by acting in *Sissignora*, a star vehicle fashioned just for her. After this performance she is considered the most "sorrowful" of Fascism's movie sweethearts.

Sissignora is the story of a servant girl's subservience. The girl is Cristina Zugno, an orphan housed at the Young Girls' Protection Institute. An acid-tongued Rina Morelli finds her a good position as a maid for Misses Robbiano, two bad-tempered spinsters.

For seventy-five lire a month (in times when the song, "If I only had a thousand lire a month" was in vogue), the dutiful Cristina is subjected to every kind of physical and moral abuse. She wears her hair in braids, or wound on the top of her head: the perfect picture of innocence and submissiveness. The two spinsters are inordinately fond of their nephew, their only relative, a sailor who is both wild and something of a Don Juan. Cristina loses both her honor and her job.

The Robbiano home is only the first of the young maid's trials and tribulations. Sent away by the two women, she goes to work for a family that goes bankrupt and doesn't pay her wages. Then she works for a widow too deeply involved in her lover to realize that her little son is dying. Cristina is infected too and dies miserably in a hospital.

The sad ending of *Addio giovinezza!* and the tragic finale of *Sissignora* turn Maria Denis into a tragic heroine. But her luck is even worse in a melodrama meant to pull the heartstrings of "the masses," *Le due orfanelle* [The two orphans] (1942) where Carmine Gallone gives her the role of Luisa, a blind foundling, abandoned on the steps of a church, who is destined to be victim to a series of hapless encounters. After being separated from her stepsister, kidnapped by a nobleman, she finds refuge with a woman who exploits her by forcing her to go begging.

Denis could hardly have avoided an appearance in *Nessuno torna indietro* [No one turns back] (1943) a patchwork of Italian movie stars; Blasetti gave her the role of Anna, a farmer's daughter and a boarder at the Grimaldi Institute. In contrast to her previous roles and her look as a loser, Denis is the only character in the movie who fulfills her dreams of love.

Despite this exception, Denis remained the tragic heroine of Fascist cinema in Italy. Not long afterwards she was the only Italian artist with a role in Marcel L'Herbier's *La Bohême* (1943) where she played the ill-starred Mimi to a background of Puccini's music.

Maria Denis was one of the few Italian movie stars to give an authentic touch to roles of humble women, tormented by destinies of ordinary misery.

During the last years of the war, this woman, with her early neorealistic calling, was often seen around Rome in the company of the infamous Pietro Koch, jingoist of the political police, accused of being responsible for a host of atrocities. As a result, after Liberation Maria Denis was accused of being a collaborator. The fair dove of heartrending melodrama might well have met the end of Luisa Ferida if Luchino Visconti had not testified at her trial on her behalf.

[see also p. 138]

Assia Noris

Although she often played the part of the sweet little middle-class ingenue, and of the fresh-faced salesgirl, in reality the blonde "Sweetheart of Italy," Assia Noris, was of noble origins – and she was inordinately proud of the fact. Many of those who knew her during her golden years recalled her as a terrible snob.

Her father, Count von Gerzfeld, an officer in the Russian imperial court, fled immediately after the Russian Revolution, first to Crimea and then to France. While she claimed that she was twelve at the time of her movie debut, in 1931 to be exact, Assia, or Anastasia, was born in St. Petersburg on February 26, 1912. She grew up in France and studied at the famous Lycée des Jeunes Filles in Cannes.

When she made her debut on the Italian screen, making an immediate hit with the genuine charm that burst from that innocent face, she had already separated from her first husband, Gaetano Assia. On the set she became famous for her hot temper and leading lady obstinacy as well as her brazen reminiscences of Russian nobility. But like magic, as soon as the director shouted "Action!" Anastasia, or Assia, turned into one of those sweet, fragile, timid birdlike women who inspired tenderness and a sense of protection. That miracle was worked especially when Mario Camerini was directing her. The best women's director of Cinecittà had lost his head over Assia and, in 1940, after a long engagement, became her husband. But not the last.

Gaetano Assia managed to last two years and the good Camerini heroically reached three. Then Anastasia Noris von Gerzfeld's second marriage spectacularly broke up as well.

Collector of husbands, Assia had drawn another Italian director to the altar before Camerini – Roberto Rossellini, a young man at the time. According to Noris, the marriage was never consumated. "He was a young, handsome, brilliant playboy. He had also inherited a fortune. So we married in a Russian church and I was very happy,

Assia Noris as a simple girl in Darò un milione *(1935). From left to right: Franco Coop, Gemma Bolognesi, Vittorio De Sica.*

although being as young as I was, I was also very frightened. But we never had an intimate marriage, I can't say why. My father came to get me at the hotel in Sanremo, a hotel where I never set foot again. And after forty-eight hours the marriage was annulled." Just what did happen in that hotel room?

Assia closely resembled Dora Nelson, the heroine of the movie of the same name, a frivolous, faithless vamp. And apparently, when Mario Soldati, Camerini's assistant director on the set of *Il signor Max* (1937) directed Noris in *Dora Nelson* (1939), he truly did want to mock her.

Dora Nelson was not the only picture where Assia Noris rediscovered her Russian origins. In 1942, when she was at the peak of her career, she played the part of Mascia in *Un colpo di pistola* [A pistol shot], based on the famous story by Alexander Pushkin. Wrapped in the airy crinolines designed by Maria De Matteis, Assia seems happy to find herself on the set of "her" Russia, not the Soviet Russia that torments Alida Valli in *Noi vivi* (1942) *(We the Living)*, but rather the romantic tsarist Russia of the eighteenth century.

In *Un colpo di pistola* a delightfully flirtatious Assia shows off a series of elegant ensembles. One particularly original outfit is a riding habit: a puffy shirt and a top hat, embellished with a ribbon fastened with a buckle. She was unable to do without hats and demanded them in abundance for all her pictures; they were also useful for "raising" her. None of her costume designers dared object, firstly because of her temper, and secondly

because she really did look good in hats. By that time she could demand and get whatever she wanted. She was one of Cinecittà's few real stars.

She spoke in something of a monotone and her style never changed as the years passed. In *Il signor Max* when she discovers the snob Max in his guise of newspaper man, she widens her eyes like a girl in a school play. She is also altogether lacking in Valli's extraordinary naturalism. But her face still manages to "break through" the screen.

Darò un milione [I'll give a million] (1935) is the picture that begins her long artistic friendship with Vittorio De Sica. They become the ideal couple in Camerini's poetic universe, acting together in his most important movies: *Ma non è una cosa seria* [But it's nothing serious] (1936), *Il signor Max* (1937), and *Grandi magazzini* [Department stores] (1939).

A typical representative of middle-class sweethearts, Noris had a fondness for floral dresses and scarves. She put aside the platinum blonde of her debut and accepted hair-dos more befitting her middle-class ladies, with generous curls. Her look couldn't help but please romantic Fascist Italy, too syrupy to be real.

Unlike Alida Valli, an adaptable sweetheart who took on a variety of roles, Assia Noris almost always acted the same parts especially in the pictures directed by Camerini for whom Assia was ever the fragile Lauretta of *Il signor Max*.

Una romantica avventura [A romantic

Assia Noris, Italy's sweetheart, but also a husband collector.

adventure], Camerini's next-to-last picture directing Assia Noris, is a genuine star vehicle, an important costume movie created just for her. Assia acts three – yes three – parts: the heroine Annetta, a middle-class country girl, ingenuous and eager to experience society; Annetta twenty years later, embittered by age; and her daughter Angioletta (another term of endearment) who elopes. With a touch of pride, Assia explained the triple role in purely economic terms: "When they paid Noris, they wanted to get their money's worth. So that's why I had to do everything." But to tell the truth, *Una romantica avventura* seems to be Camerini's gift of love to a woman so ungrateful that she was unaware of it. The movie was based on Thomas Hardy's *The Loves of Margery* but it was shot during the war, at a time of proud hostility towards the hated Albion. Indeed, every reference to the original England was carefully erased.

Here too there are traces of Noris' imaginary biography. She plays a proper middle-class girl from the country. Her father owns a brick factory and she works on a farm. Camerini shoots her intent on caring for silk worms, with a scarf around her head and a polka-dot blouse. But Annetta dreams of a different world. And when she meets the nobleman Leonardo Cortese, she asks him if she can go to a party at the castle. So the fairy tale takes shape. The hollow of a centuries-old oak tree becomes a dressing room, and the handsome Count leaves a magnificent white silk gown for her to find. A radiant Assia Noris dons it and out she comes, dazzling and wrapped in silk and airy veils, a vision of ribbons and bows. The evening darkness is lit up with this floating vision.

For a moment, Annetta resembles Cinderella on her evening of glory: at the ball the Count only has eyes for her. But when the girl confesses that she already has a sweetheart (in other words, admitting that she is a brazen liar), the nobleman seizes the lovely gown and throws it into the fire. Annetta's dreams go up in smoke.

Still infatuated with her Count, Annetta ends up making do with her boyfriend, the good Gino Cervi, an honest, hard-working laborer who readies everything for their wedding and even chooses the furniture.

Her marriage to her good-hearted fiancé is not really what she wanted and she spends the next thirty years regretting it. She hates the calluses on his laborer hands and the furniture he has chosen. She dreams of Count Leonardo Cortese, the gilded mirrors and silver candlesticks. And her husband's loving patience makes it all the more unbearable. "How could you put up with me all these years?" an embittered Annetta asks her husband. And she cries and cries and cries, crocodile tears, as Assia Noris had always done.

Alida Valli

When she appeared on the screen for the first time, fresh from her studies at the Centro Sperimentale, Alida resembled a Myrna Loy ingenue. With her radiant smile, a well-scrubbed but interesting beauty, a delicate nose and oh-so-slight bucked teeth, she looked like a fawn nibbling grass.

In her first important role, she made her debut alongside Angelo Musco, who was her partner in *Il feroce Saladino* [Saladin the fierce] (1937). The comedy, with oriental pretensions, was directed by Mario Bonnard and dedicated to the most popular competition of the thirties organized by Perugina, Italy's largest chocolate and candy manufacturer. Alida dances with her belly covered only by veils and oriental trinkets. She in fact manages a highly successful belly dance and sings, dubbed:

> A flower is all that you need
> to tell of the heart that suffers
> and trembles and lives,
> only for you…

This was Cinecittà thumbing its nose at Hollywood. Alida, Italy's new Ginger Rogers, was unknown but extremely attractive. She was only sixteen, but it was already easy to tell that she would go far. She was born on May 31, 1921 in Pola, in the province of Istria which passed from Austria to Italy after World War I. Her real name was Alida Maria Altenburger. Her father, Baron Gino von Altenburger, taught philosophy at the Pola lyceum and wrote musical reviews for the city newspaper, the *Corriere Istriano*. Her mother was Slovenian. At the beginning of the thirties

Assenza ingiustificata (1939): from high school student to young woman, Alida Valli grows up alongside "doctor" Amedeo Nazzari.

Alida Valli with Osvaldo Valenti in **L'amante segreta** *(1941).*

the Altenburgers settled in Como.

Alida was very young when she moved to Rome with the intention of becoming an actress. According to legend, she took up permanent vigil under Alessandro Blasetti's window to force him to let her do a screen test at the Centro Sperimentale. Whatever the case may be, Alida soon proved her rare talent. She left school at the end of the first year to launch herself into the scremmage.

After a few ingenue roles, Alida linked her name to that of the Austrian director Max Neufeld who directed her in a series of successful comedies, starting with *Mille lire al mese* [A thousand lire a month] (1938).

In her debut role Alida plays Magda, a girl who wants wedding bells to crown her dreams of love. But her fiancé is unemployed: no money, no wedding! The radio croons the melody of a famous song by Carlo Innocenzi:

If I could only have
a thousand lire a month
without overstating
I am certain I could find
happiness so fine.
A modest job I'd like to have
without any make-believe,
I only want to have a job
so that I can find
the peace I seek…

Directed by Max Neufeld, Alida also acted in *La casa del peccato* [House of sin] (1939), *Ballo al castello* (1939) (Ball at the Castle), *Taverno rossa* (1940) (The Red Inn), and also, in 1940, *La prima donna che passa* [The first woman who comes by]. But most important of all there was *Assenza ingiustificata* [Unexcused absence] (1939) one of the most classic examples of the "white telephone" film style. The white telephone films characterized the cinema of the Fascist regime, with settings and stories that were false, detached from reality, lavish and ostentatious, oozing with romantic froth.

Here Valli plays Vera, a badly behaved high school student who earns herself a suspension. The girl fakes illness, aided and abetted by Dr. Amedeo Nazzari, ready to sign bogus health certificates and thrilled to lead the young lady who, in the meantime has been expelled from school, to the altar.

Neufeld fashioned a comedy that went down as easily as champagne, a tasty confection that was a cross between a school movie and a white telephone film. The picture was effortlessly made, without being overly contemplative or overly rehearsed, but Alida Valli was still perfect. She is spirited and lively, with the charm of an Audrey Hepburn, part-woman and part-girl.

Mille lire al mese, Assenza ingiustificata, and Neufeld's other movies made Valli incredibly popular. Girls wore "Alida Valli hair-dos," young men wrote her passionate love letters, hordes of aspiring fiancés sent her flowers. Cameramen used gauze and filters to soften her close-ups, but Alida went on treating filmmaking like any other job. She never once threw a temper-tantrum or made a scene on the set.

Docile, she accepted orders from directors, make-up artists and costume designers. Alida was Cinecittà's anti-star. But her movies rarely gave her the feeling that she was doing anything that would go down in the history of cinema. "I discovered the pleasure of making pictures when that crazy man Soldati asked me to act in *Piccolo mondo antico (Little Old-Fashioned World).* But the episode was like a pearl among the rhinestones…"

In the movie she plays Luisa, a middle-class girl who marries a young aristocrat against the wishes of his cold-hearted grandmother, a powerful, overwhelming guardian. The setting is Lombardy in 1850, ruled by the Hapsburgs (Alida, herself from Istria, continued to play exclusively northern Italian roles). Italian patriots are waxing enthusiastic over Piedmont's independence and count Cavour. Even Franco, Luisa's husband, is a fervent patriot.

Between 1939 and 1942, Alida Valli was one of the industry's busiest actresses, shooting four or five movies a year. The Fascist regime, proud of this actress produced by the national "laboratory" of the Centro Sperimentale di Cinematografia, awarded her, encouraged and pampered her. And the public adored Alida. She was naturally talented, modern, and extremely photogenic. What more could they ask?

Notwithstanding her twenty years, Alida played another schoolgirl role in 1941 in *Ore 9 lezione di chimica (Schoolgirl's Diary),* one of Mario Mattoli's best pictures. Just as in *Assenza ingiustificata,* Valli plays the part of an unmotivated student, Anna, failing in Latin, arithmetic, and most dismally, chemistry.

Her father is a rich industrialist, a widower, with no time to take care of her. He places her in the Valfiorita boarding school, a chic institution for the female offspring of the upper classes. Anna casts flirtatious looks at her chemistry teacher, a darkly handsome Andrea

Checchi. Not a single one of his students is able to concentrate on her lessons when he is teaching. Neglecting carbon sulphide and iron dioxide, the girls study the good-looking teacher's new polka-dot tie, honoring him with sketches and bits of poetry.

Alida was a great success seated at her desk in *Schoolgirl's Diary*. She acted so naturally that it was easy to overlook the fact that her beauty was over-ripe for a scholastic career.

Alida wisely went back to women's roles. Mattoli used her talents to start his lucky series of "movies that talk straight to your heart": poignant melodramas that left an indelible mark on Italian taste of the time. In *Luce nelle tenebre* [Light in darkness] (1941) Alida plays Marina, the good-hearted sister of Clara Calamai in another of her frivolous vamp roles.

Both sisters fall in love with a young engineer, the brooding Fosco Giachetti. But while Marina hesitates and is destroyed by true love, the shrewd Clara devours him whole.

Alida also starred in the second of Mattoli's series *Catene invisibili* [Invisible chains] (1942).

In this movie she plays the daughter of a rich industrialist, the owner of steel mills throughout Italy. Cold-hearted, cynical and proud of her position in society, Elena is struck by remorse when she hears of her father's death. She realizes how distant she always was, and to honor his memory tries to help a wild hoodlum, an illegitimate son of her father.

Alida Valli's enigmatic, extraordinary beauty allowed her to play any character. With just a few changes of make-up and costume, the rich upper middle-class girl of *Catene invisibili* turned into a Soviet peasant girl, Kira Argounova in *Noi vivi* (1942) *(We the Living)* and *Addio Kira* (1942). Divided into two parts because of its length, the latter picture was a maudlin melodrama, heavy with verbose dialogue and blunt ideological simplifications. Not even Hollywood managed to put such a ridiculous USSR on the screen.

Kira Argounova is a white Russian, a refugee in Crimea. A few years after the October Revolution, she returns to her family in St. Petersburg and falls in love with a melancholy nobleman, Leo, carefully watched by the secret police. Kira, anti-Communist, of course, is arrested for conspiracy. She is saved by Commissar Andrej Taganov, played by Fosco Giachetti, madly in love with her. In order to help Leo and send him to a sanatorium, Kira becomes Andrej's mistress.

"Do you always look at people as if you were trying to read their inner thoughts?" asks the brooding Leo, played by Rossano Brazzi. In this movie, where sinister Soviet women rant and rave about female emancipation, Alida's brightness gleams like a guiding star. She is almost always dressed in men's clothes, and in some scenes she resembles Greta Garbo's first serious "Soviet" appearances in *Ninotchka* (1939).

Right after 1945 she received menacing letters from people longing for a return of Fascism. Actually, Alida is the one who should have resented the Regime – or the course of history at least – since the war had interrupted her career at its peak, when Valli was in her flowering twenties and fresh from the recent triumph of *Little Old-Fashioned World*.

In the postwar period, Alida, who was only twenty-four in 1945, was young, beautiful and highly talented. But she was still the star of another era. The collapse of Fascism turned the country inside-out, changing the terms of its dreams and imagination. It seemed like a hundred years had passed during the last two years of war, and Liberation was the dawning of a new century.

Italy had crossed a stormy river and part of the legend of Alida Valli had been left on the other bank.

[see also p. 70]

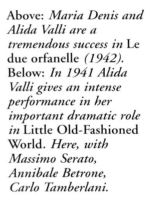

Above: *Maria Denis and Alida Valli are a tremendous success in* **Le due orfanelle** *(1942).* **Below:** *In 1941 Alida Valli gives an intense performance in her important dramatic role in* **Little Old-Fashioned World.** *Here, with Massimo Serato, Annibale Betrone, Carlo Tamberlani.*

Mariella Lotti

With their rounded curves and easy-going natures, the stars of Fascist cinema would never have had a chance in the motion pictures of the eighties and nineties, partial to sinuous and slender swanlike women. Milan-born Anna Maria Pianotti, stage name Mariella Lotti, might well have been the only one who could have competed with the top models of today.

Her figure made her the delight of costume designers like Gino Carlo Sensani, who could encase her tiny waist in sadistic corsets, inventing incredible and complicated crinolines for her, without ever making her look anything but elegant.

Similarly, her long Northern face, could take the showiest of hair-dos. Period wigs and coiffures failed to make her look ridiculous. In reality, Mariella's photogenic quality conferred dignity on the eighteenth and nineteenth-century characters she played. Lotti thus frequently found herself in the role of a noblewoman of distant times, even of the Middle Ages, in the midst of court intrigues and drawn swords, living in pasteboard castles: *Kean* (1940), *Il ponte dei sospiri* [The bridge of sighs] (1940), *Marco Visconti* (1941), *Il cavaliere senza nome* [The nameless knight] (1941), *La Gorgona* (1942).

Lotti, who always paid close attention to any curl out of place, detested brusque movements that risked the arrangement of her coiffure. Actually, Mariella also had a weakness for statuary poses. A certain stiffness is part of her often distant beauty. However Lotti was one of those actresses who could pour out charm on the screen in gallons.

Her Renaissance look was greatly appreciated by the Fascist regime who watched over her and offered her enticing opportunities to advance her career.

Mariella Lotti was born on December 27, 1921 into a middle-class Lombard family in Busto Arsizio near Milan. Her older sister Carol preceded her onto the set but without any great success. She had only a tiny part in *Gli uomini, che mascalzoni...* [Men, what scoundrels] (1932) and other minor roles. Mariella on the other hand, wanted to break into the movies the right way and studied acting at the Centro Sperimentale.

Her blonde beauty, not at all Mediterranean, was perfect for costume movies and adventure stories.

Photogenic and engaging, she worked in a series of movies directed by Scalera, starting with *Il ponte dei sospiri*, where she played the gentle daughter of the Doge. At the beginning of the forties, she was one of the three official blondes of the Fascist cinema, along with Vivi Gioi and Vera Carmi. She had the naïve quality of young Joan Fontaine but fans and reporters of the time compared her with Loretta Young and Joan Bennett.

She almost always had a title in her movies: marquise, countess, daughter of the Doge, the Prince's niece. In Camillo Mastrocinque's popular comedy, *I mariti* [Husbands] (1941), with just the right touch of haughtiness, refined and with her lovely nervous curls, the little duchess Emma flits from one drawing-room to another, in love with an illusion.

She was given a completely different role by director Franciolini in *Fari nella nebbia* [Beacons in the fog] (1942), a movie in the naturalist vein, a forerunner of neorealism. Here Mariella has to give up the noble blood of her countesses and marquises to play a truck driver's wife: a loose woman who abandons her husband and ultimately returns to the fold, purified by an inner crisis.

Mariella wears cheap dresses in *Fari nella nebbia*, the kind found on the racks of bargain basements. But it was almost impossible to transform the blonde countess into the humble truck driver's wife. Whatever they put on her looked elegant. She recalls, "They put a cat-fur cape on me, but it looked like lynx. What could the costume designer do?"

Ultimately, Mariella's lovely golden curls were tied back behind her neck in a sort of bun and she finally looked like an ordinary woman, the wife of truck driver Fosco Giachetti, who was after Luisa Ferida.

One of the most touching wartime motion pictures was *Nessuno torna indietro* [No one turns back] (1943), a realist

Mariella Lotti's beauty and elegance are highlighted in movies such as I mariti (1941). With Giacomo Moschini.

At the peak of World War II, Mariella Lotti was already a serious actress in excellent dramatic roles.
Left: *With Massimo Girotti in the episode* Ricorda di santificare le feste, *from the movie* I dieci comandamenti *(1944-45).* **Below:** *With Cesarino Barbetti, Lotti in her greatest role in* La freccia nel fianco *(1943).*

melodrama narrating the heartbreaking farewell to childhood of seven young girls attending the Grimaldi Institute, a dormitory for female university students.

While she had the reputation of being a protégé of the regime, Lotti did not manage to get the role she wanted most: Emanuela, the most elegant of the seven girls. That part went to Doris Duranti who had friends in even higher places. Mariella had to make do with playing Xenia, a much more submissive character, at least at the beginning of the movie, where Lotti displays a very uncharacteristic modesty.

Alberto Lattuada directed Mariella in a memorable movie, *La freccia nel fianco* [Arrow in the side] begun after July 23, 1943 and interrupted by the war on September 10 while the crew was shooting on location at Arosli, in Abruzzo. The picture was finished in the summer of 1944 and was released in the middle of 1945 in an Italy that had undergone deep changes in the meantime.

A phone rings, but no one answers: Madam Nicoletta has just been killed. This is no "white telephone" movie: with *La freccia nel fianco* (1943), blonde Mariella Lotti became a postwar star, where high-class ambience was out of place.

It is not hard to distinguish the first part of the picture (shot in 1943) from the second (shot in 1944), also because the two roles correspond to two different parts of the story. In the first part Mariella Lotti is a solitary eighteen-year-old who refuses every marriage proposal she receives and makes friends with a twelve-year-old boy, as solitary as she. A sublime love. In the second part, Mariella is twenty-eight and settled into a middle-class marriage. But she has a secret sorrow… the memory of that boy, the dream of an impossible love affair, of youth that has fled.

Mariella's full maturity was ruined by history: she was a woman seriously harmed by ensuing events that coincided with her career as a great actress.

[see also p. 139]

Dria Paola

Assia Noris, Maria Denis, Mariella Lotti and Alida Valli were the prototypes of the sweethearts of Fascist cinema. But of course they were not the only interpreters of this inert and sugary model of femininity.

One sweet young thing who appeared on the scene at the end of the twenties was Rovigo-born Dria Paola, a subdued star who straddled two eras. She made her debut in *Sole* [Sun] (1929), a mythical, long-lost picture – with the exception of one fragment – that culminated the era of silent movies. Her second picture, *La canzone dell'amore* [Love song] (1930), opened the era of talking pictures. And both movies marked important pages in the history of Italian cinema.

Dria Paola was obviously a composite stage name, the fashion at the time, of two first names, like Leda Gloria, Isa Miranda, or Paola Barbara. Her real name, on the other hand, was so strange it sounded false: Etra Pitteo.

She was born on November 21, 1909 in Rovigo, where she attended vocational schools and studied piano and violin. She started acting when very young in plays produced by a small Rovigo theatrical company under the watchful eye of her mother, Jone, who followed her like a shadow all the way to Rome. Dria

Paola really wanted to study medicine. Instead, she had to make do with being named an honorary student at the University of Padua.

Her debut coincided with young Blasetti's and he gave her the starring role in *Sole*, Giovanna; the beautiful daughter of a hunter in the Pontine marshes, a daring opponent of the land reclaimers.

Blasetti's realism in *Sole* was of strategic importance for the Italian cinema. Since its story called for an almost all-male cast, Dria Paola had little to do. But she did have the chance to show off her modern, somewhat naturalistic beauty. That was how it happened that Gennaro Righelli chose her for *La canzone dell'amore*, the first complete talking Italian movie with a musical score.

Her figure was not a curvaceous one and the draping clothes Dria favored accentuated her lankiness even more; her high forehead, her long arms, tapering fingers and thin, somewhat artificial mouth. Dria had an unusual nose – long and pointed, with generous nostrils and a slightly drooping tip. She was one of those women who seem to have a perpetual cold; perfect for tearful parts.

La canzone dell'amore was a great success with the critics and an even greater success with the public. One might have expected a more brilliant career for the star of a picture that had beaten every box office record. Instead, Dria Paola chanced upon a series of particularly unfortunate movies, such as *Vele ammainate* [Lowered sails] (1931) directed by Anton Giulio Bragaglia, where she played the role of a kind-hearted barmaid in a tavern who sang for the customers, attracting the attentions of a good-looking captain. But it just wasn't enough.

Elio Steiner, her male lead in the successful *La canzone dell'amore*, appears by her side in a number of inconsequential pictures, such as Malasomma's thriller *L'uomo dall'artiglio* [Man of claws] (1931), but also in films of note, including the musical biography *Pergolesi* (1932), ennobled by Sensani's costumes, and the charming comedy directed by Righelli, *Pensaci, Gicomino!* [Think, Gicomino!] (1932). Here Dria plays an unwed mother, the

In 1930, Dria Paola has the leading role in the first Italian talkie, La canzone dell'amore. *Here, with Elio Steiner.*

daughter of janitor, Angelo Musco.

Wan, ashen and sickly, Dria gradually perfects her stereotype of the unhappy maiden, victim of an undeserved destiny or the cruelty of men. Her melancholic, resigned beauty is perfectly suited for the melodrama *La cieca di Sorrento* (1934) *(The Blind Woman of Sorrento).*

To underline the blindness of Beatrice di Rionero, Dria Paola's gaze is lost in the distance and her eyes circled with soot. The heavy make-up looks like a throwback to the by-gone era of silent movies, which really was not all that distant. This is 1934 after all. With her darkened eyes and white grease paint, pale and listless, the blind Dria falls instantly in love with the engaging young doctor who takes her on outings and organizes boat trips complete with mandolines. And kisses her. "How kind you are," she says.

At the end of the thirties, although still young, she was forced to reappraise her image as an actress: from famous starring roles in movies such as *La canzone dell'amore* and *The Blind Woman of Sorrento* – she resigned herself to being a co-star. And sometimes directors even gave her supporting roles, such as in *L'albergo degli assenti* [The hotel of the missing] (1939), where Dria is a diaphanous pregnant wife, kidnapped, along with her husband and other hostages, victims of organized crime.

Her star was definitely waning. And after another film with a lengthy cast, *La pantera nera* [The black panther] (1942), Dria Paola retired forever from the silver screen.

Caterina Boratto

Many sweethearts of Fascist cinema had the mournful look of cattle being led to the slaughter-house. Caterina Boratto was of a different mold. She was a staunch, independent woman, capable of making and sticking to decisions, at least when it came to her heart. And that was not to be underestimated for a little blonde from Mussolini's Italy.

Born in Turin on March 15, 1916, Boratto leaped into the limelight in 1936, playing the role of the daughter of tenor Tito Schipa in the melodrama *Vivere!* [Live!] based on one of the singer's famous songs, "Live, without sadness. Live..." as the verse went. Rumor had it that this catchy tune brought bad luck. Caterina Boratto, for her part, had nothing to complain about.

She had never dreamed of becoming a motion picture actress; her studies and efforts were aimed at making a name for herself in the world of music. She received a degree in piano studies from the Turin Conservatory at the age of seventeen. And she continued studying voice. Caterina loved sports. Fencing, horseback riding and, most especially, swimming. Newspaper reports from the period mention

her winning a regional championship. Her father, an Italian from New York, died very young. Caterina was brought up by her mother, another robust woman from Turin. The state-run radio station, EIAR was headquartered in Turin during those years and Caterina sang into its microphones after winning an audition before composer Pietro Mascagni.

Distributed in Italy by Metro-Goldwyn-Mayer, *Vivere!* was an enormous success. Caterina Boratto found herself with a three-year contract with Livio Pavanelli's Appia Film. Pavanelli was quite rightly interested in exploiting the Boratto-Schipa team's popularity with another musical. And this led to *Chi è più felice di me!* (1938) *(Who's Happier than Me!),* where Schipa was no longer Boratto's father but her fiancé.

Tall, slender, swanlike, and Turinese right down to her bones, Caterina Boratto was already unconvincing as the daughter of the robust southern-born tenor, but as his fiancée, she was even less so! Schipa, born in 1889, had seen twenty-seven springs more than she and was several centimeters shorter. Love does wonders. So does music.

Caterina Boratto's cold beauty.

33

Caterina Boratto was finally given a chance to sing with her own voice in this picture. And she proved she could. Even Louis B. Mayer admired her golden voice, which led to a venturing across the ocean. The dream of Hollywood could have made her into one of the top stars. Instead, it brought an end to her career.

Boratto endured three years of Hollywood limbo without being allowed to enter Paradise. She returned to Italy in 1942 empty handed and her name almost completely forgotten.

Livio Pavanelli remembered her, though, and organized a second meeting for her with Guido Brignoni, the director who had brought her luck before. He offered her the female lead with Amedeo Nazzari in the sentimental nineteenth-century melodrama *Il romanzo di un giovane povero* [The novel of a poor young man] (1942). Boratto was perfectly suited to lace and long skirts. She settled admirably into the role of an elegant goddess-like young lady of the Roman bourgeoisie. In Marco Elter's historical film *Dente per Dente* [A tooth for a tooth] (1943), based on Shakespeare's *Measure for Measure*, she is a noblewoman named Isabella, loved by a duke (Alfredo Varelli) and blackmailed by the sinister Carlo Tamberlani. And in the popular comedy *Campo de' Fiori* (1943) she sits having afternoon tea at the fashionable Rosati Café on Piazza del Popolo in Rome, brimming with contempt for fishmonger, Aldo Fabrizi. It was no matter that her elegant, snobbish mask hid the drama of a poor, unwed mother. The image of Caterina Boratto bequeathed to us by Fascist motion pictures is that of an elegant snob, tall, slim, but somewhat stiff, with a long chin, utterly Northern, almost British, as distant as Garbo. And actually, Boratto's profile was somewhat similar to the mythic star's – from certain angles.

[see also p. 152]

Vivi Gioi

For a moment, let's skip ahead to 1946. The war is just over and *enfant terrible* Giuseppe De Santis is shooting his first picture, *Caccia tragica (Tragic Pursuit)*. He gives Vivi Gioi the role of the dark lady; the mistress of a terrorist, of a sadistic, drifting Nazi. She is forced to wear a wig because her head has been shaved by the partisans, according to the practice used with collaborationists. She sings "Lili Marlene," and her cohorts call her by that name. She is hysterical and pained, seething with hate for everything and everyone.

The clever De Santis used this powerful portrait to rewrite the story of star Vivi Gioi, one of the women who symbolized the "white telephone" Fascist cinema. Her angelic look was turned inside out here, which is exactly what had happened to Calamai in *Ossessione*

[Obsession] (1943).

Vivi Gioi's locks – cut by the partisans to dishonor her – were some of the most beautiful of Fascist Italy. Blond and flowing, they fell over silk robes and endless strings of pearls in classics of the era of the white telephone films (the rosy, artificial cinema of the Fascist period) such as *Bionda sotto chiave* [Blonde under lock and key] (1939), *Vento di milioni* [Wind of millions] (1940) and *Dopo divorzieremo* [After we divorce] (1940). Aside from being one of Cinecittà's natural blondes, Vivi Gioi counted on a certain resemblance to Lale Andersen, the Nazi nightingale who launched the song "Lili Marlene," whose captivating notes managed to insinuate themselves inside Italian minds without the Ministry of Popular Culture having to lift a finger. Exploiting her resemblance to Andersen, Vivi Gioi had sung the song for Italian soldiers at the front, both in the theater and into the microphones of the Fascist-run state radio, thus becoming a sort of Italian Lilli Marlene. And Giuseppe De Santis found the perfect punishment for her in his Dante-inspired inferno.

Let us go back in time, January 2, 1919, birthdate of Vivi, whose real name at the Civil Registry of Livorno where she was born was Vivian Trumphey. Her mother was Italian and her father Norwegian, her family an important one, with her grandfather, Gianni, owner of a large import-export firm.

A wild young thing, she ran away from home and fell in love with Vittorio De Sica. She was not yet seventeen when she acted with her idol in Camerini's comedy *Ma non è una cosa seria* [But it's nothing serious] (1936). In deference to the handsome Vittorio, she called herself Vivian Diesca, an anagram of De Sica. But love is serious business, Vittorio slipped away and Vivian married someone else. But marriage was not for her and they separated shortly afterwards.

Twenty years old, with a divorce behind her, and her pockets bulging, Vivi was a regular at gambling casinos, from Venice to Cannes, from Sanremo to Nice. It seems she supported herself by gambling... Then a series of events brought her back to Cinecittà where she started her real acting career with the new name of Vivi Gioi.

Her second debut is in *Bionda sotto chiave*, a graceful comedy by Zavattini redolent of the white telephone genre.

There was no denying that this Carol Lombard of Fascist Cinecittà was also extremely photogenic. She was uncommonly beautiful: deep-set eyes, a wide, full mouth, hollowed cheeks and a touch of the snob about her. Her trademark was elegance. Apparently the designer Biki dressed her for next to nothing: she was walking publicity.

Gioi wavered between starring and supporting roles in comedies like *Dopo divorzieremo,* where Lilia Silvi took all the credit. Here Vivi plays a postulant named Grace Peterson who is forbidden to marry. This was not the only movie where she played an American; the same thing happened in *Harlem* (1943).

She also played a foreigner in an Italian-German co-production, *Giungla* (1942) *(Jungle)* directed by Malasomma. Here our blonde diva is called Virginia Larsen and is a doctor in the Antilles, surrounded by blood-thirsty natives and lovelorn physicians busy healing malaria and broken hearts in an obviously fake jungle setting.

In this adventure-story role, Vivi was looking for a dramatic character that would heighten her image. But it was only a modest success. The episode movie *Bengasi* (1940), directed by an inspired Genina did much better. Genina offered her another fairly dramatic role, that of an Italian woman in North Africa who is in love with a melancholy Amedeo Nazzari. But the scope of her character was limited (in spite of the fact that she was reputed to have been paid a record 100,000 lire).

She preferred returning to the sophisticated, autocratic genre, such as *Sette anni di felicità* [Seven years of happiness] (1943), to the sentimental comedies of the Fascist regime's "telephone films," still as "white" as ever. But not for much longer…

[see also p. 140]

Above: *Vivi Gioi's beauty reflects Hollywood standards of typical glamour.* **Left:** *Though set in New York,* Dopo divorzieremo *(1940) was a "white telephone" comedy typical of Fascist cinema. From left to right Lilia Silvi, Amedeo Nazzari and Vivi Gioi.*

Vera Carmi

Unmistakable with her tearful gaze, Vera Carmi contemplated her partners with huge languid eyes, as beautiful as they were photogenic.

She was born on November 23, 1917 in Turin and made her debut on the screen as Vera Del Monte at the age of twenty-three, playing a small role in Ferdinando Maria Poggioli's masterpiece *Addio giovinezza!* [Good-bye youth!] (1940).

Her type of looks, so fine and so northern, were used primarily in middle-class roles. Wavy ash blond locks above her wide, honest forehead were the faithful mark of a well-balanced, respectable destiny.

Although photogenic and enchanting, Vera Carmi could occasionally appear cold. At times she seemed to give up her role as actress, consoling herself with hats (she used large numbers of them, just like Assia Noris) and shimmering fabrics. Which is what happens in the courtroom melodrama *Labbra serrate* [Closed lips] (1942), the final chapter of director Mario Mattoli's four-part series, "Movies that talk straight to your heart." Vera took the role originally written for Alida Valli, that of Anna Massani, the daughter of an aging judge.

She plays a young doctor who courageously acts as an assistant at gruesome operations. An electric saw cuts open a skull, but Anna smiles with a professorial air while good Giachetti almost faints.

Middle-class, emancipated and progressive Vera affirms, "There is nothing wrong with women expressing a little superiority over men from time to time." Moderately feminist, she allows herself the affectation of an occasional cigarette, but has no objection to playing romantic songs on the family piano in the parlor. No deceit lies behind her smile. It is maternal, reassuring and holds the promise of conjugal joy. Her vision of love is anti-romantic, as befits an honest medical student. If the man is serious enough, no moonlight preambles are needed.

Her refinement apparently emanated the charm of Northern Europe and the Blue Danube, because more than once, Vera found herself in the part of a lovely Hungarian; for instance, in *Villa da vendere* [Villa for sale] (1941) and *La fortuna viene dal cielo* [Fortune comes from the sky] (1942).

In this beguiling Hungary, comedies of errors are the daily bread of a life too perfect to be authentic. In the ups and downs of these comedies, Vera Carmi is perfectly at ease. In *Villa da vendere*, she marries handsome Amedeo Nazzari. In *La fortuna viene dal cielo* – thanks to a stolen brooch that passes from hand to hand – she loses a fiancé but finds a husband.

Vera played a very special role, almost surreptitiously acting with the mastery of a great actress, in *Giorni Felici* (1942) *(Happy Days)*. The story was set right in the midst of wartime but in spite of that, Gianni Franciolini painted a light, faithful portrait of the romanticism of the Italian youth of a thoughtless, well-to-do, indolent society. It is the story of the holiday romances of five young people, who share the closeness of many summers spent together in a magnificent villa surrounded by woods. This dreamy coterie of friends is jolted by the arrival of an aviator who plummets by chance from the sky, like good luck, or bad... The pilot is handsome Amedeo Nazzari and faint-hearted Lilia Silvi and Valentina Cortese both fall in love with him, making their respective boyfriends, Paolo Stoppa and Leonardo Cortese, jealous. Vera Carmi plays Nietta, their "elder

Vera Carmi in a "white telephone" comedy typical of the period: Villa da vendere (1941) which, however, was set in Budapest.

sister" – almost the mother of the youngsters. She is the most serious of these young ladies, the only authentic woman, completely above any sentimental fluttering. She is the only one who doesn't face the handsome stranger with a broken heart, the only one who doesn't threaten suicide. But when aviator Nazzari takes off in his rickety aircraft, Nietta watches the sky and weeps. She too had a heart...

Making her film debut at the beginning of the forties, Vera Carmi was the last real sweetheart of Fascist cinema. There was not even enough time for her to create an image for herself. War was already upon them. The panorama of the Italian motion picture industry was devastated and the faces of that era were scattered like leaves to the wind.

[see also p. 146]

Maria Mercader

The blonde enchantress of Fascist Cinecittà was an angel from Barcelona, Maria Mercader. A name that tinkled like a flurry of little bells. A sassy little upturned nose, a disarming smile, she enjoyed immediate success and played in a great number of films, almost always in the leading role. As protagonist, she embodied the dream of every young Italian girl during the war years: to fall into the arms of handsome Vittorio De Sica.

Born in Barcelona on May 6, 1918, one of Maria's grandmothers was French and the other Irish. She nevertheless considered herself one hundred percent Spanish with her Castilian mother and Basque father. She belonged to the best Catalan society, lived in the most elegant part of town, vacationing on the sophisticated beaches of San Sebastian. She of course studied in the élite all-girl boarding schools for the wealthy and cringed hatefully at the sight of red revolutionaries. When republican fervor broke out, the Mercaders – staunch monarchists – sought refuge in neighboring France.

Maria got an early start as an actress. She was cast in the leading role of a small Spanish production, *Molinos de viento* [Windmills] (1936), and then, while in exile in France, acted in *L'Etrange nuit de Noël* [A strange Christmas night] (1939) co-starring with the very handsome Jean Servais. It was in Italy, however, that she eventually found her cinematic Eldorado. The only time anyone else snatched the leading role from her was in *La gerla di papà Martin* [Papa Martin's pannier] (1940); on every other occasion Maria was the leading lady. She was also one of the busiest actresses, appearing in at least eleven movies in the year 1941.

In *Il re si diverte* (1941) (*The King's Jester*), a movie based on *Rigoletto*, Maria is Gilda, the lovely daughter of the horrid jester Michel Simon. She is like a little doll. Her tiny head

framed by platinum curls seems a little smaller than it should be.

In the pseudo-Hungarian comedy *Se io fossi onesto* [If I were honest] Maria Mercader is instead like a lovely statue, dressed in an endless assortment of beautiful clothes as if it were a fashion show. On the set she meets Vittorio De Sica for the first time. She is the daughter of a wealthy family, and he, an unemployed engineer: it is love at first sight. Cupid also pointed his arrow at the couple in real life. De Sica, Mercader. It was to be one of the most enduring relationships in Italian cinema, a love that had to be kept secret for the time being since De Sica was married to Giuditta Rissone. Unfortunately, divorce was out of the question in Fascist Italy.

De Sica's attraction to Maria is first expressed during the making of *Un garibaldino al convento* [A Garibaldian in the convent]. He persuades her to do away with the long fake eyelashes she is so fond of, as well as all other artifices which make her look like a little doll. He gives her a more natural, authentic look, even though she never loses the image of an aristocrat from another time: Mariella, the

Vera Carmi's emerald green eyes were considered the most enchanting of 1940s Italian movies.

child of a broken family, but obstinately attached to her blue blood lineage.

Un garibaldino al convento is a contemporary version of the school movie genre. In it director De Sica, who keeps the cameo part of Nino Bixio for himself, wants to explore, with a light touch, the themes of friendship, love, and envy in the corridors of a nineteenth-century boarding school for high society girls.

This role, for twenty-three-year-old Maria Mercader, is like a refreshing bath of reality: for the first time her acting reveals genuine emotion, all the feelings and preoccupations of a girl from a by-gone era: secret love, a forbidden book, that sense of dignity which only a twenty-year-old can possess.

The blond angel only dyed her hair black twice in her career, to play in Vittorio Cottafavi's two comedies *I nostri sogni* [Our dreams] and *Nessuno torna indietro* [No one turns back], both made in 1943. The first was a brilliant but conventional comedy along the lines of Cinecittà's productions of the time. *Nessuno torna indietro*, however, was considered a prototype of cinematic neorealism and as such was hailed by young Luchino Visconti, who also praised Maria's acting.

Perhaps, with the collapse of the Regime imminent, the lovely blond actress felt the need to break away from the image of her too-sweet type of beauty, a symbol of Fascist cinema. *Nessuno torna indietro*, based upon the "verismo" book by Spanish writer Alba de Céspedes, didn't really seem to be the film for her, and Alessandro Blasetti expressed his doubts about including her in the cast. It was Alba De Céspedes himself who warmly supported the young actress' involvement in the production. And this was how the blonde angel became Vinca, a wretched young girl. Her black hair makes her almost unrecognizable. Vinca cannot forget her beloved fiancé who has been killed in combat during the Spanish civil war.

It is an intense and vibrant role, very different from anything Mercader has ever acted before. It is also the only movie that she wishes her children to see, "the only decent one in which I had a decent part," she remarked.

Nevertheless, the character of the dark-haired Vinca is not the role for which Maria Mercader will be most remembered. Her portrayals of happy dreamy young girls are more original, and more authentically "her" as, for example, the marquis' daughter in *Un garibaldino al convento* which, without betraying her natural talent as a beautiful little statue, also gave her the opportunity to express genuine sincerity. Maria will remain in her public's memory just like that, with all the enchantment of her cascade of blonde curls, cute little upturned nose and that gaze worthy of a princess.

Above: *Born in Spain, Maria Mercader's second homeland became Italy.* **Below:** *Maria Mercader with Leonardo Cortese in her best movie,* Un garibaldino al convento (1942).

Marina Berti

In 1942 a talented young man, a documentary maker who had also worked as assistant to the director Soldati in *Piccolo mondo antico (Little Old-Fashioned World)* (1941), had the chance to direct a feature film all of his own, *Giacomo l'idealista* [Giacomo the idealist] (1943), based on the book of the same name by Emilio De Marchi.

This twenty-eight-year-old hopeful was Alberto Lattuada and he wanted to cast a complete unknown in the female lead. Elena Maureen Bertolini was half-English, half-Italian and her credits included just small parts in two films of 1941, *La fuggitiva* [The fugitive] and *Divieto di sosta* [Stopping prohibited] and who was currently working as a model at "La Merveilleuse" in Turin. They had been introduced by Count Bonzi, Clara Calamai's future husband.

Elena Maureen, known as Marina to her friends, was little more than a girl. Despite her high cheekbones and the typically Mediterranean intensity of her animal-like beauty, she was in fact born in London on September 29, 1924, daughter of an Italian immigrant who did not stay long in his adopted country. Marina studied in Florence where she also tried her hand at radio broadcasting.

In *Giacomo l'idealista* she plays Celestina, a humble orphan who lives in the castle of Count Magnenzio and is betrothed to the idealistic but penniless writer Giacomo. After she is seduced in her sleep by the master's son, she is taken away and abandoned far from the town in order to hush up the scandal.

Meanwhile Giacomo, who turns out to be not such an idealist after all, is handsomely paid off. Far from her loved one, poor Celestina is tormented by his memory; so much so that she tries to find her way back to the castle. Caught in a blizzard, she eventually reaches her goal exhausted and dies in the arms of her beloved.

Her performance in the role of the romantic heroine did not go unnoticed. Maureen Bertolini, renamed Marina Berti, carved out a small niche for herself in the history of wartime screen goddesses.

She nearly always played the victim. Righelli directed her in *Storia di una capinera* [Story of a blackcap] (1943), a star vehicle inspired by the novel of the same name by Giovanni Verga. Here we find Marina, as photogenic as

ever, in a convent. She plays the novice Maria Anselmi, as she prepares to take her vows. However, the outbreak of an epidemic means that all the novices are sent home.

Back in her village, Maria falls in love with her half-sister's fiancé. She is consumed with passion, but the sense of guilt is unbearable. Maria returns to the convent, where she takes her vows, but dies soon afterwards. This part, as one of Verga's classic tragic heroines, was to become a prestigious platform for an actress hungry for great roles.

Photogenic and distinctive, Marina Berti was one of the most alluring objects of desire in Fascist cinema. The misfortunes that rained down on her slender body increased its erotic appeal. Marina's beauty always had a taste of sweet temptation.

This occurs again in *La donna della montagna* [The woman from the mountains] (1943) where Amedeo Nazzari marries her even though he is haunted by the memory of his late wife. However, the filming of this mountainside *Rebecca* was interrupted by the war in September 1943, when the cast had just finished filming on location in Cervinia. The movie was badly edited and was only released at the end of the war, as was another of Marina's films, *La porta del cielo* [The door to the sky] (1944).

Marina Berti took her chances in postwar Italian cinema – assuming the new pseudonym of Maureen Melrose – and then tried her luck in Hollywood. Maybe she was banking on her London roots, but it seems they were to little advantage.

Marina Berti with Massimo Serato in **Giacomo l'idealista** *(1943).*

[see also p. 150]

Sweethearts and fiancés of the Italian movies of the '40s.
Above: *Vera Carmi, Lilia Silvi, Leonardo Cortese, Valentina Cortese, Paolo Stoppa in* Happy Days *(1942)*.
Below: *Lilia Silvi, Carla Del Poggio, Irasema Dilian in* Violette nei capelli *(1942)*.

SCHOOLGIRLS OF CINECITTÀ

Between the thirties and the forties, Fascist cinema enriched the Olympus of its stars. In an increasingly authoritarian panorama, the regime had to replace the actresses from abroad who were starting to disappear from Italian screens. They were uprooted and supplanted by young healthy saplings, in the enriched soil of Cinecittà.

So all at once, almost by magic, a whole new crop of young actresses began appearing, producing a new generation. The naive purity of adolescence was a flag to wave, synonym of the honesty of the soul, ideological fidelity and clean feelings. All of these maidens were part of dreamlike love stories rooted in the world of fantasy. The lasses were bait to lure Italian audiences far from everyday reality.

But where did these Italian adolescents live? As always in Italian society, during Fascism, the lives of these girls were embedded in the warm womb of the family. The scenario offered little inspiration to the imagination of screenwriters. The only alternative was the school world, which was legitimatized by the very popular book *Cuore* [Heart] by Edmondo de Amicis.

The four or five hours a day spent at school were too short to get up to much mischief, so boarding school became the favorite setting. Here was a place where the girls could have a fuller life experience. They could study, play, plot and, above all, dream. For this reason the boarding school (with its working-class variation of the orphanage and the nineteenth-century version of the convent school) became the strategic location for Fascist cinema.

The boarding school girls studied – and almost always detested – home economics, geometry, chemistry, history, music, German (but never English, the language of the perfidious Albion), and commercial correspondence. They were child-women who were mainly interested in scanning the horizon for any possible Prince Charming. As the cleaning lady of the Audax Commercial School (where Maddalena, with zero in conduct, and the day student Irasema Dilian, are both students) puts it, "Women can do without history and math, but they can't do without powder and lipstick," in *Maddalena... zero in condotta* [Maddalena... zero in conduct] (1940).

Looking at the movies of the Fascist years, we get the impression that almost all Italian girls lived in boarding schools. This was, of course, far from true. But these places were a substitute for basic values: religion, first of all, and a "military" vision of existence. The boarding schools were like convents, given the frequent presence of nuns and lay sisters. But they were also reminiscent of barracks, with aprons as uniforms, marching in lines, and the discipline that reigned, at least in theory, thanks to the inflexible vigilance of watchdog-teachers armed with operetta meanness, regularly the butt of the students' pranks.

Thanks to the abundance of convent schools, boarding schools, and all-girl high schools, hallowed sanctuaries of virginity, the young actresses of Fascist pictures found a wealth of roles in movies with almost all-female casts. Any kind of character could be found in the microcosm of a boarding school: sentimental or devilish, treacherous or angelic, craven or proud, scapegoat or smart-aleck. So while these movies were vehicles of an ideology that today we would define as "anti-feminist," it is a paradox that Fascism offered Italian actresses a much richer, wider range of parts and professional opportunities than were available to actresses in later eras. During the sixties and the seventies, in spite of the Bellocchis and Bertoluccis, the screen presence of women was almost always limited to secondary roles, in the shadow of the unbridled importance of male stars.

So at the end of the thirties and beginning of the forties, boarding school movies became a type of genre dedicated to women. It was abandoned after the war, being deemed too full of sentimental triviality. It was reborn in later times and elsewhere: in America during the eighties, for instance, in a completely different cultural and social scenario. Then, after the fall of taboos and barriers between the sexes, the sometimes voluntarily demented "college movie" mixed boys and girls together in an orgy of riotous fun and fluttering underwear.

Lilia Silvi

There was a moment, between 1940 and 1942, when this twenty-year-old with an impertinent air seemed to be one of Fascism's brightest stars. Lilia Silvi's winning card wasn't beauty, but a malleable face that she could do just about anything with: she had the infantile, affected expression of children who make faces, wiggle their bodies and stick out their tongues. Her smiles were over-exuberant, childish and clownlike, but this heap of exaggeration was enlivened by a prodigious friendliness and a contagious optimism that turned Silvi into a force of nature, adored by audiences of all ages and

overshadowing more alluring, talented actresses.

This earthquake girl was the antidote to the mawkish demeanor of the sentimental sweethearts, like Adriana Benetti, who lowered their eyes and suffered in silence. Not even Lilia refused sentimentalism of course – it was the era's daily bread – but she rid it of its force and thus made it bearable.

At the beginning of the forties Lilia was partner in all of six movies with Fascist Cinecittà's number one male heartthrob, Amedeo Nazzari. It was a winning match that did wonders at the box office. Of all of Nazzari's female partners, Silvi was the one who managed to hold her own with the most authority. Her spirited wiggles counteracted the monolithic Nazzari, bombastic hero of honesty.

Lilia always played the role of the good-hearted ingenue, frivolous but capable of rolling up her sleeves when needed and even willing to make sacrifices for her girlfriends, often more beautiful, richer and luckier in love than she. She stuck her nose in other people's business, especially their sentimental business, lavishing advice and suggestions. Her heart was very, very tender. But she believed in friendship more than in love.

Lilia Silvi – her real name was Silvana Musitelli – was born in Rome on November 23, 1922 but the movie mags of the early forties made her a year younger to render her portrayals as a tomboy more credible. She immediately revealed a talent as a child prodigy, studying dance at the school of the Rome Opera House and music at the Conservatory of Santa Cecilia. She started her acting career at the tender age of four, at nursery school.

Italian audiences fell in love with her in Max Neufeld's school movie *Assenza ingiustificata* [Unjustified absence] (1939), the story of a love affair between high school student Alida Valli and physician Nazzari. The seventeen-year-old Lilia is cast in the role of one of Alida's classmates, a schoolgirl who creates havoc in the classroom and steals the scene from the leading lady more than once.

She truly reaches stardom in *Giù il sipario* [Curtain!] (1940) a comedy set in theater circles where she plays the daughter of head actor and company manager Sergio Tofano, and flirts with Andrea Checchi. But even more important for her career was *Dopo divorzieremo* [After we divorce] (1940) an American-style sophisticated comedy directed by the great Malasomma where Nazzari is called Phil Golder and Lilia Silvi turns into Fanny Sullivan. The screenplay was written by

Sergio Amidei, future father of neorealism who for the moment was passing the time with the romantic "white telephone" Fascist cinema genre. It was Amidei who first grasped the potential of the couple Silvi-Nazzari: a little slip of a girl, slightly comical, flanked by her cavalier.

The movies for which Lilia Silvi would be remembered were shot at the height of the war. Nunzio Malasomma, the director best suited to helping her pace her acting, directed her in *Scampolo* (1941). Here she plays a vagabond, a sort of Charlie Chaplin in skirts. She is nicknamed "Scampolo" (Scrap) by a police chief who arrests her for vagrancy and then tells her, "You've got too much stuff for a child and too little for a woman. You're a little scrap of a thing!" So here she is, this mite of a child. She scrapes together a little money by working for an ironing lady. Once, making a delivery, she meets Tito Sacchi, alias Amedeo Nazzari, a temporarily broke engineer who does, however, have a brilliant plan for building a railroad in Sardinia. At the moment though, he doesn't even have enough money for a clean shirt. Scrap helps him out.

The image of an industrious little ant suited Lilia, the humble, hardworking girl who irons, sews and cleans. She later plays a workaholic seamstress in *Violette nei capelli* [Violets in her hair]). A heroic little woman, step by step she manages to climb mountains. Whatever she doesn't know, she learns fast. For someone who has studied very little, she has a fine mind. And she inevitably gets what she wants, especially in love. That dashing blade Amedeo Nazzari, big, strong and as handsome as the sun, is her greatest, most unattainable ambition. It is the love story of the little Cinderella who captures the heart of prince Nazzari. This outsider in the race of life who beat her more combative, better-educated rivals, played out one of the great popular daydreams of the female working class of Fascist Italy. The laundresses, the serving girls, the waifs, those at the bottom of the urban social ladder, lost themselves in this fantasy. The dream of the "private secretary" was not very far in the distance.

The young critics who created neorealism considered Lilia Silvi a tedious dreamer. Her performance in *La bisbetica domata* [The taming of the shrew] (1942) got bad reviews and Silvi went back to her old stereotype with a dignified *Giorni felici* (1942) *(Happy days)* and *La vispa Teresa* [Lively Teresa] (1943) that took her back to the characters of her beginnings.

In *La vispa Teresa*, Silvi acts and sings with her own voice imitating the "complete" actress Deanna Durbin, the mischievous Hollywood star to whom she was often compared. But this movie is also Lilia's declaration of surrender. She accepts the fact that there are no other roads for her and resigns herself to her stereotype. *Il diavolo va in collegio* [The devil goes to college] (1944) is another picture along the same lines, the most classic and mannerist of the school movies, directed by the French Jean Boyer when the collapse of the Regime is already accomplished.

Lilia would always remain one of the great popular "phenomena" of Fascist Cinecittà; after the war she failed to attain a position as prominent or as popular as the one which she had known only a few years before. Her distinctive image was too heavily imbued with the female model, Fascist-style, of the light comedies typical of the era. Intellectuals and directors of neorealism saw Lilia Silvi as a symbol of a style of filmmaking that committed the blunder of encouraging daydreaming.

Carla Del Poggio

Three out of ten in chemistry, two in German, four in history. And, naturally, zero in conduct: this was Maddalena Cenci's (or, Carla Del Poggio's) report card: the most famous high school student of Fascist cinema. Vittorio De Sica noticed her among the students at the Centro Sperimentale di Cinematografia (Rome's famous movie acting and movie-making school) and launched her as the lead in one of his most important movies, *Maddalena... zero in condotta* [Maddalena… zero in conduct] (1940). It wasn't at all a bad start. The fifteen-year-old Neapolitan Carla Del Poggio managed to do it all with a lot of smugness, entering the movie world, which would change her life, at full gallop and eventually even marrying a Milanese filmmaker, the director Alberto Lattuada.

Her real name was Maria Luisa Attanasio, and she was born in Naples on December 2, 1925. She certainly didn't have much to do with the poor and folksy Naples with its tiny side streets and colorful laundry hanging from windows. Maria Luisa belonged to an upper middle-class family of the city: a beautiful house, domestics, ballet school, holidays in Capri and lots of horseriding. She had ridden horses since the age of six (she would ride a horse with no double in the movie *Un garibaldino al convento* [A Garibaldian in the convent] (1942) and was such a perfect rider that she took part in competitions which were eagerly followed by all Neapolitan high society.

The movies never became a chance of escaping from reality for her, but her career was a result of her parents' desire who, instead of keeping her far away from the movie business in the normal stardom cliché, encouraged her to join it. Her mother had always wanted to be an actress herself. Her father, a cavalry officer, had actors like Eduardo De Filippo as friends

A romantic version of Carla Del Poggio, between Lilia Silvi and Enzo Biliotti in **Violette nei capelli** *(1942).*

and believed in an unconventional kind of education, based not only on formal education certainly, but also on gaining some kind of distinction. After junior high school, with war threatening, it appeared impossible to send her to England to learn English, and she was therefore enrolled in the school of cinematography founded by the Fascist regime, the Centro Sperimentale di Cinematografia. This was a highly educated choice and typical of the prevailing attitudes of the liberal upper middle class.

But the future Carla Del Poggio had no intention of becoming an actress: this very special school she was attending was only one experience out of many more to come, she hoped, in her life. However, in the summer of 1940 a telegram from Vittorio De Sica arrived, saying he had a sentimental school comedy in the works. He had been struck by a group photo of the new students of the Centro Sperimentale, in which Maria Luisa appeared, with the pseudonym Carla Del Poggio, a name of her own invention. Her mother immediately flew to Rome to supervise. *Maddalena... zero in condotta* brought Carla Del Poggio immediate success.

The character seemed to have been created especially for her: Maddalena Cenci, a student in the Scuola Privata Commerciale Audax (a professional high school), lives on 3 via Tomacelli, a street in central Rome. At home, lunch is served by a butler in a white jacket. Breakfast is served in her room by a maid. An upper middle-class little girl, exquisitely spoilt

– an only child – who sails through school books and tender love intrigues with devil-may-care boldness. The students of Audax do not have to wear a pinafore (like other Italian children) and Maddalena shows up in cute little skirt suits. On her collar she wears a mother-of-pearl brooch, usually with a scarf, and has a fine wristwatch.

Despite the very bad grade in conduct, she is pure, as is her girlish image. Sincere, strong, and generous, she willingly takes the blame in order to save the young teacher Vera Bergman from being fired. All of Carla Del Poggio's characters are victims of this common trait of loyalty, that is never compromised even when she is up to things like selling her school books: Maddalena only does this after having been expelled from school. Her expulsion is in fact a heroic act, because she has saved her teacher's job. Moreover, as the Audax school doorman says, "Women can do without history and math in life."

Friendship comes before love for Maddalena and other characters played by Carla Del Poggio. *Violette nei capelli* [Violets in her hair] (1942) is also the tender story of a friendship between women in which Carla co-stars again with Irasema Dilian, who appears as her sister. Carla and Irasema were friends also off the set and their mothers often got together to chat over their common problems as "star mothers."

In *Violette nei capelli* Carla Del Poggio is Mirella, a girl brought up in a freak family situation: first weaned by her musician father on anti-middle-class ideals, she is an

impassioned athelete and spends her time skiing, playing tennis, skating and doing gymnastics.

Vittorio De Sica, faultless in casting, gives her the part of the wealthy Caterinetta in the eighteenth-century period movie *Un garibaldino al convento* (1942), a lovely costume comedy, where once again Carla performs in a plot based upon female friendship. This time she co-stars with the "blonde angel" Maria Mercader, who is three years older and has already won De Sica's heart. Maria Mercader, playing Mariella, belongs to a noble family who feels contempt for Caterinetta's background. The two girls end up together in the type of military boarding school that appeared in Fascist movies and manage to overcome their families' conflict, becoming two very good friends.

Once again friendship is regarded as a very strong moral value by Carla Del Poggio and – just like Maddalena with a zero in conduct – Caterinetta refuses tattling as an escape. On the contrary, she stoically accepts to be punished in the place of her friend, for having been found with a copy of *Le ultime lettere di Jacopo Ortis* [The last letters of Jacopo Ortis]. This was an important eighteenth-century Italian classic by Ugo Foscolo about true love and political ideals, considered a dirty book by censors. Honest, open, and straightforward, Caterinetta always says exactly what she thinks. The beginning of the movie shows her "giving it" to a group of naughty girls, mimicking them Lilia Silvi-style. She loves animals and

has lots of pets: a surreal banquet at her home is suddenly interrupted by an eruption of geese, pigs, ducks and other creatures invading the dining hall and happily stomping over the precious linen.

In *Un garibaldino al convento* Carla is surprised to find out about the secret love affair between the marquis' daughter and the Garibaldian Leonardo Cortese, hiding out in the keeper's shack. Finding them in each others' arms she feels a sudden pang of jealousy. It is only a naive kind of feeling – which makes it even more charming – since she is hurt that her girlfriend has said nothing to her about it.

Her role as a careless teenager brought her success but was also her limit. As an actress, however, Carla was able to survive the stereotype which Fascist Cinecittà had created for her and eventually accepted the advent of neorealism. This transformation also coincided with her own adulthood and the physical changes that marked the end of the bloom of youth and beginning of her life as an adult woman.

"I would love to write a story especially for you, since you now seem to have acquired those qualities to play more mature characters," Luigi Zampa told her on the set of the comedy *C'è sempre un ma!* [There's always a "but!"] (1942). However, Giuseppe De Santis, Pietro Germi and above all her husband Alberto Lattuada (she would be his muse at least five years), would be those to actually do so.

[see also p. 141]

Carla Del Poggio as a teenage brat in Un garibaldino al convento *(1942) with, from left to right, Clara Auteri Pepe and Dina Romano.*

45

Irasema Dilian is a success in Schoolgirl's Diary *(1941).*

Irasema Dilian

Even more than the character of Maddalena herself in *Maddalena... zero in condotta* [Maddalena... zero in conduct] (1940), the truly unforgettable character is the "privately tutored student," a role which Vittorio De Sica offers to a young girl who, just like Carla Del Poggio, is a newcomer to cinema: Irasema Warschalowska, the daughter of a Polish diplomat. In the film credits her name appears as Eva Dilian, but from her second movie on, she would become famous as Irasema Dilian.

Born on May 27, 1924 in Rio De Janeiro, Irasema studied music and, even more intensively, classical ballet (as a professional dancer, she would later perform dance scenes without a double as in *Violette nei capelli* [Violets in her hair] made in 1942) and, at the age of only fifteen, made her debut as the private student in *Maddalena... zero in condotta*. Thus, like Carla Del Poggio, Irasema got her start by playing a character very similar to her real self, a privileged young lady from a well-to-do family who was educated at home by private tutors. It isn't

really explained whether this is because she is too slow a student or just too wealthy to go to school.

"I'm a private student," she tells the business correspondence teacher Vera Bergman, "I hardly ever come to school. My mother told me that before taking my exams I should attend at least a few classes. Teachers, though, normally come to *me*... I'm a private student!" The word "private," pronounced by Irasema with that high-pitched tone so distinctly hers, like the ring of a Chinese vase, makes the other girls giggle. They begin chanting the syllables of the magic word: "pri-vate, pri-vate, pri-vate..." Irasema twists her hat anxiously and looks around in dismay. Carla Del Poggio, who sits next to her in class, never calls her by her real name, but simply "private."

Extremely spoilt but not really bad, a bit gullible but not dumb, she abides by her schoolmates' moral code of solidarity. Even though she rarely shows up at school, when she does, she immediately tries to gain the group's acceptance.

After this film, Vittorio De Sica offers Irasema Dilian a role in *Teresa Venerdì* (1941) *(Do You Like Women?)*. Unlike the chic schoolgirls of the Audax Private School, the Istituto di Santa Chiara, a convent boarding school, is frequented by very poor orphan girls. With her well-bred air, Irasema cannot be cast as a poor abandoned orphan and De Sica invents an amusing character just for her, a budding poetess who speaks in rhymes and whose name is Lilli Passalacqua.

Draped in veils like a nymph, daddy's pampered little girl paces the sumptuous halls of her house desperately searching for the perfect rhyming word. Sympathizing with her predicament, mother tries to help, but Lilli shakes her head smiling and with her shrill voice tells her, "Mom, give up, you're no good at this!" The butler, however, is extremely gifted, and while dishing up tortellini in tomato sauce comes up with the perfect word. "But do you think that *I'm* going to accept a rhyme from a *butler*?" huffs the poetess.

It is generally believed that Irasema Dilian — like other actresses her age, such as Lilia Silvi — is incapable of handling other roles that depart from the stereotypes she has played with such success. However, much to everyone's surprise, she takes a completely new direction, proving that she is indisputably a great actress. She performs superbly in three difficult movies, *Ore 9 lezioni di chimica* (1941) *(Schoolgirl's Diary)*, *Violette nei capelli* (1942) and *Malombra* (1942).

Halfway between a comedy and a melo, *Schoolgirl's Diary* is again the usual school movie of the Fascist era. Unlike her role in *Maddalena... zero in condotta*, however, in this film Irasema portrays the model student, Maria, always in the first row and always ready with even the most difficult answers. She has thoroughly mastered the law of multiple proportions and the impossible formulas taught by their young chemistry teacher, Andrea Checchi, for whom many of the girls are swooning, especially Anna, alias Alida Valli.

The entire film is based upon the antagonism between these two girls, who have absolutely nothing in common. Alida Valli is strong and healthy, extroverted and cheerful; Irasema is dark and taciturn, frail and sickly. Dilian masterfully builds up the characterization of a courageous girl who can never bring herself to smile, tortured by some unavowable sorrow. During the night she leaves her bed and furtively runs to the waiting arms of a man in the college garden. Who is this stranger? Alida suspects it is their wonderful chemistry teacher and beside herself with jealous rage, breaks the girls' vow of mutual loyalty and tells the headmistress Giuditta Rissone everything she has seen.

Irasema cannot possibly confess who the man is, since it is her own father hunted by the police. With her restrained and intense interpretation, filled with silences, hesitations, and half smiles, Dilian proves her talent as a real actress. This superb performance is subsequently confirmed in *Violette nei capelli*, where she portrays the ballerina Oliva, a fragile child in love with an older musician. A love story related by Carlo Ludovico Bragaglia with great tenderness. Pursuing her artistic dream, Oliva stumbles into an impossible and self-destructive love affair with a much older man, who is always away and, she suspects, already has a family of his own.

The desperately sad air that the ballerina Oliva emanates in her most painful moments also appears on Edith's face, another of the sensitive characters Irasema Dilian plays during the same years, in *Malombra*, set against the nineteenth-century backdrop so typical of Mario Soldati's period works. In this movie of sublime decadence, Irasema portrays the daughter of an aging Hungarian hussar living in exile in Italy. During the entire first part of the story, Edith is a ghostly memory in her old father's mind, who has in fact not seen his daughter for many long years. Then, suddenly, the girl appears before him, emerging from the shadows of lake Como.

Her blonde hair is striking against the grim elegance of the costume designed for her by Maria De Matteis. Edith weeps in her father's arms, for it has been over fifteen years since she has last seen him. Though portraying a Hungarian woman, she now speaks perfect Italian without the slightest trace of the fluty resonance of the private student in *Maddalena... zero in condotta*. In *Malombra* audiences discover a grown-up Irasema with full sensuous lips ready for love. And, in fact,

she is living a romance – though platonic – in real life with writer Corrado Silla, alias Andrea Checchi. They see each other often, go for long walks together along the streets of Milan. She begins giving him impossible Hungarian lessons, a feeble camouflage for her true emotional attachment.

Irasema's popularity rises steadily, but the threat of war is also growing. She has now turned eighteen and, unlike Lilia Silvi who still acts in teenage roles though she is much too old for these parts, Irasema manages to make the transition to the roles of young women. With wonderful results too, as in Bragaglia's *Fuga a due voci* [Fugue for two voices] a delightful sentimental musical comedy which is released, unfortunately, in April 1943, with the fiasco of the Regime's collapse imminent. In the most tragic war years, Irasema fled to Franco's Spain, which in any case seemed to offer a bit more security, and there made a few more movies, among them a Spanish version of *Maddalena... zero in condotta*, in which she plays Carla Del Poggio's former role. Upon her return to Italy, Dilian became one of the many languid "sweethearts" created by the new Cinecittà. As many of the actresses of her generation, she could not help feeling the overwhelming bitterness of having had to interrupt her career right at the peak of her success.

[see also p. 143]

Irasema Dilian in **Violette nei capelli** *(1942).*

Adriana Benetti

Adriana Benetti usually portrayed the victimized fiancée, as in **Four Steps in the Clouds** *(1942).*

Diction lessons at the Centro Sperimentale could never alter Adriana Benetti's round accent typical of her native Emilia in northern Italy. At the end of her first year of studies, Vittorio De Sica catapults her into an important movie, in the leading role, no less, when he casts her in *Teresa Venerdì (Do You Like Women?)*. Thus, this completely unknown actress becomes the most famous orphan in Italian cinema.

Born in Comacchio, in the province of Ferrara on December 4, 1919, Adriana Benetti grew up in a family of farmers similar to the one in *Quattro passi tra le nuvole* (1942) *(Four Steps in the Clouds)*. She was the kind of dreamer – there were lots of them in the thirties and forties, particularly in rural Italy – who went to the cinema every day of the week and adored the big Hollywood productions, imagining she was Carole Lombard in the arms of Fred MacMurray.

Behind her defenselesss little girl appearance she hid an iron will: she placed first in the competitive entrance exam for the Centro Sperimentale. This little brunette of peasant stock managed to win over such important film directors as Luigi Chiarini and Alessandro Blasetti precisely because of her common beauty. She certainly wasn't the woman tigress nor the artificial Fascist "white telephone" dolly, nor even the blond well-brought up young lady. She had bright luminous eyes and a natural look just like any number of young Italian women one might see on the bus, running errands, or shopping in the local markets. Petit, with thick dark hair, always tossled, tiny little shoulders, small breasts. A typical Italian girl, nothing exceptional.. and this was precisely why she became just the right interpreter of a kind of cinema that aspired to reality: one that Luigi Chiarini, Umberto Barbaro, and Francesco Pasinetti had on their minds. As true founders of a Regime style, they held up Soviet realism as their model. These same ideals were also fervently shared by Vittorio De Sica when he made *Do You Like Women?* This film begins Benetti's career as a weeping woman. When she cries she is absolutely real. When she isn't crying, she has those shiny moist eyes just before tears. She was even a cry baby out of character, in real life: while shooting, she used to burst into tears every time De Sica corrected her acting.

Those watery eyes also come in handy when she gets her second part in *Avanti c'è posto* [There's room up front] (1942). Adriana Benetti represents the opposite of the obnoxious types portrayed by the middle-class well-fed, cheerful, naughty girls like Carla Del Poggio or Chiaretta Gelli who are always ready to play tricks on someone. They had been brought up in an affluent world. Instead, Benetti is puny, ruffled, and scared, with a gut-wrenching longing for love. Naturally the audiences, typically sentimental, more readily identified with her melancholy characters. *Four Steps in the Clouds*, another movie in the neorealistic vein, was also received enthusiastically. In this film Adriana is again flanked by a very talented male partner, and, in the footsteps of De Sica and Fabrizi, it is now Gino Cervi to co-star with her as a pastry vendor.

With the character she portrays in *Four Steps in the Clouds*, Adriana Benetti returns to her rural origins. Maria, in fact, comes from a family of farmers. And like Adriana, she leaves the countryside to seek fortune in the city. But the unfortunate girl in the movie is seduced and abandoned. She is on her way home, pregnant, anticipating her family's reaction when they discover their daughter is an unwed mother, when on the train she meets Gino Cervi, a good and sensitive man, who pities her and agrees to pretend to be her husband – at least for a few hours.

Maria weeps a lot in this film too. "I don't even know why I'm crying," she confides to the stranger Gino Cervi. Later, after having revealed everything to her mother, she bursts out sobbing "I wandered through the streets half mad. I wanted to die!"

Slowly the Benetti stereotype begins to change: from a very poor girl she becomes middle-class. This is confirmed in 1943 when she appears in movies such as *Gente dell'aria* [Sky people], in which she plays a test pilot's daughter who falls in love with Gino Cervi, a courageous pilot, and then in *Quartieri alti* [Rich neighborhoods] in which she is a provincial girl from Rovigo in northern Italy, who moves to Rome to go to school.

But it is certainly not this character which will be her most enduring portrayal. For audiences, Adriana Benetti will forever be the orphan "Teresa Friday" and the poor humble little girl. They will not easily forget those frightened eyes searching men's faces in the hope of finding a friendly smile, perhaps even love, but above all, a father's protection.

Valentina Cortese

The diaphanous blonde who casts a slow sidelong glance on life is Valentina Cortese. She looks like a porcelain statuette, especially in her first movies, which take her back to distant times. Mournful and emotional, she faces every problem with whines and sobs. In *Quattro ragazze sognano* [Four dreaming girls] (1943) she tries to open a bottle with a pair of scissors and hurts herself lamenting, "Oh, what if I get an infection now?" In *Giorni felici* (1942) *(Happy Days)* she injures her bare foot on the hook of fisherman Leonardo Cortese. And again you can hear her peevish complaining.

Born in Milan on January 1, 1925, Valentina developed a mad passion for the stage at an early age. "I remember coming back home from school and locking myself in my room, letting my hair loose in front of the mirror and starting to act." She was just sixteen when, during a tour of Cinecittà, she ran into stage director Guido Salvini. She had met Salvini the previous summer in Stresa, where she was on holiday with her grandmother. Valentina had amused herself directing and acting in some improvised skits for children. Guido Salvini, who had enjoyed those summer performances and was preparing a movie about the theater world, then offered her a part as a young girl in *L'orizzonte dipinto* [Painted horizon] (1941).

These were the golden years of Lilia Silvi and Carla Del Poggio who were extremely popular among Cinecittà's flocks of starlets: the demand for teenage actresses was growing. At her age (she was only fifteen), and with her talent, Valentina Cortese could have easily been a big success in the school-movie genre. However, oddly enough, her first roles took her back into the distant past amidst lace and crinoline. In *La regina di Navarra* [The queen of Navarra] (1942), she is princess Eleanor of Austria, an undemanding part. Just as modest, but more prestigious, was the role

Valentina Cortese with Amedeo Nazzari in La cena delle beffe *(1941).*

Alessandro Blasetti had offered her a year before in *La cena delle beffe* [The dinner of derision] (1941): Lisabetta, one of three mistresses abandoned by hot-blooded Neri, alias Amedeo Nazzari.

Even the film *Il bravo di Venezia* [The good man of Venice] (1941) sends Valentina back in time. In the Venice of the Doges she is Alina, the niece of a treacherous banker and the mistress of artist Rossano Brazzi.

Valentina Cortese with tough-looking Amedeo Nazzari in Happy Days *(1942).*

Alina is frail but stubborn, qualities that many of Valentina Cortese's characters will later share. Her precious sixteenth-century gowns, which keep her from moving freely, promise a lovely full bosom.

With her big innocent eyes she is a forerunner of some of the characters that will later be portrayed by Audrey Hepburn. Only the film *Soltanto un bacio* [Only a kiss] shows a grown-up Valentina; in all the other movies of that period she appears in teenage roles. She seems very young in *Happy Days*, a light-hearted comedy of summer teenage romance, in which she is Marianna, a silly and deliciously sentimental young girl. Fluffy blonde curls, bicycle rides and shorts that reveal fantastic long slender legs: Marianna is in love with her cousin Oliviero, alias Leonardo Cortese (homonyms by pure coincidence), who enjoys bullying her.

The movie which represents the biggest challenge as a good cryer will be *Primo amore* [First love] (1941), in which she is again painfully in love with Leonardo Cortese. In this movie – as in *Happy Days*, which follows a year later – Valentina and Leonardo are again cousins. Cortese is a girl from Amalfi, desperately in love with her cousin Pietro, a jazz musician who has grown up in the States. Out-smarted by Jane Blue, alias Vivi Gioi, Valentina goes almost mad with grief and attempts suicide. She is rescued, but immediately after this falls seriously ill. A song dedicated to Valentina by her beloved cousin will save her.

Between 1942 and 1943 Cortese finally found a place in the sun upon the crowded Olympus dedicated to sentimental stars. She was therefore included in the most famous all-star movie of those years, *Nessuno torna indietro* [No one turns back] (1943) by Alessandro Blasetti, who gave her one of the seven leading roles. Her character's name is actually Valentina, a girl still very much a child, who bites her nails and loves eating chocolate. But teenage dreams – for her as well as for her girlfriends – are about to come to an end, and even Valentina is doomed to a gloomy marriage.

Although Valentina Cortese interpreted quite a few movies during the Fascist period, she left no mark on the cinema of those years. Paradoxically, the evanescence of her image would help her to continue her career in the postwar years. Other teenage actresses like Lilia Silvi or Chiaretta Gelli never managed to break away from the stereotypes which Fascist moviemakers created for them. For Valentina, however, it wasn't difficult to have people forget her and start all over again. The decade after the war was intense and full of satisfaction for Cortese, not only in Italy but also in Hollywood, where she was given the new name, Valentina Cortesa.

[see also p. 84]

Loredana, one of the last Italian sweethearts of the war years.

Loredana

The gentle little lamb, Loredana, or officially, Loredana Padoan, got her start grazing innocently in Cinecittà's meadows, nibbling on minor character roles. Her big kind eyes would make her suitable for the naive sweetheart roles, a likely victim at the hands of base scoundrels.

Born in Venice on March 24, 1924, Loredana Padoan had first gone to teachers' training school before attending dance, music, and acting classes. Mario Camerini had her debut with a very small part in *Grandi magazzini* [Department stores] (1939) as a strikingly pretty sales clerk: a peaches-and-cream beauty tormented by an obsessive and impossible customer. Between 1940 and 1942 Loredana appeared in a great number of movies, usually in very minor roles, except when she played the supporting female role as Neala, in the adventure movie *Il figlio del corsaro rosso* [The red pirate's son] (1942), and the only female character in the sequel *Gli ultimi filibustieri* [The last pirates] (1942), both based upon adventure novels by Emilio Salgari.

Graceful and delicate, there was something special about Loredana who managed to attract notice among the pageant of sweetheart starlets available at Cinecittà.

1942 was her lucky year, when, at eighteen she was offered the leading role in *La signorina* by director Laszlo Kish. She is Lulu, a chaste young woman who has grown up in the home of a writer, Nino Besozzi. When she becomes of marriageable age, her well-intentioned stepfather begins looking for a suitable match for her. However, when he discovers that the betrothed is anything but worthy, he marries Lulu himself instead.

Lulu's daughterly affection turns into true love. As is often the case with Cinecittà's sweethearts, Lulu falls in love with a man who is old enough to be her father.

Between 1942 and 1944 Loredana eventually entered as a full-fledged "sweetheart" into Cinecittà's pantheon of such actresses, but she continued to be offered both leading parts as well as minor roles.

Loredana's docile fragility, however, will always be bound to a spectacular costume film on the life and loves of the painter Raffaello Sanzio (Raphael), *La fornarina* [The baker's daughter], shot between 1943 and 1944. The movie was packed with women of the Reich: Lida Baarova and Anneliese Uhlig make numerous appearances in Renaissance gowns of breathtaking cleavages and nudity. Loredana, however, is the innocent lamb, the young girl suffering from a bad heart, Maria Dovizi da Bibbiena, shy and god-fearing. Long golden locks, lowered eyes, she confesses to Raphael, "I live thinking of your painting." And in secret she kisses a drawing, a gift from the adored artist.

Postwar cinema offered very few opportunities for Loredana. Even her marriage to Giuseppe Rinaldi didn't last beyond the forties. In 1949 as Loredana, barely twenty-five, was separating from Rinaldi, she also bid farewell to any artistic activity forever.

Bianca Della Corte

Two big eyes full of melancholy like the sea of her beloved Naples, Bianca Della Corte peers from the screen at her audiences with a slightly ecstatic and inquisitive smile. In *Ore 9 lezione di chimica* (1941) *(Schoolgirl's Diary)* she has round plump cheeks like a ripe peach. In other movies she is more grown-up, a little lady, with a mischievous little smile hidden behind ready lips.

Born in Naples in July 1917, she made her debut with a part as a seamstress in *Addio giovinezza!* [Good-bye youth!] (1940), Emma, the faithful friend and colleague of cute Dorina, alias Maria Denis. They go for walks and skating together. They pick up two stalwart medical students; the star, Maria Denis, gets good-looking Adriano Rimoldi, and Bianca has to settle for the duller Carlo Minello. Emma in the film wisely knows that no medical student will ever marry a poor seamstress. She tries to reason with her girlfriend who is just too in love to listen.

Bianca Della Corte's debut is promising, especially thanks to her natural friendliness which helps the budding young starlet hold her own alongside Maria Denis, the established star of the movie. In some instances, such as at the skating rink, in fact, it even appears possible that Bianca could steal the scene from Denis.

Against the backdrop of an ancient *belle epoque* Turin, skillfully recreated by Ferdinando Maria Poggioli, the twenty-three-year-old Neapolitan Della Corte coos happily with her morose sweetheart. Unfortunately, this successful debut was not followed by any important performances and after some rather poor parts, Bianca ended up in the gynaecum of *Schoolgirl's Diary*. At twenty-four she was too old for teenage roles, but Mario Mattoli had her wear two braids tied up in cute little ribbons and she became Luisa, Alida Valli's best friend. A funny chatterbox, she makes the perfect partner for Alida Valli, as she mimicks their gloomy chemistry teacher, Andrea Checchi.

A highlight in Bianca's career was a very important role she played in *Il conte di Montecristo (The Count of Montecristo)* (1942), which was released in two parts. Della Corte appears in the second part only, *La rivincita di Montecristo (The Revenge of Montecristo)*, in which she is Haydée, the leading young actress. She is even dressed in an oriental costume as the daughter of the pasha of Janina. After marrying the count of Montecristo, she wears western-style clothes. This role is very different from the lovely little characters of her past portrayals. Della Corte is seen almost as an avenger when she causes the suicide of the magistrate De Villefort, one of her husband's persecutors.

In *The Revenge of Montecristo*, Bianca is the only Italian actress in an otherwise all-French cast. Most likely it was during the filming of this movie, mainly shot in France, that the young Neapolitan woman met writer Félicien Marceau, destined to become her life companion. For him, she would leave the world of cinema forever.

Bianca Della Corte as Haydée, the "righter of wrongs," in the second part of the French movie The Count of Montecristo *(1942) with Pierre Richard-Willm.*

Above: *Anna Magnani with Federico Collino in* Do You Like Women? *(1941). During the 1930s and beginning of the '40s Magnani was only offered parts as music hall singer or maid.* Right: *the two real vamps of Italian cinema, Elli Parvo and Clara Calamai.*

covered with a flowered apron. The heat is stifling. We can almost smell the pungent odor of her sweat. "You've got shoulders like a horse," she says to Massimo Girotti in a lecherous voice.

My God, Clara, where are your evening gowns, your mink stoles and cute little hats? The only way to recognize this Clara is to look into her wild eyes with the same gleam of sin as the courtesan's in *La cena delle beffe*.

Visconti's drastic transformation is nothing more than a re-styling. In reality, Calamai is still pure seduction even in *Ossessione*, a negative character drenched in erotic insinuations. She continues to be branded with the trademark of original sin, despite the fact that the giddy courtesan is now an adulteress in a detective story. The only real transformation involves the character's moral world. In *La cena delle beffe* Calamai's degeneration is lighthearted, in *Ossessione* it is dramatic.

Calamai represented a type of femininity that was much too modern, a type that Italian motion pictures at the beginning of the forties viewed as immoral. So, Ferdinando Maria Poggioli decided to cast her in the part of a rich American heiress in *Sorelle Materassi* [The Materassi sisters] (1943). Here she is transformed into the archetype of North American feminine beauty. She wears shorts, smokes, drives a car. She becomes the woman who introduces the recent fashions of the New World to Europe. A sort of demon…

In May 1944 Calamai married Count Leonardo Bonzi, an explorer who also made documentaries. She followed him in his frequent wanderings to far-off continents, populated with wild beasts and exotic birds or, otherwise, waited for him in their lovely home in Milan, with her faithful dog Piera to keep her company.

[see also p. 148]

Elli Parvo

One of the most famous busts in Italian motion pictures belonged to Elli Parvo. It could be glimpsed under a diaphanous veil in the Venetian movie *I due Foscari* [The two Foscaris] (1942) shot right in the midst of the war, a year after Clara Calamai's famous nude scene in *La cena delle beffe* [The dinner of derision] (1941). Along with the placid damsel Calamai, and the savage Duranti, Elli Parvo was the high point of Fascist eroticism. But in contrast to the other high priestesses of sex, she never became a major star. According to some, she didn't have a powerful enough paramour. Nevertheless, a look at her filmography shows that what she really lacked was a variety of roles. The same animal eroticism was forced upon her in almost all her films and she ended up by becoming monotonous, locked in a prison of character parts.

Her stage name, Parvo, is a mystery. In Latin, *parvus* means "small." What did this giantess of Fascist Cinecittà have that was so small? Absolutely nothing. Large breasts, a large mouth, large hips and an enormous, powerful jaw line. The name Parvo did not come from Latin (in spite of the Mussolini-inspired cult for all things Roman). It came from Pardo. Before redubbing herself Parvo, this pre-war Anita Ekberg called herself Elli Pardo. It was a name that recalled the pounce of a leopard, perfect for a woman who brandished her breasts with barbarous energy. But the name Pardo had Jewish echoes to it, and Elli romanized it to avoid any trouble during the war. Her real name was terribly commonplace: Elvira Gobbo.

Born in Milan on October 17, 1915, she inherited the stature of a Hapsburg from her Friulian mother and German father. Her magnificent green eyes contrasted with jet-black hair.

Elli Parvo wasn't very noticeable between 1937 and 1940. In those years, she appeared in

Elli Parvo and Viviane Romance are two fiery and sensuous girls in Carmen *(1942).*

purely decorative parts in movies by famous comics such as the De Filippo brothers, Gandusio, Musco, Totò, Macario.

After 1940 Elli – increasingly taciturn, statuesque and forbidding – concentrated her efforts on melodrama. Her hair as dark as coal, she was the husband-stealer who lured men away from sweet, honest maidens, fragile, and almost always blond little defenseless birds confronting the claws of the eagle of sex.

A very sinister Elli Parvo appears in *I due Foscari*, where she plays a jealous, vindictive theatrical actress. Abandoned by her former lover, she marries an elderly judge desperately in love with her, Memo Benassi, and schemes against the man who has abused her love. "What a fury of a woman," Benassi tells her, "you're like a tigress." Make-up artists accentuate her high cheekbones to turn her into a Doris Duranti-like tiger-woman. The French director Christian-Jacque casts her in a small but prominent part in his *Carmen* (1942). She plays the worker in the Seville tobacco factory who fights and comes to blows with Carmen, played by Viviane Romance – a battle of tigers.

"I've been wanting to scratch your eyes out for a long time, you witch," screeches Viviane Romance.

"Damn you, you bitch!" growls Elli Parvo. The two women fly at each other in a fury of kicking, scratching, biting, and end up on the ground in a wrestling match.

She was particularly suited to the role of the "lost" woman. Young Roberto Rossellini, fascinated by young women like Roswita Schmidt with strong jawlines, gives her the female lead in a movie with a tormented story, full of Visconti-style eroticism, *Desiderio* [Desire]. It was started in 1943 with another title, shot during the bombings, and released after the war. Begun by Rosellini and completed by Marcello Pagliero, the picture is certainly no masterpiece, but it is definitely the most inspired acting of Elli Parvo's career. She paints the vibrant portrait of a debauched woman desperately trying to redeem herself. Her unreal marble-like beauty becomes alive, modern and immediate. With her great bust barely hidden under a black slip, her long hair cascading over the pillow, and all rhetoric gone from her gaze, this is one of the most exciting movie scenes of the period. Moviegoers could actually breathe the sultry atmosphere of that bedroom. Unfortunately, *Desiderio* was released late and badly. After only one day of viewing, it was confiscated and subjected to numerous cuts by censors. So Elli's image would remain tied to the panting eroticism of her routine characters: Lolita de Fuego in *Il fanciullo del West* [Little boy from the West], the extremely bad girl of *I due Foscari*, the wild woman of *Carmen*, a man-eater who hunts down and torments sweet little blondes, slightly exaggerated, a bit of a caricature of herself.

[see also p. 101]

Anna Magnani

The myth of the neorealistic Nannarella belongs to the postwar period and Rossellini's manifesto *Roma città aperta* (1945) *(Rome, Open City)*. But Anna Magnani's fiery woman-of-the-people roles began in Fascist motion pictures, in characters like Elide, the fruit and vegetable vendor in *Campo de' fiori* (1943). From the beginning of the forties, Magnani – bolstered by her success in variety – was able to make a brazen on-screen exhibition of her Roman dialect that was an outright offense to the purist linguistics of the Regime. It was a way of speaking that didn't conform to the respectable settings of the pictures in vogue. Unpolished but sincere, Magnani's women said exactly what they thought. They were often music hall singers on their days off, dancers, often mistresses, and never entrapped in the prison of a family.

Her forte was playing music hall characters like the Fanny of *Cavalleria* [Cavalry] (1936). Set in the Turin of the *belle époque*, Magnani plays a singer with bouncy blond curls who utterly bewitches army lieutenant Enrico Viarisio. Then come the roles as Vanda Reni in *La fuggitiva* [The fugitive] (1941), a variety artist and unwed mother who lives in a room in the Grand Hotel; the music hall star Lulu in *Finalmente soli* [Finally alone] (1942); and, above all, the soubrette Loletta Prima in *Teresa Venerdì* (1941) *(Do You Like Women?)*. Striking her chest, Loletta warbles at the top of her lungs:

Here in my heart, in my heart,
is my love, my love…
Here in my bos'm, my bos'm
is my love, my love.

All of Anna Magnani's music hall singers grew out of the "crude woman" stereotype. They tried to hide the genuineness of their vulgarity under an artistic varnish. They were ashamed of their origins which was why they attempted to appear refined and respectable, though sometimes the most spontaneous insults exploded from their working-class hearts and mouths. "I'm just too refined, you pig!" shouts Loletta in *Do You Like Women?* where she plays a second-rate music hall singer interested in good-looking Vittorio De Sica's money.

All of these roles of down-at-heel singers are a bridge between variety and motion pictures. But they also come at just the right moment to draw out that combative verve that would make Nannarella's fortune.

In 1943 Anna was at the peak of her popularity as a music hall singer. Over the past year she and Totò, Italy's most famous

comedian, had become a fixed pair in Michele Galdieri's revue, *Volumineide*. Her comic talent shone in numerous parodies of heroines of literature from Anna Karenina to Malombra (Soldati's film with Isa Miranda was still fresh in people's minds). Carlo Ludovico Bragaglia tried to bring one of these characterizations to the musical *La vita è bella* [Life is beautiful], a star vehicle for the singing virtuoso, Alberto Rabagliati.

Magnani's breakthrough, from caricatures to authentic parts, came with *Campo de' fiori* (1943), written by a young Federico Fellini for the comedian Aldo Fabrizi. The story was set in the fruit and vegetable market of Campo de' Fiori in Rome, historical site where Giordano Bruno was burnt at the stake in 1600. Magnani plays the part of Elide, a working-class woman who has a fruit and vegetable stand. Her heart still belongs to fishmonger Fabrizi, who, after having seduced her, has left her and now dreams of improbable affairs with high-class women. "Who would want that blockhead?" cries Magnani, brandishing a huge cabbage in Fabrizi's direction.

At the end they fight. She screams at him for wanting "other flounder to fry" and the corpulent fishmonger tries to push her head under the fountain. This bit of theater blends perfectly with the atmosphere of the market and is told with a taste for truth that is already redolent of neorealism.

Though never a real beauty, Magnani makes herself frankly ugly to become a market woman in black rags with a shawl thrown over her shoulders.

The respectable bourgeois lady vainly courted by the fishmonger is an icy Caterina Boratto, who makes Magnani seem like a wild animal in comparison. Ice and fire. The contrast heightens the intensity of Magnani's working-class character. And when Fabrizi chides her for not being genteel enough, of not having the right manners, she growls, "That's how I am. I've got no manners. I'm not one of *them*!"

With *Campo de' fiori*, the Roman dialect that Fascism had banished from the screen experienced a sudden brilliant comeback. Anna Magnani staked her claim to becoming queen of the cinema of the future, anxious to throw open its windows to the world, unfortunately closed for so long, a cinema that many already had smoldering inside of them for a long time.

While waiting for history to turn the page, Magnani goes back to her caricatures of wrathful music hall singers, where a base vulgarity hides under the façade of the artist, both in *L'ultima carrozzella* [The last carriage] (1943) and the comedy *Il fiore sotto gli occhi* [A flower right before you] (1944). But this star of vaudeville knows very well that she can do much better…

[see also p. 67]

Anna Magnani is stiff and ridiculous with Virgilio Riento in one of her last movies before the end of the war La vita è bella *(1943).*

*Doris Duranti with
Amedeo Nazzari in*
È sbarcato un marinaio
(1939).

*Luisa Ferida with
Fosco Giachetti in*
Fari nella nebbia
(1942).

STARS IN BLACK SHIRTS

Which Cinecittà stars were really involved with the Fascist regime? All of them and none of them.

They were all stars of a quasi state-run motion picture industry (or at least one heavily sponsored by the Regime) and they were also public figures. Consequently, Italian actresses of those years could hardly decline to take part in ceremonies, celebrations, meetings, inaugurations and demonstrations. But very few of them embraced the Fascist rites with any real conviction.

The black shirt was men's attire and the association of many a movie star was limited to the role of mistress, accomplice, kept woman or queen. The only black garments they wore were black lingerie.

Calamai's erotic air in *La cena delle beffe* [The Dinner of derision] (1941) is permeated with the kind of morbid sensuality that some, for instance Pasolini in *Salò o le 120 giornate di Sodoma* (1975) *(Salò or the 120 Days of Sodom)*, attributed to Fascism. In the same way, the role of Giovanna di Morreale played by Elisa Cegani in Blasetti's *Ettore Fieramosca* (1938) was that of a female warrior close to the Fascist worship of war.

Rumor had it that Maria Denis, the shy servant in *Sissignora* [Yes Ma'am] (1941) welcomed the attentions of Pietro Koch, active in the Fascist police who was executed after Liberation. Denis, in fact, was investigated after the war by agents of the political police in Milan. Then there was Mariella Lotti, who apparently had the backing of His Excellency Galeazzo Ciano.

But in all eras – and in all regimes, even up to our own present times no doubt – movie stars have had "secret" relations and hushed up affairs with important politicians offering the seduction of power and the right backing for a career. It is almost an organic part of the world of entertainment.

However, in the mythology of the Italian motion picture industry, only three actresses go down in history with truly "black" souls. Dark lady Doris Duranti – aside from the parts of man-eater she played on the screen – proudly flaunted her role as the "favorite" of Fascist big-wig Alessandro Pavolini. He was commander in the Black Brigades during the more than one hundred days of Salò and power behind the throne of the Ministry of Popular Culture, the Fascist propaganda wing. Luisa Ferida, of Emilia Romagna, was introduced to the pleasures of cocaine by her lover Osvaldo Valenti. The partisans executed the two of them together, accusing them of betrayal and of torturing the Regime's opponents. Finally, there was the innocent Miria di San Servolo, otherwise known as Maria Petacci, the sister of Claretta, Benito Mussolini's official mistress, executed with him.

Doris Duranti

With its weakness for angelic women, Fascist cinema did not produce many vamps. Actually, it produced only one, Doris Duranti, the "dark" lady of Cinecittà. The three elements of her universe were Love, Luxury and Pleasure. She was not the only woman who let herself be led by these three guiding stars, but she was one of the few who had the courage to admit it.

On the screen she dominated men. Her type of femininity had a witch-like quality to it, together with a strong exotic element. She became an Abyssinian, a Mongol, a Slav, and an Albanian in her movies. She had the advantage of high cheekbones, full African lips and slightly almond-shaped eyes. There was no chance of her ever being able to act the role of the good mother, a shy serving-girl or well-to-do fiancée.

Off the screen and on the stage of life, her behavior almost surpassed that of her most devilish characters. Aside from her extraordinary fondness for alcohol and, sometimes for cocaine (but she wasn't alone in this), she went through men with a

After Clara Calamai's nude breasts, Doris Duranti takes up the challenge as well in Carmela (1942).

vengeance, showing a particular liking for the powerful. This man-hunter – and her prey were almost always married – had no pretensions about appearing moral.

Though the daughter of an anarchist who detested the Fascists, Doris strongly supported the Regime. It was not only due to her relationship with a thoroughbred of Fascist ideology like Alessandro Pavolini, or because she shared certain ideals – starting with a self-destructive taste for transgression; it was also because of her scorn for its opponents. Duranti hated partisans and anti-Fascists because they persecuted the mistresses (of Mussolini or Valenti) while sparing the wives. She would have met the same fate as Luisa Ferida if she hadn't escaped to Switzerland first.

She stole husbands on the screen as well, which might have been the reason that female audiences despised her. "In some way, all women would have liked to be like me, but they hated me." To make up for it, Doris drove men wild, much like Clara Calamai, but more so. Like Clara Calamai, she reveals her breasts for the camera. This is in 1942, on the set of *Carmela* a year after *La cena delle beffe*.

This dark star was born on April 25, 1917. Paradoxically enough, she was born in the city where the Italian Communist Party was founded, Livorno.

Doris Duranti, a transgressive star in the Italian firmament.

She ran away from home before she was even seventeen, chasing fantasies of older men who promised the moon in exchange for a kiss. One of them was Nino Besozzi, Cinecittà's national heartthrob. Naturally he promised the girl from Livorno a future as a star.

Doris believed him, and her mother was forced to move to Rome to act as a chaperone for her daughter, the aspiring leading lady. It was a little like what would happen many years later to Romilda Vallani from a town near Naples and her daughter Sofia Scicolone who came to be known as Sophia Loren.

1936: Fascist Italy is proud of its provinces far beyond the sea. And it is in Africa that Doris Duranti reaches definitive stardom. After a small part as a curious tourist in Augusto Genina's film *Squadrone bianco* (1936) *(White Squadron)*, she is cast in the starring role of *Sentinelle di bronzo* [Bronze sentries]. This is a teary melodrama set in the colonies with an almost all-male cast, based on the novel by Marcello Orano and Sandro Sandi, *Marrabò*.

Doris was not at all alarmed at the idea of turning herself into a dark Abyssinian woman, Dahabò, virgin of the forest. She put herself in the hands of make-up artist Euclide Santoli, the magician of Cinecittà, who smeared chocolate-colored greasepaint on her from top to toe and plaited her hair in a forest of braids. Sophia Loren, another exotic creature of the silver screen, would endure similar treatment in one of her roles.

Doris kept company with princes, captains of industry and ministers. One them, the greatly feared Alessandro Pavolini, Mussolini's thirty-eight-year-old right hand man, fell in love with the tigress from Livorno. He too was married. Doris met him while she was shooting *Carmela*, a passionate melodrama filmed during the bombing of Tirrenia.

Theirs was another love affair that grew out of the shadows of the war. It was made even more dramatic by the sense of the imminent end hovering over all of the Duce's men. Pavolini was one of them and possibly the least detested among them. He was a tried and true party official, one of the few Fascists who did not use his power or that of the Party to accumulate personal wealth. Doris was not only seduced by the scent of power, which she always adored, but, above all, by the solitude of a man caged in unhappiness. One night, to declare his love, he took her with him to walk in a cemetery!

In the aftermath of July 25, 1943, as the statues of Mussolini were being torn down, plainclothes men knocked on Duranti's door looking for Pavolini, "What do you think, that I'm hiding him under my bed?" Everyone knew about the affair between the actress and the taciturn Fascist official. Rumor of the affair even reached the ears of the Duce himself. Mussolini took the married minister harshly to task because the liaison harmed the Party's image. Pavolini pleaded wih him, "Duce, Signora Duranti is very important to me." In his private viewing room in Villa Torlonia, Mussolini ordered the projection of *Il re si diverte* (1941) *(The King's Jester)* where he could admire Doris Duranti dancing almost completely nude, covered with only a few veils. The next day he summoned his faithful Pavolini. "I saw that Duranti of yours. How well I understand you..."

Strange man, Pavolini. As Minister of Popular Culture, he could do as he liked at Cinecittà. But he was unable to offer Doris luxury and jewels because he lived off his salary and because, first of all, he had a family to support. Actually, it was apparently Doris who supported him during difficult moments. It is even said that she once gave him the money to buy Christmas presents for his family.

All he gave her were love poems – but he did offer her the chance to become the sex symbol of Italian movies, keeping the censor from blocking a few pictures where Duranti appeared steeped in sexuality. This was particularly true of *Carmela* and *Calafuria* (1942) two melodramas that were authentic tributes to the wild beauty of an actress at the peak of her splendor and power.

The fact that Doris had already reached stardom was confirmed by two other star vehicles created just for her. One was *La contessa Castiglione (The Castiglione Countess)* (1942) where she plays a Mata Hari of the Italian Risorgimento, a haughty leading lady swathed in a spectacular wardrobe and surrounded by marble staircases – and the other was the Tolstoyesque *Resurrezione* [Resurrection] (1943). They were created for her, but added nothing to her prestige as an actress. Alessandro Blasetti directed her in a different kind of movie, a work entitled *Nessuno torna indietro* [No one turns back] (1943). Here Doris temporarily puts aside her standing as star in favor of being in the cast of a memorable work narrated with infinite delicacy.

Duranti is a platinum blonde in *Nessuno torna indietro*, as she in *Resurrezione*. In the latter she plays Caterina Maslova, a Slav peasant, seduced by Prince Dimitri, played by Claudio Gora. Caterina sinks into the

depths of prostitution and is condemned to a forced labor camp in Siberia for having killed a man. Even her striped prisoner's uniform looks charming on her.

She ran the risk of wearing it for real some time later when the Nazis took over control of the territory after the fall of Fascism. The SS came to arrest her at the Hotel Excelsior in Florence and took her to the Gestapo. Due to an anonymous letter, her name had been included in a list of Jews who were to be deported to the death camps in Poland. She was thought to be Jewish (although she wasn't) because her mother's maiden name, Vitali, was Jewish in origin.

As she writes in her memoirs, on the night between April 13 and 14, 1945, Doris made love with her handsome Fascist Robespierre for the last time. Fourteen days later he was shot by the partisans and hanged by his feet in Milan. Duranti crossed the Swiss border with her faithful director of production Eugenio Fontanna who never abandoned her. Pavolini spent an enormous sum to save her, twenty thousand Swiss francs, used to pay for a false passport (under the name of Dora Pratesi) and the help of some smugglers.

Duranti asked the border police for political exile. She was supposedly in bad health (thanks to an obliging doctor's report) and was admitted to a clinic in Moncucco. The Italian partisans, who made insistent claims for her extradition, never managed to have her sent back to Italy. If they had, she would have met the same fate as Luisa Ferida.

Doris Duranti's slightly oriental features were suited to adventure movies such as **Capitan Tempesta** *(1942). Here, with Adriano Rimoldi.*

[see also p. 137]

Luisa Ferida

A fierce gaze, the manners of a street urchin, gypsy eyes, pure Roman blood and a haughty bearing. This was Luisa Ferida, awarded best Italian actress in 1942 for her role in *Fari nella nebbia* [Beacons in the fog]. But her name is remembered today for a more sinister event: she was the only Italian motion picture actress to be shot by the partisans at the end of the war, at the Liberation from the Nazis.

The sentence was carried out in Milan, on via Poliziano, on the same spot where the Fascists had killed the brother of a partisan in the Pasubio brigade years before. The fatal bullets were shot by Marius and Poker, the code names of two partisans. It was exactly three o'clock in the morning on April 29, 1945. Another body would lie next to hers, Osvaldo Valenti, her colleague, lover and perhaps Fascist Cinecittà's biggest ham-actor. For the benefit of passersby, two signs were placed on the bodies: FERIDA and VALENTI.

Luisa of course – Luisina for her friends – was not shot for the parts she played but for her activism in the ranks of the Decima Mas, the élite division of the troops of Salò, comprised of fanatics who pledged themselves to the death led by Prince Valerio Borghese. As Osvaldo

Luisa Ferida with Amedeo Nazzari in the adventure movie **Il conte di Bréchard** *(1937).*

Valenti's mistress during the last days of the Republic of Salò, Luisa Ferida also wore the uniform of the Decima Mas. She too had been given a rank and seemed proud of the power her uniform secured.

It is said that outrageous parties and orgies were held in their villa in Venice. Those who knew them recalled their faces ravaged by drugs. Some told of their complacent participation in the despicable reprisals against relatives of partisans. Still others affirmed that Osvaldo and Luisa were regulars at the Villa Triste, the headquarters of the infamous torturer, Koch. It is even said that Ferida went to dance naked before the partisans after they were tortured. The picture is a macabre one: shreds of truth probably mixed with slander, gossip and the gruesome Valenti myth.

There is no doubt that the couple joined Koch's bands in their rounds, bellowing out songs of the Regime at the top of their lungs. And in her autobiography, even Doris Duranti testifies to the fact that it was common to take cocaine and other drugs. Nor could Duranti forego painting a biting portrait of her fellow actress. "Although Luisa was a fairly good actress, she was irreparably marked by her working-class origins. She dressed without taste and spoke without intelligence. Valenti made her his mistress and tried, poor thing, to be her Pygmalion. He changed her hair-do, made her improve her makeup, always too heavy, and got her to wear sexy but well-cut clothes. The result was that he looked like he was escorting a bedecked, exhausted breeding mare…"

Luisa turned thirty-one years old a month before she was sent before the firing squad. Her real name was Luisa Monfrino Farnet and she had been born in Castel San Pietro, near Bologna, on March 18, 1914.

Of humble origins, she arrived in Rome at the age of sixteen after spending her childhood in a boarding school. Before making a name for herself in the movies, she had acted in the Repertory Theatrical Company of Bologna.

In 1935 and 1936 Ferida acted in a handful of pictures that would make her famous. Hers was a working-class beauty: lively, impoverished and passionate. It was said that she was the most "typically Italian" of the nation's actresses. That might have been the reason why Luisa Ferida became the official partner of the actor who best embodied the "heroic" Italian type, Amedeo Nazzari. At his side she starred in three movies in only twelve months: the country melodrama *La fossa degli angeli* [The angels' grave], the tragic comedy *I fratelli Castiglioni* [The Castiglione brothers], and *Il conte di Bréchard* [The Count of Bréchard], a film set during the French Revolution. In the first, she is cast as a peasant girl being fought over by two rough-and-ready types who work in the marble quarries of the Apuane hills. In the second, she is an unwed mother sent away by her landed family for her "sin," and becomes a factory worker to support her infant. In the third – one of her rare appearances as a blond – she plays a lower-class girl who saves the life of the nobleman Nazzari during the French Revolution, marrying him and rescuing him from the prospects of the guillotine.

Luisa had the eyes of a gypsy and the look of a warrior. In the seventeenth-century setting of *Un'avventura di Salvator Rosa* (1940) (*An Adventure of Salvator Rosa*), Ferida perseveres with her lower-class stereotype. Actually, Alessandro Blasetti underlines these qualities even more, casting her in the role of a rough peasant girl that allows Luisa to pull out her claws. She plays the part of Lucrezia, a bloodthirsty peasant woman who believes that you get what you deserve, even when confronted with the Spanish nobles infesting the Neapolitan countryside, laying heavy taxes on hard-working peasants.

Hers was an earthy, gloomy sort of eros. Italian audiences of the period would never forget the scene in which Lucrezia is tied to a pole and stripped naked by a jailer about to flog her. We can add a second image of turbid eroticism: that of *La cena delle beffe* [The dinner of derision] (1941), where Ferida aggressively confronts her ex-fiancé, Amedeo Nazzari who is tied to a cross and exposed to her panther-like nails... Here was the specter of sado-masochism that would rear its head again with accusations that the actress was accomplice or spectator to the atrocities Koch's henchmen committed against the partisans.

Under the seventeenth-century blouses designed by Gino Carlo Sensani, bounce Ferida's generous breasts. Beating to the rhythms of war beneath Lucrezia's ample chest in *An Adventure of Salvator Rosa* is the heart of a wild beast. Blasetti goads her to a frenzied pitch: all the fury of the Third Reich is contained in Luisina's gaze. She is ready to wreak battle against injustice, against the noble good-for-nothings who deviate the flow of rivers, leaving fields dry, in order to bring water to their villas' useless fountains.

Blasetti makes Luisa Ferida's raging eyes the symbol of the struggle against the bourgeoisie. Born and brought up in the region of Emilia Romagna just like the Duce, she becomes the symbol of the Fascist rebellion against parasites, agitators and fops. She is a working-class woman fired by a sacred cause. In the colossal production *La corona di ferro* (1941) (*The Iron Crown*) Blasetti creates an even more violent role for her. She is Tundra, a warrior horsewoman, driven by her deep resentment for the entire human race.

Cruel towards men, generous with animals, Tundra rides through the woods, free and alone. She rescues a deer caught in a trap, "Go free, you who can!" She knows nothing of love. She rides horses like a man, dresses like a man, fights and commands like one too. She wears thigh-high boots and a sword at her side. "Hey, boy," shouts Massimo Girotti as he chases her through the woods. Then suddenly, a cascade of dark graceful curls fall from Tundra's hat: a shiver of sensuality is unleashed when Luisa Ferida and Massimo Girotti struggle, rolling on the ground, in a wrestling embrace.

Love and violence become one in Ferida's form of eroticism. Girotti slaps the fiery Tundra but the tender Elisa Cegani realizes that it is a show of love. "Yes, he hit you but it was as if he had kissed you." Luisa Ferida's black soul that represents all the sentiments of a hunted, wounded losing beast, glows.

Like Lucrezia in *An Adventure of Salvator Rosa*, Tundra in *The Iron Crown* fights for

Luisa Ferida, the dark star of Cinecittà.

63

Luisa Ferida by Fosco Giachetti's side in Nozze di sangue *(1941).*

freedom; but she is the daughter of a queen and leads a handful of rebels in a plot against the usurper, King Sedemondo. In comparison to Lucrezia, Tundra is more brutal, overwrought, almost evil. She speaks to her men with a disdainful, imperative, Mussolini-like tone. Once again, Luisa Ferida's beauty is heavy with ideological significance and this will be remembered after the fall of Fascism.

Elisa Cegani plays a straightforward, wax-like model of femininity in *The Iron Crown*, Tundra's exact opposite. She recalled Luisa Ferida as a fragile, timid child. But no matter. By that time Ferida's myth was that of a wild woman.

The story goes that it was during the shooting of *The Iron Crown* that Luisa sank into her relationship with Osvaldo Valenti, whom Blasetti had cast as the treacherous Prince Eriberto, a sort of fighting machine. The wild tiger and the cruel warrior: what a perfect combination! A great actor and eccentric character, Valenti was a snob who, at that time, despised the vulgarity of the Fascist regime – later he hated superficial turncoats. He was a cocaine addict, an

Italian-style dandy and a sham right down to the core.

Having become a full-fledged member of Fascism's Olympus of stars, Luisa Ferida could sit back and enjoy the packaged movies put together just for her. But she also had to deal with the insidious image that was turning out to be more than a little oppressive. "I'm not a hellcat," she stated in a January 1941 interview. Unfortunately, by that time, Luisa was a prisoner of her stereotype image as a man-eater. In the tedious rural melodrama *Nozze di sangue* [Wedding of blood] (1941), Goffredo Alessandrini cast her in a dark lady role, Joan Crawford-style. She played Nazaria, an aggressive, tigerlike woman. "Every time I see you my blood boils," the slimy Nino Pavese says to her.

The two-year period 1941-42, which was the heyday of Fascist motion pictures, coincided with the most inspired period of Luisa's Ferida's career. The release of *Fari nella nebbia* (1942) straddled these two golden years. *Fari nella nebbia* was a pre-neorealist melodrama about daily disenchantment with which Ferida tried to erase her image as a ferocious, vengeful beast.

The darkly handsome truck driver Fosco Giachetti is desired by two women: his legitimate wife, a cold, narrow-minded Mariella Lotti, and his loving mistress, Luisa Ferida. Although here too she plays a husband-stealer, Ferida finds in this character – Piera – features unknown to her past roles. Here she is gentle and compliant, docile and hopeful. She waits for her man at home, tries to learn to cook, offers solace and reassurance.

Osvaldo Valenti's name appears in the credits of Ferida's movies with increasing frequency. The two actors are practically a permanent couple. Luisa was madly in love with him and hoped to have a child, but suffered two miscarriages. According to legend she was obsessed by her desire for maternity and carried a baby's bootie with her at all times, a remnant of unfulfilled motherhood.

Luisa goes back to playing a Sicilian peasant woman in Ferdinando Maria Poggioli's *Gelosia* [Jealousy] based on a masterpiece of "verismo" literature, *Il marchese di Roccaverdina (The Marquis of Roccaverdina)* by Luigi Capuana. Aristocrat Lupi gives his mistress, Agrippina, in marriage to a man whom he then murders out of jealousy. Agrippina, a provocative peasant, wrapped in black shawls, swears vengeance, "I will have no peace until my husband's murderers are avenged!" Like the Russian Fedora, Agrippina pursues a murderer who is really her lover. The sentimental relationships of Ferida's characters were frequently turbulent, with often someone to avenge or murder. Love and death went hand in hand down the road to melodrama.

Actually even Luisa Ferida's life – and most especially her death – seemed to belong to the screenplay of a passionate melodrama, one that she played right up to madness, to death itself.

When *La locandiera* [The innkeeper] was released, Fascism had already fallen. Luisa and her beloved Osvaldo had already begun their long pilgrimage through northern Italy that would lead them first to Emilia, then Venice and, finally Milan, to that volley of machine-gun bullets on April 29, 1945. Luisa had made her choice, out of love, and when it was time to settle the score, she found herself on the losing side.

Only God knows the truth of the crimes with which she was charged. But we can safely say that the character of the wild woman she had played was so firmly etched in the popular imagination that it finally became one with reality. The anti-Fascist partisans were not really shooting Ferida; they were shooting the raging Tundra of *The Iron Crown*, the husband-stealer of *Nozze di sangue*, and the hellcat of a dozen other movies.

Luisa Ferida in **Fedora** *(1942) is a Russian princess thirsty for vengeance.*

THE NORTH STAR OF POSTWAR CINEMA

Anna Magnani

[see also p. 56]

In the firmament of Italian postwar cinema, she was without doubt the true guiding star of Cinecittà...

Magnani was not just one among many. She was an actress who went beyond the rules of the game, the womanly woman, the throbbing soul of postwar Italy, something like what Bette Davis was to America and Jeanne Moreau was to France: the symbol of a nation, the emblem of a way of life, of a style.

Pina, the heroine of *Roma città aperta* (1945) *(Rome, Open City)* is a character who symbolically opens a new era: she has inside her the desperate strength of an Italy which has decided to roll up its sleeves. Aggressive, uncombed hair, abrasive, this Magnani is sometimes even ugly, but her great heart is open wide. And no one would dare doubt her ability to win. She would! She would! Pina in *Rome, Open City* is shot down by Nazi rifle fire as she races after the truck that is carrying off the man she loves. But she is in fact running at full speed towards the postwar period: upon Magnani's vital energy is founded the idea of femininity that the Italian cinema develops with the superwomen of the fifties and sixties, from Sophia Loren to Gina Lollobrigida, from Giovanna Ralli to Claudia Cardinale. Even an actress of the Antonioni school like Monica Vitti will follow in the footsteps of Magnani.

The femininity of "Nannarella" (as Italians affectionately called Anna Magnani) was an entirely Mediterranean and earthly idea of femininity that wiped out with one stroke the incorporeal beauty of the women of the artificial "white telephone" style. Enough of the fluttering butterflies of the Fascist cinema! Nannarella was the diva with a human face, an actress who poured her dramatic personal experiences into the heroines she portrayed on the screen.

Magnani surmounted the boundaries between fiction and reality, just as did the new Italian cinema which some called by the strange name of neorealism. She, who lost the leading role in *Ossessione* [Obsession] (1943) because she was five-months pregnant when Visconti finished casting, was the only great neorealistic diva of the Italian cinema, the only one who in order to appear real did not have to be discovered out walking the streets...

Between 1945 and 1950, already an established variety star, Anna Magnani interpreted the roles of women of the people in a dozen films. Gennaro Righelli directs her in two bizarre comedies: *Abbasso la miseria* [Down with poverty] (1946) and notably *Abbasso la ricchezza (Peddlin' in Society)* where she plays the role of a fruit seller who gets so rich on the black market that she can afford the luxury of living in the home of an absentee count. But then, she naively loses all her money and is obliged to return to her fruit shop: "Money is a real misfortune," Magnani says in her inimitable Roman

Anna Magnani reveals tremendous dramatic potential in her first, and rightly famous, postwar movie **Rome, Open City** *(1945).*

dialect which will become the official idiom of the Italian cinema.

In Luigi Zampa's *L'onorevole Angelina (Angelina)*, Nanarella plays the role of another iron woman of the people, Angela Bianchi, a rabblerouser capable of stirring up women's consciences. It was even proposed that she run for office, but she refused. It was 1947, less than a year before the head-on clash between the lay and the clerical forces in the 1948 elections which would see the victory of the center-right government. You don't wash your dirty laundry in public. Better to be an old-style kind of diva! Magnani hid herself in a traditional Italian star vehicle: *Assunta Spina* (1948) in the role that was associated with the divine Francesca Bertini. Nannarella also felt herself to be divine.

Meanwhile, as her husband Goffredo Alessandrini was definitively leaving her, her relationship was growing with Roberto Rossellini, the young director of *Rome, Open City* who dedicated *Amore* (1948) *(Ways of Love)* to her – a two-episode film custom-made to fit her acting talents. In the first part, *La voce umana (The Human Voice)*, a cinematographic transposition of the famous monologue by Jean Cocteau, an unusually bourgeois Magnani is the universal image of tormented womanhood suffering for love. In the second part, *Il miracolo (The Miracle)*, she

is a vagrant with mystic tendencies. Seduced by a hobo, she goes through her pregnancy alone and gives birth to a child whom she is convinced has been conceived by divine intervention.

1948 was not only the year of the great clash between the center-right and the united left. The movie magazines reported spicy tales of Magnani's tempestuous love for Rossellini, a love which already had hurricane clouds forming on its horizon. But the storm didn't break until Ingrid Bergman arrived in Italy to play the lead in *Stromboli terra di Dio* (1949) *(Stromboli, God's Land)* for Rossellini. The Hollywood star fell in love with the talented director and he with her.

Nannarella immediately wanted to take her revenge as woman and actress: while Rossellini was with Ingrid and the troupe were working on the little island of Stromboli, she too was shooting an island film only a few miles away – *Vulcano* (1950) *(Volcano)* – where she was courted by a handsome Rossano Brazzi and directed for the first time by a great Hollywood director, William Dieterle.

Fiery and passionate in all aspects of her life, Magnani could not pass up the protest march in Rome's Piazza del Popolo on February 20, 1949 organized by the Committee for the Defense of Italian Cinema.

Portrait of a caustic mother: Anna Magnani with Tecla Scarano in **Bellissima** *(1951).*

She got up to launch an appeal: "Help us! Help Italian cinema or it is dead! Don't let us die." As a woman of the people she was inclined to take leftist positions, even if Anna openly declared she hated politics. And most of all she hated political women.

Once she had left the Rossellini circle, Nannarella entered Visconti's entourage. He gave her the role of the mother in *Bellissima* [Ravishing] (1951). As the wife of the construction foreman Spartaco, she dreams of a radiant film career for her timid little girl. Swindled, disappointed and humiliated, she picks up the pieces of her shattered dream and returns to her humble reality.

Magnani is a loser with greatness, an actress who knows how to imbue her defeats with heroism and at the same time also humanity. This also is her lot in her only great French film, Jean Renoir's *La carrosse d'or* (1952) *(The Golden Coach)*, where Renoir makes her into a muse of the *commedia dell'arte*. But Magnani is also a tiger; she never refuses a match with her rivals, not even the most belligerent of them. It is thus that in *Siamo donne* (1953) *(We the Women)* she again finds herself side by side with Ingrid Bergman who in the meantime has had three children by "her" Roberto Rossellini. But the two women appear in two different episodes of this film, with Bergman being directed by Rossellini and Magnani once again by Visconti.

In 1956 Magnani became the first Italian actress to win an Oscar. She received it for a role that Tennessee Williams wrote especially for her, *The Rose Tattoo* (1955), directed by Daniel Mann. In this film Nannarella is an immigrant who adores her man, a smuggler who operates in Florida. When the police kill him, she has the body cremated and continues living in the morbid memory of that love until the day she discovers that he had in fact been unfaithful to her. Only a meeting with a Sicilian truck driver (Burt Lancaster) keeps her from going out of her mind.

Between Hollywood and Cinecittà, Magnani reached her heyday as a diva, but this coincided with the autumn of her womanhood: these were uneventful years for her. She even dressed in an improbably glamorous way that falsified her. She refused the part of the mother in *La ciociara* (1960) *(Two Women)*, thus missing out on another possible Oscar, because she was offended at the idea of playing the mother to Sophia

Loren, who at first was considered for the role of the daughter. But she accepted the part alongside Giulietta Masina of a convict incarcerated in the Roman prison Le Mantellate in *Nella città l'inferno* (1958) *(And the Wild, Wild Women* or *Caged)*.

But her career would not end in this way. The right direction was provided by a young new director, Pier Paolo Pasolini. In his *Mamma Roma* (1962) Nannarella is once again the old fiery tigress. She *is* Mamma Roma, an ex-prostitute turned fruit vendor (the same job as in *Peddlin' in Society*), a woman who stubbornly wants the best for her son. Her Mamma Roma is none other than Pina in *Rome, Open City* with a few more years behind her. She has the same fighting spirit, the same womanly passion, even if she is acting against the backdrop of a different Italy.

Anna Magnani is the actress who, symbolically, opens the great era of the Italian postwar cinema with *Rome, Open City* and ends it with *Mamma Roma*. And it is thus that she thoroughly deserves to be considered the guiding star of Italian divas.

The great Italian actress' first steps towards an international career. Anna Magnani as Colombina in The Golden Coach *(1952).*

THE SEVEN STARS OF THE BIG DIPPER

Alida Valli

[see also p. 27]

*Alida Valli and Amedeo Nazzari in **Last Meeting** (1951), Valli's first Italian movie after her return from Hollywood.*

Clear as water, pure as snow, sharp as ice, the Istrian actress Alida Maria Altenburger, known as Alida Valli, was a typical timeless star. At the end of the war she was already famous for the films she had made during the Fascist era. She confronted the new Italy with Mario Mattoli's *La vita ricomincia* [Life begins again] (1945) in a mildly neorealistic style. Her beauty, slightly drawn, was still in the taste of the Fascist era. But Alida broke off brusquely with the Regime. In her home in Rome, Via dei Monti Parioli 18, there was even a certain concern for the many menacing letters received from nostalgic Fascists who reproved her for having broken off and, most of all, having refused to collaborate with the cinema of the Republic of Salò.

Her classical oval face, her elegance, her acting style appealed to David O. Selznick who offered her a fabulous contract. Alida was not yet twenty-six when she went to Hollywood with her husband Oscar De Mejo, a young composer of light music. The Italy that Alida was leaving was rife with political and social conflicts that were tearing the country apart.

In America Alida was called simply Valli (only her last name, as would also happen with Anna Maria Pierangeli, rebaptized Pier Angeli). But in Hollywood they realized that she spoke English badly and that her teeth needed fixing. So, without hesitation they filed away some protrusions and remade her mouth to perfection. Intensive English lessons made her more credible as an American woman. Hitchcock exalted the mystery of Alida's beauty in *The Paradine Case* (1947) and Carol Reed directed her in *The Third Man* (1949). At once she became a star of the first magnitude. This is clear from the partners she plays opposite: from Gregory Peck to Fred MacMurray, Joseph Cotton, and Frank Sinatra; from Glenn Ford to Orson Welles. For the rest, her look fit well with Hollywood standards. Alida seemed a Mediterranean type of Ingrid Bergman. Her eyes were magnetic, her glance deep. The authoritative weekly *Life* wrote: "Hollywood has a big new star."

The American experience was a little shorter than the seven years originally contracted with Selznick. But Alida had gained international stature and on her return to Europe she disembarked in France as the lead in a melodrama by Yves Allegret, *Les miracles n'ont lieu qu'une fois* [Miracles only happen once] (1951). Partnered by Jean Marais, Alida, by now in her thirties, was radiant, splendid. Hollywood had further refined her image at a time when the other Italian actresses were wading deep in the truths of neorealistic films. That is why on her return to Italy, Alida seemed to come from another age. The refined quality of this Valli was a mixture of two types of glamour: the artificial Italian "white telephone" kind, and the American, Hollywood kind. Alida's image had nothing in common with neorealism.

But the Italy of the fifties by now wanted its women fleshy with maternal breasts. There was a desire for the ampler woman. Alida had nothing in common with that kind of woman, exuberant and muscular. Her beauty was better suited to lady-like or womanly roles such as the parts she plays in *Ultimo incontro* (1951) *(Last Meeting)* and *Il mondo le condanna* (1953) *(The World Condemns Them)*, two melodramas by Gianni Franciolini who attempted to relaunch her as a star in the eyes of the greater public by pairing her with the very popular Amedeo Nazzari. In *Last Meeting* Alida is a lower middle-class woman, wife of an Alfa Romeo mechanic. She allows herself a love affair with Jean-Pierre Aumont and is then blackmailed by the malevolent Vittorio Sanipoli as in the most classic melodrama. In *The World Condemns Them* she plays an ex-prostitute who attempts suicide. Saved by a gallant industrialist, the poor creature vainly tries to climb out of the slime, but she is obliged to kill a man and must take refuge in a convent. Alida looks aristocratic even in the garb of a prostitute. There is an abyss between her and the Gina Lollobrigida of *Pane, amour e fantasia (Bread, Love and Dreams)*, for whom the Italians of 1953 go crazy. Gina's cheeks are as rotund as her hips, while Alida Valli has a sculptured, hollowed, dramatic face. Age was beginning to harden her features. She was not an easy diva to deal with. She was a great actress for somewhat specialized tastes. The Italian cinema, which was following other routes, had little to offer her.

Italy in 1953 – according to many – was drifting towards communism and the De Gasperi government defended itself with any means at its disposal. In a social climate raised to boiling point by the approval of the "fraud law" (designed to minimize the Communist Party's electoral gains), there suddenly appeared a film that interpreted the Italian Risorgimento as a failed, or at least, betrayed revolution: it was *Senso* (1954) *(The Wanton Countess)* based on a novel by Camillo Boito and directed by Luchino Visconti. Alida plays the lead as countess Livia Serpieri, a free-thinking woman, drawn into a murky adultery. It was her most important role during the fifties. Alida, whose carriage and perfect oval face always enhanced the work of the costume designers, whether radiant or in the grip of passion, now very tender, now distorted by jealousy. It

Alida Valli gets her big break in Luchino Visconti's The Wanton Countess *(1954). Here, with Farley Granger.*

was a role and an interpretation that were worth a whole career (even if Visconti is supposed to have wanted Ingrid Bergman originally).

Unfortunately the film was received according to criteria of an exclusively ideological nature. Exalted by leftist critics and Visconti supporters, *The Wanton Countess* was denigrated by the conservative press. At the Venice Film Festival it was the center of a real battle and was defeated: the Golden Lion went to Renato Castellani's *Giulietta e Romeo (Romeo and Juliet)*. The Volpi Cup for best actress was not awarded at all, perhaps to avoid having to honor the Valli of Visconti, and yet, in competition there were also Giulietta Masina for *La strada* and Barbara Stanwyck for *Executive Suite*.

Despite her performance in *The Wanton Countess*, Alida Valli found no other roles suitable to her talents and she turned to the theater, primarily Ibsen and Pirandello. She only returned to the screen in 1957 for Antonioni's *Il grido (The Cry)* where she plays Irma, a tormented woman, the lover of Steve Cochran and the protagonist of a complicated round of relationships; abandoned by her husband who has emigrated abroad, she lives with a laborer with whom she has a baby girl. When she receives news of her husband's death, the laborer wants to marry her but she confesses that she no longer loves him. It is an important film that deals with Antonioni's theme of personal crisis on a working-class level generally pre-empted by neorealism. Alida Valli's beauty is chilling. Her austere style is efficacious and well-suited to the existential suffering of Antonioni's characters.

But Alida becomes more and more of an exception. Her image is far from the style of Italy in 1957, a country which is already tasting the delights of the economic boom, daydreaming about the millions of "Double or Quits," buying refrigerators on credit, and the first mass-produced economy car, the Fiat 500. Alida is far from the kinds of fantasies which are nourished by the "Lollo-Loren" rivalry. She belongs, instead, to international films which offer her deluxe roles such as Claude in *La diga sul Pacifico* (1957) *(This Angry Age)*. Here Alida is perfectly at ease as the mistress of a businessman. She has an affair with an Anthony Perkins much younger than herself, but she is convincing and beautiful all the same. Perkins, crazy about Alida, sings to her "One Kiss Away From Heaven…" which in reality is the English version of the Neapolitan song *Malatìa* by Armando Romeo.

Another important role for her in 1957 is in the young director Gillo Pontecorvo's *La grande strada azzurra* [The big blue street] where Alida plays the wife of Squarciò (Yves Montand), a poacher fisherman destined for a tragic end. It is an honorable role even if a supporting one. But Alida was losing her fight with time and a cinema that wanted fresh flesh to celebrate its rites.

Relegated to character parts, Valli was cast in French and Italian films of various kinds: melodramas, comedies, light detective stories. Many young French directors, more or less connected with the *nouvelle vague* (the French New Wave of the sixties), gave her strange characters to play as did Georges Franju in *Les yeux sans visage* (1960) *(Eyes Without a Face)* Jacques Deray in *Le Gigolo* (1960), Philippe Agostini in *Dialogue des Carmelites* (1960) *(The Carmelites)*, Henri Colpi in *Une aussi longue absence* (1961) *(The Long Absence)* and Claude Chabrol in *Ophélia* (1962). Her presence was a way of quoting from Italian and American film classics so much loved in the France of the early sixties.

The Italian cinema was much more stingy towards Alida, offering her very little, almost nothing, even if in 1967 Pier Paolo Pasolini tried to bring her back with a substantial role in *Edipo Re (Oedipus Rex)* where she makes an excellent Merope. Three years later Bernardo Bertolucci offered Alida a made-to-measure role in *La strategia del ragno* (1970) *(The Spider's Stratagem)*, restoring fame and prestige to her in much the same way that Pasolini had done for Magnani in *Mamma Roma*, a little less than ten years earlier.

Alida Valli in **The World Condemns Them** *(1953).*

Giulietta Masina

Giulia Anna Masina, Giulietta for her friends and for posterity, got her start in radio and the theater.

Radio had access to everyone and the Italians became fond of the voices of their favorites. In 1942 Giulietta began to be known through the radio program, *Cico e Pallina*, with the sparkling dialogue of the young humorist, Federico Fellini. Giulietta played Pallina, a very naive little woman, in a role created especially for her by Federico whom she married in 1943.

Pallina made headway in the theater. She was no vamp. On the contrary, she excelled in comical and grotesque characters to whom she gave a vein of poetry and a trace of melancholy. After the war she made a fleeting appearance in the Florentine episode of *Paisà* [Peasant] (1946). Two years later she had a more important role in *Senza pietà* (1948) *(Without Pity)* directed by Alberto Lattuada. It is the part of Marcella, a young woman on the skids who becomes involved in the hell of Tombolo, a pine wood in Livorno which is a den of smugglers and prostitutes, a kind of Tuscan Far West.

Italy really was a kind of Far West where women were weak and defenseless and the American liberators were hungry for "segnorine," army slang for prostitutes, who could be found on any street corner. Misery reigned. The newspapers of the period recorded cases of mothers who took to the streets in order to feed their children. The Giulietta of *Without Pity* is one of these. Her femininity, deprived of sex appeal, is ordinary, simple, far from the standards of cinematic beauty. While the majority of Italian actresses banked on their attractiveness, Giulietta built her career on her dramatic talent. For this she was appreciated by the critics who continued to award her prize after prize, by the directors who considered her a rare case of an intelligent actress, and by women who could quite easily identify with her.

The Italian woman of the forties and fifties was much more like Giulietta Masina than Alida Valli or Gina Lollobrigida. She was a silent loser like the majority of the characters Giulietta interprets. *Luci del varietà* (1950) *(Lights of Variety)* wins her more prizes. She plays the part of Melina Amour, a variety artist abandoned by her man (Peppino De Filippo) who is infatuated with the stupendous Carla Del Poggio.

Masina's destiny as an actress was curious. Despite the fact that she was one of the "greats" of Italian cinema, she wore the stigmata of the character actress and was often given supporting roles as in Roberto Rossellini's *Europa '51 (The Greatest Love)* where she plays the part of a woman from

the slums who is helped by the bourgeois Ingrid Bergman.

A character player deluxe, Giulietta Masina managed to confer dignity on typical character parts as in *La Strada* (1954) where she plays sweet Gelsomina, a real acting triumph. Tiny and ingenuous, Giulietta creates a character for herself which she will carry with her throughout her career: the loyal and credulous woman (sometimes a wife, sometimes only a companion) who is good and defenseless and always, unfailingly betrayed by the meanness of others. She moves along the razor's edge of pathos, between tears and grimaces, like a sad clown. It would be difficult to say whether it was Giulietta who resembled Fellini's characters or, on the contrary, they who were inspired by her.

One thing was certain, all of Giulietta's characters were cut from the same cloth. For example, the prostitute in *Le notti di Cabiria* (1957) *(The Nights of Cabiria)* (a role that won her yet again another Nastro d'Argento prize), is nothing other than a Gelsomina of the world of vice. Above and beyond the characters that she played, Masina glowed with innate candor, with chaste ingenuousness, for her capacity to find wonder in the most ordinary things in life.

Thus even outside Fellini's world, Giulietta Masina continued to be a Gelsomina as in the case of *Fortunella* (1958) by Eduardo De Filippo. But her preferred scenario was Fellini's: *Giulietta degli spiriti* (1965) *(Juliet of the Spirits)* which was a true hymn to the talent of this actress. Here she is no longer a ragged vagrant, the miserable helper of Zampanò, the wandering player, but a rich lady of the Roman upper class. Ten years had passed since *La Strada*. In Christian Democratic Italy the economy was booming. Wealth was making slow but steady progress. Fellini gleefully explored the middle class and its monsters. But even in this changed scenario, Giulietta Masina continued to play the role of the innocent and gullible: she is the defrauded partner, the woman who is always betrayed.

As ever she is the victim of betrayal. In *Juliet of the Spirits* the discovery that her husband Giorgio (Mario Pisu) has a mistress sets her on a kind of vertiginous voyage. Only after having skirted madness does Giulietta emerge victorious. Masina is a loser who always keeps afloat. She manages to survive a million woes which she brings upon herself out of pure innocence. It is the others who are beaten down, the sirens, the superwomen. They are swept away in the vortex of their own voluptuousness. This too is a sign of the moralistic attitude that the Italian cinema has always taken towards its women.

Gelsomina and Zampanò, two extraordinary roles for Giulietta Masina and Anthony Quinn, in Federico Fellini's compelling movie **La strada** *(1954).*

Silvana Mangano

If Gina Lollobrigida will go down in cinematic history for her neckline in *Phryne*, Silvana Mangano will win her share of immortality for the tight mid-thigh pants she wears in *Riso amaro* (1949) *(Bitter Rice)*. If Gina is the "bersagliera" and Sophia the pizza baker, Silvana Mangano is the rice-picker.

Italy's most fascinating rice-picker came to films, like "Lollo" and Loren, by way of beauty contests. Miss Rome of 1947, Silvana Mangano worked as a fashion model for the Mascetti atelier. Her Italy was that of the couture houses and fashion shows: "Made in Italy" was booming thanks to a clever policy of price cutting. Even a model like Silvana earned good money. Hats were her specialty. Movies offered her small parts such as the one in *L'elisir d'amore* [Elixir of life] (1946) where she played Nelly Corradi along with a Lollo who was still another unknown like herself.

The year is 1948: the national elections in the spring have split Italy in two with the Communists and the Socialists forming a united front against the center forces. The Communist leader Palmiro Togliatti is seriously wounded in an assassination attempt: a general strike is called.

But it was precisely the 1948 elections that offered another scrap of notoriety to Silvana who appeared on a poster urging voters to do their duty and vote. It was quite a chubby Silvana who in that same year entered another beauty contest announced in the magazine *Cine Illustrato*: the girl with the most radiant smile won a trip to legendary Hollywood. Among the jury members were Orson Welles and Gregory Ratoff. Silvana dreamed and made plans: she

Silvana Mangano attains stardom for her performance in Bitter Rice *(1949). Here, with Vittorio Gassman.*

didn't like her surname much and if she became famous she would shorten it to Silvana Mango. Her big break came when Lucia Bosè refused an important role in Giuseppe De Santis' second film, *Bitter Rice*, a social melodrama set in the rice fields of Vercelli. Silvana's screen test excited De Santis: she was perfect for the part of the rice-picker. Even her surname was approved. To hell with Mango!

Statuesque, standing sturdily on two athletic legs that rise strong out of the water of the rice fields, Silvana seems like a goddess of the lakes. Thanks to her beauty, *Bitter Rice* takes on the flavor of a Greek tragedy. The rice-picker Silvana is courted by Raf Vallone, but then she becomes the woman of a ruffian, the crazed Gassman. After having betrayed her fellow-workers, she punishes herself with a spectacular suicide, the victim of destiny and society.

At least on paper, the female lead of *Bitter Rice* was supposed to be Doris Dowling, an American actress in the role of another rice-picker: the woman who redeems herself and gets onto the side of the just. But during the shooting, Silvana's presence began taking over, day after day, putting poor Dowling ever more in the background. Extremely photogenic, Mangano was like a statue in the flesh. By comparison, Dowling, who thought she had finally got her chance, seemed insignificant. It was not only a question of appearance, but of personality.

Mangano's debut turned into a real triumph, hailed by both critics and public. Silvana, with a Sicilian father and an English mother, had a revolutionary appeal: the diva of the future. She was neither a Mediterranean nor a Nordic type, but a mixture of the two. She combined the sovereign indolence of a southern feline with a cool northern gaze. And hers was not only an Italian success, since *Bitter Rice* circled the globe becoming neorealism's biggest hit, thanks as well to Silvana Mangano, the image of a new eroticism.

Her rustic sex appeal became a symbol of Italian social contradictions in those years of struggle between pro-Soviet passions and American temptations.

In a word, with Silvana Mangano a very present-day star was born. It was clear at once that she was a future diva, not least because of her marriage to the producer of *Bitter Rice*, Dino De Laurentis, one of Lux Films' most brilliant tycoons. Silvana too belonged to the Lux Films' stables and they gave her her first truly starring role in *Il brigante Musolino* [Brigand Musolino] (1950), where she could dust off her rustic sex appeal by the side of Amedeo Nazzari. She had already been his partner in *Il lupo della Sila* (1949) *(Wolf of the Sila)* a type of Calabrian western.

Silvana began to earn a reputation as an actress who threw away her best opportunities, and as being the most apathetic figure in Italian cinema. "I must admit I have never had any special liking for movies. I accepted the part in *Bitter Rice* more for money than for the desire to undertake a career in films," she once confided. Unlike Lollo and above all Loren, who lived in and for films, Silvana was very detached from her work as an actress. She even looked down upon it. Perhaps it is this very detachment that gives her such an air of aristocratic arrogance.

Whatever the case may be, Mangano appeared in an important melodrama, *Anna* (1952) directed by Alberto Lattuada, a director who, like De Santis, was at his best in creating feminine characters. In this film, too, Silvana is the center of a fight between two loves and two men, one of whom represents good and the other evil. And once again, as in *Bitter Rice*, her partners are Raf Vallone and a sneering Gassman. Silvana plays Anna, a nightclub dancer who decides to expiate her sins by becoming a nun. (She feels guilty for the death of Gassman whom her fiancé, Raf Vallone, has killed in a knife fight.) But her novitiate is troubled by a chance encounter with her ex-fiancé who is brought wounded into the hospital where she works. Anna nears the point of renouncing her vows, but then resigns herself to her destiny.

In the guise of a novice Mangano is no less striking than she was in *Bitter Rice*. Moreover her chaste look is undermined by her dance performances. Dubbed by Flo Sandon, Silvana sings *El negro Zumbon*, which becomes a hit thanks to Lattuada's film. The nun's habit completely hides her lovely body, but it has the advantage of emphasizing her face, framing it, enhancing her features. The erotic aspect is entrusted to her mouth, fleshy and sensual and no less impressive than her long, bare legs in *Bitter Rice*.

Unlike the other great stars of the Italian cinema of that period, Mangano avoided exploiting her fame too intensively. On the contrary, her natural indolence and the lack of a need for money induced her to spare herself. Even at the peak of her popularity, she never made more than one movie a year – very few if one remembers that Loren and Lollo were shooting three or four at the same time. Silvana revealed herself to be a skillful actress with a robust dramatic temperament. She preferred quality to quantity. In *Ulisse* (1953) *(Ulysses)* directed by Mario Camerini, she plays the double role of Penelope and the sorceress Circe. She has a changeable look suitable to noble as well as common characters, and she can even be credible as a

Silvana Mangano in the role of Jocasta in Pier Paolo Pasolini's pagan myth of Oedipus Rex (1967).

bourgeois as happens in *Mambo* (1954), where she falls under the influence of a cynic who once more assumes the guise of Vittorio Gassman. Just as in *Anna*, in *Mambo* she plays a nightclub dancer and performs a famous dance number created by Katherine Dunham, thus launching the mambo, a dance which became the rage in the second half of the fifties.

Mangano returned to playing more refined characters in *La diga sul Pacifico (This Angry Age)* (1957) and then in *La tempesta* (1958) *(Tempest)* where she interprets the part of Masa "the captain's daughter" created by Pushkin. Only at the end of the fifties did Silvana discover her comic vein in *La grande guerra* (1959) *(The Great War)* by Mario Monicelli. Consequently, in the course of the sixties she was able to shoot excellent comedies with Alberto Sordi such as *Crimen* (1960) *(And Suddenly It's Murder!)*, *La mia signora* (1964), *Il disco volante* (1964) *(The*

Silvana Mangano again plays opposite Vittorio Gassman in **And Suddenly It's Murder** *(released in Great Britain as* **Killing in Monte Carlo***).*

Flying Saucer), and *Scusi, lei è favorevole o contrario?* [Excuse me, are you for or against?] (1966). It was said that Sordi was in love with her and that he was only waiting for the break-up in her marriage with De Laurentis. Partnered by Sordi on the set and off, Silvana rediscovered her smile and found that she could act in a genre that before had been considered closed to her: comedy. In the early sixties her career was taking this direction. And yet her most important role of the decade remains the part of Edda Ciano in Lizzani's *Il processo di Verona* [The Verona trial] (1963). In this film Silvana recites one of the most wonderful telephone monologues in the history of Italian movies: the call that Edda makes to her father Benito Mussolini in the desperate attempt to save the life of her husband, Galeazzo Ciano, accused of treachery and condemned to death by the Special Court of the Republic of Salò. In the sixties Mangano on the screen is an upper-class wife, now cold, now ambiguous, now spiritual.

In *Le streghe* (1967) *(The Witches)* Silvana interprets five roles, directed by Franco Rossi, Vittorio De Sica, Luchino Visconti, Mauro Bolognini, and Pier Paolo Pasolini. This gallery of characters had been expressly written to set her talent into relief.

In her next film, Pasolini throws a mythological, pagan aura over Silvana's beauty, giving her the role of Jocasta in *Oedipus Rex* (1967). Hieratic, sharp,

enveloped in an atmosphere of Greek tragedy, this Mangano seems much more abstract than she was as the sorceress Circe in *Ulysses*. Her stonelike poses, like a magnificent pagan statue, recall if anything, the rice-picker in *Bitter Rice* who goes to meet her destiny with a tragic sense worthy of Euripides. But the Silvana Mangano of the sixties is much less rigid, much more of an actress, even if she has deliberately cast off much of her obvious sex appeal.

One year later, when Italy, along with the rest of Europe, is passing through the sacred fire of student dissent, Pasolini gives her another important role: the wife of the industrialist in his *Teorema* (1968) *(Theorem)*. She is the mother and Massimo Girotti the father – two symbols of postwar Italy who, having taken off the rags of neorealism, change into busy middle-class people. Pasolini puts them into a crisis about their roles in the family and society. Mangano in *Theorem* is a ghost of a woman, a bourgeois who is unknowingly oppressed by class relationships, but who is also a human being thirsting for truth. Suddenly she rediscovers herself through physical love. She even starts picking up young men in the street. Her crisis mirrors the image of an Italy which, having brilliantly passed through the reconstruction years, seems to be suffering satiation at the table of the economic boom.

[see also p. 192]

Eleonora Rossi Drago

A slim and elegant actress, with a typical fashion model's gait can certainly not call herself Palmira Omiccioli... Thus Palmira, who in the meantime had married a certain Cesare Rossi, became Eleonora Rossi. This is the name that appears in the credits of two films in 1950: *Due sorelle amano* [Two sisters love] and *Altura*. Eleonora is a charming brunette with regular features and strong, stunning legs. At twenty-four she already has the look of a high-class woman.

In order not to be confused with the actress Luisa Rossi, she searches for a more unique surname and becomes Eleonora Rossi-Drago with a big, big hyphen which will, however, disappear before long. Comencini directs her in *Persiane chiuse* (1951) *(Behind Closed Shutters)* where she plays Sandra, a lower middle-class girl who throws herself into the maze of the underworld in order to find a sister who has disappeared in the midst of a prostitution ring. *Behind Closed Shutters* is a film that plays on the contrast between Sandra's fine purity and the corruption of the surrounding milieu. Rossi-Drago's popularity began to rise at once. In Italian films, which were going through a swelling wave of neorealism, it was not easy to find such classical beauty. Eleonora dominated the movie scene along with Silvana Mangano during the early fifties; they were two equally sensuous women who both seemed to glide, rather than walk, above the ground.

In Eleonora's languid eyes all kinds of dramas and secrets lie hidden. She is a passionate woman, but with such style! In *Tre storie proibite* (1952) *(Three Forbidden Stories)* she is a girl of good family but a little rebellious. After running away with a good-for-nothing, she becomes a drug addict. Vainly she tries to remake a life for herself. She tries for a job as a typist but gets trapped when a staircase collapses under the weight of hundreds of aspiring job applicants. The unfortunate creature dies after death throes which scan her life in flash-back.

Equally unfortunate is the character which Eleonora plays in *La tratta delle bianche* (1952) *(Frustrations)*. Here a sinister Gassman and a good Ettore Manni contend for her. Even though pregnant, the good girl takes part in a dance marathon to get money to pay the lawyer for her man who has got himself in trouble. After several days of rumba, beguine, and fox trot, she dies on the dance floor.

In *Sensualità* (1952) *(Enticements)* too, where she plays an Istrian refugee, Eleonora dies. But this time she is killed by her husband, Marcello Mastroianni, who has discovered her with his brother-in-law Amedeo Nazzari.

Unhappy about having one of the most unusual noses of the Italian cinema, Rossi-Drago underwent plastic surgery. But what a shame! Having lost that curious profile (the point a little large, the nostrils rather pronounced) she also lost a part of her personality as an actress.

The myth of Eleonora, however, held up even with a new nose. Her fans called her simply Nora to avoid the long drawn-out "eleonorarossidrago." But the sound of her name was so harmonious; its vibrations conjured up elegance, class. She was the "lady" of Italian movies, rather like what Greer Garson was for Hollywood.

The beauty of this Italian cinematographic Circe was intangible. The many woes Eleonora went through on the screen left no trace on her. The priestess of the new postwar rites, Rossi-Drago, was a woman incapable of living a normal life and was destined to remain alone with her beauty as happens in *Le amiche* (1955) *(The Girlfriends)* and in *Donne sole* [Women alone] (1956). In both films Rossi-Drago relives the years spent in the world of high fashion when she walked down the runway as a model. In *Donne sole* she is a model seduced by a prince who then betrays her trust. In *The Girlfriends*, Antonioni gives her the part of Clelia, a woman of common origins who makes a career thanks to her natural refinement and class, sacrificing her own emotional life for the sake of her career.

At the end of the fifties, Eleonora interprets a series of important roles as a bourgeois woman. In *Un maladetto imbroglio*

Eleonora Rossi Drago, center, in one of her best movies, **The Girlfriends** *(1955).*

Eleonora Rossi Drago with Jean-Louis Trintignant, her young lover, in Estate violenta *(1959).*

Even Giuseppe De Santis, a director of stories of peasant and proletarian women, invented a middle-class role for Eleonora. In *La garçonnière* [The bachelor flat] (1960) Eleonora plays the rich wife of Raf Vallone occupied in keeping an eye on an unfaithful husband and helping to set his economic troubles straight.

But Eleonora Rossi Drago's most important role is unquestionably the one in *Estate violenta* [Violent summer] (1959), the love story of an officer's widow and a boy many years younger. In the setting of the decadent small town Riccione in 1943, Eleonora plays a bourgeois woman determined upon rejecting the hypocrisy of a society that is coming apart at the seams and living her life intensely despite her age. Splendid in her maturity, Rossi Drago in *Estate violenta* is a sensual woman. Against the background of an Italy with no ideals left, the war and the relationship with a boy, the exquisite eroticism of this film is highlighted. Thanks to this film, Eleonora wins the only Nastro Argento (Silver Ribbon) prize of her life.

(1959) *(The Facts of Murder)* she is a lady of the Roman bourgeoisie who, on returning home, surprises a housebreaker and is killed. In *L'impiegato* [The employee] (1960) she is a Milanese manager obsessed with efficiency who vainly tries to instill the philosophy of American-style marketing into a group of lazy Roman employees. She torments poor Nino Manfredi, but ends up falling in love with him.

Strangely enough, after such a fine role, Eleonora's career comes to a sudden halt. Rossi Drago (more and more often her name appears without the hyphen) faces the sixties as a thirty-five-year-old woman, an age which offered very little to a woman in the film industry. Rossi Drago remains the sensual interpreter of a kind of femininity composed of elegance and jewels, a refined wardrobe and grandeur – a model not to be underestimated, even if it sides against the neorealistic cinema for the sake of provocation.

"Rossi Drago," the producer Tonino Cervi recalls, "was perhaps one of the last divas, highly neurotic and insecure. She often cried. The last time I saw her she hugged me and cried, as if I reminded her of something lost and forgotten, something that had been much loved. She hob-nobbed with the rich because she thought in this way some of their security would rub off on her, the security she did not have."

With Amedeo Nazzari in Pride, Love and Suspicion *(1952).*

Lea Massari

A Roman woman of a well-to-do family, Anna Maria Massatani was a student of architecture. The set designer Piero Gherardi tried to lure her into movies without success. The one who did succeed, instead, was the director Mario Monicelli who at the end of 1954 fulfilled an old idea of Emmer's – to bring to the screen the novel by Grazia Deledda, *La madre* [The mother], which in its movie version was entitled *Proibito* [Forbidden]. Miss Massatani too, who plays the part of Agnese (the girl loved by a priest) gets a new name: Lea Massari.

But Lea Massari would acquire fame only two years later playing in Renato Castellani's *I sogni nel cassetto* (1957) *(Dreams in a Drawer)*. She is the student bride living in a furnished room with her beloved husband, a medical student in his last year. "You look like two little birds on a branch to me," Cosetta Greco tells her. Massari in *Dreams in a Drawer* is a little girl playing house. Castellani, with his extraordinary gift for nursing along actors discovered off the street, helps her create a very tender portrait of an ingenue. But the rosy romanticism in which the film is immersed ends on a pathetic tone when the young bride dies in childbirth.

This child-wife was one of the most charming heroines of the Italian cinema of the fifties. Lea Massari was no great beauty and not even a *maggiorata* (a "big" woman). With her doe-like eyes, strange, unmistakable upturned nose, dimpled cheeks, her hair sometimes in two braids tied with a ribbon, she was like an intoxicating comic book figure made more likeable by the chirping speech of the excellent Adriana Asti who dubbed her voice. The Massari of *Dreams in a Drawer* was one of the few Italian actresses who knew how to use her whole body to express a character.

In the wake of this success, Lea was given a role in *Capitan Fracassa* on television. An ingenuous, clowning and sometimes crudely expressive actress, Massari did not change her style even for the role of Anna in Antonioni's *L'avventura* (1960) *(The Adventure)*. From young bride in love she goes to fiancée in a crisis without abandoning her pouts or her grating expressiveness. During an excursion to the Aeolian Isles, Anna mysteriously disappears after seeking, in vain, understanding from her fiancé (Gabriele Ferzetti). This is a character that is only seen for a limited time in the film, but her absence weighs on all the rest of it.

Antonioni's image of this Massari is that of a bourgeois in flower, conscious of her own rights as a woman, the most important of which is the right to love and happiness.

After a short though successful theatrical break with Arnoldo Foà, Lea Massari returned to the screen in *La giornata balorda* (1960) *(From a Roman Balcony)* directed by Mauro Bolognini and *Il colosso di Rodi*

Lea Massari, child-woman in Dreams in a Drawer *(1957).*

(1961) *(The Colossus of Rhodes)* by Sergio Leone. In *From a Roman Balcony* she is in the guise of a good bourgeois Roman lady who has a relationship with the good-for-nothing Jean Sorel. In *The Colossus of Rhodes*, on the other hand, she plays Princess Diala, a hot little number. The color film flatters her dark complexion conferring a slightly oriental air on her. A few little beauty marks grace her cheeks, her eyelashes grow longer. Lea Massari's vivacity seems to be a little toned down by the ancient Greek costumes, but the romantic aura of *Dreams in a Drawer* sticks to her. Here too Lea dies tragically. "I had so many dreams..." she whispers to her muscular hero Rory Calhoun as she dies.

The Italy of the early sixties was full of dreams and Lea Massari was a good dreamer.

As the years passed Lea Massari became more and more fascinating: her eyes retained their childlike beauty, while her features became more marked and gave her a more defined personality. The price of her stock as a diva remained stable. And yet Massari never managed to reach the level of real stardom: she was an excellent actress who remained locked in the vestibule of *divismo*. She could not find roles to equal the quality of the one created for her by Castellani in

Lea Massari with her faithful pup on the set of **Una vita difficile** *(1961).*

Dreams in a Drawer. Not even a movie like *Una vita difficile* [A difficult life] where she partnered an Alberto Sordi at the peak of his popularity, enabled her to make the decisive leap.

Nanni Loy gives her a less bourgeois role in *Le quattro giornate di Napoli* (1962) *(The Four Days of Naples)* where she is a simple girl called Maria involved in the uprising against the Nazis. It is a fine part, but it gets lost in a deliberately complex plot involving several main characters. The same can be said of the part that Zurlini writes for her in *Le soldatesse* [The women soldiers] (1965), where she is Toula, a Greek girl who during the war prostitutes herself for food and who is repatriated by the authorities along with her sister and other unfortunate women.

The child image of Lea Massari develops into a languid subtlety that cannot find a place in the Italian film scene of the late sixties. French cinema seems to understand her better: Lea plays the hero's wife in Sautet's *L'amant* (1969) *(The Things of Life)* and the incestuous mother in Louis Malle's *Le souffle au coeur* (1971) *(Murmur of the Heart)*.

It is again Valerio Zurlini who casts her in the fine film *La prima notte di quiete* [First night of calm] (1972) as the wife of Alain Delon, infatuated with his beautiful young student Sonia Petrova. But Massari's talent doesn't find an outlet in characters on the level of her class. She would have to take refuge in television to find a great role – in Sandro Bolchi's version of *Anna Karenina* (1974) where she is a splendid and moving Anna.

Claudia Cardinale

The Tunisian Claudia Cardinale belonged to the next generation. The difference in age between her and the Loren-Lollo duo was insignificant: the Cardinale boom took off in 1961, seven or eight years later than Gina's or Sophia's which dated back to 1953-54. Yet in those seven years the face of Italy had changed, and the image of women in films had evolved at the same pace. The breasts of the *maggiorata* woman, a sublimated image of maternity, was the last fruit of a matriarchal society. At the beginning of the sixties, the myth of the superwoman gave way to a naughtier type of femininity: the new woman was made up of pouting and puerile smiles. In the wake of Roger Vadim's successful film *Et Dieu créa la femme* (1956) *(And God Created Woman)* the Bardot kind of woman appeared on the scene. Moreover, 1962 would be the year of *Lolita*.

"I was supposed to become a schoolteacher, Claudia recalls, but in Tunis where I lived with my family, one day I won a beauty contest and the prize was a trip to Italy. So, I went to Venice. There, some people in movies noticed me and for two months I attended the Centro Sperimentale but without too much interest. It was in Tunis that I turned on the radio and heard the news that Vides Films had put a young Tunisian actress under contract. It was me! I went back to Rome and did a screen test for an exclusive seven-year contract with Vides. I was a minor and had to have my father's consent. The Vides contract was an American-type one as was the case in those days – like a book filled with clauses regarding pay, physical weight, what you could and could not do. In effect, it gave some guarantees of subsistence, but you had to put yourself completely in their hands. For example, it stated that I could not cut my hair without first getting approval."

After her Tunisian debut in *Gobu*, Claudia appears in *I soliti ignoti* (1958) *(Big Deal on Madonna Street)* and its sequel *Audace colpo dei soliti ignoti* (1959) *(Fiasco in Milan)* in the part of Ferribotte's sister: she is a typical Sicilian girl of that time whom her brother keeps under lock and key. A small but well-constructed role. Claudia Cardinale's career was guided with a sure hand by the Vides producer Franco Cristaldi who made a good guess at the potential of this opulent brunette with the intense eyes and the elegant carriage.

Instinctive and a bit dour as she was, Claudia seemed suitable for roles of ordinary girls. In Pietro Germi's *Un maledetto imbroglio* (1959) *(The Facts of Murder)* she is Assunta, the servant girl, thanks to whom Nino Castelnuovo gets into the luxurious apartment in Via Merulana where he will be forced to murder Eleonora Rossi Drago. In *Rocco e i suoi fratelli* (1960) *(Rocco and His Brothers)* she plays Ginetta, Vincenzo's fiancé. Cardinale's harsh southern beauty caught the imagination of Luchino Visconti and she became one of the muses who inspired his films.

But the character that most reveals Claudia Cardinale to the general public is that of another Sicilian girl, Barbara Puglisi, in Mauro Bolognini's *Il bell' Antonio* [Handsome Antonio] (1960). In this movie, based on one of Vitaliano Brancati's best novels, Claudia Cardinale is a girl from a good Catanian family married to Marcello Mastroianni who, however charming he may be, doesn't manage to consummate his marriage. After the annulment, Barbara marries a very rich nobleman and is destined to a life of unhappiness. Even if her rank as an actress and star kept her from playing character parts, Cardinale was – together with Stefania Sandrelli – the quintessential Sicilian girl in the Italian cinema of the sixties. In 1963 Luchino Visconti gives her the role of Angelica Sedara in *Il gattopardo (The Leopard)*, and in 1967 she plays the lead in another classic that is set in Sicily, Damiano Damiani's *Il giorno della civetta (Day of the Owl)*.

The film that consecrated Claudia Cardinale's place as a star more than any other, however, was Valerio Zurlini's *La ragazza con la valigia* (1960) *(Girl with a Suitcase)*. Claudia interprets the role of Aida, a bit of a vamp, who is drawn into a love affair by a cynical Corrado Pani who immediately abandons her and orders his sixteen-year-old brother to do away with her. But the boy falls in love instead. The film was a great success for Cardinale, hailed as a sensitive actress, capable of shaping such a fascinating and original female character. Claudia has a mysterious kind of beauty even when playing ordinary characters, but she can also play a bad girl quite credibly as she does in another film of Bolognini's *La viaccia* (or, *The Love Makers*) (1961), where she is the prostitute Bianca.

Shadowy, closed up in the mystery of her sphinx-like eyes, Cardinale speaks very little on the screen, partly because the voice in her first films is not her own. It is the excellent Adriana Asti who dubs her, in another Bolognini film as well, *Senilità* [Senility] (1962), inspired by the Italo Svevo novel. To hear her own voice one had to wait for *La ragazza di Bube* (1963) *(Bebo's Girl)* directed by Luigi Comencini where she plays Maria, a country girl, who falls in love with the ex-partisan Bebo, who is involved in a political assassination. This character also comes from a novel, and was created by Carlo Cassola. Claudia seemed destined to interpret heroines borrowed by the cinema from literature, and in fact her fragile, mysterious beauty lent itself well to contemporary literature, to the icy heroines who go through identity crises.

Bebo's Girl was an important movie for Claudia and immediately won her a Nastro d'Argento (Silver Ribbon) prize. That raw, toneless voice of hers, so absolutely out of place with her fairy-tale, slightly oriental beauty, made her image even more unusual. It made her seem like a cracked crystal vase on the verge of shattering into a thousand pieces. In comparison with two down-to-earth beauties like Loren and Lollo, Claudia was a mystery: she did not belong either to heaven nor to earth. She was the ideal actress to interpret Carla in Francesco Maselli's film *Gli indifferenti (Time of Indifference)* taken from Alberto Moravia's famous novel.

Thanks to this film Claudia's fame also exploded abroad. The French saw in her a second Brigitte Bardot, and imitating B.B.,

Claudia Cardinale is the cumbersome and fascinating "Fata Armenia" in the title episode of the movie **Sex Quartet** *(1966).*

Claudia Cardinale and Alain Delon are the splendid leading couple in **The Leopard** *(1963).*

named her C.C. In 1963, after her appearance in *Otto e mezzo (8½ or Eight and a Half)*, Cardinale tried to gain entrance to international films and obtained a role in *The Pink Panther* (1964) directed by Blake Edwards who used her oriental look to cast her in the part of the Indian princess who is robbed of a famous jewel. After this small role she landed others, sometimes bigger ones, as in Henry Hathaway's *Circus World* (1964), *Blindfold* (1965) by Philip Dunne, *Lost Command* (1966) by Mark Robson, and Richard Brooks' *The Professionals* (1966).

But Claudia continued to give her best in Italian films like Luchino Visconti's *Vaghe stelle dell'Orsa* (1965) *(Sandra)* in the guise of a modern Elektra. Despite the title quoting Leopardi, it is a modern-day version of Aeschylus' *Orestes* set among the bourgeoisie of Tuscany in the sixties. Fleshy and feline, immortalized by Armando Nannuzzi's baroque black and white photography, and by then also a mature woman, Claudia Cardinale was a kind of Kerima, but more subtle. Sometimes fragile, sometimes aggressive, she was ready for a wide range of roles, even that of a frontier woman: she is the only woman in the cast of Sergio Leone's great classic *C'era una volta il West* (1968) *(Once Upon a Time in the West)* . She had the look of an intellectual star, the ideal interpreter for rambunctious and quarrelsome characters.

In 1967 her professional and personal attachment to the producer Franco Cristaldi led to a marriage of no long duration. Cristaldi's place in Claudia's heart was soon taken by another man of the cinema, Pasquale Squitieri.

Monica Vitti

The Roman girl Maria Luisa Ceciarelli finished her studies at the Academy of Dramatic Art in 1953, the year Lollo played *la bersagliera*. She was no *maggiorata* (anything but a "big" woman). However she certainly didn't lack talent: she could play comic as well as dramatic roles, if only she could find herself a more artistic name. For example, she might call herself Monica Vitti. Why not?

Like many talented girls, Monica Vitti did a bit of everything: theater, dubbing, an occasional small movie part and screen tests for *Nella città l'inferno (And the Wild, Wild Women)* and *Le ragazze di piazza di Spagna* (1952) *(Girls of the Spanish Steps)*. Her voice was slightly hoarse and whiny, even worse than Claudia Cardinale's, but interesting, like the timbre of a real actress. She certainly knew how to act. Everyone disapproved of her nose – what was called an aristocratic nose. Her hair was a mixture of red and blonde and she wore it in a pony tail or gathered at the back of her neck. She almost always wore dark colors. She used little or no make-up. There was a severe air about her. Her image could hardly have been further from that of the nymphets who crowded the beauty contests ready to do anything and everything to get into the movies. For Monica Vitti, acting was a profession.

The turning point came when she dubbed the voice of Dorian Gray in *Il grido* (1957) *(The Cry)*. The meeting with Michelangelo Antonioni would change her life. The director from Ferrara made Monica Vitti his cinematic muse.

Antonioni first directed her in the theater and then on the set in *L'avventura* (1960) *(The Adventure)*, a film that hit the screens of the Cannes Film Festival like a hurricane. Blonde, impassive as the sphinx, Monica suddenly became the diva of the cinema of incommunicability. Against the background of wild nature on the islands of Lipari, Monica Vitti's expressive power recalled that of Ingrid Bergman in *Stromboli*. In *The Adventure* too, Vitti is a woman alone facing the impossibility of love, the protagonist of a drama reflected in the bleak landscape of an island of barren rock. Compared to Rossellini's Bergman, who is a refugee with no resources, there is a change in social status: the Monica Vitti of *The Adventure* is a bourgeois woman. The Italy of 1960 is already a rich country that has rid itself of every last ghost of the postwar era and feels the need to overcome the taste for neorealism. Monica Vitti with vertigo in her eyes is the woman of this Italy projected towards the future.

During the mid-sixties Monica shares in Antonioni's most prolific artistic period. She

[see also p. 195]

is his woman-symbol, the artist who can express the bourgeoisie's existential crisis: its obsession with emptiness, emotional impotence, the desperate sense of futility. Antonioni's themes are all written in Vitti's tender and absent look in *La notte* (1961) *(The Night)*, *L'eclisse* (1962) *(The Eclipse)* and *Deserto rosso* (1964) *(The Red Desert)*. Sometimes blonde as in *The Adventure* and *The Eclipse*, sometimes brunette as in *The Night*, and sometimes chestnut as in *The Red Desert*, hers is a beauty full of questioning: she belongs to the modern cinema which repudiates the psychological introspection of the nineteenth-century memory, in order to explore new frontiers of expression. Vitti is a "mental" diva. In Antonioni's films her acting, absolutely atypical, is riddled with silences, eyes lost in the void and all those actions that in films were considered insignificant.

Monica's beauty was neither of the ampler woman-type and even less that of the nymphet. She was the bourgeois woman, slightly aristocratic, who likes to dress in a casual but elegant style – pullovers, blouses, raincoats. If she were expressed in a color this Vitti would be gray, but certainly she would not be called a colorless woman. Her charm, composed of nuances, struck above all the imagination of the intellectuals.

For the Italian public Monica Vitti still smacked of existentialism, still meant love crises and neurotic personalities. Monica had to struggle to change this image, to impose a new one. Her notable talent helped her in this task. Little by little she began affirming her comic talent. She acted together with Alberto Sordi in the surreal *Il disco volante* (1964) *(The Flying Saucer)* directed by Tinto Brass. She took part in several episode films in sparkling and amusing roles. She is plaintive in one of the best episodes of *Alta infedeltà* (1963) *(High Infidelity)* and plays the lead in Blasetti's episode, *La lepre e la tartaruga (The Hare and the Turtle)*, of the film *Le quattro verità* (1964) *(The Three Fables of Love)*. But the movie that is the true turning point of her career is Joseph Losey's *Modesty Blaise* (1966). A character inspired by a popular comic strip, Modesty Blaise is a beautiful spy in Her Majesty's secret service. With a tattooed thigh, bizarre costumes based on black thigh boots and an incredible arsenal of arms that live up to any of James Bond's, Monica is a very lively heroine, witty and comical. Her sophisticated humor takes on a tinge of sensuality.

This role, that made her much more famous than any of Antonioni's ever did, was a clear sign to Monica to turn to comedy. She performed

well in roles in *La cintura di castità* (1967) *(The Chastity Belt)* set in the Middle Ages where she is the sweet Boccadoro, the wife of the crusader Tony Curtis; and in Luciano Salce's frivolous little farce *Ti ho sposato per allegria* [I married you for fun] (1967) where she is the nutty wife of Giorgio Albertazzi; and most of all in *La ragazza con la pistola* (1968) *(Girl with a Pistol)*.

Girl with a Pistol presents us with a Sicilian Vitti, the classic "seduced and abandoned" Assunta. Assunta pursues her seducer even as far as England, determined to avenge her honor, pistol in hand. But in smoky London, the dark southern girl, clothed in black and her many prejudices, is slowly transformed into a modern woman. Discovering new love she forgets her homicidal intentions. The film is an x-ray of a backward mentality tastefully and skillfully exposed by an extraordinary performer. In this role, greatly acclaimed abroad as well, Vitti finally found the popular and box office success which only *Modesty Blaise* had brought her. But *Girl with a Pistol* also procured her an endless series of awards from the Nastro d'Argento to the David di Donatello, to the San Sebastian Festival's prize as best actress.

In the seventies Monica Vitti's career followed the course drawn by this fine characterization, and she affirmed her place as the only great comedy actress of the Italian cinema of the time.

[see also p. 194]

Monica Vitti, Michelangelo Antonioni's muse, in **The Night** *(1961).*

Monica Vitti with Gabriele Ferzetti in Antonioni's masterpiece **The Adventure** *(1960).*

THE SEVEN STARS
OF THE LITTLE DIPPER

Valentina Cortese

[see also p. 49]

A restrained, icy young woman from Milan, Valentina Cortese appeared to be far from the kind of woman popular during the "white telephone" era of the Fascist regime. Her beauty even had something androgynous about it.

At the dawning of the postwar period Valentina Cortese was only a little over twenty. She was one year younger than Marina Berti and had a long career before her. The first role she got with the new Italian cinema was that of a sweet schoolteacher in the country in *Un americano in vacanza* (1945) *(A Yank in Rome)* by Luigi Zampa. She is courted by a gallant American soldier who makes her a serious proposal of marriage before he leaves Italy. This character seems to prefigure, in a way, Valentina's future: she was indeed destined to marry an American – the actor Richard Basehart.

After the role Pagliero gives her in *Roma città libera* [Rome free city] (1946) Valentina Cortese plays a substantial role in the two-part movie *I miserabili* (1947) *(Les Misérables)* where she has a double role: Fantina in *Caccia all'uomo (Man Hunt)*, the first part, and Cosetta in the second part, *Tempesta su Parigi (Storm over Paris)*. Fantina is one of the most unlucky characters to be created from the pen of Victor Hugo and for the occasion Cortese adopts the perfect appearance of a victim. She gets into every kind of trouble and woe; she weeps and despairs. Obliged even to resort to prostitution to feed her little Cosetta, the fruit of her "sin," Fantina is saved by the good man Jean Valjean who also takes care of the child.

Again in the setting of the French nineteenth century, Valentina goes from Victor Hugo to Stendhal interpreting the leading role in *Il corriere del re* (1948) *(The King's Messenger)*, Gennaro Righelli's last film inspired by *Le rouge et le noir*. She plays the part of Louise, the young and sensitive wife of the crude provincial mayor, inevitably destined for betrayal. Evidently the Valentina Cortese of that period corresponds to the stereotype of a French woman because almost at the same time she plays the role of a Parisian Jewish woman, Esther, in the melodrama *L'ebreo errante* (1947) [The wandering Jew]. Even Valentina Cortese's first American film, *Black Magic* (1949), is taken from the work of another great French writer, Alexandre Dumas. In actual fact, it is a co-production with some prominent American actors like Orson Welles and Akim Tamiroff. Valentina, who is only the second female lead, appears in gypsy guise.

It is mainly due to the overseas success of *A Yank in Rome* that Twentieth Century Fox decides to put Valentina Cortese on contract. "The idea of leaving my people and Italy gives me sleepless nights. And then there is the problem of the language which I don't speak! But Fox has been so kind as to give me a year at their expense so that I can learn English..."

In the Mecca of the film world, make-up men and costume designers take over to shine up her image. Her hair is cut short: Val, as her new American friends call her, becomes a tomboy. Her surname too is slightly altered and is now, Valentina Cortesa.

In Hollywood "Cortesa" shoots *Thieves' Highway* (1949) and *The House on Telegraph Hill* (1951) for Fox who has kept her under contract. But she is also loaned out

Valentina Cortese with Jack Palance and Norman Wooland in the historical spectacular **Barabbas** *(1961).*

to MGM for *Malaya* (1949). Both *Thieves' Highway* and *Malaya* are predominantly male films that give her very few opportunities. But *The House on Telegraph Hill* is a star vehicle made to her measure. In it she interprets the role of Karin, a Polish widow deported by the Nazis. In the concentration camp she makes friends with another widow, Victoria, who, before being deported, has managed to save her son, sending him to a very rich aunt in America whom he has never seen. Victoria dies of privation while Karin only just barely survives. With Victoria's documents, Karin goes to America in her place. The rich aunt has died leaving everything to the child who has been put under the tutelage of a distant relative, Alan. This man receives Karin (Victoria) with open arms and marries her. But he soon shows himself to be a scoundrel who intends to get his hands on the inheritance by killing the child with the help of his mistress who has infiltrated the home as a governess. Karin saves herself at the last minute, and Alan is the victim of his own machinations. The evil Alan is played by Richard Basehart who seriously fell in love with Valentina and led her to the altar. Two years later they had a son, Jackie, who would try to follow his parents' careers – unsuccessfully – when he grew up.

Between 1950 and 1952 Valentina also made many co-production films such as *Crossroads of Passion, Unwanted Women, Shadow of the Eagle,* and *The Secret People* (an English film never released in Italy). During this period Valentina Cortese was the most international of Italian actresses. She alternated between costume productions and genre films. Her quiet, restrained beauty could adapt itself to any role.

In 1955, after having played important secondary roles in big biographical productions such as *La contessa scalza* (1954) *(The Barefoot Contessa)* and *Fuoco magico* (1955) *(Magic Fire)*, Valentina Cortese confirmed her acting skill in *Le amiche (The Girlfriends)*. Directed by an Antonioni at his best, she interprets the part of Nene, a potter who sacrifices all her artistic aspirations for the love of a failed painter, who neglects her

for other women. In the novel by Cesare Pavesi, *Tra donne sole* on which the film is based, the figure of Nene is a rough sketch. Antonioni develops the part to suit Valentina.

In *The Girlfriends* she has the beauty of women who suffer inwardly. Antonioni's silences stand in high relief on her lips. Her eyes cast down, her mouth resolutely closed, and her eyes disillusioned, Valentina follows her love like an automaton. The result is a figure steeped in painful melancholy. Nene is the typical Antonioni loser, a victim in love, in work, and in life. Pavese would probably have liked this Valentina Cortese too, because among other things she had a certain resemblance to Constance Dowling in many of her films.

In the sixties she made few films but acted in a lot of plays. She interpreted small parts in *Barabba* (1961) *(Barabbas), La vendetta della signora* (1964) *(The Visit)* and *Quando muore una stella* (1968) *(The Legend of Lylah Clare)*.

Her most important role in the sixties was the one Fellini gave her in *Juliet of the Spirits* (1965). The deranged friend of the gentle Juliet, she brings her a "spirit exorciser" back from Los Angeles as a present. Very heavily made up, flamboyant, flying high, Fellini's Cortese in *Juliet of the Spirits* is a woman who looks older than her forty years. She is one of those masks with which Federico Fellini enjoyed ridiculing the myth of feminine beauty.

Valentina Cortese in one of her most memorable roles: the unfortunate Nene in The Girlfriends *(1955). Here, with Madeleine Fischer, Franco Fabrizi, and Gabriele Ferzetti.*

**Lea Padovani in
Scandal in Sorrento
(1955).**

Lea Padovani

Lea Padovani is the typical actress with a paradoxical career that promises to be a smash hit but goes into eclipse.

A talented student at the Academy for Dramatic Art, she got her start – by virtue of her remarkable physical charms – in variety when the enterprising Macario launched her in the musical comedy *Febbre azzurra* [Blue fever]. In this the production, Lea is a religious fanatic who ends up by chance on a desert island where the virus of nymphomania is raging and, of course, she comes down with it. Padovani is twenty-five and in her skimpy costume she is stupendous.

In 1946 she also made *Una mela per Elena* [An apple for Elena] directed by Dino Falconi. But she aspired to serious theater and performed in a number of dramas und comedies.

After this, she devoted herself entirely to the cinema where she had made her debut in 1945 under the auspices of Macario in the creaking revue-comedy *L'innocente Casimiro* [Innocent Casimiro]. Her first slightly important role was the one Aldo Vergano gave her in *(Il sole sorge ancora)* (1947) *(Outcry)*. Slovenly, badly dressed, in knee-

high socks, Padovani plays Laura, an anti-Fascist worker who leads her man, Vittorio Duse, to the partisan struggle. Elli Parvo, the early *maggiorata* (generously endowed) woman with the vamp look, plays her antagonist.

In *Outcry* Lea Padovani is the incarnation of the positive woman of neorealism. The international success of this manifesto film of the new Italian cinema won her an important role in another social protest film, *Cristo fra i muratori* (1949) *(Give Us This Day)* directed by Dmytryk and produced by Rod Geiger who distributed Rossellini's masterpieces in America. In this film, Lea exhibits the same neglected appearance as in *Outcry*. She is Annunziata, a poor Italian girl who goes to New York to marry Geremia, an Italo-American construction worker in Brooklyn. What attracts her most is the mirage of finally having a house of her own. In reality, the unfortunate Geremia does not have the money to actually buy the house. He only barely manages to pay the first installments. The owner loans the house to him for a few days, for the honeymoon. Then begins for Annunziata a life of privation in two small rooms in a city housing complex. The couple have four children, work and save, but the fruit of all their efforts is wiped out in the crash of '29. Geremia dies under the rubble of a demolition job undertaken without observing any of the most elementary safety precautions. Annunziata is given an indemnity with which she can finally buy the house she had always wanted.

The Annunziata of *Give Us This Day* is a highly dramatic figure who confirms Lea Padovani's image as an actress committed to progressive films. In that same period Lea had a strange adventure with Orson Welles who had signed her to play Desdemona in his *Othello*, a film which seemed to be jinxed. The shooting was broken up over a period of four long years.

This is the way Padovani recounts that experience: "At that time I was still silly, intransigent, immature, stubborn. Orson, for his part, was terribly in love with me. What an extraordinary man, when I think about it. What intelligence! He told me that he had never loved a woman so much before me... We started shooting *Othello*. In the evening I found messages on the dressing-room mirror that he had left me written in lipstick: 'Your eyes are so big, so marvelous!' or else I found photographs of beautiful cars, and written on them: 'This car belongs to Lea Padovani!' Things went on like this for a while. He said he had to marry me at all costs, that until then he had considered women to be little more than objects, pastimes. Even Rita, and all the others. He said he had possessed women just as he would have a good lunch or taste a fine wine, but with me it was different. For my part I was extremely embarrassed by such ruthless courting... I ended up jilting him right in the middle of the film, and that was the end of that!"

The success of *Outcry*, followed by that of *Give Us This Day*, for which Padovani lost the Volpi Cup at the Venice Film Festival by a hair's breadth to Eleanor Parker, seemed destined to open the doors of the whole world to her. But with the Cold War at its height, Padovani's aura of a woman of the people with libertarian tendencies didn't help her to make a career in America, nor did the fact that she had been directed by the "ex-communicated" Dmytryk.

Even in Italy, film people tainted with Communism had no easy life of it: producers wanted a quiet life and grew fat on government subsidies. Furthermore it was said of Padovani that she did not have the necessary appeal for leading roles. Many distributors refused to accept her name as a guarantee for the success of high-budget films.

Back in Italy, Lea found herself in the casts of films which were neither up to her talent nor to her international success. It was a truly strange situation.

Thus she had recourse to character parts which she managed to ennoble thanks to her talent. She was often given the part of an outcast woman: she plays a prostitute in three important films: *Roma ore undici* (1952) *(Rome, Eleven O'Clock)* directed by De Santis, the comedy *Una di quelle* (1953) where she is partnered by Totò and Peppino De Filippo, and the drama *Donne proibite* [Forbidden women] (1953). For the rest, Lea Padovani was past thirty and her intense look did not suit the lower middle-class vocation of the Italian cinema.

And yet Lea Padovani's talent was well above the average and she lost no opportunity to confirm it as in the second episode of the film *Tempi nostri* (1954) *(Anatomy of Love)*, "Il pupo." She is a poor little bride who, together with her husband, searches Rome looking for a church in which to abandon their child whom she is carrying in her arms. They visit quite a few without finding the right one. And, after one last attempt they decide to keep the baby. This neorealistic kind of role, which made the young Sophia Loren's mouth water too, earned Lea Padovani yet another artistic award – a Nastro d'Argento prize for her career. The year before she had received the Grolla d'Oro at Saint Vincent, but all of these prizes did nothing to launch her in great style.

It is a more serene and popular image that she gets to depict in Dino Risi's comedy *Pane, amore e...* (1955) *(Scandal in Sorrento)* which belongs to the light neorealistic genre.

Here Lea plays donna Violante, the chaste spinster who rents an apartment to the police marshal De Sica. This feather-brained character, who also reappears in the sequel *Pane, amore e Andalusia* (1955) [Bread, love and Andalusia], disproves the unappealing image which has dogged Padovani throughout her career. But at this point, Lea is past the age of making a new start. She receives the kind of wife roles that are suited to every "lovely lady." In the comedy *Il seduttore* (1954) [The seducer] she is Norma, the wife of an Alberto Sordi who devotes himself to pursuing the most improbable amorous adventures. A down-to-earth woman but with a soft heart, Norma runs their restaurant almost single-handedly.

From 1955 on, Lea Padovani worked mainly for television which showed much more respect for her talent.

Having drastically reduced her movie commitments, Padovani found time to return to the theater: she played in a memorable production of *Cat on a Hot Tin Roof* (1957) with Gabriele Ferzetti and Gino Cervi. Popular in England too, she acted (in English) in *The Rose Tattoo* and had a reunion on the London stage with Sam Wanamaker, her partner in *Give Us This Day*. Meanwhile movies offered her very little – a minor role in *La maja desnuda* (1958) *(The Naked Maja)* and a small part as a widow in *La noia* (1963) *(The Empty Canvas)*.

Lea Padovani and Marcello Mastroianni in the episode The Baby *from* Anatomy of Love, *released as* A Slice of Life *in Great Britain (1954).*

Ethereal and inaccessible Lucia Bosè in Cronaca di un amore *(1950), with Masimo Girotti.*

Lucia Bosè

In the Italy of the Reconstruction many farmhands became industrial workers, attracted by the mirage of a few more lire in wages. Lucia Bosè's father, a farmhand from San Giuliano Milanese also made this move. But the money was still not much. Like the little Sofia Scicolone (the later Sophia Loren), Lucia too had a coat made from the rough wool of a soldier uncle's overcoat.

Not yet fifteen, Lucia rolled up her sleeves and went to work as a waitress in the Galli cakeshop on Via Victor Hugo where she served coffee and cream-filled pastries. But the Milanese patrons came mostly to admire her long legs and beautiful provocative eyes. One day Luchino Visconti happened to come into the Galli cakeshop, and between roll and coffee, he made a prophecy to the lovely waitress. "Miss, one day you are going to be in films, I am certain of it!" Her road to glory passed through Stresa where the cakeshop waitress became Miss Italy of 1947, over a number of other contestants such as Gina Lollobrigida, Gianna Maria Canale, and Eleonora Rossi (the future Rossi Drago). Her life was suddenly turned upside down: invitations, chic gifts, a thousand photographs and, most of all, Milanese high society...

At the end of 1949, Giuseppe De Santis, who had already given her a screen test for *Bitter Rice* but had preferred Silvana Mangano, transformed this svelte Milanese girl into a shepherdess from Ciociara in *Non c'è pace tra gli ulivi* (1950) *(No Peace Among the Olives)*. Bosè wears peasant clogs as if they were high heels and her rags as if they were costumes from the designer Shubert's atelier. At that time Lucia was the woman of the duke Visconti, a Lombard industrialist and a relative of Luchino. And yet in *No Peace Among the Olives* she doesn't seem at all out of place. De Santis maintains that the mountain girls of Ciociara are svelte and haughty, just like Lucia Bosè. Shot from below, in the style of Soviet silent films, Lucia looks upwards as a sign of peasant dignity.

Bosè is a kind of restless gazelle, full of life and difficult for De Santis to control. Compared to Silvana Mangano, she lacks the statuesque build of a pagan divinity and the fascination of a sinning angel that was stamped on Silvana's face. But Lucia Bosè's eyes have a more genuine sparkle of peasant cunning: stolen glances, winks, self-satisfied smiles. One need only think of the scene of her dance under the olive trees where – to distract the attention of the local *carabinieri* – Lucia performs a country *saltarello* not lacking in sensuality.

There is an incredible abyss that separates the country vamp from the next role she is given immediately afterwards by Michelangelo Antonioni in his first film, *Cronaca di un amore* (1950) [Chronicle of a love]. Here Lucia is transformed into an elegant, introverted society woman, wife of a busy Milanese industrialist whose jealousy annoys her. But she is still involved in a youthful love affair. Lucia's rather gloomy beauty hovers like a splendid bird of evil omen over the self-satisfied Milanese financial aristocracy. Garbed in sadness, with a frozen look in her eyes, her beautiful shoulders often bare, Bosè displays a thousand gowns, revealing that model's carriage that makes her so convincing in *Le ragazze di piazza di Spagna* (1952) *(The Girls of the Spanish Steps)*.

A third kind of Bosè is immediately added to the neorealistic and bourgeois ones: Lucia Bosè, the comedienne of films such as *Era lei che lo voleva* [She was the one who wanted to] (1953), *Vacanze d'amore* [Love holiday] (1954), and *Accadde al commissariato* [It happened at the police station] (1954). In this last film Lucia is partnered by her new boyfriend, Walter Chiari, one of the historic seducers of Rome's *dolce vita*. He plays the part of the absent-minded husband. She is a cute lower middle-class wife, unfaithful and dishonest, who passes off her lover's presents as just lucky finds. But the cuckolded husband also has a mistress, and all because of a mink coat all the machinations come to the surface.

This Bosè is neither fish nor fowl. She is too aristocratic to get entirely bound up in this comedy, and too dishonest to be a truly respectable woman. Fortunately, Lucia had already interpreted two much more subtle and tasteful comedies: *Parigi è sempre Parigi* [Paris will always be Paris] (1951) and *The Girls of the Spanish Steps,* both directed by Luciano Emmer.

In *The Girls of the Spanish Steps,* which is a pinnacle of Italian comedy, Lucia seems to pass through the whole history of her real life again: she plays a girl from a poor quarter of Rome (Garbatella) who, thanks to her charms, becomes a model for a famous atelier – that of the Fontana sisters.

This Bosè knows how to be sentimental while being vigorous in a well-constructed role acted with deep commitment. She plays the cards of her big, sad eyes, her natural elegance, and her dying-swan beauty. With a light hand she draws the character lineaments of a little seamstress who wants "something more" of life and gets it even without renouncing the good sentiments of her sub-proletarian background.

It was just this character, much more than the peasant melodrama of De Santis or the existential dramas of Antonioni, that made Lucia Bosè's popularity rise. Lucia received tons of mail from her fans who were, for the most part, young, even very young, women. In her portrayals of romantic girls, Lucia Bosè's admirers saw the bitterness of their own lives and the little dreams they nurtured in the secret corners of their hearts. Of course many of them had impossible ambitions of becoming actresses. One girl from Sant'Alberto di Ravenna, for example, wrote: "Miss Lucia, I am a seventeen-year-old seamstress and it has always been my dream to become an actress one day. Unfortunately my situation doesn't permit me to do so since I cannot afford to travel to a lot of cities. I only finished fifth grade and I wanted to continue school, but that too was impossible because my parents couldn't support me. I wanted to ask you, is it true that there is no hope for those like me who can't go to the city? Or can there be some hope even for an ordinary seamstress like me? It's almost advice I am asking for. I have written you all this as if to a good friend."

If the little seamstress from Sant'Alberto di Ravenna saw Lucia as a close friend, it was certainly not because of *Cronaca di un amore* but rather for *The Girls of the Spanish Steps,* or perhaps her second film with Antonioni *La signora senza camelie* (1953) *(The Lady Without Camelias)* where Bosè plays the part of a poor shop girl who with great effort rises to become a film actress.

Neorealism, with its theory of discovering actors off the street, created many illusions that were frequent above all in the poorest strata of Italian society: seamstresses, shop girls, dish washers, chambermaids, all had their heads full of theses fancies. The Italian cinema of the period reflected upon these dreams and produced films that ruthlessly exposed the entertainment world: *Vita da cani* (1950) *(It's a Dog's Life)*, *Bellissima* [Ravishing] (1952), *Lo sceicco bianco* (1952) *(The White Sheik).*

The Bosè of *The Lady Without Camelias* has a sunken face, is shadowy, pale, unreal: one of Antonioni's ghosts. And yet this role was written with quite a different actress, with sunny Gina Lollobrigida, in mind. After having read the script Gina refused the part, afraid that it would damage her image as a winner of a woman. With Bosè, shapely but not really a *maggiorata,* the character is seen in a different light: she becomes ethereal, a woman consumed by the cinema which acts like a drug, a cancer, in her.

Lucia appears just as unearthly in *Roma ore undici* (1952) *(Rome, Eleven O'Clock)* a film involving the entwined stories of several characters directed by De Santis on the subject of female unemployment: for a single post as typist, hundreds of girls present themselves, all crowded onto a staircase that ends by collapsing. One of the girls dies. The plot was inspired by a true story to which another film of the period makes reference: *Tre storie proibite* (1952) *(Three Forbidden Stories)* by Genina. In this motley kaleidoscope of common feminine figures, Bosè's svelte elegance is even more striking, the only bourgeois woman in a gallery of proletarians. In order to go and live with a penniless

Michelangelo Antonioni cast Lucia Bosè in a magnificent role in The Lady Without Camelias *(1953).*

painter she has renounced the comforts offered by her family. Now she finds herself destitute, but she still looks high class.

During the shooting of *Muerte de un ciclista* (1955) *(Death of a Cyclist)*, an Antonioni-style film by the Spanish director Juan Antonio Bardem, Lucia Bosè met the real love of her life, Luis Dominguin, one of Spain's most famous toreadors. After their marriage, Lucia announced that she was going to quit her acting career, but this news was quickly contradicted by the facts: she was cast in a French film directed by Buñuel *Cela s'appelle l'aurore* (1956) [That's called dawn], where she plays the part of Clara, an Italian widow who has an affair with Georges Marchal. She appears more mature, her features a bit more sculptured. This is her farewell to the movies... one had to wait three years to see her on the screen again in Jean Cocteau's *Le testament d'Orphée* [Orpheus' testament] where she is partnered by her husband Dominguin. Then came a break of ten long years.

Lucia Bosè only reappeared on the screen at the age of thirty-seven in 1968 in *Sotto il segno dello scorpione* [Under the sign of the scorpion] by Paolo and Vittorio Taviani, after having spent a decade far from the cinema that might have been the greatest period of her artistic growth.

The cinema of the fateful year 1968 seemed very different, very hostile to her most of all, who still had the aura of the fifties about her. After 1968 Lucia returned to the screen, and even quite often went from French, to Spanish, to Italian productions working with important directors such as Federico Fellini, Jaime Camino, Mauro Bolognini, and Daniel Schmid. But her new films added little to the image of the Lucia Bosè of the fifties. That profile of hers with the slightly backward slope of the forehead, would live again in her son Miguel, born at the time of *Cela s'appelle l'aurore* and who, as a rock star, would inherit a masculine version of his mother's sex appeal.

Virna Lisi in one of her first movies Il cardinale Lambertini *(1954).*

Virna Lisi

At seventeen what could a blonde with no great pretences to being a *maggiorata* (a physically endowed woman) do, except play the ingenue?

Virna Pieralisi came to movies with her surname shortened to Lisi and the pale look of a girl-next-door. Between 1953-54 she made half a dozen Neapolitan films, some of them musicals, from *Napoli canta* [Naples sings] to *Desiderio 'e sole* [Desire is the sun], from *Piccola santa* [Little saint] to *Luna nuova* [New moon], where she is always the wan little blonde who is a victim of an infamous destiny. Now seduced and now abandoned, now beaten and now raped, poor Virna always finds a good reason to lament. Her tear glands, excited by onions, work overtime. The role of the victim is one that Virna drags along with her even outside the realm of the Neapolitan genre. For example, in the melodrama *Violenza sul lago* (1954) [Violence on the lake] by Leonardo Cortese and set in Latium, she falls in love with a young singer, Giacomo Rondinella, who rapes her in a fit of madness. In despair, the girl kills herself.

Virna Lisi is neither a beauty queen nor a scandal maker. Even off the set she plays the part of the respectable bourgeois, somewhere

between Lualdi and Pierangeli. To protect her from bad influences in the movie jungle, her parents keep a sharp watch over her. In general she is chaperoned by her mother, father or sister. Virna's popularity begins to rise thanks to a remake of the famous *Ore 9: lezione di chimica* (1941) *(Schoolgirl's Diary)* which Mattoli proposes as *Le diciotenni* [Eighteen-year-olds] (1955). Virna plays the part that was Irasema Dilian's in the first version: the high school girl, by now a young lady, unjustly accused of having an affair with the handsome professor (in this film a physics rather than chemistry teacher). Very blonde, the head of the class, hated by her rowdier classmates (above all by her enemy Marisa Allasio), Virna is a more respectable little Miss than ever: she doesn't even lack a touch of unpleasantness. Swarming around her are the offspring of the good families of the fifties who are not so different from the girls of the Fascist-era bourgeoisie. They have new crazes like the cha-cha-cha and photoplay magazines, but the substance is the same: money, respectability and lots and lots of sentiment.

As she grows up, Lisi loses that victimized look and becomes a rather mysterious woman who knows how to keep secrets, even quite impressive ones, as happens in *La donna del giorno* (1956) *(The Doll That Took the Town)*, a movie directed by the very young Francesco Maselli. Here Virna interprets the part of a fashion model who, to get herself publicity, concocts a false rape scenario and ruins the lives of three unfortunate men who are falsely accused of the crime. For three quarters of the film, Virna enjoys the role of the woman of the hour and carefully keeps her secret. Once more she has the victim look, but in this case she is bluffing. Later she repents and kills herself by flinging herself from a trolley bus.

After this film, Virna truly became the woman of the hour.

Unlike some stars, Lisi accepted some fairly negative roles. Her rather ethereal beauty was suited to costume parts in *Caterina Sforza,* (1959) and to the classical *Romolo e Remo* (1961) *(Romulus and Remus)*. But Virna also ventured into comedies with Totò in *Sua Eccellenza si fermò a mangiare*

(1961) [His excellency stopped to eat].

Her international reputation grew when she played the second female lead in Joseph Losey's *Eva* (1962) and the heroine opposite Alain Delon in *La tulipe noir* (1963) *(The Black Tulip)* directed by Christian-Jaque. As she reached full maturity, her movies became less prudish. Her image as an actress began taking on the tinge of an elegant and discrete eroticism: black slips, daring mini-skirts. That inimitable mole under her lip seemed to take on new meaning, a decorative little brown spot almost at the corner of her mouth.

Virna's long, long, slim nude legs make men tremble in *The Phone Call*, an episode in the scandal-film *Le bambole* (1964) *(Bambole!)*. On a hot, erogenous, Sunday afternoon in August she is the unattainable object of her husband Nino Manfredi's desire; he ends up by turning to the nymphomaniac next door. Dressed only in a black slip, Virna dedicates herself to an endless telephone call to *mamma* while Manfredi makes his futile advances... The straps of her undergarment keep slipping down, revealing her nude shoulders and much of her breasts. This episode throws new light on Lisi's comic vein just at the time when her brilliant smile lights up the TV screen in a toothpaste commercial.

Virna is just as beautiful and just as skimpily clad as she acts alongside Jack Lemmon in the movie *How to Murder Your Wife* (1964) directed by Richard Quine. She suddenly discovers that her blonde, rather frozen beauty is well-suited to the Hollywood idea of glamour in the sixties.

Virna Lisi's mischievous, seductive look in the episode The Telephone Call *in* Bambole! *released in Great Britain as* Four Kinds of Love *(1964). Here with Nino Manfredi.*

A new look for Virni Lisi, finally a serious actress in **The Birds, the Bees, and the Italians** *(1966).*

Virna's American adventure is not brilliant, but she has partners of the calibre of Frank Sinatra and Tony Curtis.

Virna hopped from film to film, shooting in the United States, France, and Italy, as her star burned brighter and brighter. Pasquale Festa Campanile offered her two sophisticated parts. Pietro Germi transformed her into a cashier in a provincial coffee shop in *Signore e signori* (1966) *(The Birds, the Bees and the Italians)*, a biting comedy of manners that attacks Italian provincial hypocrisy. Like Giovanna Ralli, Virna Lisi was an actress who didn't fear turning thirty. On the contrary, at thirty she was just hitting her stride. The loss of innocence invested her with an extraordinary fascination that shines out in *Le dolce signore* (1967) *(Anyone Can Play)*, *Arabella* (1967), and *Tenderly (The Girl Who Couldn't Say No)* (1968). Once more Virna combines elegant beauty with shrewd trickery. In Franco Brusati's *The Girl Who Couldn't Say No*, she is something entirely different: a free, dreamy woman whose head is full of fantasies and diffidence about marriage. After 1968, the year of protest, Virna proved her eternal fascination by experiencing a new golden age.

[see also p. 196]

Sandra Milo

Her name was Alessandra Marini and she was listlessly attending university precisely in the years when the *maggiorata* revolution (the revolution of the *very* "endowed woman") was exploding. Actually, she was fairly ample herself. So then, why not give the movies a try? Yves Montand was a distant cousin of hers. In order to establish family connections with the Venus di Milo too, whom some people said she resembled, she changed her surname to Milo.

She was already twenty when she made her screen debut playing the part of Gabriella in *Lo scapolo* (1956) [The bachelor] directed by Pietrangeli. Here she plays a stewardess wrapped in her lovely uniform, one of the many women who try to entice Alberto Sordi down the aisle. She is beautiful, very beautiful, and she quickly makes a career in both Italian and French films playing supporting roles in first-rate productions such as Jacques Becker's *Les aventures d'Arsène Lupin* (1957) *(The Adventures of Arsène Lupin)* and *Le miroir à deux faces,* (1958) *(The Mirror Has Two Faces)* by André Cayatte.

But her first leading role is an entirely Italian production with Vittorio De Sica as her partner in one of the "marine" films of Commander De Robertis *La donna che venne dal mare* (1957) [The woman from the sea]. She is Danae, a curvaceous Italian spy employed in sabotaging British ships from Gibraltar during World War II.

In the first years of her career, Sandra Milo's success was based entirely on her beauty. Her roles were nothing more than purely decorative parts in many movies: the attractive Tatania in *Totò nella luna* (1958), the ingenuous prostitute Olga in *Il generale Della Rovere* (1959) *(General Della Rovere)* the girl of too easy virtues who lusts after jewels and expensive lingerie in Autant-Lara's *Le jument vert* (1959) *(The Green Mare's Nest)* and the prostitute seeking redemption in Pietrangeli's *Adua e le compagne* (1960) *(Love à la carte)*. The seductive Sandra Milo even dares to offer a bonafide school of seduction intended for Italian TV viewers in *Confidenziale* (1960), a commercial success written by Lina Wertmüller and directed by Luciano Emmer. These are roles that make her popular but type-cast her as a frivolous woman and sometimes a bit of a goose, which it will be difficult for her to shed.

Sandra is the scatterbrained *maggiorata*, always ready to be courted, an Italian version of the Marilyn Monroe of *Gentlemen Prefer Blondes* and *Some Like It Hot*. In reality, like Marilyn, Sandra is a sensitive woman not lacking in brains but simply oppressed by the stereotyped roles she is given.

One of the first films in which Sandra

speaks with her own voice is *Love à la carte.* In this film Antonio Pietrangeli tells the story of a group of prostitutes who find themselves shelterless when the Merlin law closes the state-controlled brothels. Silly on a level somewhere between the pathetic and the comical, this is the movie which establishes Sandra's career. By one vote she misses getting the Volpi Cup at the Venice Film Festival (the prize goes to Shirley MacLaine for Billy Wilder's *The Apartment.*)

Wanting to get away from the stereotype of the "joyful goose," Sandra takes on the first great dramatic role of her career, that of the romantic heroine in *Vanina Vanini* (1961) *(The Betrayer).* This film, which her companion, the producer Moris Ergas wanted very much for her, was created as a classic star vehicle for Sandra Milo and put into the expert hands of director Roberto Rossellini. Vanina is a romantic princess in Rome under the Papal State who falls in love with a young Carbonist prisoner escaped from the Castel Sant'Angelo. Based on a story by Stendhal, it had already been filmed before by Gallone in 1940 with Alida Valli in the lead. It tells of the desperate passion of a woman deeply in love. This is an intense, concentrated Sandra Milo, great in her innocence and the force of her love, directed by an inspired Rossellini.

By now resigned to the idea of having to play frivolous types, Milo tries at least to give herself a more sophisticated image. Thus in *Fantasmi a Roma* (1961) *(Phantom Lovers),* another elegant comedy by Pietrangeli, Sandra plays the part of Flora, the lovely ghost of a girl who has killed herself for love. Together with some other fellow ghosts, she throws a pitiless eye on the Rome of the 1960 Olympic Games. She is a comely ghost, tied to a romantic vision of life. Pietrangeli's romanticism is less dramatic than Rossellini's. But all things considered, Flora might just as well be the ghost of Vanina Vanini (if Vanina had not preferred a convent to suicide).

By then twenty-eight, 1963 was an important year for Milo who performed in two of her most important roles: *La visita* [The visit] and *Otto e mezzo* (8 $\frac{1}{2}$). In *La visita,* one of Pietrangeli's important films, she plays Pina (a historic name from postwar Italy, since it was the name Rossellini gave to Anna Magnani in *Rome, Open City*), a forty-year-old provincial woman who dreams of finding the man of her life through a lonely-hearts ad. But the man, who comes from the capital, Adolfo, turns out to be an egoistic scoundrel.

La visita is one of the few Italian films that revolves primarily around a woman. Sufficiently aged by the costume designer Piero Tosi, who widens her hips with padded underwear, Milo finds a truly dramatic part in this bitter Italian comedy. But paradoxically, not even here does she abandon her stereotype. It is just as well. With maturity she has at last become conscious of the human wealth to be found in these light-headed women she plays. And as if to emphasize this achievement, Fellini arrives that same year to offer her and her persona of a provincial Marilyn Monroe, the part of Carla in *8 $\frac{1}{2}$,* the shapely and foolish mistress of the film director Guido Anselmi. In the subsequent *Giulietta degli spiriti* (1965) *Juliet of the Spirits,* Sandra is given even more to do, interpreting no less than three roles: Iris, an erotic and licentious little ghost, a more indecent version of Flora in *Phantom Lovers;* Susy, a woman who invites Giulietta Masini to her villa which has been transformed into a sexual paradise; and Fanny. Both Fellini films bring Sandra Nastro d'Argento prizes as supporting actress and complete her consecration as a diva.

The Fellini-type of woman has two faces, Giulietta Masina's and that of Sandra whom Fellini affectionately calls Sandrocchia. If Giulietta represents the pathetic soul, Sandra represents the other side of his feminine universe: the excessive woman, the one who induces to sin, joyfully, a true treat for the eyes and the heart. This Sandra Milo is a typical movie dream figure: showy, decorative, and as empty as a cardboard backdrop. No moral judgement is intended by this characterization; the world of Fellini is a world of fantasy, a sky into which aerostatic creatures are released. Thus even Sandra Milo's big breasts, put into relief by Piero Gherardi's low necklines, become lighter than air!

Sandra Milo, as she appears in her films of the 1960s.

Rosanna Schiaffino

One of the most appetizing Italian beauties of the sixties was the Genoese Rosanna Schiaffino, daughter of Yasmine, a woman of Egyptian origin, and a rich building tycoon. *Mamma* Yasmine represented for Rosanna what Romilda Villani was for her daughter Sofia: a confidante, a friend, a support, and a press agent. Together they moved from Genoa to besiege Cinecittà.

Cleverly guided by *mamma*, Rosanna tried her luck in beauty contests. Her graceful and svelte little figure flitted across the covers of magazines, in Italy *(Le Ore)* and abroad *(Life)*. Once her curves became fuller, Rosanna seemed ready for a grand debut on the variety stage like the many other cover girls who had preceded her. But the theater didn't interest her. She was a post-*maggiorata* (not of the era of "endowed" figures). She already had the mentality of the sixties. She hungered for the movies alone.

Yasmine had transmitted a pinch of her oriental beauty to her daughter. Rosanna was different from all the other Italian actresses of the period precisely because of this exotic touch, particularly the almond slant of her eyes. Thus she was suited to all the fantastic and adventure costume films that were proposed to her. And she would make a lot of them, from *Orlando e i paladini di Francia* (1957) [Orlando and the paladins of France], where she is a legendary Angelica, to *Teseo contro il Minotauro* (1960) *(The Minotaur)* in the double role of Arianna and her twin Fedra, to *Le miracle des loups* [The miracle of

the wolves] (1961) and *Lafayette* (1961).

The American director William Dieterle directed her in *Dubrowsky* (1958), a film taken from Pushkin's masterpiece "The Black Eagle" which had already been filmed by Riccardo Freda. Here Rosanna interprets the role which before had been played by Irasema Dilian. Schiaffino returned to modern Italy thanks to two social-realist movies: *La sfida* [The challenge] (1958), produced by Cristaldi's Vides Films and directed by newcomer Francesco Rosi, and *La notte brava* [Brave night] (1959) written by Pier Paolo Pasolini and directed by Mauro Bolognini.

In *La sfida* Schiaffino plays the part of Assunta, the simple Neapolitan bride of an up-and-coming *camorra* (Neapolitan mafia) boss trying to gain control of the produce market. In this terrible underworld, Rosanna is a young woman who can pull out her claws when the moment calls for it. Ingenuous and sweet as a young betrothed girl of the proletariat, Assunta follows her fiancé in his mad rush towards the good life and prepares herself to become a nouveau riche. She leaves her low-class neighborhood to live in an apartment with a panoramic view in the exclusive neighborhood of Posillipo, buys designer clothes and elegant furniture, and treats herself to the splendors of a fabulous wedding. But her rise is interrupted by the death of her husband who is killed for not respecting the rules of the code of honor.

She plays a rougher type of woman in *La notte brava* where, as a Roman woman from the slums, beautiful and of easy morals, she goes from man to man with impressive ease. In one night she passes from the arms of Franco Balducci to those of Jean-Claude Brialy and Laurent Terzieff, pursuing the promise of a wad of banknotes. Rosanna shows Brialy her provocative bare back and makes love in the burnt-out fields near the building sites on the edge of town. She shows off her beauty with all the vulgarity of a whore: it is a realism straight from the imagination of Pasolini. Brunette, wild, and aggressive as a starved beast, Schiaffino, in this role and in *La sfida*, created for herself such standing as a star that she was able to live off the earnings of it for some time. To manage her career there was another producer, the young, independent Alfredo Bini, who became her husband in 1963.

Among other qualities, Rosanna speaks English and French well enough to act in films outside Italy. Thus she enters the rich circle of international co-productions. After 1962 she makes very few Italian films, working rather with such directors as Jean Dreville, André Hunebelle, Gérard Oury, Vincente Minnelli, Carl Foreman, Ken Hughes, and Terence Young. Steeped in

Costume movies were perfect for beautiful Rosanna Schiaffino's figure, as in **El Greco** *(1964).*

glamour, Rosanna is suited to the feminine figures of this cinema without cultural frontiers.

The flavor of her beauty is undefinable, multiform and supra-national, but not lacking in personality. Schiaffino is a pliable figure who can interpret a vast range of types from the European bourgeois to the mysterious oriental. Above all she lends herself to the kitsch of crazy hair styles and the extravagant characters invented by the movie scripts of the sixties: bizarre and superficial creatures steeped in murky naturalism. The most vivid of the characters interpreted by Rosanna in her "international" films is probably in *The Victors* (1963), where once again she wears the guise of a southern Italian girl.

But her most important films in this decade are still the Italian ones starting with the delicious episode, entitled *Illibatezza*, directed by Rossellini in the film *Rogopag* (1963) where Rosanna is a hostess who works in the Far East and has to ward off the clumsy but insistent attentions of an American tourist.

Equally important is Schiaffino's role in *La corruzione* [Corruption] (1963), another of Bolognini's film frescoes, but rather more delicate than *La notte brava*. She is Adriana, a girl whom the very rich Alain Cluny engages to induce his son, Jacques Perrin, to give up the idea of becoming a priest. Naturally, Schiaffino has the right arguments for convincing him. Stretched out on the deck of the family yacht, Adriana wears the skimpiest of bikinis and displays her utilitarian morals. She is a cynical character who lashes out furiously, is attached to

nothing but money and knows how to use her body with professional ability.

However, Rosanna Schiaffino's body is at its most scandalous in *La mandragola* (1965) *(Mandragola)*. The eroticism of director Alberto Lattuada draws inspiration from the literary works of Machiavelli, but the Renaissance period dished up in this comedy is pure 1960's kitsch. Schiaffino is a woman so beautiful as to be famous throughout Europe. Her aging husband, Romolo Valli, cannot give her a child. Phillipe Leroy with the help of Jean-Claude Brialy organize, from Paris, a Boccaccio-style trick on the poor man that will make him a deceived but happy husband.

In *Mandragola*, Rosanna appears chastely nude, her long hair falling onto her breasts with studied precision. As is her habit, she shows her back entirely bare, but she doesn't limit herself to being a lovely statue. In this film, which is a star vehicle for her beauty meticulously constructed by her husband-producer Alfredo Bini, Rosanna reveals an unsuspected talent for comedy which is later reconfirmed in *Scacco alla regina* [Checkmate to the queen] (1969) where she takes on the guise of Margaret, a famous actress, overbearing and a bit sadistic.

Even with ten years as a winner behind her, Rosanna Schiaffino never entered the ranks of the greatest stars. She still worked intensely, but her luster as an actress began to dim even though she still had very important roles as in *La betìa* [The beast] (1971), a Renaissance peasant-life fresco. Here she goes wild in the role of a little peasant girl with an insatiable sexual appetite. This was her last truly important part.

Rosanna Schiaffino with Luciano Rossi, Richard Johnson, and Anthony Quinn in The Rover *(1966).*

Stefania Sandrelli

Like Pampanini, Bosè, Lollo, and Loren, Stefania Sandrelli also got her start in beauty contests. But if those famous stars of the fifties are connected to the splendors of Stresa and Salsomaggiore – that is to say, the golden age of the Miss Italy contests – Sandrelli is a little provincial Miss of the sixties. Even the figures she played were connected to the small-town flavor of her beauty: slightly gloomy, turbid, and a bit passive.

Photogenic ever since she was a baby, Stefania Sandrelli was a truly precocious cover girl. They took her picture on the beach and when she was playing, either at home or out on her bicycle, and these photos popped up in the pages of magazines everywhere. The weekly *Le Ore* dedicated a cover to Stefania. Movies became an attainable dream. The beautiful girl from Viareggio moved to Rome and quit school, horrible school...

Miss Cinema Viareggio of 1960 was a fifteen-year-old brunette with an indecisive air about her, but with lots of pep. After the tiny part that Mario Sequi gave her in *Gioventù di notte* [Night youth] (1961), she

Stefania Sandrelli, a mischievous and sensuous young village woman in Seduced and Abandoned *(1964).*

is cast as Lisa in Luciano Salce's *Il federale* [a term referring to a commanding officer in the Fascist regime] (1961).

In the early sixties the nymphet fever was spreading, little girls who were already women troubled the fantasies of adult males. The "Lolita" myth found fertile soil in French and Italian movies. Stefania's lovely adolescence grafted itself onto this branch. This is quite evident in a famous film of the time, Pietro Germi's *Divorzio all'italiana* (1961) *(Divorce Italian Style)* where Sandrelli, not yet sixteen, plays the part of Angela, the little cousin of Baron Cefalù (Marcello Mastroianni), hopelessly in love with her to the point of plotting his wife's murder.

With her eyes looking submissively up and her mouth slightly open, Sandrelli has the look of a wounded lamb. But beneath her appearance lies unsuspected grit, an entirely feminine kind of energy. She is lovely, damnably, photogenic and provocative – like a green apple that cannot yet be eaten. She called herself a "force of nature" and she may not have been mistaken.

She had the good luck to be cast in landmark films of the epoch such as *Sedotta e abbandonata* (1964) *(Seduced and Abandoned)*, another masterpiece by Pietro Germi. Here she plays sixteen-year-old Agnese, a Sicilian girl from the province of Agrigento, the victim of prejudices and traditions. On a torrid summer day, her sister's fiancé seduces her. Pregnant, Agnese is locked up in the house by her Sicilian father who will force the man to marry her.

In *Seduced and Abandoned*, Sandrelli exudes an almost lugubrious fascination. Always dressed in black, with raven hair, she wanders through the white streets of the town like an angel. Compared to her prosperous looking sisters, her nymphet figure stands in relief. "You're skinny! You look like a spider!" her mother complains. But her chubby sisters are sexually uninformed. Stefania, on the contrary, conceals a boiling sensuality under her mourning dress, to which the village males are not insensitive.

Her father, magnificently played by Saro Urzì, slaps her around pitilessly for three quarters of the film. With her dishevelled hair, the poor girl implores, howls, weeps in the vain effort to escape from the storm of blows that rain down on her. Squirming, she exposes the upper edge of her black stocking under her skirt and allows a glimpse of a promising white thigh. Hers is the eroticism of the victim.

Little by little, Sandrelli made a name for herself in both Italy and France for a modern look, but also for an easy and expert style of acting that was suited to all kinds of roles. She even acted in a film of Jean-Pierre Melville, *L'aîné des Ferchaux* [The eldest

Ferchaux] (1963). But Stefania was not one of those workaholics who make three, four, or even five movies a year like Sophia Loren or Silvana Pampanini in their prime. She made only a few, very good ones.

Antonio Pietrangeli, on the basis of research regarding the provincial hopefuls who flocked to Rome, the Hollywood-on-the-Tiber, developed a marvelous character once intended for Sandra Milo: that of Adriana Astrelli, a girl from Pistoia, innocent and carefree, who goes to Rome to make her fortune. But among a thousand jobs and a thousand encounters, she never finds the right one. Seemingly insensitive, Adrianna ends up by committing suicide.

Pietrangeli was convinced that Stefania was the right actress for this role, but he was in for a long fight to win over the producer who wanted a confirmed star for such an important role: Natalie Wood, Brigitte Bardot, Claudia Cardinale, or Silvana Mangano. In the end, Sandrelli got the part. In the meantime she shot *La bella di Lodi* [The beauty from Lodi] (1963) and was earning something of a name for herself in France as well. Thus was born *Io la conoscevo bene* [I knew her well] (1965), one of Pietrangeli's most touching comedies. Stefania constructs a personage that is heartbreakingly human. It is the role of a lifetime.

Soft, tender and defenseless, the Sandrelli of *Io la conoscevo bene* seems born to be sacrificed on the sword of misfortune. She, the girl who was always ready for anything

and dreamed great dreams, accepts humiliations and ever more degrading jobs. She appears to be immune to all disappointments, but in reality, beneath that air of insensitivity lies deep suffering.

This role showers stardom on Stefania Sandrelli which is confirmed by less significant films such as *Tendre voyou* (1966) *(Tender Scoundrel)* which, however, gives her the chance to act with a star of the calibre of Jean-Paul Belmondo. In *L'immorale* (1967) *(The Climax)*, where she is one of Ugo Tognazzi's women, she is again directed by Pietro Germi and again plays another small-town figure, gloomy and provocative. Sandrelli's eyes are full of that languorous and sleepy eroticism which – rightly or wrongly – is attributed to the Italian provinces: a mixture of boredom and sexuality. In 1972 Germi directs her again in another fresco of the Italian provinces, *Alfredo, Alfredo*, quite a significant film where we find her co-starring with Dustin Hoffman, the "little big man" of the new Hollywood.

Towards the end of the sixties, Bernardo Bertolucci, another depictor of great provincial frescos, directs her in two important films: *Partner* (1968) and *Il conformista* (1970) *(The Conformist)*. These are movies where Stefania Sandrelli's allure appears frozen in morbid eroticism. In *The Conformist* there is also more than a hint of a lesbian relationship between Sandrelli and Dominique Sanda when they sensually dance together cheek-to-cheek.

Stefania Sandrelli and Marcello Mastroianni in the famous movie of the early 1960s, Divorce, Italian Style *(1961).*

[see also p. 170]

97

The fifties exploded with a dazzling show of breathtaking legs and busts of some of the most superb actresses in Italy. Left: Sophia Loren. Above: Gina Lollobrigida. Below: Silvana Mangano, with other "rice-pickers" in Bitter Rice. *Opposite page: the generously endowed* maggiorata *Silvana Pampanini.*

THE MILKY WAY

A Hymn to the Bust

At the beginning of the fifties Italian cinema gave birth to a new image of woman: the physically endowed figure, *la maggiorata*. Gina Lollobrigida provided the archetypal model in the episode from *Altri tempi* (1952) *(Times Gone By)* directed by Blasetti and entitled *Il processo di Frine (Phryne)*. Lawyer Vittorio De Sica, in his defense harangue of his client Mariantonia, pronounces this term for the first time. Inoculated by De Sica, the virus of the *maggiorata* began infecting entire sections of the Italian cinema of the fifties. But what exactly was, technically speaking, that surplus that made a woman *maggiorata*? Extra curves and just in the right places.

The woman considered a *maggiorata* of the fifties was not just generally ampler. The surplus had to be located in a precise place: namely, her bust. Mariantonia of *Phryne*, for example, is chastely clothed, but her dress, precisely at bust level, has a little window... The *maggiorata* can (and must) have other physical attributes, but her breasts are the focal point of her femininity. Thus with *Phryne* the war of the plunging neckline is declared. An essential role in this war was played by the Italian costume designers. Blandished by the stars, they dedicated all their talents to creating designs that exalted "those" dimensions. Sophia Loren's neckline in *L'oro di napoli* (1954) *(The Gold of Naples)* takes up the cudgels with that of Lollobrigida in *Phryne*: it is a battle of Titans! The necklines of the two stars in these films truly

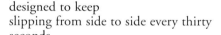

smack of the fifties. Gina's, created by Dario Cecchi, is a masterpiece of irony, an exquisite peek-a-boo. Sophia's in the episode *Pizze a credito (Pizzas on Credit)* in *The Gold of Naples* is as vaporous and soft as the pizzas that donna Sophia kneads with her own hands, and her dress seems purposely designed to keep slipping from side to side every thirty seconds.

The bust of the *maggiorata* was a spotlight that illuminated all the rest of the body which, for its part, had to be worthy of that intense scrutiny. There were busty actresses who nevertheless could not live up to their own bodies; such as Flora Lillo, or Mara Berni in *Buonanotte avvocato!* [Good night lawyer!] (1954), and even Gianna Maria Canale, the queen of the Amazons.

Bust-ology in the '50s

The boom of the *maggiorata* produced many changes in the Italian cinema of the fifties.

For example, it changed the casting criteria as well as the basis for recruiting new actresses. After 1952 it became unthinkable to make a film without at least a couple of roles for hypertrophic dolls, if only as pure ornament. The first phase of neorealism having ended, the Italian cinema – above all the average film – took its distance from reality and became more abstract. Extravagant busts were cast in roles where the characterization didn't in the least call for them. Thus one saw "endowed" housemaids, ampler secretaries and students. And even the extras were *maggiorata* types: *maggiorata* customers entering shops to be served by *maggiorata* sales girls. Physical amplitude became the refrain of an epoch.

The fairy tale of the actress discovered on the street, which had its origins in neorealism, was exploited by a thousand

Franca Marzi was probably the first real sex symbol of postwar Italian cinema.

flavor of an epoch is connected to such frivolities as this, which influence the look of urban landscape and even, perhaps, the mood of the people. The fifties wiped out the melancholy of the immediate postwar years: Italians were already setting the table for the banquet of the economic boom.

Prehistory of the *Maggiorata*

The *maggiorata* look, consecrated and celebrated by "Lollo" in *Phryne* in 1952, did not come bursting out of the blue. In the preceding years, from 1946 to 1951, there were actresses on the scene, whom we might call "prehistoric" *maggiorata*. They were the path-beaters for the boom to come that was detonated between 1952 and 1954.

Superfemininity made its first appearances in the Italian cinema right after the end of the war. The concept of the "big" woman was still hazy, but the Italian postwar cinema immediately cast its eyes about for that absent-minded looker, that saucy doll whom the Fascist regime had relegated to boring nursemaid roles. The concept of the *maggiorata* was intrinsic to the Miss Italy contests organized so vociferously at Stresa and Salsomaggiore ever since 1946. If the philosophy of the superwoman had not at least been in the air, who would have wasted their time with such exhibitions of feminine flesh? The parades of girls at Stresa and Salsomaggiore were a laboratory for experimentation that ended in the creation of the new Italian woman.

The postwar period was marked by the desire for renewal, imprecise and generalized, but no less dogged for all that: anything would do as long as it was different from the past... And so films too changed. The stories that were told had a different flavor, and the casts were full of new faces. Many new actresses got a foot in the door. The producers were seeking a new look, different from the cinematic woman of Fascist times. In the "white telephone" movies of the previous era, woman was an almost ethereal creature.

One of the carnal rarities under Fascism was Greta Gonda, the blonde man-eating music-hall singer in Jean Boyer's film *Il diavolo va in collegio* [The devil goes to college] (1943). But with regard to voluptuousness, Marisa Vernati wasn't kidding around either, as the provocative vamp and kept woman of *Perdizione* [Perdition] (1942) and in Malasomma's comedy *In due si soffre meglio* [Suffering is easier when you're two] (1943). Other than these exceptions, however, the twenty years of Fascism had little to show in the way of

producers, directors, or those who were presumed to be such, circulating around Rome, the capital of the then great swindle called cinema. And even the most anonymous big busts were signed up in the streets for roles and screen tests. The trick worked.

The myth of the *maggiorata* expanded even beyond the bounds of the set and into everyday life. It even changed the way of walking. The male "observer," used to aiming his sights low, at the hem of the skirt, in order to fix his eyes on a girl's legs, now raised his look to chest level. But a woman's way of walking altered too — at least that of the most shameless ones — and they no longer concentrated their attention on their hips, but on their busts. To make their endowments more obvious, these women adopted an erect, vaguely martial posture. And meanwhile the beauty industry came up with treatments for the woman intent on amplifying her image with bouncier breasts.

The focus of femininity having been moved upwards, the exhibition switched from the rear to the front. In this way everything became much clearer — even the comments of the rapacious male took on a more "honest" tone, so to speak, in that they now must at least be made to the woman's face rather than her back... Altogether there was more cheekiness making the rounds on the part of both men and women.

This little breast-centric revolution made for a sunnier landscape in Italy's daily life of the fifties compared to a decade earlier. The

flesh. Even the bare breasts of Clara Calamai in *La cena delle beffe* [The dinner of derision] (1941), which made such a rumpus, were in reality pretty meagre stuff, and the scandal they provoked was purely ideological. Pre-war women had a weak and sickly look, perhaps to emphasize the male and the myth of his heroism, which was exalted for the purposes of war. The ensuing peace-time era sought the brazen superwoman instead, all body, the predestined heroine of furious sexual battles. In the new cinematic woman, well-nourished and sunny, the Italians saw the antidote to their hunger and misery of those years of reconstruction. The stomachs of people were inversely proportional to the generosity of the proto-*maggiorata* ampler women. The game of desire.

Thus, in the brief span of two or three years, between 1946 and 1948, there appeared gaudy, muscular beauties, such as Franca Marzi, Silvana Pampanini, Isa Barzizza and Gianna Maria Canale. And before long their stars shone brightly, while extraordinary things began to arrive from America: the music of Benny Goodman, the films of Rita Hayworth. It seemed to be the beginning of a new epoch in a world full of promise.

Elli Parvo

[see also p. 55]

Elli Parvo was the Franca Marzi of the "white telephone" Fascist genre films. Roberto Rossellini directed her, in a pre-neorealistic melodrama entitled *Scalo merci* [The goods station] – begun during the war but completed only afterwards by Marcello Pagliero who re-baptized it *Desiderio* [Desire] (1946). It was the most appropriate title for a film in which the brazen Elli had the audacity to show herself in bed, barely wrapped in a sheet, with her gorgeous legs bare, her hair messed up, her mouth languid and still hungry for sex.

When the curtain was raised on liberated Italy, Elli was already thirty. But age did not keep her from cultivating the look of the femme fatale. It helped that *Desiderio* wasn't released until 1946 so that what made the rounds was the image of an Elli Parvo at 27, in the role of a fallen woman, consumed by vice and destined for suicide.

Parvo has a gloomy, agitated look that recalls the Clara Calamai of *Ossessione* [Obsession] (1942). Her beauty is a little bony, but Elli offers it in large portions, often wearing necklines that strain the limits imposed by the code of decency. Although she was connected with the films of the Fascist regime, Elli was appreciated by the younger generation of directors who used her mostly in negative roles, as in *Il sole sorge*

ancora (1947) *(Outcry)*. In this classic Resistance movie, Aldo Vergano gives her the part of a noblewoman suspected of collaboration. Elli battles in good simple fashion with Lea Padovani for the love of a man, but does not manage to take him from her rival. As in *Desiderio*, in *Outcry* she also ends up committing suicide.

After these roles, Elli never managed to escape type-casting as an evil or, at least, odious woman. In *I fratelli Karamazov* [The Brothers Karamazov] (1947) she plays Grushenka, the easy woman who sets the old Karamazov and his eldest son Dimitri against one another. Elli exerts an almost morbid fascination on men: she is the personification of wild, extra-marital desires that destroy others and bring on self-destruction. And her appearance does not contradict these roles, not even in *Legge di sangue* [Law of blood] (1947), another rural drama where men resort to murder in order to possess her.

Brazen, arrogant, powerful, Elli was not the physical type made for withstanding the passing years. Already in 1948 she went from playing leading roles to supporting ones, as in *Il cavaliere misterioso* [The mysterious knight] (1948) where she is just one of the many women of a Casanova Vittorio Gassman. After 1950, Elli, who was by then thirty-five, only interpreted small parts in a series of melodramas and was reduced to playing a caricature of a vamp in comedies like *Totò terzo uomo* [Third man Totò] (1951).

The pin-up Elli Parvo, a **maggiorata** *of the early days, still continues to portray the sinful woman.*

Silvana Pampanini in **La principessa delle Canarie** *(1954).*

Silvana Pampanini

Pampanini. The name alone was enough to evoke a landscape: all hills, round, full of curves...

Silvana Pampanini of Rome should really have been the winner of the first Miss Italy contest. At the event held in Stresa in 1946 she barely lost to the timid Rossana Martini of Empoli whom the jury considered to be the real Italian beauty. But a public poll saw Pampanini triumph: the announcement that Rossana Martini (destined to become Nino Crisman's wife) had won, unleashed violent controversy. Silvana was lifted bodily and carried around in triumph. She was the true Miss Italy by popular demand.

One understands that Silvana must have had something exceptional about her to provoke such a row. The film business didn't let her get away and Silvana made her debut at twenty-two in a Scotese film, *L'Apocalisse* [Apocalypse] (1947) showing herself to be extraordinarily photogenic. But her first important role was in *Il segreto di Don Giovanni* [Don Giovanni's secret] (1947) by Camillo Mastrocinque. She seems a little

self-conscious as she kisses her partner, the baritone Gino Bechi, but she is pardoned any such defects for the sake of her uncommon beauty: she is much more than a pin-up; she is a statue of living flesh. Luscious, supple, buoyant to the last hair on her head, Silvana Pampanini is the authentic antidote to the sadness of a defeated nation, her opulence a slap in the face to postwar misery.

Art was a hereditary affliction of the Pampanini family: Silvana's aunt Rosetta was an excellent opera singer, famous throughout the world. Silvana sang too. But quite honestly, her larynx was not considered the best part of her anatomy.

In Silvana, the film-going Italian public found a likeable actress without frills. The public decreed her the best. Silvana was a womanly woman, the image of simplicity and genuineness: full cheeks, big eyes, soft hair. Occasionally she could even be a femme fatale. Her admirers called her the Italian Rita Hayworth, but they referred to her affectionately as Ninì Pam Pam.

Very little is known of Silvana Pampanini's love life. She who was usually an extrovert, became highly reserved when it came to this question. Around 1953 there was insistent talk of a relationship with the actor Folco Lulli. The two allowed themselves to be photographed together frequently, even far from the set. They indulged in carefree excursions in the snow. The romantic chroniclers embroidered on the facts.

In reality, Pampanini was a girl without whims. She brought to the cinema the frankness of the variety soubrette. She was a kind of feminine Totò. In the film *I pompieri di Viggiù* [Firemen of Viggiù] (1949) she plays the part of the fire chief's daughter who has run away from home to become a soubrette. In the episode *Censura e bikini* [Censorship and bikini], where she wears a very chaste two-piece bathing suit, Silvana seems too concerned with keeping the suit on to concentrate much on her acting. In *47 morto che parla* [47 Deadman who speaks] (1950) she is the music-hall singer Marion Bonbon who takes part in the trick played on the miserly Baron Antonio Peletti, alias Totò.

It is said that Totò was very much in love with Silvana and was constantly sending boxes of chocolates and bouquets of flowers to her dressing room. And it seems to have been just for her that he wrote his most famous song, *Malafemmina*.

With a candid smile, Silvana minimized the whole business: "Totò, I love you very much, but like a father!" Furthermore Silvana liked to call herself the "lily" of the Italian cinema, giving to understand by this, that she was a rare case of purity in a rotten world such as that of the movies, with its easy morals and extramarital affairs. She was almost always chaperoned by her parents. Who could doubt her good faith?

The characters Silvana Pampanini played were always in a light vein – very often soubrettes, cabaret singers, merry socialites.

This prehistoric *maggiorata* only had to face the question of her credibility as an actress around 1952, when Lollo and Loren began to attract attention. Silvana Pampanini's first serious attempt at a dramatic role goes back to *La tratta delle bianche* (1952) *(Frustrations)* where she plays the part of a dance-hall singer who tries to rebel against the pervading corruption. On this occasion her voice is dubbed, while it is really she herself who sings the song *La testa gira* [My head is spinning].

Pampanini tried to round out her image as a complete actress in movies such as *Bufere* (1952) *(Dangerous Woman)*, *Vortice* [Vortex] (1953), *Noi cannibali* [We cannibals] (1954), and *Schiava del peccato* [Slave of sin] (1954), but she still needed someone to dub her voice. Pleasantly querulous and with a nasal drawl, it was not out of place in the surreal comedies of Simonelli, Bragaglia and Mattoli, but a melodrama like *Vortice* demanded a different vocal timbre. One of Pampanini's more important roles is in Luigi Zampa's *Processo alla città* (1952) *(A Town on Trial)* where she plays the part of Lilliana Ferrari, a prostitute in the squalid Hotel Tortorella in Spaccanapoli, involved in the trafficking of the Neapolitan *camorra* mafia. Here Silvana sings a song, symbol of those condemned to death, *Tradimento* [Betrayal], but she is dubbed by Nilla Pizzi.

Despite Pampanini's heroic efforts in *Processo alla città*, her best characterizations remained those in light comedy. Her work in the star vehicle *La presidentessa* [Madam President] (1952) by Pietro Germi is highly enjoyable. In this movie she plays Gobette, who generously displays her stupendous endowments from Mother Nature, especially her legs, almost always shown off by showy garters. The lovely Gobette is involved in a series of embarrassing situations with the chief judge of the court who wants to "censure" her.

The image of Pampanini, the actress, was re-evaluated by Giuseppe De Santis, the director who discovered the other shapely Silvana (i.e. Mangano) of the Italian cinema. In *Un marito per Anna Zaccheo* (1953) *(A Husband for Anna)*, he entrusts her with the part of a Neapolitan woman, respectably poor, but very beautiful, pining over an unhappy dream of love. De Santis' premise in this melodrama – which at the time was unjustly underestimated – was an original one: that women are sometimes the victims of their own beauty. Anna Zaccheo was a role made to measure for Silvana Pampanini.

In one scene Silvana poses for a fashion photographer in a magnificent wedding gown. During the romantic fifties, marriage was the dream of almost every girl, but for Anna Zaccheo it seemed to be an impossible goal. Pampanini's torment appeared to be sincere.

In *A Husband for Anna* De Santis proved that Pampanini had talent to give away.

Girded with her popularity, Pampanini threw herself into arduous star vehicles such as *La bella di Roma* [The beautiful girl from Rome] (1956), where she had a Magnani-type of role: Nannina, a fiery Roman woman who exploits her charms in order to make a niche for herself. After a thousand affairs, her relationship with the young boxer Antonio Cifariello heads for a quiet marriage. Here, skillfully directed by Luigi Comencini, Silvana shows herself to be a complete actress, even capable of treating ironically her larger-than-life image of a womanly woman.

This very convincing interpretation was preceded by an equally good performance in Franciolini's *Racconti romani* [Roman tales] (1955) where she plays a wife grieving over a ne'er-do-well husband. After these successes, it is strange that Pampanini could find no other important roles in Italy. She fared better in France where she shot *Koenigsmark* (1953) with Solange Térac, and Abel Gance's *La Tour de Nesle* (1954) *(The Tower of Nesle)*. In the latter movie, spiced with orgy scenes, Pampanini demanded a stand-in to do the nude scenes.

After having dominated Italian cinema for the first half of the fifties, Silvana's career began to decline – perhaps unjustifiably early. The intense and superficial way her

Silvana Pampanini demonstrated her great talent when De Santis gave her the chance in such films as A Husband for Anna *(1953). Here, with Massimo Girotti.*

image was exploited from 1950 to 1953 backfires. But what mostly goes against her is the lack of planning in her career. If Sophia Loren docilely allowed herself to be guided by Carlo Ponti along the road that led to an Oscar, if Silvana Mangano was used parsimoniously by De Laurentis, and Giovanna Ralli had an Amidei who wrote custom-made parts for her, Pampanini had no such equally effective Pygmalion. Between the end of the fifties and the beginning of the sixties she set out on the road to international moviemaking but involved herself with minor-league directors. She shot a movie in Mexico with Pedro Armendarez, then in Egypt working with Folco Lulli in a film directed by Andrew Marton.

Hers were the sad, sad sixties and Silvana Pam Pam lamented: "Here in Italy if you don't have a man backing you, husband or lover or whoever, you can't get ahead. The producers only call you when they have no choice, when the public demands you and you alone. But as soon as there is another actress the public likes – even if less than they may like you, but who has a guardian angel – then they don't offer you any more good parts."

The most important role offered her in the sixties was probably Dino Risi's *Il gaucho* (1964) *(The Gaucho)* where she played the part of a fading diva, a cruelly autobiographical role.

Franca Marzi

Franca Marzi of Rome started her acting career right after the end of the war, but she had already had the experience of several seasons in vaudeville (in Luigi Visconti's troupe, the famous Fanfulla) and in variety.

The comedy *I due orfanelli* [The two orphans] by Mario Mattoli, and Giorgio Ferroni's melodrama *Tombolo paradiso nero* [Black paradise Tombolo] both made in 1947, were her visiting cards. Franca was an explosion of feminine beauty. Only just twenty-one, she was already a goddess. In *I due orfanelli* she is a Parisian aristocrat, Suzanne, who plots to kill Totò: what an operetta villain! Her acting skills, still crude, cannot bear the scrutiny of close-ups and visibly embarrass her. But her body lines are perfect: Franca Marzi wears deep, deep necklines verging near the tips of her breasts, and Totò surreptitiously peeps at them.

Tombolo paradiso nero shows us Franca Marzi's other, more dramatic side: a dark lady of the Livorno pine woods called Tombolo, where a year later Alberto Lattuada, set his film *Senza pietà* (1948) *(Without Pity),* she is involved in illegal trafficking and a prostitution ring. With her rough gangster look, Franca does not win much sympathy. She is haughty and forbidding even in the opera film *Follie per l'opera* (1948) *(Mad About Opera)* where she makes a brief appearance as Carmen while Gino Bechi sings the aria of the toreador. She doesn't even have a word to speak and only casts torrid glances at Bechi.

Indeed, Marzi rarely plays a likeable character. She has a hard look even in the comedies with Totò such as *Fifa e arena* [Crazy arenas] (1948) where Mattoli teases her femme fatale role in a loving way. Here she plays the part of another Carmen, the president of the Seville Women's Bullfighting Club. Franca Marzi does her Spanish act: necklines that reach down to the limits of decency, languid cigarettes, incendiary glances. She doesn't even allow herself a smile. She is a little lugubrious with that tiny birthmark in the corner of her eye.

From 1949 to 1953 she made more films than any other Italian star – she, who was nicknamed "meatball" by Edgar Ulmer, her director in *I pirati di Capri (The Pirates of Capri).* In 1951 alone she was cast in sixteen films, a record good enough for the Guiness.

An actress of "volume," physically as well as cinematographically, Franca Marzi constantly posed as the femme fatale in any situation. At the peak of her fame, Franca complained about the vamp look which she felt was stifling her. She would have liked to be less of a vamp and more of an actress: "It is awful to get that kind of start. No one believes I can do anything else. I would like them to see me looking plain, even ugly, but capable of really acting in a serious role. On the set the directors tell me to stare down the man who is to be the victim of my charms, to smile and nothing else! "

But it was not easy to make a victim out of of a superwoman of her league. A few directors tried, but Franca nevertheless remained tied to her cliché of a goddess-like manhunter. The public liked her precisely because of this stereotype.

Furthermore, from 1953 to 1954, with Lollo's success as Phryne and Loren's as the pizza baker, the popularity of superwomen soared. As the myth grew, someone or other discovered that Franca Marzi had been playing this cliché part for years. Her massive hips and lovely vampish rump had anticipated the times.

Churning out dozens of roles in minor comedies and melodramas, Franca managed to refine her acting abilities. Thus, towards the middle of the fifties, in such comedy films as *Il medico dei pazzi* [Doctor of the crazies] (1954) or dramatic roles like *Suor Maria* [Sister Maria] (1955) she appears much more at her ease, cleansed of that hardness noted in the earlier films.

With her marriage to the European champion prize fighter Franco Festucci, and above all upon becoming pregnant for the first time, her flourishing beauty took on

Above left, opposite page: *Silvana Pampanini and Marc Lawrence in the highly dramatic film* Frustrations *(1952).* Lower left, opposite page: *Silvana Pampanini and Antonio Cifariello in* La bella di Roma *(1955).*

Stately and provocative Franca Marzi in Fellini's Nights of Cabiria *(1957).*

even greater proportions. But just when pregnancy was forcing her to call a halt to her career, Federico Fellini noticed Franca and this was her break into the circle of serious films. "But Federico, what do you want with me, fat as I am right now?" Fellini wanted her for *Le notti di Cabiria* (1957) *(The Nights of Cabiria)* in the part of Wanda, friend and sister-hooker of the gullible prostitute Cabiria, alias Giulietta Masina. Beside tiny Giulietta, Franca seems more corpulent than ever. Together they make a grotesque pair. Masina, with her nervous acting style, spins around like a top; Marzi moves with the slow grace of a hippopotamus. Masina is a little woman who lives in a dream world; Marzi stands for everything down-to-earth and rational. They are two characters full of pathos, and a kind of female Laurel and Hardy team.

For *The Nights of Cabiria*, the costume designer Piero Gherardi works out a look with Fellini that emphasizes Franca Marzi's corpulence: scanty, sleeveless T-shirts, skimpy blouses and dresses unable to contain her masses of flesh. The necklines, deep as ever, fully expose two magnum-sized breasts separated by an inviting little gulf. Hats like carrot-colored mops and her hairdo with bangs make her face look even rounder. This Franca Marzi is almost deformed. Even the famous birthmarks seem bigger than usual.

Marzi's matronly femininity in *The Nights of Cabiria*, is Fellini affectionately mocking the look of the many *maggiorata* stars that everywhere fill the screens in the fifties. The humanity of the character and the vigor of Marzi's interpretation win her important recognition: the Nastro d'Argento (Silver Ribbon) award for best supporting actress in 1958.

The role of Wanda is the point of no return in the career of Franca Marzi. From this moment on she ceases to be the femme fatale. Franciolini tried to turn her into a middle-class type in one episode of his *Racconti d'estate* (1958) *(Love on the Riviera)* where she plays Clara, a still attractive mature woman who falls for an unscrupulous youth.

Her sixties career would be in a lower tone. She was the still provocative woman of the lower or middle class, the mother who has not stopped being desirable to men of her own age or even younger, the florid aunt involved in love adventures. Even if she was past the age, Franca Marzi remained bound to an image of flavorful eroticism.

Gina Lollobrigida

She goes charging ahead and nothing can resist her, just as her nickname *la bersagliera* tells us. (A wink at the swift-moving troops of the Italian infantry with their trumpets and plumed hats). Sunny Gina belonged to the category of the muscular beauties. She was the picture of health, a big, dark girl, well-built, ideal for the beauty contests that were the rage of postwar Italy. At Stresa, where hordes of Venuses were contending for the Miss Italy prize, Gina came in third. Excellent placing when you consider that in 1947 there were contenders like Gianna Maria Canale, Lucia Bosè, and Eleonora Rossi Drago.

These were years when the cinema was renewing itself and seeking fresh feminine bodies. The contests where Miss Italy was elected were farms for raising milky beauties. Italy was going through its infancy as a liberated country, working at it with difficulty, but with great enthusiasm. There was a place in the sun for everyone: all you had to do was roll up your sleeves and not be too fussy.

Like her rival, Sophia Loren, Gina Lollobrigida also got her start in the photoplay mags, under the pseudonym of Diana Loris, before finding the right road to film acting. Between 1948-49 along came her first starring roles in two of Costa's opera films: *Follie per l'opera (Mad About Opera)* and *I pagliacci (Loves of a Clown)*. Lux Films offered her various opportunities, but the

first role that really suited her was Margherita in *Vita da cani* (1950) *(It's a Dog's Life)*, a film about the world behnd the scenes of the vaudeville theater. This came only shortly before *Luci del varietà* (1950) *(Lights of Variety)*. Gina is a country girl who runs away from home, vivacious and bursting with health, and makes her fortune as a soubrette. Lollo also has the chance to show off her singing abilities: "Il mio muchacho ha una fattoria nell'Ecuador" ("My guy has a farm down in Ecuador…").

In those years there was no shortage of roles in Italian films for a superwoman like Gina. She played ingenue or victim in many minor films. But her personality received its due only in *Fanfan la Tulipe* (1951) *(Fanfan the Tulip)* where besides her beauty she has the opportunity to display other qualities: charm, vivacity, temperament. In gypsy dress, co-starring with a blazing Gerard Philipe, Gina seems to be a tigress, but she is also a statue of flesh, a monument to femininity. Her opulent bosom, put into full evidence by plunging necklines, is a forerunner of her role in the *Phryne* episode directed by Blasetti in *Altri tempi* (1952) *(Times Gone By)*. This enchanting little story has a certain importance in the history of Italian exhibitionism, marking the birth of a new phenomenon: the *maggiorata* (well-endowed) woman. The plot was simplicity itself. Lollo is Mariantonia, a woman of the people who has poisoned her mother-in-law. During the trial, her lawyer (brilliantly played by Vittorio De Sica) pleads her extraordinary beauty as grounds for her innocence, although she has confessed to the crime. "The law prescribes that the mentally retarded be absolved. Well then, why should there not be absolution for a physically developed person like this extraordinary creature…?"

In the film Mariantonia is acquitted. Outside the film Gina is a triumphant success: she becomes the archetype for the new look of the Italian movie actress, the endowed *maggiorata*. So Gina Lollobrigida finds herself at the head of an army of superwomen who go marching across the movie screens, ready to invade the nation.

The costume designer, Dario Cecchi, son of the famous writer Emilio Cecchi, invents a very special neckline for Mariantonia, which puts Lollo's bosom into exhilarating relief. The bottom part of her dress (a long, darkly sober dress) suddenly opens from the waist in two diagonal lines that progressively widen letting one see a white blouse which in turn has a very low neckline. From this rhomboid opening which chastely closes again at the neck, aggressively erupts a protruding bosom that is barely contained by the blouse. The effect is clamorous to say the least. It seems as if the dress, incapable of

containing so much vitality, is bursting open from the pressure of the two escaping cannon balls.

The success is so stunning that Gina appears with the same neckline in other films of the time, such as *Il maestro di Don Giovanni* (1953) *(Crossed Swords)* where her ampler look is entrusted to a masterful costume designer, Vittorio Nino Navarese, who in the following years goes on to win an Oscar.

The figure of Mariantonia in *Phryne* combines discretion and provocation, respect and mockery, feminine naughtiness. In Italy the myth of the *maggiorata* ignites like straw taking fire. Women themselves are its victims who allow themselves to be seduced by ads such as the following:

TO GET YOURSELF A LOVELY BOSOM
Protuberant, firm, perfect:
ask for the free brochure from
Ugo Marone Co.,
Piazza A. Falcone No. 1 – Naples

The bosom actually becomes an investment. Women with a lovely abundant bust need nothing else. Thus in *Phryne*, Mariantonia never says a word. It's simply not necessary. Her glances, her winks, her neckline do all the talking. Her presence

With Gina Lollobrigida in the episode **Phryne** *from* **Time Gone By***, released as* **Infidelity** *in* **Great Britain** *(1952), the myth of the fantastically "endowed"* **maggiorata** *was born.*

alone is enough, as long as it is absolutely superb! Thus feminine *divismo* gave a new twist to the neorealistic habit of picking actresses off the street: since acting talent had become a secondary consideration, the number of aspiring stars began growing in leaps and bounds.

Gina becomes the ideal woman. Italian and French designers are inspired by her head-spinning vital statistics. So greatly in demand for films, she allows herself the luxury of turning down the lead in Michelangelo Antonioni's *La signora senza camelie* (1953) *(The Lady Without Camelias)* which was then given to Lucia Bosè, the little Milanese girl who had beaten her at Stresa in the 1947 Miss Italy contest. By now a star, Gina plays alongside actors such as Errol Flynn and Humphrey Bogart in various films. But she also picks up the challenge of more artistically ambitious works based on novels like *La provinciale* (1953) *(The Wayward Wife)* by Mario Soldati, where for the first time Gina dubs her own voice, and in Luigi Zampa's *La romana* (1954) *(The Woman of Rome).*

The most sparkling of Gina's star vehicles is a film that reinterprets some neorealistic themes and situations in a light vein: Luigi Comencini's *Pane, amore e fantasia* (1953) *(Bread, Love and Dreams)* where she again appears in the guise of a simple, ordinary girl. In fact, here she is a true peasant, poor and fatherless. With a raggedy farm-girl look, carefully studied to emphasize her physical charms, Gina is a veritable hurricane of impetuousness and sweetness. *La bersagliera* "the girl of the rifle regiment" – the nickname given to the character she plays, and which will stick – was on the cover of all the magazines. Equally famous was her rivalry with the other great star of the time, Sophia Loren, no less of a *maggiorata* and equally clever in playing roles of a girl of the common people. The skirmishes between Lollo and Loren, exaggerated deliberately by the press, were one of the main topics of conversation in the fifties. There were discussions about which was the better paid, but of course both were carrying home money by the bucket.

Gina *la bersagliera* capitalized on her success of *Bread, Love and Dreams* and

Gina Lollobrigida attained great popularity in the role of the "bersagliera" in **Bread, Love and Dreams** *(1953).*

its sequel *Pane, amore e gelosia* (1954) *(Bread, Love and Jealousy)* throughout all the fifties and sixties by churning out an interminable series of international films that rubbed her glamour to a high sheen but did little for her prestige as an actress. She traveled constantly, earning the title of Italy's ambassadress of beauty to the world. She was received at the White House and the Throne of England. Peron and the Shah of Iran showed her the honors reserved for heads of state. Hollywood opened its doors wide to her. Marilyn Monroe confided to her, "Do you know that they call me the Lollobrigida of America?"

In Italy Gina didn't do much beyond that. To French and American films she sold dearly her image as the "world's most beautiful woman," but this international aspect deprived her of her grit, her explosive, rustic impetuosity which seemed to be caged by the Hollywood stereotypes of superstardom. Nevertheless, Gina made some important films with directors such as Robert Z. Leonard, Carol Reed, Jean Delannoy, Jules Dassin, John Sturges, King Vidor, Robert Mulligan, Basil Dearden and Melvin Frank. She was the personification of beauty, classic and wild at once: she was *la Lollo!*

Above: *From national popular actress to international star, Gina Lollobrigida with Sir Ralph Richardson in* Woman of Straw *(1963).*
Below: *Gina in* Mare matto *(1963).*

Gianna Maria Canale

Gianna Maria Canale in a typical "super-vamp" pose.

Miss Calabria was a beautiful typist who immigrated to Florence. In the 1947 election of Miss Italy she came in second just behind Lucia Bosè. Her name was Gianna Maria Canale. Hers was a sculptural beauty, aggressive and with something wild about it.

When a girl like that walks down the street, men's heads turn. The director Riccardo Freda came across her and was electrified. He followed her, found out where she lived, and telephoned her. Gianna Maria had acquired a strong Tuscan accent, she was rude to him, almost prickly. Freda explained to her that he was the director of *Aquila Nera (Black Eagle)* (1946). Gianna Maria had seen this film and had liked it. Thus from a casual encounter an actress was born, Gianna Maria Canale, another archetype of the *maggiorata* at the end of the forties. And so began her long love story with Riccardo Freda.

Gianna Maria became the muse of Freda's films, and was the female lead of all the films he made between 1948 and 1953, five years in which the prolific director worked at an incredibly frenetic pace. Canale's debut was in *Il cavaliere misterioso* [The mysterious knight] (1948) where the generous Miss Calabria plays the countess Lehmann, one of the many women of the Casanova Vittorio Gassman. Working with her in the film was another forerunner of the *maggiorate*, Yvonne Sanson, and the necklines of the eighteenth-century costumes do honor to the bosoms of both ladies.

Riccardo Freda served up Gianna Maria Canale in every imaginable sauce: a lovely South American in *Guarany* (1948), a fourteenth-century woman in *Il conte Ugolino* [Count Ugolino] (1949), the antagonist of Franca Marzi in *Il figlio d'Artagnan* [Artagnan's son] (1949), *La vendetta di Aquila Nera* [Revenge of Black Eagle] (1951) and in *Vedi Napoli e poi muori* [See Naples and die] (1952); the daughter of Amedeo Nazzari in *Tradimento* [Betrayal] (1951), a patriotic noblewoman in *La leggenda del Piave* [Piave legend] (1952), the lover of a muscular Massimo Girotti as gladiator in *Spartaco* (1952) *(Spartacus, the Gladiator);* all characters that give Gianna Maria Canale the opportunity to put her natural blessings on full display. She plays the star with unremitting seriousness, both on the set and in private life. Very rarely do these characters sparkle with irony. One of the few times she is comical is when she plays in *Totò le Mokò* (1949) in the guise of Viviane De Valances, a French woman who is infatuated with a Totò of the Casbah whom she asks to prove his love in a duel. Gianna Maria brandishes her lethal breasts like two pistols pointed against Enemy Number One. And yet it is rare that this protuberant bosom, emphasized by a statuesque posture, is ever censured. Rather it is her belly button that perturbed the censors and convinced Freda to take the scissors to *Teodora* (1954) *(Theodora, the Slave Empress)* where Canale puts on the guise – scanty, to tell the truth – of the Byzantine empress and performs a lustful belly dance. Gianna Maria Canale was so beautiful and so much a star that she was ill-suited to the rags and miseries of

With Amedeo Nazzari in Il tradimento *(1951), a film in which Canale takes on a serious role and tries to break with her former sex-symbol image.*

postwar Italy. She always played roles in costume films. Her ventures into the twentieth century were rare. Memorable among them were Giorgio Bianchi's melodrama *L'ombra* [The shadow] (1955) where she is the cruel antagonist of Marta Toren who repents at the moment of death, and the "contemporary" *Donne sole* [Women alone] (1956), a sort of *Le amiche* (1955) *(The Girlfriends)*, but less Antonioni-like, where Canale shows off a luxurious wardrobe in the role of a model who, having married a producer, can finally start out on the road to a longed-for film career.

Her connection with Freda being over, after having run alongside him in the "Cinema rally" and appearing in the Gothic mystery *I vampiri* (1957) *(The Devil's Commandment)*, Gianna Maria Canale continued to be present in genre films. To hold off the risk of a rapid decline, she embarked on the venture of international films. Landing on the coast of Britain, she made two films in 1958: *The Silent Enemy* and *The Whole Truth* with Stewart Granger and George Sanders. But both were treated with charitable silence.

Gianna Maria Canale's true vein was stylized Italian mythology, and it was thanks to this that she was able to survive as an actress. In a peplum, her somewhat wooden build takes on new life, thanks as well to the colorful costumes in films like Francisci's *Le fatiche di Ercole* (1958) *(Hercules)* where Canale shows off her beautiful bare legs in the role of Antea, the queen of the Amazons who entices Jason. She is again queen of the Amazons two years later in a film by that name directed by Vittorio Sala (1960).

Gianna Maria's breathtaking beauty is put in high relief by technicolor that flatters her dark complexion. The deep rose of her skin ignites, just as did Maria Montez's flaming beauty. This color density applied to the body of Canale signifies passion, battles, bloody clashes. Thus Gianna Maria becomes the typical diva of adventure movies. She escapes from this cliché only when Vittorio De Sica casts her as a middle-class wife in *Il boom* (1963). Sylvia, daughter of a general, marries an Alberto Sordi who is in such financial straits that he is obliged to go so far as to sell an eye. Thirty-six years old at this point, Canale has the air of a somewhat rumpled beauty, but she is still not entirely lacking in charms. If anything, she is too wild to be a bourgeois woman. That feline – and a bit vulgar – flash in her eyes is not suited to a real lady.

Gianna Maria Canale was one of those purely physical actresses who do not manage to survive the decline of their beauty. On the threshold of forty she took refuge in character roles before disappearing into the vortex of oblivion.

Sophia Loren

The story of Sophia Loren reminds us of the Ugly Duckling's and is a true Cinderella fairy tale: an underprivileged girl transformed into a movie queen.

Poor and fatherless, war-starved Sophia as a little girl was all skin and bones in postwar Naples. But her mother, an artist manqué, inspired her with the desire to succeed. And, with great pains, Sophia started to climb... She began a career in photoplay magazines and already by 1950 had gained a degree of notoriety. The world of the photoplay, one of the most important cultural phenomena in postwar Italy, was booming.

These magazines were the movies of the poor and they had a vast market, millions upon millions of readers. In the pages of *Sogno* [Dream] and *Cine Illustrato* [Cinema illustrated] Sofia Scicolone abandoned her cacophonous name and became Sofia Lazzaro. She received hundreds and hundreds of letters from her fans and even a few marriage proposals. In short, she was already a kind of star. But her real dream was the movies. She sat in the waiting rooms of producers for long hours with very few

The first pictures as a successful star: Sofia Lazzaro becomes Sophia Loren.

111

Sophia Loren, a tigress, in The Miller's Wife *(1955).*

results: work as an extra and microscopic bit parts. She too entered beauty contests with varying succes. Entirely ignored in the election for the Queen of the Adriatic Mermaids, she came in second in the Miss Latium contest and won the title of Miss Elegance at Salsomaggiore in the Miss Italy contest.

The turning point came when a Milanese producer, Carlo Ponti, accepted her in the lists of his protégés and became interested in more than just her acting career. Sofia's popularity suddenly began to rise and her appearances became more substantial. Sofia Lazzaro said her goodbyes to the photoplay public.

Her first important role was that of Leonora Guzman in the film of Donizetti's opera *La favorita* [The favorite] (1952). But Sophia had to go through another transformation before becoming a true movie actress. Another name was needed, something more exotic, something that had a better ring to it than Sofia Lazzaro. "Something like Marta Toren," suggested Gustavo Lombardo, the boss of Titanus Productions, to whom Ponti had for the time consigned Sofia. Thus was born Loren. Another masterstroke was the change from the banal Sofia into the aristocratic Sophia. And presto! The ugly duckling was

transformed into an international swan!

Her first undertaking with the new name was *Africa sotto i mari* (1952) *(Africa Under the Seas)*, a narrative film in which Sophia almost always appears in a bathing suit. That body of hers really seemed to be the best thing she had going for her. From 1952 to 1954 she made one film after another – in the lead. But these were minor comedies. She still had a long way to go to polish her image: she had Luxardo photograph her, she studied diction and, above all, acting. In *Due notte con Cleopatra* (1954) *(Two Nights With Cleopatra)*, one of Mattoli's sparkling comedies, Sophia begins to show what she's made of. It is nothing less than a dual role: as a brunette she plays Cleopatra, and as a blonde, the slave girl Nisca. In Italy there is talk of *maggiorata* ("big") women. Sophia is a belligerent contender in the rivalry with Gina Lollobrigida and, playing alongside Totò, she acts in a charming episode of the film *Tempi nostri* (1954) *(Anatomy of Love)* where she is photographed together with Totò by Silvio Bagolini. Sophia moves her body in a rather slovenly way, like an ignoramus wearing a mink coat who doesn't know what it is worth. Meanwhile her popularity continues to rise visibly.

It is another episode film that definitively consecrates her as a star: *Pizzas on Credit*, in Vittorio De Sica's *L'oro di Napoli* (1954) *(The Gold of Naples)*. Loren's part is that of a woman called donna Sofia and seems written to measure for her. In reality it was thought up in 1947 by Giuseppe Marotta. Donna Sofia is "la pizzaiola," the beautiful pizza baker of Materdei, a poor quarter in the heart of Naples. During a visit to her lover, she loses a precious ring her husband has given her. To account for the loss, she says she lost it while making dough for the pizza her husband sells on credit. Thus begins the hunt for the ring that could have ended up inside any one of the countless pizzas sold in the neighborhood. The story is set in the misery-ridden Naples of Commander Lauro, the mayor-shipping tycoon (who makes presents of shoes to his electors: one shoe before the election and the other after the results are in). It is the picturesque Naples of the most unimaginable and intricate swindles. Donna Sofia cries at the top of her lungs: "Pizza! Get your pizza! Come and have a snack! Who wants my good pizza?" And her cuckolded husband, Giacomino Furia, the considerate pizza baker, echoes her in his nasal voice: "Here you eat... and don't pay!"

It is bound to be a success. In her native Naples Sophia once again finds the inspiration that makes her throb with life and truth and become more beautiful than ever. The characterization soon wins her enormous fame. While Lollo flushes with the success of *Bread, Love and Dreams* (1953), Sophia is confirmed as her most dangerous rival in the constellation of Italian stars. The pizza girl of *The Gold of Naples* becomes a role model. To give just one example, her image of healthy, streamlined beauty is used by an important food company, Locatelli, to launch a new mozzarella called "La Pizzaiola" (the Pizza Girl). And Sophia ties her image to many other products such as Lux beauty soap "used by nine out of ten stars."

Loren and Lollo declared war on the battlefield of movies and interviews. Sophia stepped on her rival's toes by stealing her part and her partner in *Pane, amore e...* (1955) *(Scandal in Sorrento)* where she plays a "bersagliera" from Sorrento who calls herself, provocatively, donna Sofia, the braggart. Italians once more split into two camps, the Lorenites and the Lollo-ites. Soon the overpowering quality of these two goddesses put all the other Italian actresses in the shadows. Sophia and Gina were the image of Italy the winner, just as the two bicycle champions Fausto Coppi and Gino Bartali who shared the adoration of bike racing fans.

The fact was that Loren and Lollo appeared on the scene almost simultaneously, and imposed themselves with two characters of great popularity who had several traits in common. And in fact, their careers too were curiously similar. They were two archetypes of a muscular and cheeky kind of beauty. They both came from the world of the photoplay magazines and portrayed ultra-common types of women. Both of them aimed for Hollywood and eventually went through a prestigious American period.

After *The Gold of Naples*, Loren tries to further smooth out the rough spots in her image by playing a number of sophisticated comedies such as *Peccato che sia una canaglia* (1954) *(Too Bad She's Bad)*, *Il segno di Venere* (1955) *(The Sign of Venus)* and *La fortuna di essere donna* (1956) *(Lucky to be a Woman)*. Sophia presents herself as a kind of Italian Katherine Hepburn. Above all, partnered by Marcello Mastroianni she is brilliant and convincing. She is less persuasive in a star vehicle directed by Mario Soldati, *La donna del fiume* (1955) *(Woman of the River)* which tries to impose on her an intensity like that of Silvana Mangano.

This attempt, which cannot be considered entirely successful, nevertheless foreshadows the dramatic roles Sophia is given in Hollywood. In fact, Carlo Ponti is preparing with meticulous care her move across the Atlantic to launch her internationally.

In America Sophia fares much better than her rival Lollobrigida, who has made a similar leap. The American Loren continues to play Mediterranean roles: a Spanish woman in Stanley Kramer's *The Pride and the Passion* (1957); a Greek woman in Negulesco's *The Boy on the Dolphin* (1957); an Italo-American in Delbert Mann's *Desire Under the Elms* (1958) and in Martin Ritt's *Black Orchid*; a North African heroine in

Sophia Loren in her most famous movie, **Two Women** *(1960), for which she was awarded the most highly coveted honor for an actress, the Oscar.*

Legend of the Lost (1957) by Henry Hathaway; an Italian woman in *Houseboat* (1958) and in *It Started in Naples* (1960), both directed by Shavelson.

Sophia Loren has a much more chameleon kind of beauty than Gina Lollobrigida, the type that lends itself well to Hollywood's maxfactorization and which also allows her to play "American" roles such as *That Kind of Woman* (1959) and *Heller in Pink Tights* (1960).

Loren was one of the biggest topics of gossip in Italy during the fifties and sixties for, among other things, the complications in her relations with Ponti who was still married though separated. Her love affair enraged some conservatives and bigots who considered her a concubine and buried her in an avalanche of insulting letters and even denunciations. In 1957 Sophia and Carlo got married in Mexico *per procura*, taking advantage of the tolerant Mexican law regarding marriage and divorce. But according to Italian law Ponti was formally a bigamist.

Meanwhile Sophia was enjoying a stranglehold on the covers of the picture magazines throughout the world with her love affairs, her films, her pregnancies (which were never carried through) and her relationship with Carlo Ponti.

In 1960, Sophia was a consecrated star and agreed to wipe the Hollywood make-up off her face and dress in the rags of an entirely Italian character again in De Sica's film *La ciociara* (1960) *(Two Women)* based on a novel by Alberto Moravia. It is an austere and dramatic role which suddenly confronts us with a different Loren, more mature, more real, full of maternal concern for her daughter who is a victim of the horrors of war. This performance was rewarded with an Oscar and an interminable series of other acknowledgements. It brought her definitive beatification. From this point on she alternated between starring roles in colossals of the calibre of *El Cid* (1961) or *The Fall of the Roman Empire* (1964), and delicious Italian sketches entrusted to the sagacity of Vittorio De Sica such as *La riffa* *(The Raffle)* in *Boccaccio '70* (1962), *Ieri, oggi, domani* (1963) *(Yesterday, Today and Tomorrow)* and *Matrimonio all'italiana* (1964)

(Marriage Italian Style).

A special place in her career is occupied by *C'era una volta* (1967) *(More than a Miracle)*, Francesco Rosi's realistic fable where we see Loren as a peasant in the arid Campania of the seventeenth century, walking barefoot and participating in a dishwashing contest – a strange mixture of realism and glamour embellished with the exquisite color photography of Pasqualino De Santis. The year 1968 surprised Sophia with a new pregnancy and she was entirely occupied with making sure that this time it would come to term. This too was an excellent subject for photographers and journalists who tried in vain to discover her hide-out. Carlo Ponti had tucked her away in a suite on the eighteenth floor of the Hotel Intercontinental in Geneva. Carlo Jr., called Cipi, was born at the close of 1968. The child was presented to the world at a press conference exactly as if he were a film. The image of a radiant Sophia protectively cradling the new-born baby in her arms circled the globe crowning her myth of actress and womanly woman.

[see also p. 197]

Opposite page: *Sophia Loren, star of American super-productions, in* The Fall of the Roman Empire *(1964).* Below: *A very beautiful, radiant, passionate Loren in* More Than a Miracle*, released in Great Britain as* Cinderella, Italian Style *(1967).*

*A typical Italian beauty,
Giovanni Ralli.*

Giovanna Ralli

Giovanna Ralli is seven years old when she appears in her first film, Vittorio De Sica's *I bambini ci guardano* (1943) *(The Children Are Watching)*. She only has a tiny role as again seven years later in another feature film destined to make history, *Luci della varietà* (1950) *(Lights of Variety)* where Ralli is not yet a woman but gives evident signs of her future as an "endowed" *maggiorata*. Young actress in Peppino De Filippo's theatrical company, the Italians only discovered her between 1951-52 when she played the part of Aldo Fabrizi's adolescent daughter in the three films of the series *La famiglia Passaguai* [The Passaguai family] which dealt with the anxieties of an Italian girl growing up during that period, treated in an amiable comic light.

With the passing of the years, Giovanna became one of those girls that make men turn their heads – just as happens in one episode of *Amore in città* [Love in the city] (1953). Although she was a born Roman, she was often given the role of a Sicilian girl. Her smoldering looks suited the stereotype of the gloomy and feline southern girl. But her first important role was in a Roman setting: an episode directed by Franciolini in *Villa Borghese* (1953) where Giovanna plays the

part of an impetuous and vindictive girl. After a fight with her boyfriend, she accepts out of pure spite the attentions of Vittorio De Sica in his usual gallant vein.

Villa Borghese lays the foundation for the Ralli stereotype. The Italian cinema of the fifties relegates her to roles of an impetuous but generous Trastevere girl. She is ever the twenty-year old with a heart of gold who aspires to an honest, sincere and marriage-bound love, but who demands utter faithfulness from her fiancé. At his first false step she is ready to raise her voice as well as her fists. And she hits hard.

Giovanna Ralli picks up the mantle of Anna Magnani: she is the other side of the sentimental and sickly femininity of the sweet little girlfriend portrayed by Marisa Allasio. She too is poor but beautiful, but more vigorous, energetic, and in harmony with her impressive body. Romantically tied to Sergio Amidei, one of the leaders of neorealism, Giovanna often got important parts in films he wrote. Giovanna Ralli's type of the fiery Trastevere girl is temporarily Tuscanized by Valerio Zurlini in *Le ragazze di San Frediano* [Girls of San Frediano] (1954), where she once again must fight off her scamp of a boyfriend, Antonio Cifariello.

Two feature films directed by Gianni Franciolini were primarily responsible for consecrating this image of the lusty common girl: *Le signorine dello 04* [The 04 girls] (1955) where Giovanna is a self-possessed telephone girl who dreams of Prince Charming; and *Racconti romani* [Roman tales] (1955) where she is a pugnacious fishmonger who doesn't mind sending to the devil those customers who can't make up their minds between the trout and the pike. But she also sends her boyfriend, Antonio Cifariello to hell quite often too!

She won the Grolla d'oro (Golden Goblet) award for her interpretation in Luciano Emmer's *Il momento più bello* (1957) *(The Most Wonderful Moment)*. Here she plays the part of a nurse engaged to a gynecologist, Marcello Mastroianni, a disciple of painless birth. Just when she discovers she is pregnant, however, her husband seems to be losing interest in her.

Giovanna is often a woman in need of affection who feels neglected. Almost always she reacts energetically with insults, spitefulness or even blows. Her fights with Mastroianni are particularly impressive on the screen, so that in 1959 Gianni Puccini gets the couple together again, this time in a comedy, *Il nemico di mia moglie (My Wife's Enemy)*.

Ralli, who discovered her most comic vein in variety, went on the boards in the 1957-58 season as leading lady with Rascel's troupe doing plays by Garinei and Giovannini. The show, called *Un paio di ali* [A pair of wings], was also made into a movie entitled *Come te move te fulmino* [I'll shoot you since you moved] (1958). At the end of the fifties, Giovanna Ralli, already a brazen womanly woman, interprets three roles for Rossellini specially written for her by Sergio Amidei: the young mistresss of De Sica in *Il generale Della Rovere* (1959) *(General Della Rovere)*, the chubby black-marketeer in *Era notte a Roma* (1960) *(Wait for the Dawn)*, and the Calabrian woman in *Viva l'Italia* (1961). The most important of these is the part of the common woman Esperia in *Wait for the Dawn*. Here Rossellini revisits in a post-neorealistic key his masterpiece *Roma città aperta* (1943) *(Rome, Open City)* and gives Ralli a typical Magnani kind of role. In a Rome occupied by the Nazis, Esperia is the aggressive but big-hearted Trastevere girl. She is capable of rebelling against wrongs committed against her and of helping out her anti-Fascist boyfriend, a Renato Salvatore destined to die. Sensitive and quarrelsome, just like certain of Magnani's characters, she also knows how to take risks. She hides an American, an Englishman and a Russian in the attic who have escaped from a prisoner-of-war camp. For this role of a heroic woman with an internationalist bent, Rally received the prize at Karlovy Vary in 1960, what was then the most important film festival behind the iron curtain.

Giovanna Ralli was one of the few actresses during the fifties whose real voice was almost always used, though in *Viva l'Italia* it was Rita Savagnone who dubbed her. Among the historic *maggiorata* ("endowed"), she was also one of those who managed to grow older gracefully, passing from the pin-up stage to being a real actress. So it is that in the sixties Ralli is the fascinating "Nun from Monza" in the film of the same name directed by Carmine Gallone. Gallone also directs her in the subsequent *Carmen di Trastevere* (1962), which transfers to Rome the story by Prosper Merimée which also inspired Bizet's opera. Shot almost entirely outdoors in the most picturesque Roman locations between Piazza Santa Maria in Trastevere, Vicolo del Moro, Via della Paglia and Via dei Genovesi, it seems to be made solely to enhance Ralli's working-class look, the only true Carmen of the Italian cinema.

Another important role of the sixties for her was *La fuga* [The escape] (1964), Paolo Spinola's first movie. Once again we are dealing with a part written especially for her by the good Sergio Amidei: a girl with a tortured mind who escapes into a fundamentally lesbian friendship with the lovely Anouk Aimée. A Nastro d'Argento (Silver Ribbon) part. Giovanna returns to being a Sicilian, as the heroine inspired by Pirandello adapted by Amidei: Santuzza Azzara in *Liolà* (1964) directed by Blasetti.

Santuzza deceives Ugo Tognazzi as Liolà, making him believe she is expecting a child by him. Only in this way can she persuade him to go ahead with a dangerous undertaking regarding a well. Tognazzi co-stars with her again the same year in Carlo Lizzani's *La vita agra* [Harsh life] where Giovanna momentarily abandons her common-woman stereotype to interpret the part of a left-wing journalist.

At almost thirty, Ralli is still at the peak of her popularity. Loved by the public for her roles as a frank and instinctive woman, she attempts the transatlantic leap that had already been attempted by Loren, Lollo, Pierangeli and many other Italian actresses. In America Giovanna plays a handful of roles none of which is highly successful. Perhaps the best of them is *What Did You Do in the War, Daddy?* (1966) a comedy with a military setting directed by Blake Edwards where she goes back to playing a hot-headed Sicilian. She also appears in the cast of a good mystery directed by Brian Forbes: *Deadfall* (1968).

In Italy she is later directed by Ettore Scola in the fine *C'eravamo tanti amati* (1974) *(We All Loved Each Other So Much)* drawing a delightful portrait of a Sandra Milo-type character – that of the big, ingenuous babydoll, wife of a Vittorio Gassman on-the-make. Here she is the daughter of building speculator Aldo Fabrizi who, almost a quarter of a century earlier, had been her daddy in the series *La famiglia Passaguai* [The Passaguai family].

Giovanna Ralli shows great dramatic talent in **Wait for the Dawn** *(1960). Here, with Renato Salvatori.*

Above: *Sylva Koscina with Rossano Brazzi, Mario Passante, Monica Vitti, and Gianrico Tedeschi in the episode,* The Hare and the Turtle, *from the film* The Three Fables of Love *(1963). Right: Sylva Koscina as a middle-class wife.*

Sylva Koscina

Born in Yugoslavia, Sylva Koscina studied physics at the University of Naples. But she was also Miss Di Tappa at the Tour of Italy bicycle race in 1954 and, above all, a fashion model.

She made a fleeting appearance in the part of an aspiring actress in *Siamo uomini o caporali?* [Are we men or caporals?] (1955) before making a flying catch at her great opportunity: she is Giulia, daughter of the train engineer Andrea, in Pietro Germi's *Il ferroviere* (1956) *(The Railroad Man)*. Pretty, and even too elegant for the part, Sylva Koscina immediately confirms her talent in *Guendalina* (1957) where she has no difficulty playing the part of a young mother. But her daughter, a charming Jacqueline Sassard, steals the show.

A lead player in popular comedies like *Nonna Sabella* [Grandmother Sabella]

(1957), *Ladro lui, ladra lei* [He a thief she a thief] (1958), and *Poveri millionari* [Poor millionaires] (1958), Koscina alternated cleverly between roles as vamp and as ingenue. She represented women in the search for social upward mobility, the image of an Italy that had left its worst problems behind.

Sylva was suited to sophisticated comedies like *Mogli pericolose* [Dangerous wives] (1958) where she makes a direct sentimental challenge to poor Giorgia Moll. But she also seemed at ease draped in a peplum: she makes a marvelous fiancée for Hercules in *Le fatiche di Ercole* (1958) *(Hercules)*, a prototype of this kind of film. *Il vigile* [The policeman] (1960), where she plays her own self, gives us a true example of her popularity: in order to win her over, Alberto Sordi, then a traffic officer in real life, let her go without a ticket. Sylva, guest on a television program, thanked him on the air, thus getting him into lots of trouble.

An actress noted for her carriage, Sylva has an "important," entirely feminine way of walking on the screen (and at times she professes it as in *Mogli pericolose* where she lectures Giorgia Moll on how to walk like a lady). In many of her roles she gives the impression of modeling at a fashion show, head high, mouth very slightly open, eyes lost in the distance. She is the elegant actress of the sixties with an aristocratic manner bordering on snobbery.

In the first half of the sixties Sylva Koscina became the wife of Raimondo Castelli, a small producer connected with Minerva Films. She managed to keep well afloat with roles that were anything but negligible such as the dramatic part in Damiano Damiani's *Il sicario* [The hired killer] (1961). In *La lepre e la tartaruga (The Hare and the Tortoise)*, an episode in *Le quattro verità* (1963) *(The Three Fables of Love)*, the director Blasetti constructs a deliciously sophisticated duel between her and Monica Vitti. Then, in 1965 Sylva takes part in *Giulietta degli spiriti (Juliet of the Spirits)* as one of Juliet's sisters. But she also becomes a television personality who is often the

special guest on variety shows.

After passing thirty, she too tried playing the American card. She partnered actors such as Kirk Douglas in *A Lovely Way to Die* (1968) and Paul Newman in *The Secret War of Harry Frigg* (1967), but without luck. Her fame being a bit tarnished, it was given a boost in the second half of the sixties with her appearance, photographed bare-breasted, in the Italian edition of *Playboy* magazine. There was nothing obscene in the exquisite photography by Angelo Frontoni, but the simple fact of such a popular actress appearing in the slick pages of a for-men-only magazine provoked a scandal.

Thus the image of Sylva, based on an elegant and slightly snobbish femininity was enriched with a touch of the erotic. This occurred also because in that period Mauro Bolognini's *L'assoluto naturale* (1969) *(He and She)* was released complete with a "chaste" full nude shot. This was a sign of the radical change Italian cinema and society were undergoing.

Sylva Koscina posing for Angelo Frontoni in all her magnificence.

Anita Ekberg

A historical event of the fifties was the arrival (or perhaps one should say debarkation) of Anita Ekberg.

This goddess-like woman of the North, Miss Sweden in 1951, was maxfactorized in Hollywood where she established herself in a series of comedies as a big, blonde, rather silly woman of the early Marilyn Monroe type. She came to Italy for the first time in 1956 to take Arlene Dahl's place in King Vidor's colossal *War and Peace.* Aldo Tonti devoted lingering close-ups to her as Elena, Henry Fonda's unfaithful wife. When Federico Fellini called her in 1958 for *La Dolce Vita* (released in the U.K. as *The Sweet Life)*, it was not exactly for her acting talent that he wanted her, but rather for what she represented – that is, the myth of Nordic beauty, the woman who had gone through the Hollywood gilding process. So it was that in *La Dolce Vita* Anita – or Anitona as Fellini called her with affection and a

pinch of malice – plays little more than herself.

The Ekberg of *La Dolce Vita* was twenty-eight years old. She was the image of a ripe femininity full to the bursting point. The night bathing scene in the Trevi fountain when Anita, in her evening gown wades into the water, is one of the most famous images in movie history. It could be considered the symbolic image of postwar cinema, just what the Odessa Steps sequence in *The Battleship Potemkin* (1926) is to silent films.

"This scene really happened before I met Fellini," Ekberg relates. "One night I was out shooting photos with Pier Luigi and, not wearing shoes, I cut my foot. So I went looking for a fountain to wash it in and I happened onto the Trevi Fountain piazza. It was August. I was wearing a cotton dress with pink and white checks. The upper part was like a man's shirt. So I pulled my skirt up and stepped into the fountain, saying to Pier Luigi 'you can't imagine how cool this water is. You come in too!' Pier Luigi told me to stay still and began to shoot pictures of me. Those photos sold like mad. But the difference was that I waded into the fountain in August, whereas Fellini had me wade into it in January."

Anitona is the true 'battleship Potemkin' of movie femininity. For Fellini she represented what Moses was for Michelangelo. Upon her image of a colossal woman he also built that little jewel, *Le tentazioni del dottor Antonio (The Temptation of Dr. Antonio)*, part of the episode film *Boccaccio '70* (1962). Here Anitona's opulent curves are enlarged by a billboard on which

Ekberg advertises milk. A few months before, Anita had done a TV ad for beer with Fred Buscaglione, but naughty Fellini thought that this human milk cow with the prosperous breasts was more suited to advertising milk. And it is thus that Anitona disturbs the dreams of Dr. Antonio Mazzuolo (Peppino De Filippo). The Ekberg of *Boccaccio '70* represents cyclopean femininity, the maximum in temptation and the maximum in sin for the Italian male of the sixties: a Latin macho always on the lookout for conquests, hypocritical and a bit bigoted, just like Dr. Antonio. Aside from these two historic roles, Italian films offered Ekberg very little of interest. Her career as an actress, then in decline, only brought her minor roles such as that of the baroness Olga in Alberto Sordi's *Scusi, lei è favorevole o contrario?* [Excuse me, are you for or against?] (1966).

Lisa Gastoni

During the first years of her career, Lisa Gastoni was, to all effects, an English actress. Born in Alassio to an Italian father and an Irish mother, this big blonde with the enormous eyes full of promise moved to England where she was cast in roles as a Mediterranean vamp. Lisa also appeared in some good quality films such as *You Know What Sailors Are* (1954) by Ken Annakin, or *Doctor in the House* (1954) by Ralph Thomas. But she was limited to supporting roles.

At the end of the fifties, Italy was importing lean, blonde British beauties like Margaret Lee and Belinda Lee. In their wake, Gastoni also went back home wearing the aura of a British star. Her name might have been Italian, but physically Lisa was a northern type.

In 1961, after her marriage with Constantin Manos, Lisa Gastoni interpreted several roles as an English woman in Italian genre films. In *Le avventure di Mary Read* (1961) *(Hell Below Deep),* a pirate story set in the seventeenth century, she is an unconventional lady devoted to theft and fraud. Mary Read loves dressing up in men's clothes. She enrolls as cabin boy on a galleon and after various vicissitudes she gains control of the ship and dedicates herself successfully to piracy. It is a Gianna Maria Canale type of role spiced with an androgynous flavor.

In the nineteenth-century *Duello nella Sila* [Duel in Sila] (1962), Lisa Gastoni is again a British citizen named Miss Parker, a journalist come to the deep Italian South to interview a famous bandit. Even when she cast off her guise as a beautiful English-woman, Lisa continued to play roles of the foreigner. In *Diciottenni al sole* (1962) *(Eighteen in the Sun),* she is a brazen German woman on vacation; in *Eva* (1962), a Russian.

Comedy offers Gastoni her first roles as an Italian, beginning with *Rogopag* (1963) where she is Tognazzi's little bourgeois wife in the episode *Il pollo ruspante* [The scratching chicken]. She also has a comic role in *Il monaco di Monza* [The monk of Monza] (1963), an eighteenth-century genre film with Totò, where she plays the part of the marquise Fiorenza, the prisoner of a perfidious Nino Taranto who wants to force her into marriage. We again find Taranto in Bragaglia's parody *I quattro moschettieri* (1963) *(The Four Musketeers)* where Lisa returns to her British roles in the part of Lady De Winter (which Lana Turner had played in a more serious film version of the novel by Alexandre Dumas directed by George Sidney).

In the first half of the fifties, Lisa

dedicated her florid beauty to genre films. She used her Nordic look as the guiding star of Italian science-fiction movies. In *I criminali della galassia* (1966) *(The Wild, Wild, Planet)* and its sequel *I diafanoidi vengono da Marte* (1966) *(The Deadly Diaphanoids)* directed by Anthony Dawson, alias Antonio Margheriti, she assumes the evocative name of Jane Fate. She adopts showy space suits and a futuristic look.

An actress with no connections to the emergent artistic *cinema d'autore* of the young independent directors of the Italian New Wave, Lisa was only truly recognized in the second half of the sixties when, already past thirty, she played the lead in a number of films by important directors such as Lizzani, Samperi, and Lattuada. In *Svegliati e uccidi* [Wake up and kill] (1966) she plays Candida, lover and then wife of Luciano Lutring, a Milanese boy who for love of her becomes a bandit. Gastoni's image undergoes a brusque change towards realism: Lisa here is a submissive, fragile, very real woman. This role, so different from all those that preceded it, won her the Nastro d'Argento award (Silver Ribbon) and gave her a boost towards the *cinema d'autore.* But Lisa Gastoni will be remembered above all for the role of Lea, aunt of the cruel Alvise in *Grazie zia* [Thank you auntie] (1968), the first film by protest director Salvatore Samperi.

Above: *Lisa Gastoni made a great many movies, but it was in* Svegliati e uccidi *(1966) that she attained true recognition as a serious actress. Here, with Robert Hoffmann.*

Opposite page, above: *Anita Ekberg in* Zarak *(1956), a spectacular Hollywood production.* **Below:** *Anita Ekberg with Marcello Mastroianni in the movie which brought her international fame,* La Dolce Vita *(1959) or* The Sweeet Life, *as released in Great Britain.*

STAR CONFETTI

The Sweeties

With the end of the war, Italian movie imagery returned to the full-bodied passionate woman, but the pin-up *maggiorata* trend couldn't shake off the other type of cinematic femininity: the sweeties in the bloom of their youth with their deep silences and languid sighs.

The sweetie didn't actually have to be betrothed: many of them, like Lorella De Luca and Alessandra Panaro in *Poveri ma belli* (1956) *(Poor but Handsome)*, weren't engaged at all: they were unclaimed fiancées. Sometimes they might be happily married (or even pregnant) like Lea Massari in *I sogni nel cassetto* (1957) *(Dreams in a Drawer)*, cooing away just like a schoolgirl out on her first date no matter her swollen tummy. Others who played blissful wives with sweetie looks were the three young brides in *Auguri e figli maschi* [Congratulations and male children] (1951) Delia Scala, Giovanna Pala, and Maria Grazia Francia; the unfortunate Gabriella Pallotta in *Il tetto* (1956) *(The Roof)*; and cute Jacqueline Sassard in *Nata di marzo* [Born in March] (1957).

They were usually typecast as shy, sickly, and vulnerable women, ready to slip into the starlet persona, although they never gave up their childish ways. The sweeties were women who weren't aware of their sex appeal, even though their daddies and big brothers sometimes surprised them trying on a garter – and then "they'd get it!" The sweetie type was more like a state of mind, or even better, a state of heart. They were girls with a love dream and they only knew one way to attain it: marriage, a home, and babies.

If they usually seemed to be at home in a naive daydreaming world, it wasn't always true that it was a happy one, as for the victim sweeties like Milly Vitale, Maria Grazia Francia, Cristina Gajoni or Eva Vanicek, who would suddenly burst into tears because of an impossible love affair or a cruel destiny caused by the meanness of men. Maria Grazia Francia in *Non c'é pace tra gli ulivi* (1950) *(No Peace Among the Olives)* was probably the most wretched sweetie to appear on the Italian screens: beastly Folco Lulli gets her pregnant on purpose and so she is forced to marry him and endure a humiliating life for the rest of her days.

But the sweetie could also have a cunning wit. She often played the flirt, like Elsa Martinelli in *Donatella* (1956), seducing the Roman aristocrats with her foxy looks; Marisa Allasio in *Poor but Handsome* challenging the bullies on Piazza Navona with her coy sweetie smiles; or lovely Claudia Mori in *Cerasella* (1959) and Carla Gravina in *Esterina* (1959). Sometimes Alessandra Panaro could be seen playing the little temptress too.

However, the sweeties were nice girls with a natural kind of charm even if they played naughty. They overestimated themselves, thinking they would be able to control their emotions. However, even they were ready to melt for Mr. Right. The sweetie wasn't cynical, nor did she have a destructive attitude towards men just for the sake of overpowering them.

Sometimes, the cunning sweetie could be naughty. Marisa Allasio was a typical example. In Mario Mattioli's movie *Le diciottenni* [Eighteen-year-olds] (1955), she tortures Virna Lisi, who is already a victim sweetie type. In *Poor but Handsome*, a fundamental movie in sweetie history, Marisa is really as mischievous as can be, tricking Maurizio Arena and Renato Salvatori, wearing their briefs only, to appear before passers-by in Piazza Navona.

The favorite role of the sweetie is playing someone's sister, ready to fall in love at first sight with her best friend's brother, as in *Poor but Handsome*, where Lorella De Luca has secretly fallen for Alessandra Panaro's brother and Panaro, in her turn, has fallen in love with Lorella De Luca's brother. However, the sweeties also played secretaries. In this case they would fall in love with their boss, as long as he was handsome enough, as what happens to Giovanna Turi in *Terza liceo* [12th grade] (1954). If the boss was a bit of a devil, however, like Mario Carotenuto, the sweetie would have to watch it!

Many of the sweeties were actually schoolgirls. They were painfully in love with the teacher, like Marisa Allasio in *Le diciottenni*, who is crazy about her good-looking physics teacher. Cute schoolgirl parts were especially played by Anna Maria Pierangeli in *Domani è troppo tardi* (1950) *(Tomorrow is Too Late)*; by Marina Vlady, Anna Maria Ferrero, Eva Vanicek and Brunella Bovo in the college movie *Fanciulle di lusso* (1953) *(Luxury Girls)*; and by Giulia Rubini, Roberta Primavera, Giovanna Turi, Anna Maria Sandri and Ilaria Occhini in *Terza liceo*. Italian movies were indeed filled with all-girl high schools and boarding schools.

Sometimes, the schoolgirl sweetie was a real brat. Take Giulia Rubini, for example, the schoolgirl daughter of a sculptor in *Terza liceo*; she even pretends to go on a hunger strike, but only to get her way in love. The sweeties lived exclusively for love… as, for example, the five young women in Zurlini's film, *Le ragazze di San Frediano* [The girls of San Frediano] (1954).

Opposite page: *The most popular sweethearts of the Italian movies in the post-war period: Marisa Allasio, Alessandra Panaro, and Lorella De Luca in* Poor But Handsome *(1956).*

The Sweetie Style

The sweeties were delicate-looking girls with big eyes, perfect little faces, tiny shoulders, and cherry lips. Carla Gravina in *Amore e chiacchiere* [Love and gossip] (1957) was a prototype, with her plain teeny-weeny frocks, and dowdy shapeless suits more like pinafores. And the Lea Massari of *I sogni nel cassetto* (1957) *(Dreams in a Drawer)* had the perfect look of the sweetie.

If the pin-up *maggiorata* revealed as much as possible, the sweeties hid themselves. If the deep neckline of the *maggiorata* sex-symbols was meant to whet men's appetites, the sweeties' could only inspire innocent feelings. They had nothing to hide; their honest appearance matched their dainty feelings.

The sweeties were chameleon-like on the movie screen; they camouflaged themselves to vanish in the crowd. They disliked dressing extravagantly, wearing too much makeup or being exhibitionists. They didn't have the "international walk" that comedian Totò referred to. The sweeties' looks were as normal as could be, with the natural style of the girl-next-door. And their shyness became legendary.

The pony-tail was the hairstyle hit for the sweeties. But pig-tails (with ribbons too!) could fit the stereotype just as well; such as miserable Anna Maria Sandri's in *Terza liceo* [12th grade] (1954), until radical-chic Ilaria Occhini shows up to drag her to the nearest hairdresser's. The sweeties also act in childish ways, although they are obviously grown-up women. Their fresh femininity is devoid of eroticism: the troubled teenage nymphet is another trend, imported from French movie culture and set in a particular time. The sweetheart of the Italian cinema is never a Lolita.

Physically the sweetie is a weakling, no tonus in her. Sometimes, she walks with a stoop like Carla Gravina who became famous for her slouch, a trifle 'existentialist', we might say, because she does look lonesome. Others almost have a scoliotic back posture. The typical sweetie is thin, really thin. She barely eats. Fussy. Her mother is always scolding her because she doesn't eat enough. Stefania Sandrelli in *Sedotta e abbandonata* (1974) *(Seduced and Abandoned)* looks like she could use a bottle of vitamin supplements to pep her up. It was also because of the costume designers, who were not only very smart at highlighting the curves of the *maggiorata* stars, but seemed also to take a strange pleasure in drowning the sweeties' waif-like bodies in oversized clothes.

Cinecittà, the state-owned Italian film studio, promoted many sweeties playing teacher roles, starting right from Maria Denis who played the title role in *La maestrina* [The schoolteacher] (1942). As teachers, they were sometimes harrassed by a bunch of bratty schoolgirls who might also be romantic rivals. They were usually miserable and gloomy, but like Gigliola Cinquetti in *Testa di rapa* [Thickhead] (1966), they were always welcome in the countryside.

The sweeties played the parts of maids – another typical job for them. The maids were a subtype: humble common girls having newly arrived from small provincial towns or even from rural villages. The most representative of these after World War II was Maria Pia Casilio in *Umberto D.* (1952), who becomes a stereotype of the gossipy, nosy maid, a characterization that was destined to endure.

Maria Pia Casilio also found more demanding roles, such as that of the innkeeper's daughter in *Racconti romani* [Roman tales] (1955). However, she also showed a talent for comedy. She was lively, while the others usually behaved like cry babies: like Anna Medici in *Una domenica d'agosto* [An August Sunday] (1950) or Cristina Gajoni in *Un maledetto imbroglio*

The object of Aldo Puglisi's desire in **Seduced and Abandoned** *(1964), Stefania Sandrelli, with all the qualities of blossoming femininity.*

(1960) (*The Facts of Murder*), who get themselves into some real trouble.

The three girls in *Le ragazze di piazza di Spagna* (1952) *(Girls of the Spanish Steps)*, Lucia Bosè, Cosetta Greco, and Liliana Bonfatti, are sweetie seamstresses who show great modesty and dignity. Even sweetie receptionists have their moment of success in *Le signorine dello 04* [The 04 girls] (1955). In short, the sweetie was a polymorphous animal. But the many subspecies of the stereotype had only two things in common: a boundless sentimentality and a fragile appearance.

However, we shouldn't dismiss the sweeties as women without charm. They had a lot it, they just didn't like showing it off. They were women in the bloom of their youth, with the signs of a new-born femininity. The sweeties beg, swoon, chatter, and whine. And they get

beaten up. In *Poveri ma belli, (Poor but Handsome)* Marisa Allasio, the typical sweetie with a naughty face, gets smacked by Ettore Manni, her ex-fiancé. Lorella De Luca and Alessandra Panaro get a good slapping by their big brothers; and even poor Rossella Como, by, yet again, Ettore Manni. *"Me mena sempre"* ("He always beats me"), Como blubbers. However, the sweeties seem to know very well how to create havoc, to kick furiously, to shout their heads off. They also know very well how to hit right back. This is how the audience comes to respect the energy of the iron-fisted Giovanna Ralli. And Maria Fiore and Elsa Martinelli when they get down to it, aren't kidding either. Even Marisa Allasio manages to defend herself, when needed. Nevertheless all these little ladies usually end up in the same way – in the arms of Mr. Right...

A bouquet of 1950s sweethearts featured in the movie **Le ragazze di San Frediano** *(1954). From left to right: Giulia Rubini, Giovanna Ralli, Rossana Podestà, Luciana Liberati, Marcella Mariani.*

Poor but Beautiful

The working-class sweetie appeared on Italian movie screens from the end of the forties, but only truly took hold in the mid-fifties with *Poveri ma belli* (1956) *(Poor but Handsome)*, a modest saga of the urban working class in Rome. *Poor but Handsome* was a comedy featuring a new kind of sweetie, both lively and emotional at the same time. Three actresses, Marisa Allasio, Lorella De Luca, and Alessandra Panaro, played this character in different ways.

Marisa Allasio

is the big girl know-it-all who enjoys teasing two street boys, Maurizio Arena and Renato Salvatore. Lorella De Luca and Alessandra Panaro are innocent young things secretly in love with the two handsome men. Marisa Allasio, on the other hand, hides bitter feelings of torment; she is still in love with the one who left her, Ettore Manni.

"I love kissing you guys" Maria says, flirting with both Maurizio Arena and Renato Salvatori, trying to stir up jealousies between them. Marisa Allasio was the most coquettish of all the sweeties. Right after *Poor but Handsome* she acted in *Marisa la civetta* [Marisa the flirt] (1957), a minor star vehicle tailored to her brusque manners. In 1957 Allasio was just over twenty. Physically, she had all it took to be a *maggiorata*. In *Poor but Handsome*, greengrocer Ughetto Bertucci shouts out to her across Piazza Navona, "What lovely big peppers! What lovely big peppers!" Marisa Allasio, however, had

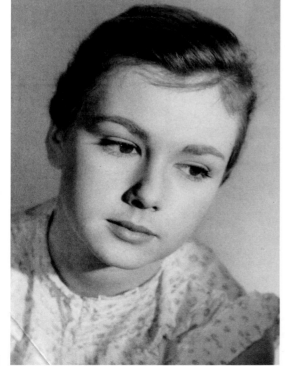

Above: *Marisa Allasio, as mischievous as ever.* Below: *Lorella De Luca is the most serious of the "poor but beautiful" fiancées.*

that dewy sentimental look which gave her her place in the sweetie stable.

As the daughter of Federico Allasio, a soccer player for the team from Turin and then coach of the Lazio team, Marisa made her way into the movie business quite easily. Her first important performance was *Le diciottenni* [Eighteen-year-olds] (1955), where she co-starred with the legendary Virna Lisi in a remake of *Ore 9 lezione di chimica* (1941) *(Schoolgirl's Diary)*. She was only a fussy schoolgirl, but already had that cheeky attitude that got her type-cast when she hit stardom in *Poor but Handsome* in the second half of the fifties. Her characters were always a bit agressive, perhaps to suit her exuberant physical proportions. Apart from *Le diciottenni*, Marisa Allasio always played the poor belle, and always with a clear petty bourgeois or working-class inflection. Poverty did not seem to bother her, she never shied away from problems or complicated affairs: in *Maruzzella* (1956) she is an orphan, secretly in love with her stepmother's lover.

In *Susanna tutta panna* [Susanna all cream] (1957), she works in a Milanese cakeshop. The customers go there to buy a special cake called Susanna, but mainly to survey her charms. Here Allasio recalls a character inspired by the life of actress Lucia Bosè, the "cake seller at Galli's." Susanna is obsessed by her lover's jealousy over her. Marisa Allasio is a showy beauty of the most glamorous kind, who is no doubt a torture for her boyfriend's manly self-esteem. Besides, she isn't at all chaste in her ways: flirting is an art. So in *Marisa la civetta* she shows us her wide range of tricks, performing as an ice-cream vendor from Civitavecchia. Marisa Allasio is a big she-cat having a lot of fun in teasing her mice, bullying Roman tough guys with her good looks. Director Dino Risi makes a sequel to *Poor but Handsome* with *Belle ma povere* [Poor but beautiful] (1957). Marisa Allasio returns to pursue Lorella De Luca's and Alessandra Panaro's boyfriends, but only for fun. All's well that ends well – in a triple marriage gorgeously arranged in a Catholic church. Then, right at the peak of stardom, Marisa Allasio left the industry to marry the count Pier Francesco Calvi di Bergolo, thus becoming related to the House of Savoy: one of the most important celebrity marriages of the fifties. Shaky Italian aristocracy sought to regenerate itself in the splendors of movie stardom. However, as a countess, Marisa Allasio was no longer allowed to play the working-class spirited flirt she had previously. The popular cinema, after all, was no place for nobility.

Even **Lorella De Luca** got married to an important man, director-producer Duccio Tessari, who of course didn't force her to quit the movie business. She found a way of regaining some popularity at the end of her career as an actress, playing in two Italian westerns directed by her husband, *Una pistola per Ringo* (1965) *(A Pistol for Ringo)* and its sequel *Il ritorno di Ringo* (1965) *(The Return of Ringo)*. She was nicknamed Hally Hammond for the occasion.

However, Lorella De Luca is remembered by Italian moms of the sixties above all as a showgirl, alongside Alessandra Panaro, yet again, in a TV quiz program called *Il Musichiere*. After the triple wedding in the happy ending of *Belle ma povere*, Alessandra Panaro and Lorella De Luca become "sisters-in-law" for the Italian audience. As sisters-in-law, they play together again in *Poveri milionari* [Poor millionaires] (1958), the second sequel to *Poor but Handsome*, but this time without Marisa Allasio who had already left the cast for her newly attained nobility.

Lorella De Luca's earliest performance, at fifteen, as Broderick Crawford's daughter, was in *Il bidone* (1955) *(The Swindle)*. De Luca was from the start a natural with the camera who went on to refine her acting at the Centro Sperimentale di Cinematografia. Before *Poor but Handsome*, she played several minor roles: the most important one being the daughter of Vittorio De Sica in the film *Padri e figli* [Fathers and sons] (1957). In all these films, Lorella De Luca nearly always is the daughter of a middle-class family, or even a richer girl; the working-class gal she plays in the trilogy *Poor but Handsome*, *Belle ma povere* and *Poveri milionari* is in fact an exception. However it was, in fact, precisely her performance in *Poor but Handsome* that brought her fame. In one scene where Renato Salvatori calls to his friend Maurizio Arena, De Luca runs to the balcony with eyes open wide trying to learn what's going on outside. "How come you're always the first to come running?" says Renato Salvatori. Like other sweeties, Lorella De Luca is the kind of young girl who would already like to be considered a woman. But when she wears a sexy garter belt, she'll get a big slap in the face by her brother, Maurizio Arena. "How on earth am I supposed to keep my stockings up?" she whines.

Always ready to cry, Lorella De Luca is a typical product of the romantic fifties.

Alessandra Panaro, her "sister-in-law," was a bit less of a cry-baby. Nevertheless they really had a lot in common. Both of them were fragile and emotional and fell in love, but kept it to themselves, in silent languor. Both wore their dresses loosely with no shapely curves to show: they were sweeties in

Alessandra Panaro, is a shy, "well brought-up" young lady.

bud. Thanks to Teresa Franchini, her drama teacher, Alessandra Panaro was launched on TV in a children's program. Not yet sixteen, she played adolescent roles in *Gli innamorati* [Those in love] (1955) and *Guardia* [Sentry], *Guardia scelta* [Selected sentry] and *Brigadiere e maresciallo* [Bragadier and marshall] (1956). However it is in *Poor but Handsome* that she becomes famous: she is Anna Maria, Renato Salvatori's shy little sister who is hopelessly in love with Maurizio Arena, the brother of her best girlfriend.

Panaro preferred playing the upper middle-class girl to the poor belle. That's why in *Amore e chiacchiere* [Love and gossip] (1957) she assumes with such ease the snobbish manners of Lolly, the daughter of the very rich engineer Paseroni, played by Gino Cervi. And again, in *Lazzarella* (1957), her most famous film after *Poor but Handsome*, Alessandra Panaro is a schoolgirl, the daughter of a tycoon, in love with a penniless Mario Girotti. Her dad's business goes bankrupt, but Alessandra stubbornly keeps behaving as a chic upper-class kid. Alessandra Panaro was able to play these bourgeois roles with a disarming freshness and wit.

In 1960, director Luchino Visconti gave her a minor role in *Rocco e i suoi fratelli* (1960) *(Rocco and His Brothers)* where she is the girlfriend of Ciro, the most sensible of the brothers. In the sixties she then performed in peplums, spaghetti-westerns (in which she became Topsy Collins), and minor comedies, though never achieving again the heights of popularity she enjoyed following *Poor but Handsome*. She left the screen after her marriage to a wealthy banker.

Antonella Lualdi

In early 1949, movie magazines advertised a competition to launch a young budding actress still nameless, known as just "Miss X" for the time being. The unknown face on the cover of *Hollywood* and on other front pages, was that of a fair-haired eighteen-year-old with lovely eyes, selected by Mario Mattoli for the main character in *Signorinella* (1949). Her identity card read Antonietta De Pascale. She would later be known in Italy as Antonella Lualdi.

In *Signorinella* Antonella Lualdi wasn't actually making her debut, since she had already appeared in an earlier film, even if just briefly: *Prince of Foxes* (1949), shot by Henry King in Italy. However, *Signorinella* was her first important performance as a protagonist; she is Maria, a young woman working for a telegraph office in a small town in Abruzzo. The mayor of the town, her boyfriend's father, doesn't want them to marry, but thanks to a freak event, Maria manages to persuade him.

Her small, dark, lively eyes, her high and honest forehead, her open smile sweetening her features: all give her that naive, shy, cute, and somehow insipid, sweetie look. She takes after the type introduced by Milly Vitale, but is more sentimental, less pathetic with more of an emotional flair.

As the blind ragged girl, Antonella Lualdi is an even tougher competitor for Milly Vitale, who is generally considered the "official" blind star of the Italian movies in the fifties. In 1952, the two of them star in two different screen versions of a tearjerker novel by Francesco Mastriani, entitled *La cieca di Sorrento (The Blind Woman of Sorrento)*, which was celebrating its centenary. The film starring Antonella Lualdi, also called *La cieca di Sorrento*, was more faithful to the novel than the version starring Milly Vitale which was only "freely adapted." Moreover, Milly Vitale is a plump and doll-like blind girl, while Antonella Lualdi is much thinner and painstricken. The box-office verdict favored Antonella Lualdi: *La cieca di Sorrento* which was released a few months before *Prigionieri delle tenebre* [Prisoners of darkness], cashed in Lires 460,000,000; the film starring Milly Vitale, less than 200,000,000 lire.

However, Antonella Lualdi's indisputable consecration as a serious dramatic actress came in *Tre storie proibite (Three Forbidden Stories)*, inspired by the same news story used by De Santis in *Roma ore 11* (1952) *(Rome, Eleven O'Clock)*. Wonderfully directed by Genina, Antonella Lualdi plays young Anna Maria recovering from a bad marriage to a well-off, but stupid gentleman.

In her first performances as a wife, she looked like a creature from Paradise, a blond angel of the hearth. Like Lea Massari in *I sogni nel cassetto* (1957) *(Dreams in a Drawer)*, Lualdi is a sweetie wife in *Cronache di poveri amanti* [Chronicles of unlucky lovers] (1954), possibly Carlo Lizzani's best movie. Milena is a Florentine shopkeeper in the first years of the Fascist era: she is calm, gentle and honest but shyly available enough to succumb to a love affair with one of her husband's friends. Despite this intrigue she manages to keep her ethereal air.

Already popular in Italy, she is introduced to the French audience when she co-stars with Gérard Philipe in *L'uomo e il diavolo* (1955) *(Scarlet and Black)*, a film directed by Claude Autant-Lara after Stendhal's famous novel, *Le rouge et le noir*. Antonella Lualdi is Matilde de la Mole, a role made famous by Irasema Dilian in the earlier movie version of the novel, *Il corriere del re* [The king's messenger] (1947). Antonella Lualdi's later interpretation is played in a more romantic and sentimental key whereas Dilian is a more spiteful sweetie.

The love of her life was an actor. On September 17, 1955 Antonella Lualdi married Franco Interlenghi to form one of the happiest couples in the Italian movie world; their daughter Antonellina eventually became an actress as well. Franco Interlenghi was Antonella Lualdi's partner also on the set, in a number of films like *Canzoni, canzoni, canzoni* [Songs, songs, songs] (1953), *Gli innamorati* [Those in love] (1955), *Non c'è amore più grande* [No love so great] (1956), *Il cielo brucia* [The sky is burning] (1957), *Padri e figli* [Fathers and sons] (1957), and *Giovani mariti* [Young husbands] (1958). But the ones that brought her success were especially those directed by Mauro Bolognini: *Gli innamorati*, in which she is a very jealous Roman hairdresser whose boyfriend is attracted to Cosetta Greco; and *Giovani mariti*, where she is courted by an eccentric bachelor whom she finally marries.

A radical change in her ingenue image occurred in *La notte brava* [Brave night] (1959), directed again by Mauro Bolognini, with a screenplay written by Pier Paolo Pasolini, already committed to the cause of youths from the working-class suburbs of Rome. In this setting, Antonella Lualdi plays a prostitute for the very first time in her career. She is a vulgar Roman girl, dark-haired, with exaggerated make-up, foul-mouthed and always ready to fight with the other girls.

With the years, Antonella Lualdi's innocence turned more fascinating and sensual. In France, her second cinematic home, she was offered important parts, such as her role in *Une vie* [A life], based on a work by Maupassant. Claude Chabrol casts her in one of his claustrophobic family melodramas, *A double tour* (1959) *(Web of Passion)*, as Leda, her name evoking mythical beauty. Chabrol's Leda is the mistress of a man whose family she intrudes on, with outrageous presence, upsetting its delicate internal workings. However, the part she plays in *I delfini* [The dolphins] (1960) is even less respectable, despite its setting in a luxurious upper-class environment. Taking after her mother (a grim-looking Germana Paolieri), who doesn't attempt to hide her nocturnal affairs from her daughter's not-so-innocent gaze; the younger woman ultimately surrenders to sly Claudio Gora's tempting ways.

In both *Il disordine* (1962) *(Disorder)* and *Hong Kong, un addio* [Hong Kong, a good-bye] (1963), films in which she seems to have lost a bit of her status as a star, Antonella Lualdi is a fascinating young wife handling a tough marriage. In *Disorder* she is Malì, a beautiful bourgeois lady who makes love with her husband (Jean Sorel) in the midst of a friend's party. In *Hong Kong, un addio*, she desperately tries to salvage a disastrous marriage arranging a romantic voyage to the Orient.

Nevertheless, her stardom was, by this time, in decline. Although she was still very beautiful, her innocence having given way to sensuality, the Italian moviemakers of the sixties did not have much to offer her: a few parts in mythological and action films like *Arrivano i titani* (1961) *(My Son the Hero* or, *Sons of Thunder)*, and *I cento cavalieri* [The hundred knights] (1964).

Antonella Lualdi as the lovely telephone operator in **Le signorine dello 04** *(1955).*

Anna Maria Ferrero

Anna Maria Ferrero with Totò in **Totò e Carolina** *(1955); she was almost always cast as a victim.*

In the frequent role of a victim, Anna Maria Guerra became popular as Anna Maria Ferrero – in tribute to the great master Willy Ferrero – for her performance in *Il cielo è rosso* [The sky is red] (1950), in which she plays Giulia, a young girl growing up amidst the debris of war. She is racked by tuberculosis and an unhappy teenage love.

In the line-up of "ingenues" presented in the film *Domani è un altro giorno* [Tomorrow is another day] (1951), Anna Maria Ferrero was the working-class girl, dishonored, exploited and blackmailed, who finally even attempted suicide. Her performances were always excellent tearjerkers and, with her sad accusing eyes, she became the ideal child actress to play in those controversial Italian movies that took another look at the most recent events in the country's history. If Milly Vitale was the first doll-like sweetheart perfect for the romanticism of minor films, and Antonella Lualdi was the naive middle-class girl ready to fall for the first man that came by, Anna Maria Ferrero was the girlfriend fit for the psychological realism typical of the movies by Claudio Gora, Léonide Moguy, Curzio Malaparte and the interior torment of the first films of Michelangelo Antonioni. She was the ideal victim to reveal the corruption of Italian society.

Anna Maria was often seen as a tormented teenager who became involved with bad boys, as in *Febbre di vivere* [Life fever] (1953), where she is the girlfriend of gang leader Massimo Serato who, after making her pregnant, tries to convince her to have an abortion. In the Italian episode of *I vinti* [The defeated] (1952) she is the fiancée of Franco Interlenghi, the rogue of an upper middle-class family. Young Francesco Maselli, at the time Michelangelo Antonioni's assistant, called upon Ferrero's image in a movie that evoked the degeneration of bourgeois provincial youth in *I delfini* [The dolphins] (1960).

She played another part as a tortured adolescent in *Le due verità* [The two truths] (1952), a mystery thriller where Ferrero is run over and killed by a street-car. At the subsequent court hearing, the public prosecutor describes her as the innocent victim of her boyfriend; but a lawyer, pleading in defense of the boy, draws a different profile of the dead girl, presenting her as a corrupt precocious young girl. Anna Maria Ferrero even manages to be a "bad" girl when she plays in the light comedy *Totò e Carolina* [Totò and Carolina] (1955), and is a country girl mistakenly arrested by the police. Carolina tries to take an overdose of barbiturates in a failed attempt to commit suicide and is entrusted to officer Caccavallo (played by Totò) to escort her back to her village. However, the girl is pregnant and the last thing she wants is to go home to her family; another difficult character, but one softened by Mario Monicelli's delicate humor and by an inevitable happy ending. Just as touching is another role in *Cronache di poveri amanti* [Chronicles of unlucky lovers] (1954), when Ferrero plays Gesuina, a gentle maid who offers shelter to poor Marcello Mastroianni, wounded by a gang of Fascists. She takes care of the young man and soon falls in love with him.

Her encounter with Vittorio Gassman, who ended his marriage to Shelley Winters for her, opened up new horizons for Anna Maria Ferrero. She played on screen and on stage alongside the "matador" and he helped her explore her gifts as an actress. She is Desdemona opposite Gassman who alternated between two roles from evening to evening, playing Othello or Iago with Salvo Randone. Between 1955 and 1957 Anna Maria dedicated most of her time to theater, sharing Gassman's conviction that cinema was an inferior art form. One of her best performances on the stage was the musical comedy *Irma la dolce (Irma la Douce)*.

Carlo Lizzani directed her in two movies set in Nazi-occupied Rome, *Il gobbo* (1960) *(The Hunchback of Rome)*, where she is the daughter of a commissioner of the Fascist police, infatuated with a delinquent who rapes her to dishonor her father, and in *L'oro di Roma* [Roman gold] (1961), this time, as the daughter of a Jew under Fascism. She acts with actor Jean Sorel in this movie and he later became her husband.

After her marriage, Anna Maria Ferrero left the movies to devote herself to her family. It is generally believed she would have become the Italian Jeanne Moreau if only she had continued her career.

Anna Maria Pierangeli

The gentlest sweetheart Italian cinema would ever know was Anna Maria Pierangeli, a fragile seventeen-year-old from Sardinia who first performed in 1950 in the movie *Domani è troppo tardi (Tomorrow Is Too Late)*, the first postwar film to openly focus on the problem of sexual education among adolescents. Anna Maria Pierangeli is Mirella, a romantic young girl driven to suicide by the base insinuations of the adults around her. As sweet as a little puppy, she is quick to burst into tears. In the sequel *Domani è un altro giorno* [Tomorrow is another day] (1951) she again plays an innocent young girl wounded by the squalidness of life. In the film, she discovers she is pregnant and, rejected by her family, she attempts suicide.

Her speciality by now being attempted suicide, Pierangeli is the poor young thing who is capable of breaking the hardest hearts of stone. She fights an unfair battle against the hypocrisy of a world blind to innocence. And, it is in this struggle that the fragile Anna Maria attains greatness.

These two successful movies sufficed to lead her to Hollywood. Using her new name, Pier Angeli, Anna Maria made her important debut in the States as the heroine of Fred Zinnemann's *Teresa* (1951).

Here, she is an Italian girl from the mountains who marries an American soldier. When she returns to the United States with her husband, she must deal with the tyranny of an over-powering mother-in-law and only manages to save her marriage after much hardship.

Unlike many of the other "sweeties" of Italian cinema, Anna Maria is not plagued by impossible love or a broken heart. She never slips into easy sentimentality, though she is certainly a victim of society's double standards, "proper" bourgeois attitudes, and conservative morality. This enhanced her credibility as an actress in Hollywood. She featured in a number of important movies such as *The Light Touch* (1951), *The Devil Makes Three* (1952), *The Story of Three Loves* (1953), *The Flame and the Flesh* (1954), co-starring with actors such as Stewart Granger, Kirk Douglas, Ricardo Montalban, Mel Ferrer, and Danny Kaye. She was hailed as the new Janet Gaynor. She lived in a Chinese-style villa in Beverly Hills, drove a big Buick, and never missed a premiere. Her popularity was so great that she even brought her twin sister Marisa Pavan to Hollywood.

Marisa shared the same ingenue family look as her sister and was cast in several important productions such as *What Price Glory?* (1952), directed by John Ford, in which she plays a young French girl. She was even nominated for an Oscar as best supporting actress for her role in *The Rose Tattoo* (1955).

Her much talked-about sister Anna Maria, rumored to be very close to James Dean, was being considered for the role of Judy in *Rebel Without a Cause* (1955). What a pity when the part was given to Natalie Wood – Anna Maria's affinity with James Dean ran very deep: they were two great stars who, behind a façade of blithe teenage insouciance, hid intense inner torments. Nevertheless, among all the true or invented love affairs, Pierangeli did finally openly admit to her romance with the Italo-American singer Vic Damone.

Probably Anna Maria's most important American movie was *Somebody Up There Likes Me* (1956) directed by Robert Wise, in which she is Norma, the wife of boxer Rocky Graziano, played by Paul Newman. Anna Maria's performance was strong and convincing and lived up to the demands of the movie's leading actor Newman, yet at the same time never losing the gentle sweetness for which the actress was famous.

Unfortunately, nothing lasts forever. By

Anna Maria Pierangeli, whom Americans re-named "Pier Angeli," in the splendid bloom of youth.

131

1958, after her appearance in *Merry Andrew* alongside Danny Kaye, her stardom gradually began to fade. She had a short-lived comeback in 1961-62, when she featured as the female lead in the Italo-American biblical spectacular *Sodom and Gomorrah*. Then, the plunge. In 1962 she divorced singer Vic Damone to marry Italian composer Armando Trovajoli, fifteen years her senior. Delicate Anna Maria was desperately seeking a father's protection. Her screen appearances during the sixties were largely Italian. She played mediocre unchallenging roles in insignificant productions. For an actress who had known the splendor of Hollywood, it was quite a step down.

Nearly forty, she went through a serious crisis as an actress and as a woman. On the tragic night of December 9, 1971 in Beverly Hills, Anna Maria swallowed a lethal dose of sleeping pills. She left the world in this final brutal act... just as another former ingenue, Marilyn Monroe, bid farewell after being seduced and abandoned by her cherished Hollywood.

Anna Maria Pierangeli, an innocent sweetheart, in her second Italian movie Tomorrow is Another Day *(1951). Here, with Giovanna Galletti.*

Rossana Podestà

Just like Claudia Cardinale and Edwige Fenech, Rossana Podestà was another actress who was born in Africa. Her parents, from Liguria in northern Italy, moved to Tripoli during Fascism's adventures in colonialism. It was there, in Zliten, that Carla Dora Podestà, later famous as Rossana Podestà, was born.

The talent scout Léonide Moguy launched her in *Domani è un altro giorno* [Tomorrow is another day] (1951), in the role of a well-off young lady, rather spoiled, but also quite sensible. Although Rossana didn't seem to take the movie business very seriously at the time, her mother did, and encouraged her to pursue an acting career. And it was thus that this rather chubby teenage youngster took her first steps out into the world of the silver screen, strictly chaperoned by her scrupulous mother.

Rossana played several small parts of little note. She was the daughter of police officer Aldo Fabrizi in *Guardie e ladri* (1951) *(Cops and Robbers)*, and then got a more important role in the fairytale-like *Sette nani alla riscossa* [Seven dwarfs on the counterattack] (1951) where she is an ethereal Snow White who lives happily ever after with a handsome prince played by Roberto Risso. With her daydreaming air she was fit for intemporal, unreal characters, and her beauty was still reminiscent of childhood.

Prospects began to look good in 1953 when she was offered a marginal but important role in Mario Camerini's epic blockbuster *Ulisse (Ulysses)*. She is a beautiful Nausicaa, and dyes her hair blonde for the role. Immediately after shooting, Mexican director Emilio Fernandez chose her to play the leading role in one of his most famous movies, *La Red* (1953). Here Rossana is a fiery Rosaria, Mexican mistress of Antonio, a runaway delinquent pursued by the police for an attempted robbery. With her lover, she flees to a deserted hide-out along the coast. One day the couple are joined by one of Antonio's accomplices, José, an escaped prisoner who has been wounded by the police. Rosaria cares lovingly for the injured José and, of course, falls in love with him. Her two contenders fight over her, and when Antonio is defeated, he murders Rosaria. *La Red* was a stylized, passionate movie used by director Fernandez to reveal Podestà's hidden sensuality, totally misunderstood in Italy where she was only offered unrewarding roles. Podestà's performance in *La Red* was acclaimed by critics at the Cannes Film Festival and she came very close to winning the award for best actress; a prize that would have been hers if it had not been for the dubbing of the movie.

In Italy, Rossana got her first truly major role in a movie directed by Valerio Zurlini, *Le ragazze di San Frediano* [The girls of San Frediano] (1954), as Tosca, one of the girls in love with the playboy Bob (Antonio Cifariello). With her humble but dainty appearance, Tosca is a strong-minded local girl, the daughter of an alcoholic coachman. She wears cheap dresses and sweaters, but when she sees Bob in the arms of a wealthy lady (Corinne Calvet), she also pretends to be a sophisticated vamp in order to compete with her rival. But Tosca is really a humble girl, a poor belle at heart. Her birdlike common-girl appeal is played to the hilt when Cifariello takes her to the beach: that weird swimsuit with all its flaps fluttering is actually as naive as her big beautiful eyes.

Rossana was a big-built girl and extremely voluptuous. Nevertheless, she was too innocent to be a true brazen *maggiorata*. Instead, she had the eyes of a little girl in love; she wasn't aware of her sex-appeal which was natural and lovely.

Hollywood tried very hard to change this image. Director Robert Wise made her look glamorous in *Helen of Troy* (1955), a movie which again launched Rossana on the international scene, where she had already

been successful with her performance in *La Red*. Though she appeared as a poor girl in Emilio Fernandez's film, in *Helen of Troy* she gave herself the Hollywood airs of a Hedy Lamarr or Virginia Mayo. "Aphrodite – you are Aphrodite!" raves shipwrecked Jacques Sernas.

A blonde Barbie doll with long long eyelashes and a Sunset Boulevard Grecian hairdo, Podestà is decked out in Hollywood's idea of ancient Greece: a pale silk voile gathered at one shoulder, fastened with a brooch of precious stones; an equally showy jewelled belt just as gracefully clasped around her wasplike waist. The skimpy outfit just barely exposing the beautiful generous breasts beneath. Her arms are also soft and chubby. As a blonde diva, Rossana still remains very Mediterranean. Her face, bony yet sweet, and that famous protruding chin, are unmistakable. By the end of the fifties she was a big star and had nothing to envy such divas as Yvonne De Carlo in *La spada e la croce* [The sword and the cross] (1958), or Esther Williams in *Raw Wind in Eden* (1958).

In the early sixties, Rossana Podestà was one of the most exciting actresses of the new Italian erotic genre, inciting scandals and

Rossana Podestà with Franco Interlenghi in the movie **Don Lorenzo** *(1952) is the perfect, though slightly spoiled, sweetheart.*

investigations. She defended herself explaining, "Personally, I adore sex in cinema. It gives good films that extra stimulus. *Le ore nude (The Naked Hours),*" continued the actress, "is a movie based on a novel by Moravia, an author particularly sensitive to the problems of sex in modern society. When I take my clothes off, I feel I'm just doing what a scene or my character calls for. I hope these scenes will be as sexy as ever and I can assure you that being nude in these films is much less difficult than wearing some of those see-through costumes with long slits up the side of some of my epic or mythological movies."

Moreover, in the sixties, Rossana's bust, which with the passing of the years was becoming a monument of Italian cinema, also became a symbol of transgression, as in Marco Vicario's *Sette uomini d'oro* [Seven men of gold] (1965) and *Il grande colpo dei sette uomini d'oro* [The big raid of the seven men of gold] (1966). These were two highly successful movies in which Podestà is Giorgia, the mistress of an imperturbable British professor, who also heads a gang of hightech burglars specialized in gold robberies.

The two movies rework 007 technological feats into stories of mystery and suspense which give Rossana the opportunity of wearing a wide range of costumes designed by Gaia Romanini to show off her body. One of the most memorable creations is the skin-tight superbly worked black body suit designed for her, that hugs her gorgeous curves outlining them as if she were completely nude.

This Rossana Podestà is reminiscent of the eroticism of the sixties, fleshy and a little kitsch, emphasized by her stupendous eyes that – with the help of contact lenses – keep changing colors.

Rossana, who several times in her career came very close to becoming a real international star, never actually broke through. At the end of the sixties her image faded slowly from the screens.

Hollywood-style: Rossana Podestà in **Helen of Troy** *(1955).*

Carla Gravina

She belonged to a subtype of the fawnlike beauty variety and was perfect for sweet love stories in sophisticated Italian comedies or teenage dramas. From Udine, Carla Gravina moved to Rome with her family at the age of thirteen. She was a tall girl, slim and vaguely Nordic, with a face covered in freckles.

Alberto Lattuada, who spotted her one day as she was leaving school, intended to offer her the female lead in *Guendalina* (1957), but the French actress Jacqueline Sassard finally got the part. Carla, who was chosen for only a minor role in the cast of *Guendalina*, soon forgot her disappointment when she was accepted to study acting at the famous Centro Sperimentale di Cinematografia.

The movie that launched her was *Amore e chiacchiere* [Love and gossip] (1957) where she plays, with some difficulty, the daughter of a sweeper in a sad love affair with Geronimo Meynier, the son of an opportunistic Christian-Democrat mayor.

With her cute little pony-tail and freckles, Carla Gravina was the perfect fiancée. However, her cheap working-class clothes in *Amore e chiacchiere* were incongruous with her warm and well-bred voice. She insisted however, on using her own voice, and her talent as a young actress was indisputable. In fact, for her performance she was awarded the prize for best actress in Locarno in 1958. At the time Gravina was under contract with Dino De Laurentis.

She explained, "He signed an exclusive contract with me as was common in those days. Nearly all the young actresses had this type of agreement, even Panaro and De Luca. Mine was for a duration of seven years, it guaranteed me a monthly starting income of so much, and each year it increased a little, but at the end was next to nothing. I don't remember anymore just how much my fee per movie was at the time, but eventually De Laurentis sold me to another producer – something that happened repeatedly, since I worked frequently for others – I think he must have come out very well considering what he gave me monthly and that paltry sum per film. Let me give you an example, and this refers only to the first year, since after two years I broke the contract: I think I used to get 200,000 lire per month plus 500,000 for the first movie. So, if someone was a success overnight during the time he was under contract, it was a real rip-off. However, these contracts were useful since at least they gave you a minimum income to survive on, without having to accept just anything." Her image as a sweetie got stronger after the very delicate romance *Primo amore* (1959) *(First Love)*. In this film she is the daughter in an upper-class Swiss family, and goes to Rome to spend a holiday with her cousin. She again has a love story across classes with Geronimo Meynier, but this time she's the rich one and Meynier, son of a veterinarian in a slaughter house, is a respectable lower middle-class man; but he is ashamed of his origins and so pretends to live in the luxurious via Monte Parioli.

Fragile and delicate, Carla Gravina was the conventional sweetie who invited protection. She had a modern kind of beauty; a strong chin, big eyes and an almost graphic profile, like a character in a comic strip.

Her childish pouts in *Amore e chiacchiere* which she uses to scold and excite Meynier, are irresistible, with an instinctive, rough, nearly wild way of acting. Carla was again a little animal in *Esterina* (1959), where she plays the part of a young daydreaming countryside maid who runs away from her employers' home with two tough truck drivers and eventually gets herself into lots of trouble. Gravina next starred in *Jovanka e le altre* (1960) *(Five Branded Women)*, as one of the five Slavic women with shaven heads convicted of treason for their connections with the invading Nazis. Mira, the youngest of them, gives birth to her child in a cave. This was the first time Gravina acted in English.

With the years, she lost her teenage air and devoted more of her time to theater. Her acting was brilliant, but became perhaps too technical over the years, as if her portrayals came more from the head than from the heart. She became Gian Maria Volonté's companion in a relationship that caused a lot of gossip, Volonté already being married.

"In those days it was hard to live a love affair like the one I had with Gian Maria Volonté, a married man; and I was pregnant with his child as well. I had a lot of problems, believe me! My father wanted me to give up the family name of Gravina and demanded that I leave home, even though I was the one who had decided to go away. Priests wrote to me telling me I was a sinner. I couldn't get any work for a while because I was banned from television for a couple of years and didn't appear in movies for a long time either. They used to say I looked too young for my age – I was 20 – but at the same time I couldn't play teenage parts anymore because I was an unmarried mother and my public image had definitely been ruined by this. I was considered a loose woman. So, I couldn't play teenage roles and I couldn't play grown-up ones because my body looked too young. I had to wait for seven years before going on the set again."

Carla Gravina returned to the movies only at the end of the sixties, finally in the part of a rather young-looking respectable married woman in *Cuore di mamma* [Heart of a mother] (1969).

Carla Gravina and Geronimo Meynier are two young likeable teenagers in **Amore e chiacchiere** *(1957).*

Elsa Martinelli

In the fifties, a decade of flamboyant and buxom women, Elsa Martinelli was like a creature from another planet: slim and very tall, like a model and, in fact, she did work in high fashion for a time for designer Roberto Capucci.

Elsa's refined manners never betrayed her modest background as one of eight children in a very poor family. Her Tuscan father had moved to Rome when he found work in the Ministry of Public Transport. In the capital, she got a job as a waitress in a small coffee shop on the outskirts of the city, then started modelling. She earned 400,000 lire per month, quite a sum considering that her father, as a civil servant, got under 12,000. She became one of the very first top models to jet-set from one part of the world to another, going from fashion show to fashion show. The tabloids hinted of an affair with Count Oleg Cassini, Gene Tierney's ex-husband.

When Elsa's picture appeared in the pages of *Life*, Kirk Douglas discovered her and offered her a part as co-star in the western by André de Toth, *The Indian Fighter* (1955), where she was cast as a beautiful Indian squaw. Elsa, who was quite fluent in English, thus broke into the motion picture business quickly and easily. With her sculpted features, strong and prominent, and her slim tall build, she was certainly no conventional beauty. In Italy, she left casting directors perplexed. Raffaello Matarazzo launched her

Elsa Martinelli, international star, draws her inspiration from Silvana Mangano's rice-picker in the typically Italian production Rice Girls *(1955).*

in *La risaia* (1956) *(Rice Girls)*, a movie based on another famous film, *Riso amaro* (1949) *(Bitter Rice)*, in which Elsa portrays Silvana Mangano's former character, the lovely rice-picker with the stunning legs.

Her performance in Mario Monicelli's movie *Donatella* (1956) is much more successful. Martinelli resembles Audrey Hepburn in her early films. As the daughter of a humble bookbinder, she is entrusted to tend a rich American woman's luxurious villa for a few weeks and this gives her a chance to rub shoulders with high society. Thanks to her honesty and kindness, she conquers the heart of a rich and handsome young man.

Her physionomy was impossible to classify: not a pin-up nor a vamp, not the typical little sweetie either. More often she played negative characters, as in *Costa Azzurra* [French Riviera] (1959), where Elsa lives a loveless life as a kept woman with Nino Besozzi; or in the erotic vampire film directed by Roger Vadim, *Il sangue e la rosa* (1960) *(Blood and Rose)*, where she has a quasi-lesbian relationshiip with Annette Stroyberg. The ambiguity of such roles finally leads to the role of a Roman prostitute in *La notte brava* [Brave night] (1959).

Elsa Martinelli was one of the rare actresses who could reconcile a strong personality with extraordinary elegance; refinement that came through even in the most squalid situations. Hollywood offered her a final role in *Hatari* (1962) directed by Howard Hawks. Here, she is a photographer sent to Africa to report on the natural reserve kept by John Wayne.

Although she had stepped into the star system right from the beginning of her career, Elsa never actually became a leading screen star. After *Hatari*, her popularity began to wane. Orson Welles gave her a minor part in the film adaptation of Kafka's novel, *The Trial* (1963) as Hilda, the wife of a warden, involved in a love affair with Anthony Perkins. Even in *The V.I.P.s* (1963), Elsa has only a minor role, upstaged by the mythic Taylor-Burton duo and plays the actress Gloria Gritti who is traveling with her mentor, a film director, vaguely recalling Fellini.

She returned to Italy to play a leading character again, and was cast in *Pelle viva* [Live skin] (1963), Giuseppe Fina's first work. Here, she is Rosaria, a girl from Puglia, who works in Milan and returns home every weekend to her infant son, born out of wedlock and who must live in an orphanage.

The sixties were years of decline. Though Elsa Martinelli was still one of the most beautiful women in Europe, she had to settle for secondary roles such as Marcello Mastroianni's mistress in *La decima vittima*, (1965) *(The Tenth Victim)*, by Petri.

SUNSET BOULEVARD

A great comet: Magnani, the only guiding star capable of showing the way. Seven very great ones, the stars of the Big Dipper: Alida Valli, Giulietta Masina, Silvana Mangano, Eleonora Rossi Drago, Lea Massari, Claudia Cardinale, and Monica Vitti. And one step below these, another seven slightly less luminous stars of the Little Dipper: Lea Padovani, Valentina Cortese, Lucia Bosè, Virna Lisi, Rosanna Schiaffino, Sandra Milo, and the tender Stefania Sandrelli. Around these orbit the lesser stars, imposing *maggiorata* types and constellations of angelic girls-next-door. Little by little, as in a planetarium, the celestial vault of the movie divas in postwar Italy began to take shape.

But to make these "heavens" complete, we must take a look at another great galaxy, that of the "silver stars." These were the mature beauties who were cast in the parts of mothers, wives, aunts and mature mistresses of the Italian cinema. They were womanly women, quiet or hysterical, serene or desperate, ambitious or modest. And it had been some time since any of them had been young girls.

A few of them, like Eleonora Rossi Drago, were young women who vested themselves in elegance. For others, their prime was only a memory by now. But the merciful screen never showed us their wrinkles or their white hair, these signs being artfully removed.

Stunning beauty, though now waning, lingers on the faces of the silver stars. They are the pressed flowers that would have appealed to Oscar Wilde. Luxury is what they love because it makes them bloom again, at least apparently. Rarely do the silver stars appear as common folk: the mature divas demand roles as society women. They desire designer clothes and impressive coiffures. What they have lost in freshness they make up for with chic.

Many lovely ladies of the postwar era already had a cinematic past. And of course they had been ingenues. Some of them came from the "white telephone" era of Fascist Italy: Maria Denis, Mariella Lotti, Doris Duranti, Caterina Boratto, Vera Carmi, Irasema Dilian. But others were born ladies, with such an innate aristocratic sense that they could never have played ingenues or young sweethearts.

THE COMPROMISED

More or less secret connections bound the actresses of the "white telephone" films (the rosy, artificial cinema of Fascist Italy) with the upper circles of the Fascist apparatus. Several clamorous episodes, such as the execution of Luisa Ferida by the partisans for her connections with the Republic of Salò, continued to project a sinister light on all the divas of those dramatic years.

Other actresses like Maria Denis, Doris Duranti, and Mariella Lotti were also more or less compromised with the Fascist regime. But they quietly and gradually managed to get themselves a certificate of democratic respectability and be recycled as "lovely ladies" back into the new Italian cinema.

Doris Duranti
[see also p. 59]

The most compromised was doubtless the Livornese Doris Duranti, an expert in roles as femme fatale and aggressive vamp. After the final fall of Fascism, Doris risked meeting the same end as Luisa Ferida. To save herself,

Doris Duranti, with her famous smoldering look of the wartime movies such as Clandestino a Trieste *(1951). With Carlo D'Angelo.*

she fled first to Switzerland and then to South America.

In 1945 Doris was already twenty-eight. She made a few films in Brazil, but found her greater fortune in the Dominican Republic, where she weaved relations with the powerful, becoming the mistress of the dictator Rafael Trujillo. From her quiet vantage point in Central America, Doris watched the growth of neorealism whose fame was spreading. She, who had never disowned her role as a beauty of the Regime, snobbishly called it the "ratty-tatty cinema."

She returned to Italy at the end of the forties when things had calmed down. In her autobiography, Doris described her return home: "I wanted to put a damper on my happiness by asking around if I wouldn't be in danger in the country where Pavolini had been hanged by the feet and where they wanted to see me dead like Clara Petacci. The amnesty had benefited the survivors. The purged had returned to their places. The Communists had been outflanked and were at low ebb."

It was 1950. Doris Duranti could confidently return to her career in movies. But she did so in a low key partly due to her age; she was then about thirty-three. The only serious attempt to revive the old splendor was made in *Il voto* [The vote] (1950) where Doris plays the lead in a role that revives one of the most famous characters in her career, Carmela, of the film of the same name directed by Calzavara in 1942. In *Il voto* she is again called Carmela. And the sea setting is the same too. But ten years have passed in the meantime and this Carmela is more adult: she is a wife, an unfaithful wife, of a fisherman who has left for a long voyage to the South Seas.

Doris Duranti still has the look of a man-eater: the passionate glance, vaguely surly, the languid mouth, the ruffled hair. She seems a bit withered, but the old fire still burns within. On the set of *Clandestino a Trieste* [Stowaway in Trieste] (1951) Doris meets Alvaro Mancori again, the director of photography, to whom during the war years she had often entrusted her image as an actress. "Alvaro of the water green eyes, Alvaro of the feverish orgasms..." thus Doris describes him in her autobiography published in 1987.

She seems a little bit less of a man-eater in *Tragico ritorno* [Tragic return] (1952), a drama where she plays the part of a woman who, believing herself to be a war-widow, marries again. Her hair is curly, her mouth sensual, her glance vampish. But she forces herself to smile like a good wife plagued by destiny. Squeezed into modest suits that square her shoulders, she looks embarrassed: the character cramps her style. Italian cinema no longer suited her.

In her autobiography Doris tells how she missed her big opportunity right at the beginning of the fifties when she rejected the assiduous courting of the American producer Sam Zimbalist who was in Italy at the time for the shooting of *Quo Vadis*. He proposed that she learn English and assured her of a career in Hollywood. Thus Doris sadly faded into the sunset. After playing herself in a theater première, *L'ora della verità* [Truth's gold] (1952) she went back to Central America taking the television journalist Mario Ferreti with her. Together they opened a chic restaurant in Santo Domingo with the nostalgic name of "Vecchia Roma" ("Old Rome").

Maria Denis

[see also p. 23]

At the dawn of the postwar era Maria Denis also had serious problems with the law. It was rumored that she had a relationship with the notorious Pietro Koch of the Fascist police. The accusation was that of collaboration.

"One fine day, or rather horrible day," she related, "some agents of the Political Squad presented themselves at my door and arrested me on order of the Milanese court. My protests were of no avail. I was openly charged with having worked for Koch's men, giving them information and being responsible for arrests. There was no concrete evidence and nobody could prove the charges. I was accused only on the basis of having been seen in a Roman restaurant in the company of Pietro Koch."

The brutality of Koch and his gang was legendary. Maria Denis was arrested at the time she was shooting the movie *Cronaca nera* [Black chronicle] (1946) where she plays the part of a nice young girl whose boyfriend is a bandit. She was kept in prison for several days, but at the trial, Luchino Visconti came to her defense and Maria Denis was allowed to resume her film work.

When she returned to the screen in 1946 she was already thirty. She looked like a middle-class lady. She had a florid beauty, suitable for an ingenue and still in the white telephone style. And she continued to play that part in *Malìa* (1946) where a perfidious Anna Proclemer steals her handsome Rossano Brazzi away from her. But her most important postwar role was the one in *La fiamma non si spegne* [The flame won't die] (1949), freely based on the life of Salvo D'Acquisto. Here Denis plays the mother of the heroic *carabiniere*. At the beginning we see her still looking young at the birth of the hero; then we see her suitably aged at the time of her policeman son's sacrifice.

Maria Denis and Gino Cervi in the movie **Cronaca nera** *(1946).*

The Italian cinema didn't offer her much more than this. She went looking for opportunities abroad. She acted in English, French, and Spanish productions, partnered by some important actors such as Erich von Stroheim and Peter Ustinov. Her last role of any importance was in the episode *Scusi ma...* [Excuse me but...] of the film *Anatomy of Love* (1953) where she played the part of a sweet middle-class lady married to Enrico Viarisio. But this episode, considered weak, was cut when the film was released.

Maria Denis abandoned films eventually to devote herself to being an interior decorator.

Mariella Lotti

[see also p. 30]

Mariella Lotti also seems to have been connected to the Fascist regime. In a film of Alberto Lattuada's, shot during the last months of the Regime, *La freccia nel fianco* [Arrow in the side], Lotti plays the part of a woman who commits suicide. But suicide was considered a taboo subject by the Fascists. Maria Lotti herself appealed to Galeazzo Ciano, whom she apparently knew well, to get special dispensation from the "Minculpop" (Ministry for Popular Culture).

Lotti was one of the greatest stars on the scene of Italian cinema during the last years of Fascism. A fading blonde, she was dedicated to the roles of Nordic or Slavic types, especially in

period movies. She was an Austrian princess in *Il cavaliere del sogno* [The dream knight] (1946) and the Russian Katerina Ivanovna in *The Brothers Karamazov* (1947). Tired of nineteenth-century roles, Mariella would liked to have given up crinolines and puffed skirts. She dreamed of interpreting modern parts. "I want to do Marie Curie..." she confessed to reporters. She also complained her image was too elegant, too chic. She wanted to have a different air about her, maybe even a little neorealistic. "I want at least once to be a poor girl, an underdog. Wear rags, perhaps, but feel more real and less like a model." The movies, however, continued putting her in white telephone-type films and giving her the usual roles.

After the war, Mariella acted in a series of films with Amedeo Nazzari, several of them being in a romantic-historical vein very similar to the white telephone style. These ranged from the Donizetti biography *Il cavaliere del sogno* (1946), to the melodrama *Malacarne* (1947). In a neorealistic vein, on the other hand, was *Un giorno nella vita* (1946) *(A Day in the Life)*, beautifully directed by Blasetti. Here Lotti plays a nun who helps a group of partisans being hunted by the Nazis. Keeping them hidden in the convent, the nuns are shot in reprisal while the partisans make their escape.

Fair-haired and well-coiffed, Mariella was at her best as a charming middle-class woman. She had an icy beauty that was even a little inexpressive, and she never lost control. She is Jean Gabin's bourgeois wife in *È più facile che un cammello* (1950) *(Twelve Hours to Live);* the

139

elegant wife of Amedeo Nazzari, the judge in *Processo alla città* (1952) *(A Town on Trial);* and the seductive French noblewoman in *Il naso di cuoio* [Leather nose] (1952). Mariella Lotti was a woman of fashion above all else. In 1947 a French magazine called her Italy's fashion ambassadress. She had settled into her stereotype of costume movies and loved nineteenth-century-style clothes. She even wore them in everyday life. Even down to the little hats…

One of the most original roles in her filmography was the Fata Turchina in *Le avventure di Pinocchio* [The adventures of Pinocchio] (1947), but this was a marginal role. She gets more more space in *Solo per te Lucia* [For you only, Lucia] (1952) where she is a radio commentator and unwed mother, the heroine of a love story and of misunderstandings with a fellow worker, a technician at the radio station. This was her last film before making a prestigious marriage that opened the doors of northern upper-class Italian society to her, but which removed her permanently from the world of the movies.

Mariella Lotti is the elegant middle-class wife of judge Amedeo Nazzari in **A Town on Trial** *(1952).*

THE LOSERS

Vivi Gioi
[see also p. 34]

Along with Alida Valli and Mariella Lotti, Vivi Gioi was one of the most representative comediennes of Fascist-era movies. She was the incarnation of the typical twentieth-century girl, easy-going and roguish, modern and non-conformist. During the war years, Vivi Gioi ventured into cabaret and, immediately afterwards, won success for her theatrical performances directed by Luchino Visconti.

After the war Vivi Gioi was twenty-six and Gaetano Amata tried to have her act again in a white telephone-style movie, *Marito povero* [Poor husband] (1945), but Giuseppe De Santis undermined that image of unstained purity letting her play the terrible Lili Marlene, the fallen woman in *Caccia tragica* (1947) *(The Tragic Pursuit)*. Accused of being a collaborator, Lili Marlene, whose real name is Daniela, has her hair cut by the partisans and hides the mark of treachery under a blonde wig which gives her quite a serene air. In reality, Daniela is a poor, hysterical wretch who has renounced her dreams to follow destructive ideologies (first Fascism, then the fight against the peasants). A wounded man pulls off her wig and Lili's strange crew-cut is revealed which makes her harder still. In a nervous fit, Lili pushes a wounded man out of a moving ambulance. Actually, Lili's hair-cropping is small stuff compared to what is done to the women in *Jovanka e le altre* (1960) *(Five Branded Women)*.

The Vivi Gioi of *The Tragic Pursuit*, wrapped in clothes almost like a man's, has an angular, ambiguous beauty. It is the outward sign of the ideological ambiguity De Santis attributes to the character. In the climax of the film when she wants to kill the peasants by exploding mines, Lili Marlene's eyes look wild, like those of a psychopath. She is mercilessly killed with a burst of machine-gun fire, shot down by her bandit lover. The comparison with Giovanna, a serious woman, a worker – played by an angelic Carla Del Poggio – who honestly wins her right to happiness, lights the fire under Lili Marlene's contradictions. The unfortunate creature realizes that she is a failure, without hope, and she falls into the vortex of mad self-destruction.

For *The Tragic Pursuit* Vivi Gioi won a Nastro d'Argento award as best supporting actress. Duilio Coletti offered her another role of the same emotional substance in *Il grido della terra* (1949) *(The Earth Cries Out)*, a film about the birth of the state of

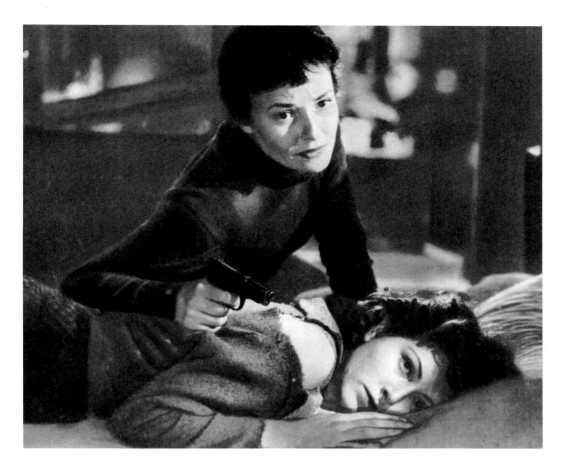

A great change for Vivi Gioi after the war in the movie The Tragic Pursuit *(1947), when her radiant beauty became bony and ambiguous. Here, with Carla Del Poggio.*

Israel where Vivi plays Judith, a fanatical partisan devoted to the cause of Jewish independence. Ferociously anti-Communist on the screen, Vivi Gioi nurtured the same opinions in real life. In the 1948 elections she took a middle-of-the-road position: "I will vote against Communism by voting either for the Christian Democrats or for the liberal block. To tell the truth, I tended towards communism, but I don't like the road the Communists are taking. I think the Christian Democrats will win the election, or else some other middle-road party. It will be much better for our country, which is in need of order, peace, serenity."

But Vivi Gioi still carried with her the air of a woman under a curse, bound also to a kind of beauty that became ever harsher with the passing years. The producers still cast her as unfortunate figures as in *Donne senza nome* (1950) *(Unwanted Women)*. Just as unlucky in real life as on the screen, Vivi Gioi did not have a long career. And the newspapers talked of a tormented love affair with Gabriele Ferzetti, one of the renowned playboys of Italian movies.

In the fifties she almost abandoned the movies in favor of the theater. The screen still saw her in a few roles, but rather small ones like Elsa Martinelli's mother in *La risaia* (1956) *(Rice Girls)*. Terribly aged and dressed in black, she is donna Rachele Mussolini in *Il processo di Verona* [The Verona trial] (1963) a typically hard and unhappy figure.

Carla Del Poggio
[see also p. 43]

After the war, vivacious Carla Del Poggio's image underwent a radical change. In 1945 she had just turned twenty and the former bothersome adolescent became an actress in the neorealistic vein. The early years of neorealism made Carla one of its muses, primarily in the films of Alberto Lattuada who also became her husband.

The film that radically transformed her was *Il bandito* (1946) *(The Bandit)* where Carla plays the sister of the war veteran Amedeo Nazzari. Back from the war, Nazzari finds his family destroyed: his parents are dead, the house in ruins, and his sister forced into prostitution. Nazzari takes her away from the brothel, but her pimp kills her and Nazzari takes vengeance, thus becoming a murderer and a bandit. In reality, Carla Del Poggio is a minor figure in *The Bandit* and disappears very early in the movie. But to see her transformed into a prostitute is terribly shocking for the Italians who still remember her lighthearted air in *Maddalena zero in condotta* [Maddalena zero in conduct]. The raw realism of *The Bandit* is a turning point in Carla's career and she is destined to become one of the favorite actresses of neorealistic directors over the next five years. She is coupled with Massimo Girotti in two films made in 1947: *The Tragic Pursuit* and *Gioventù perduta* [Lost youth].

141

Carla Del Poggio went through a complete transformation too: from a mischievous bothersome teenager she performed with exceptional dramatic talent in Without Pity *(1948).*

With their look of good honest kids, Del Poggio and Girotti embodied the type of young couple who had the responsibility of building a better society. Primarily for leftist directors like Giuseppe De Santis, these actors were the symbol of a democratic Italy that wanted to start with a clean slate, honestly, and without compromising with the past. Along their road towards the new life, Del Poggio and Girotti have to fight and suffer, but they are destined to win like all just people. It was the positive feeling that was common to social realism, to the classic western, and to Italian neorealism too.

The Carla Del Poggio of *The Tragic Pursuit* is a farm laborer on a cooperative in the Po Valley. At the beginning of the film she appears as a peasant girl seated on the back of a truck with her lovely legs bared to the knee in homage to the eroticism of De Santis. She, who was the peaches-and-cream girl of the white telephone era, in the postwar period becomes a womanly woman with childhood memories. Her innocence appears soiled by the war.

This image of mud-stained candor excited the imagination of directors like De Santis and Lattuada who interpreted the beauty of the Italian woman in a sensual key unknown to Fascist movies. In *The Tragic Pursuit*, the honeymoon trip of Carla Del Poggio and Massimo Girotti is violently interrupted. The newlyweds get a place on a truck taking government subsidies to the cooperative. But a group of paid bandits hold up the truck, a crime organized to destroy the cooperative movement. Girotti remains unconscious and the poor bride is taken hostage by Andrea Checchi who fears she will denounce him. Carla Del Poggio is the personification of positive femininity, the honest working girl, in contrast to the sick femininity of Vivi Gioi, the collaborator Lili Marlene, who under her blonde wig hides her hair cropped by the partisans to mark her treachery.

In reality, more suitable to Carla's appearance and manner would seem to be the role Pietro Germi entrusts to her in *Gioventù perduta:* a girl of a good middle-class family, Maria, daughter of an aging professor who works as a clerk in the university.

But more than anyone, it was her husband, Alberto Lattuada, who gave her highly challenging roles and had her play postwar girls as in *Senza pietà* (1948) *(Without Pity)*, where once again her image as an ingenue is thrown into the world of prostitution. Blonde, sweet and defenseless, in *Without Pity* she plays Angela, a girl who has run away from home because she is pregnant. Angela becomes trapped in the blaze at Tombolo, the pine wood at the gates of Livorno. She tries to escape together with a black American military policeman. The desperate love of Angela, the blonde fallen angel, for a black man is a slap at the racism still thriving in Italian culture – one of Alberto Lattuada's first sensational gestures of erotic transgression.

But the finest role Lattuada created for Carla was that of the small town soubrette Lily in *Luci del varietà* (1950) (*Lights of Variety)*, a figure on which the imagination of Federico Fellini also collaborated, Fellini being co-director for the occasion. Lily, or rather Liliana Antonelli, is a girl who has been nurtured on bread and comic books in one of the most backward Italian provinces. In the chorus of the ramshackle troupe of Peppino De Filippo, Lily pursues her dream of glory, and in the end she fulfills it when she is signed up as a dancer with an important variety company.

When Lattuada turned to other muses to inspire his films, Carla Del Poggio's career began to go into crisis. De Santis, who at first had her in mind for Silvana's role in *Bitter Rice* (1949), gave her only a small part in the film *Rome, Eleven O'Clock*, where she is Luciana Renzoni, one of the many unemployed girls looking for work.

Only just past twenty-five, Carla Del Poggio had already had two successful careers: one as the adolescent "brat" in white telephone films, and one as a misery-plagued woman in neorealistic war films. Her appearance was still young and modern, perhaps too much so for the times. She also played in some not very good comedies like *Cose da pazzi* [Crazy things] (1953) and a few movies in France. She is Lina, the composer Mascagni's tender companion in the opera film *Melodie immortali* [Immortal melodies] (1952). When she shoots *I girovaghi* (1956) *(The Wanderers)* with Peter Ustinov, she is taken almost always in close-ups – she is pregnant. Her acting interested her less and less. In the mid-fifties she found new verve for a while in a stage production: the musical comedy *Tutte donne meno io* [All women except me] (1957) partnered by Macario. She seemed to be the lovely Lily of *Lights of Variety* again. Certainly, Carla Del Poggio did not experience a total decline. She continued to receive leading roles even during the last years of her career. But she did prefer to withdraw from the scene little by little as if the world of movies was no longer hers.

The new-born Italian television, that tried to attract actresses who were abandoning the movies used Carla as a heroine in some important comedies and TV films. But these were only stages on her way out of the world of entertainment. Carla Del Poggio had no regrets. "Every person has his time in life. My career was premature with regard to the times, to the mentality, to my age. It was a wonderful period. But I must say that my nerves gave out. I didn't have the psychological nor physical resistance to keep it up."

Irasema Dilian
[see also p. 46]

When the war ended Irasema Dilian was barely twenty years old. Her popularity, connected to the role of the private student in *Maddalena zero in condotta* [Maddalena zero in conduct] (1946) was still very much alive in Italy.

She also shot a remake of that film in Spain, *Cero en conducta* (1946) where she played the part that was Carla Del Poggio's in the original. But Irasema was searching for new characters and it was not easy for her to find these roles. With her blue eyes, blonde hair, her clean look, she was perfect as an ingenue. She envied the transatlantic ingenues. "Joan Fontaine, Joan Leslie, Olivia de Havilland do more than just weep and smile. Here in Italy, these are usually the only expressions allowed to us ingenues," she complained.

Dramatic roles were offered to her in Spain where she was famous for *Cuando llegue la noche* [When night falls] (1946) and *Un drama nuevo* [A new tragedy] (1946). In Italy Irasema began to change her image in two films taken from Pushkin, both in which she is called Mascia: *Aquila Nera* (1946) *(Black Eagle)* and *La figlia del capitano* (1947) *(The Captain's Daughter)*. In a letter to a fan, Irasema wrote, "*The Captain's Daughter* is the only recent movie of mine in which I had a few moments when it was possible to express any true feeling. A movie actress is so bound to an intricate knot of circumstances outside her control that they suffocate and cancel out every trace of personality. Often a successful interpretation is to be considered entirely coincidental... The cinema is a bizarre and jealous monster that does not stoop to

Irasema Dilian also took a new direction and became an intensely dramatic actress in The Captain's Daughter *(1947).*

making pacts or accepting compromises. One must follow it renouncing all other things and it often repays you in incoherent and strange ways."

From her letters one gets the impression of a sensitive woman to whom the Italian cinema owed a debt seeing that in 1948 she was still waiting for her first "real film." Dilian was not dreaming of Hollywood, but true dramatic roles which were a long time coming. Despite that, she had many, many admirers. In 1948 she was the actress who received the most fan mail in Italy.

Magnificent and jewel-laden, but still innocent and haughty, Irasema is the daughter of a marquis in *Il corriere del re* [The king's messenger] (1948), Righelli's last film. But by this point she didn't want to be anyone's daughter: on January 29, 1950 she married the journalist Dino Majuri. She was becoming more and more Italian.

The dramatic role she had been waiting for finally came from Geza Radvany in the film *Donne senza nome* (1950) (*Unwanted Women*). In an absolutely different vein from anything she had previously acted, she plays the part of a Polish woman in a refugee camp. It is an excellent test of her talent. In fact, the role the of victim appealed to her. Irasema attempted it again in *I bastardi* [The bastards] (1950) where she plays a poor unwed mother persecuted by an evil destiny. But her star had begun to set. Perhaps the Italian public preferred her as an ingenue.

Thus Irasema tried her luck in other countries. She became one of the three big stars in the Mexican firmament along with Dolores Del Rio and Maria Felix. Directed by Buñuel, she played the lead in a necrophiliac love story: *Wuthering Heights* (1953), a work of strong dramatic color based on the novel by Emily Brontë.

In the fifties, Irasema Dilian became one of the most popular stars of Mexican cinema in Un minudo del bondad *(1953).*

THE BOURGEOIS WOMEN

Isa Miranda
[see also p. 11]

Isa Miranda was the "everybody's lady" of Fascist cinema. After the war she still seemed solid, very beautiful and luminous, despite her years. With the return of peace she was thirty-five years old. At that age it was hard to start from scratch, especially in the new Italian cinema with its distinct penchant for neorealism: her style was that of a charming and classic kind of woman, at times mysterious, at times a vamp. Very rarely had rags covered her lovely body. Roman patrician, a noblewoman of period pieces, bourgeois – Isa Miranda had no love of neorealism.

Instead, her postwar debut was made in a film of the purest Fascist white telephone style, *Lo sbaglio di essere vivo* (1945) (*My Widow and I*) in the role of Vittorio De Sica's wife. Here, once again she is a bourgeois woman, often unfaithful, but most appealing. Partnered by De Sica, Miranda also appeared on the stage in those years. They founded a theater company of their own, the De Sica-Miranda Company, but after 1945, with the departure of De Sica, it became the Isa Miranda Italian Prose Theater.

The Miranda of the first postwar years and the Italian cinema had very few points in common. Her husband, the producer Alfredo Guarini, quite rightly turned her towards international films, especially to France where Isa was already famous. She put on the guise of an adventurer in an insipid movie directed by R. Pottier *L'aventure commence demain* [The adventure begins tomorrow] (1947). But more notably she played the lead in *Le mura di Malapaga* (1949) (*The Walls of Malapaga*) an Italo-French co-production directed by René Clement. Isa Miranda plays the role of Marta, a woman separated from her husband, a brutal individual who persecutes her and tries to take their little daughter away from her. Marta works in a tavern in Genoa where she meets a French sailor wanted for the murder of his mistress. The sailor, Pierre, is a mature Jean Gabin; it is a meeting of silver stars.

Alongside Gabin who, notwithstanding his age, still retains with dignity his gruff charm, Miranda finds her right place as an actress. She may be a little too chic for a woman working in a wharfside tavern, but this role up-dated her stereotype of a femme fatale and suitably adapted it to her almost-forty years of age as well as to moviegoers' tastes of the times which favored bitter characters in a realistic mode. *The Walls of Malapaga* was awarded the Oscar for the best foreign film and Isa Miranda was awarded the Cannes Festival prize for best actress.

The other French role she played in those years was something much more stylized: directed by Max Ophüls, Isa Miranda is one of the women in *La ronde* [The circle] (1950), the glittering amorous merry-go-round of unrequited loves and colorful passions set in the Vienna of the early twentieth century. It is the typical Isa Miranda "international" role with Isa flying from the arms of Jean-Louis Barrault into those of Gérard Philipe.

The fourth episode of the movie *Siamo donne* (1953) *(We, the Women)* offered a carefully indiscreet look at the lives of actresses off the set. The episode given to Isa Miranda was first intended to be directed by the "women's director" Giuseppe De Santis, but instead was entrusted to Luigi Zampa. It was a first-person confession, free of the theatrical rhetoric of the times. "I live on the top floor of a house at the end of Via Nomentana," Isa Miranda's off-screen voice begins to narrate. She tells about a minor episode in the daily life of a woman: how she helps a child who hurts himself playing in the street, taking him to a first-aid station and then back home, a poor apartment house on the edge of town where Miranda lives alone with her four children. This very simple story acted out the aspirations of Isa Miranda herself to be a mother.

She could not have children, but nevertheless she filled her house with dolls that she made herself by hand. She sold them, with the proceeds going to charity.

During the second half of the fifties, Miranda worked a great deal in France. She was a charming bourgeois lady in *Avant le déluge* [Before the flood] (1954), *Le secret d'Hélène Marimon* [The secret of Helen Marimon] (1954), and *Une manche et la belle* [A game] (1957). In *Rasputin* (1954) she was the tsarina Alessandra, while in *Storie d'amore proibite* [Stories of forbidden love] (1959) she was another tsarina, Elisabeth of Russia.

Playing together with Katherine Hepburn in David Lean's romantic film *Summertime* (1955), there was a violent personality clash

on the set and during the editing, Miranda's part was cut to practically zero. Meanwhile, Italian films were offering her very little.

Between 1959 and 1963 Isa Miranda abandoned films and made a number of comedies for British television. She was not afraid of acting in a foreign language. She had done so before both on screen and on stage. Isa lived her acting life with great intensity; she had no life outside of this. And that was a cause of suffering, especially when she began to feel the weight of the years.

In 1963 Damiano Damiani and Mauro Bolognini both offered Isa Miranda, almost at the same time, character parts. In *La corruzione* [Corruption], Isa is a terribly exhausted middle-class mother. Locked up in a clinic she goes from one sleep cure to another while her son prepares to become a priest against his father's wishes. In *La noia (The Empty Canvas)* she is an equally middle-class mother but without so many problems – at least apparently.

Her acting resources, even when reduced to playing character roles, appeared to be inexhaustible. Thus Isa Miranda drew dozens and dozens of more delightful cameos, one of the most notable being that of the countess Erika Stein in Liliana Cavani's *Il portiere di notte* (1974) *(The Night Porter)*. She was an actress who found her reason for living in her art and only death took her away from it after long years spent immobile in hospital.

Isa Miranda perfectly portrays the middle-class Italian woman.

Paola Barbara's now shaky career hesitates between adventure movies and bourgeois roles. Here, with Gino Cervi in Nerone e Messalina *(1953).*

Paola Barbara
[see also p. 19]

The span of Paola Barbara's career is stupefying. It links together periods of Italian history that seem very far from each other. A broken-hearted femme fatale in *La peccatrice* [The sinner] (1940), Paola reappeared on the screens of Cinecittà only at the end of the forties when she was past thirty in the garb of a "nice lady" in heroic postwar films. Then in the midst of the sixties she participated in the heyday of the spaghetti-westerns under the imaginative pseudonym of Pauline Baards. This woman embraced three epochs of modern Italian history: the two decades of Fascism, the Reconstruction, and the economic boom.

The wife of the prolific director Primo Zeglio, Paola Barbara also had a brief Spanish career between 1943-49. Only in 1947 does she reappear on the screens of Cinecittà playing the lead in *La monaca di Monza* [The nun from Monza], together with Rossano Brazzi. In the same year she is a Sicilian woman of the eighteenth century in the adventure movie *I cavalieri dalla maschera nera* [Knights of the black mask]. Paola was thirty-five. She seemed a bit mature for the role of vamp or young sweetheart, but she was a talented actress.

In the fifties Paola Barbara was the typical "nice lady" playing the role of housewife as she did in *Il coraggio* [Courage] (1955) where she was the wife of the knight-commander Paoloni (Gino Cervi). But Paola Barbara also acted in genre films, many of them directed by her husband Primo Zeglio. For him she appeared in *Nerone e Messalina*

[Nero and Messalina] (1953), *La figlia del diavolo* [The devil's daughter] (1953), and *Capitan Fantasma* (1954). As Pauline Baards she played in three spaghetti-westerns directed by her husband under the pseudonym of Anthony Greepy: *I due violenti* (1965) *(Two Gunmen)*, *I quattro inesorabili* [The four inexorables] (1966), and *Killer Adios!* (1968).

Vera Carmi
[see also p. 36]

Vera Carmi was the typical slightly cool Piedmontese. She made her acting debut during the war and did not even have time to create an image for herself in the Fascist movie world. Thus on the eve of the postwar period Vera did not have that flavor of a re-heated dish like some of her acting rivals. Hers was a new face for the Italian cinema.

And yet Vera was almost thirty: ingenue and young lady roles were a bit limited for her. Her Turinese elegance, lovely ash-blonde hair, the eyes a compromise between grey, green and blue, the rigid posture, all made her into a total lady. In harmony with these externals, Mario Soldati gave her the part of a middle-class wife in *Le miserie del signor Travet* [The misfortunes of Mr. Travet] (1945). Her husband, the good Travet, is a modest little employee whereas she is an ambitious wife: she complains about his miserable salary and demands a rapid rise up the social ladder. Sensitive to the fascination of power, she accepts the discrete courtship of her husband's boss and probably would have no qualms about betraying her husband, given the opportunity.

Carmi, in *Le miserie del signor Travet* is the female archetype of the new Italy, middle-class and democratic. In love with elegance, she would do anything for a fur coat.

As an actress Vera was a bit cold. She portrayed the type of woman who was never overcome by passion, and in *O sole mio* (1946) *(O sole mio)*, directed by Giacomo Gentilomo, she is perfect in the part of a collaborator who betrays a group of Neapolitan partisans but changes her mind and sacrifices her own life to save her brother and a man she loves. It is unquestionably the best role that Vera Carmi ever played and she performed it in a measured and sensitive way – a disdainful spy role, but only on the surface.

Despite being thirty, Vera dominated the movie scene in the early postwar years. In 1946 she made five films; more than any other Italian actress. She had great success playing an American lady in the romantic *Addio mia bella Napoli* [Good-bye my beautiful Naples] (1946), and one of her rare ventures into comedy, *Come persi la guerra* [How the war was lost], where she partners Macario. This film became the biggest box-office hit of 1947.

The public also gave a big welcome to the long two-part movie *Fiacre n.13* [Carriage no. 13] (1948) based on a classic of French popular literature, where Vera plays the part of the mistress of a duke who is killed by his brother in an inheritance struggle. On hearing this news, the poor woman, who has had a child by her dead lover, faints and is trapped in a fire. Saved at the last moment, she loses her memory. She recovers in the second part of the movie when – by now an elderly woman – she recognizes her son who has become a judge and is re-opening the case of his father's murder.

Sweetly innocent, Vera Carmi was the typical respectable Italian petty bourgeois who did not want to "get her hands dirty." In *Natale al Campo 119* [Christmas in camp 119] (1948) she plays a Turinese schoolteacher on a trip to Rome. At the Forum she is courted by an awkward and crude Aldo Fabrizi who, with clumsy gallantry, offers to be her guide. Vera has grace and delicacy as also is the case in *Domenica d'Agosto* [August Sunday] (1950) where she is a young widow who closely watches over her daughter on vacation at a summer camp and meets Cigoli, a widower persecuted by an overbearing mistress. Between these two terribly lonely adults an undeclared love story develops made up of glances, thoughts and shyness.

At thirty-three Vera devoted herself exclusively to hundreds of varying housewife roles. She appears chubbier in two dramas of Gentilomo where she plays a governess: *La*

Vera Carmi, still beautiful and sophisticated, is an ambitious bourgeois wife in Le miserie del signor Travet *(1945).*

cieca di Sorrento (1952) *(The Blind Woman of Sorrento)* and *Appassionatamente* [Passionately] (1954). She is a somewhat treacherous governess who feels herself to be "mistress of the house." In *Appassionatamente* she has a downright disquieting and menacing look that is reminiscent of Mrs. Danvers, the terrifying governess in Hitchcock's *Rebecca* (1940). These were her final important screen appearances.

After the war, Vera Carmi was offered the most intense role of her career in O sole mio *(1946).*

Clara Calamai

[see also p. 53]

At the beginning of the postwar era, Clara Calamai celebrated her thirtieth birthday. She still carried with her the flavor of a Fascist-epoch star, but the belated success of *Ossessione* [Obsession] brought her up to date, made her modern.

1945 and 1946 were two golden years for her. For her work in *L'adultera* [The adultress], she won the newly constituted Nastro d'Argento prize. Camerini's *Due lettere anonime* [Two anonymous letters] confirmed her fame as an actress with a neorealistic image. Both movies bore the mark of the intense desire for postwar renewal: during the Fascist period no one would have dared to make a film with a title like *The Adulteress*. Here Clara Calamai, brunette and vamp, is a farm girl who marries a rich landowner, old and coarse, out of ambition. The man wants a child, but the couple remains childless. His wife has an affair with her old boyfriend and gets pregnant by him. He tries to convince her to flee with him. Finding himself rejected once again, he reveals the story to her unwitting husband who kills her lover. Desperate with remorse, the adulteress goes mad.

This was another variation on the theme of the restless wife that was treated in *Ossessione* [Obsession]. Calamai keeps to the road of *verismo* neorealistic characters but, of course, *L'adultera* is not up to the level of

Clara Calamai with Giovanna Scotto in **Due lettere anonime** *(1945) successfully proves herself a neorealistic actress.*

Visconti's movie. Clara Calamai's interpretation is much appreciated, but probably she was given the Nastro d'Argento also as a belated recognition for her work in *Ossessione*.

Even the refined Camerini scents neorealism in the air and shoots a film in that style: *Due lettere anonime*, about Rome occupied by the Nazis. Here Clara Calamai is working in a print shop. Two anonymous letters inform her that her lover is a spy collaborating with the Germans. She unmasks him, but is arrested. Destined to be deported, she is saved by the arrival of the Americans.

When Luigi Chiarini offered her a romantic role in *Ultimo amore* [Last love] (1947), her star was already setting. She appeared in a small part in the Spanish film *Cuando los angeles duermen* [While the angels are sleeping] (1947). Her career flared briefly in the gloomy drama *Amanti senza amore* [Lovers without love] (1947) based on Tolstoy's *Kreuzer Sonata*, where she played Nora, the inconstant wife of a young doctor. Still tied to the Visconti model of herself as an unsatisfied and passionate wife in search of sentimental fulfillment, Clara relives that stereotype in a middle-class vein: here her lover is a famous violinist.

After this role of an unsatisfied housewife, the rhythm of her decline accelerated: she played the widow of Fosco Giachetti as a patriot fighting the Austrians in *Romanticismo* [Romanticism] (1951), and a noblewoman in *Carne inquieta* [Anxious flesh] (1952). Clara Calamai, the intended wife of the explorer and director Leonardo Bonzi, slowly retired from the screen.

After several years of inactivity, the circle of Clara's career closed with the same Visconti who years before had revolutionized her star image in *Ossessione*. In *Le notti bianche* (1957) *(White Nights)*, one of Visconti's least neorealistic movies, she plays an aging prostitute who encounters Marcello Mastroianni in his nocturnal peregrinations. This Clara Calamai of *White Nights* is one of Visconti's phantom creatures, an apparition. Her sphinx-like smiles seem like so many winks to the audience as if to say: "Yes, it's me, it's really me…!"

Without adding anything to her fame, she made a few appearances in small television parts (for example, a minor role in Eros Macchi's *Tom Jones* in 1960) and in the movies. Another nice cameo part for her was the ex-actress in Visconti's episode *La strega bruciata viva* [The witch burned alive] in the movie *Le streghe* (1967) *(The Witches)*.

Ten years later, on the screen Dario Argento had her decapitated in a pool of blood in his *Profondo rosso* (1975) *(Deep Red* or *The Hatchet Murders)*.

Elisa Cegani

[see also p. 18]

Composed and glacial, Elisa Cegani was the perfect embodiment of the heroic female of the Fascist imagination. Fetish actress in the films of Alessandro Blasetti, Cegani was a bundle of nerves waiting to be triggered off: the great eyes, the drawn face, the sunken cheeks – it was a rather disquieting look. As an actress she was a serious artist, committed, suitable for interpreting mentally twisted characters. Unfortunately she lacked the glamour of a star and the least trace of sex appeal.

When Elisa Cegani appeared on the scene of a liberated Italy she was already a thirty-five-year-old woman. Her appearance was severe, which made her perfect for her role in *Un giorno nella vita (A Day in the Life)* as Sister Maria, the mother superior of a convent where a group of refugees is being hidden. Sister Maria is executed by the Nazis along with the other nuns as a reprisal.

With her austere face Elisa is also the ideal interpreter for historical roles such as *Eleonora Duse* (1947) in the film directed by Filippo Ratti, or the freed Christian slave in *Fabiola* (1948). With the passing years her image became stable and Cegani became more and more the ageless woman. Measured, composed, elegant, this icicle of an actress never was young in films and seemed immune to aging – her fascination was entirely "mental."

Even her roles as a lover were in an exclusively psychological vein as, for example, in *La morsa (Infidelity)*, one of the best episodes in Blasetti's movie *Altri tempi* (1952) *(Time Gone By)*. By this time a woman of forty, Elisa Cegani plays the unfaithful wife of Amedeo Nazzari who corners her in front of her embarrassed lover: a chamber piece for three voices based on Pirandello and directed with a firm hand by Blasetti.

Another of her important "psychological" roles is the countess Anna di Nemi in *La nemica* [The enemy] (1952), a drama inspired by Dario Niccodemi's play of the same name. Here Cegani is a bitter, unpleasant widow. Forced into taking in the son of her husband by another woman, Anna treats him with coldness and hostility. Despite this, the boy becomes attached to her. He grows up winning the love of everyone, but suffers because of his stepmother's hostility which he is not able to understand since he knows nothing of the situation. When Marta, the daughter of the family notary alludes to his illegitimate birth, the boy, who is now an adult, interprets the revelation wrongly; he imagines himself to be the fruit of an adulterous love affair of his mother's. He confronts her to say that he loves her despite this. Anna, countess of Nemi, is one of those roles every actress dreams of playing for its dramatic intensity – a veritable obstacle

course which Elisa Cegani, with her cold and detached manner, manages admirably.

In the fifties Elisa specialized in maternal roles, always playing women of the nobility or upper middle class. She is the woman of ice of the Italian cinema. In *La fiammata* (1952) *(Pride, Love, and Suspicion)* she plays the classical "mistress of the house" who gives a party in honor of a minister.

Even poor Lidia in the episode *Scena all'aperto* [Outdoor scene] of the film *Tempi nostri* (1953) *(Anatomy of Love)* was a noblewoman. This cameo directed by Blasetti was one of Cegani's best postwar interpretations. Lidia is a penniless marquise who has resigned herself to begging for extra work at Cinecittà, where she can play period noblewomen with credibility and dignity. Prostrate with age and misery she runs into an old suitor at Cinecittà, the count Ferdinando (played by a gallant De Sica) who makes ends meet in the same way she does. The two decide to live together to comfort each other in cherishing the memories of the good old days. It is a pathetic and humorous role that wins Elisa Cegani a Nastro d'Argento prize as best supporting actress. But how cruel this part is too, which seems to be alluding to the decline of Cegani and all the other silver stars!

As her forties came to an end, Elisa's roles as mother or wife became smaller and smaller. In *Graziella* (1954) she plays the aristocratic mother of Jean-Pierre Mocky, in *La fortuna di essere donna* (1956) *(Lucky to Be a Woman)* she is the wife of Charles Boyer, and in the delicious film *Amore e chiacchiere* [Love and gossip] (1957), the mother of Geronimo Meynier and the wife of the comical village mayor Vittorio De Sica.

In postwar times Elisa Cegani continued to appear as the elegant and reserved lady. With Vittorio De Sica in **Amore e chiacchiere (1957).**

Marina Berti

[see also p. 39]

Marina Berti was half-English. Her real name was Elena Maureen Bertolino. At the beginning of 1946 she had just turned twenty-one and her cinematic image was yet to be shaped.

In 1944, in the midst of the war, she married Claudio Gora, a good-looking young actor at the time, destined to become an excellent director and to direct his wife in some of her most important parts. Their union would turn out to be happy and fruitful. One of their five children began much later in the seventies to make a career as a television *bello* with the stage-name of Andrea Giordana.

Tall, with her straight hair pulled back, and dark, dark eyes, Marina was a forerunner by some years of Lucia Bosè's inert and sensual beauty. After the war she made her debut in Pietro Germi's first film, *Il testimone* [The witness] (1946), where she was the girlfriend of a murderer who had been wrongly acquitted. Desperate with remorse, the man confesses his guilt to her. Marina, who appeared in the credits under her stage-name, Maureen Melrose, is here a pretty and innocent young girl. She has nothing to do with the crime.

English-speaking actress Marina Berti is cast in almost all the big American productions such as Quo Vadis *(1951) in which she plays the slave Eunice.*

As Maureen Melrose, Marina also shot her second postwar film *Notte di tempesta* [Night of the tempest] (1946). It was a murky role as a victim: an orphan who is sexually molested by her stepfather and then vindicated by her brother. Set in a fishing village, the story imposes a submissive look on her. But frankly the threadbare aprons suit her very well.

There were some who reproached her for having changed her name to Maureen Melrose from sheer servility towards the allies. To them, Marina explained that Maureen was her real name and Melrose that of an actress grandmother in England. In reality Marina Berti made contact with Hollywood-on-the-Tiber because of her excellent English. But before beginning her English-speaking career she had played the part of a Jewish partisan, Dina, in *Il grido della terra* (1948) *(The Earth Cries Out)*, a movie dealing with the beginnings of the state of Israel.

Marina's first contact with American movies came in Henry King's film *Prince of Foxes* (1949), a costume movie shot in Italy where Marina had a small role together with such big names as Tyrone Power and Orson Welles. She plays the part of Angela, the lovely cousin of Cesare Borgia and the fiancée of Andrea Orsini, Valentino's lieutenant. The following year Berti was part of the cast for the colossal *Quo Vadis* (1951) in the role of Eunice, a beautiful slave freed by Caio Petronio "arbiter elegantiarum." Eunice is so much in love with her master that she refuses freedom just to remain beside him. The role of a woman sensually dependent upon a male master suited Berti's rather sleepy and passive beauty.

In fact, her image was curiously flexible. She was a one-key actress but adaptable to the stylized kind of Hollywood "antiquity" as well as to Italian social realist films such as her husband's, Claudio Gora's, first work, *Il cielo è rosso* [The sky is red] (1950). In this crude fresco about Italy's lost youth, Marina plays in tandem with Anna Maria Ferrero, both of them being innocent victims of a cruel destiny and, above all, of the war. They roam like ghosts through the desolate city outskirts, experience impossible love affairs with their misery-hardened peers, and prostitute themselves for food. Marina Berti's performance was hailed as a great acting achievement.

In 1951 Marina moved to Hollywood where she got minor roles in two movies: the comedy *Up Front* (1951) and the detective story *Deported* (1951). The American stylists tried to change her look. In *Up Front* her hair-do looks curly and vaporous. But despite this re-styling she remained a discreet Englishwoman. Marina had no luck in the film-Mecca of the world, and returned sadly

Marina Berti, here with Ernesto Almirante, appears in the impressive movie Il testimone *(1946) under the pseudonym Maureen Melrose.*

to Italy where she immediately found a passionate role in *Carne inquieta* [Anxious flesh] (1952): Femia, a sensual Calabrian woman, fiery and always in a low neckline. She runs away from home with her boyfriend, Raf Vallone, but is caught and sent to serve in the home of the Marquise di Francavilla in Sorrento whose son she seduces. Transferred to Naples she becomes the mistress of the Duke di Moliterno – a carnal role of the Doris Duranti type. Marina Berti passes from one man to another with all the gusto of a great seductress.

It was her husband Claudio Gora who offered her another important role in *Febbre di vivere* [Life fever] (1953). With her look of a weak woman, a bit passive, haughty but sensual, Marina puts on the garb of the ex-girlfriend of a hooligan, Massimo Serato, and the latter offers her to a friend who has gone to prison in his place. Naturally the poor girl has no intention of being used as merchandise for barter, but she ends up falling in love on her own with the man she is destined for. It is all quite convincing, seeing that the man in question is the handsome Marcello Mastroianni.

Another one of her characters is more realistic: Marianna Sirca in *Amore rosso* [Red love] (1953) inspired by a bucolic novel by Grazia Deledda. Marianna Sirca is a rich and charming Sardinian landowner obliged to manage by herself all her father's land holdings. Oppressed by the responsibility, lusted after by dowry chasers, she has an impossible love affair with a good young man who will become a brigand. Marianna's life ends in suicide.

With the passing years Marina Berti's icy beauty became austere and composed in a way suitable for parts of rich, powerful women. Thus, in *Casta diva* [Chaste diva] (1954) she displays gorgeous nineteenth-century costumes in the role of a patron of the arts who supports the composer Vincenzo Bellini. But it is a secondary role. After 1955 Marina Berti mostly played secondary roles, even in the international colossals where she was cast because of her perfect English and beauty. She was the courtesan Fulvia in *Ben Hur* (1959), Elisa Bonaparte in *Madame Sans-Gêne* (1961), and the Sicilian lady Filippella Risino in *Jessica* (1962).

Berti acted the last really important role of her movie career in *Un eroe del nostro tempo* [A hero of our time] (1960). At forty-one, she plays a war widow, Virginia, madly in love with a young man who soon begins to feel himself suffocated by the woman's obsessive affection. After her lover robs her and she discovers this betrayal, Virginia kills herself. This screen death marked Marina Berti's exit from the movie scene. She dedicated herself mainly to her family following this film and only sporadically would she be seen in comedies and dramatized novels.

Before her comeback thanks to Federico Fellini, Caterina Boratto plays in only one movie after the war, Il tradimento (1951), in which she is an elegant middle-class lady whom Vittorio Gassman, an untrustworthy family friend, tries to seduce.

Caterina Boratto

[see also p. 33]

The fame of Caterina Boratto had its roots solidly planted in the "white telephone" movies of the Fascist era in Italy. In 1943 Boratto had interpreted on the screen the part of the mother in *Campo de' Fiori*, but after the war she was a mother herself. Caterina moved to Turin, living happily with her husband, a doctor of solid repute. Cinecittà was only a memory for her.

But in 1951, at the respectable age of thirty-five, Caterina Boratto tried for an improbable return to the screen in the melodrama *Il tradimento* [The betrayal]. With the impeccable look of the "mistress of the house" she plays the wife of Amedeo Nazzari whose faithless business partner is trying to seduce her. But her return was only a flash in the pan and she was not heard of again.

Twelve years passed in total silence. Then Federico Fellini, with his archeological-necrophiliac taste for the beauties of the Fascist era, unearthed Boratto for a small part in *8 1/2* (1963): she is a mysterious, incredibly beautiful lady at the spa. Fellini again offered her a more substantial role in *Giulietta degli spiriti* (1965) *(Juliet of the Spirits)*. Here Caterina plays Juliet's deliriously accoutred mother – the affectionless mother who has no solutions for Juliet's problems – she is a fifty-year-old with nothing on her mind but how she looks. And how Caterina looks is uniquely beautiful in the costumes of Piero Gherardi.

Fellini's attentions gave new life to Caterina Boratto's image. On the basis of these two parts she constructed her comeback during the mid-sixties. Between 1966-68 she played a series of roles which may not have restored her old glory but did keep her name alive. Haughty, often an aristocrat, always stunningly beautiful, Boratto was suited to playing a mature mistress of the house, but also to doing witty characterizations. She is Marcello Mastroianni's sister-in-law in *Io, io, io... e gli altri* [Me, me, me… and the others] (1966), a noblewoman given to charity work in *Non stuzzicate la zanzara* [Don't tease the mosquito] (1967), a nice blonde lady in *Scusi, lei è favorevole o contrario?* [Excuse me, are you for or against?] (1966), Ann-Margret's mother in *Il Tigre* (1967) *The Tiger and the Pussycat* (1967) and Mita Medici's in *Pronto, c'è una certa Giuliana per te!* [Hello, there's someone called Giuliana for you!] (1967).

Afterwards she did a lot of television work and, in 1989 went back on the stage in works of Pirandello directed by Patroni Griffi.

THE FOREIGN LEGION

Foreign girls were more attractive: they were beautiful, very beautiful. They came from faraway lands. They were mysterious. Very often, they came from the cold mythical Nordic countries which once gave birth to such women as Greta Garbo and Ingrid Bergman. The Nordic lady very often had light blue eyes like those of the American soldiers… But sometimes foreign actresses were from the Far East, or were African or Middle Eastern. When this was the case, they were true tigresses, flesh-and-blood types like Kerima.

After World War II, Italian producers were constantly on the look out for exotic foreign beauties. However, Hollywood's stars were too expensive. So, they sought imitations, fake ones. Foreign belles abounded. They had little experience, maybe a few minor parts, perhaps slightly more, but all had fabulous exotic names which evoked mystery and adventure. If they hadn't been born with such a name, they invented one for themselves. The starlet with an exotic foreign name could make believe anything she liked, and some of the stories were quite fantastic: phantom Hollywood fortunes, great love stories with glamorous popular personalities.

Foreign actresses had unsteady luck in Italy. They made it, or disappeared completely. Some got a part in the movie which was the turning point of their lives. Others could only boast of having the right husband, which wasn't such a bad thing either come to think of it… Those foreign actresses who got their start in Italy or whose careers were definitively consecrated there, the foreign actresses who found a second homeland in Italy, at least temporarily, are treated in the following pages.

Marilyn Buferd

In 1948 the papers were filled with news of the arrival of a long-legged girl from America to play in Rossellini's *La macchina ammazzacattivi (The Machine That Kills Bad People):* it was Marilyn Buferd, Miss America 1947.

The starlet's "debarkation" in Italy was the first time the press used a publicity stunt to promote a movie. In fact, Mary Buferd had not gone to Italy to be in *The Machine That Kills Bad People:* she was already there, in Rome, long before, working as a high fashion model.

Buferd was a big bursting-with-health American girl, not yet twenty, but as huge as

a statue of Venus. She embodied wholesome and healthy America with its vitamins and thick steaks. She was already a full-bodied pin-up. When Rossellini, who was used to tailoring his roles to fit his actresses, gave her the part of a super-girl, the boys who lived in the tiny town where the film was shot, didn't know what had hit them. Before, during, and after her scenes, she generously displayed her charms in swimsuits which, for the time, were truly scandalous.

The role of the pin-up with no brains but lots of body was neither pain nor joy for Miss Buferd. She gained a lot of fame out of it, but this also forced her to always play the same roles time after time in low comedies like *Al diavolo la celebrità*, (1949) *(A Night of Fame)*, *Tototarzan* (1950) and *Io sono il Capataz* [I am Capataz] (1950). Hers was the brawny muscular beauty just begging to be shown off.

1950: the Holy Year. Someone protests that beauty contests ought to be abolished because they are works of the devil. Yet, many contests are still held and Marilyn, already crowned as Miss America, is asked to be part of the juries. She usually wears glasses for these occasions, which give her an intellectual look. In Italy, she not only receives lots of movie offers, but also an important marriage proposal: she marries commander Francesco Barbaro and gives birth to little Nicolò in 1952. The marriage does not last long, however, and its end coincides with that of Marilyn's career in Italy.

Before returning to the States, however, Miss Buferd finally landed a part that differed from those of the fleshy pin-up: it came from Mario Soldati, director of *La provinciale* (1953) *(The Wayward Wife)* in which she plays the role of Anna Sartori, Franco Interlenghi's sister. But in the end, it turned out to be only a cameo part.

Marilyn Buferd, Miss America 1947, was cast in movies in Italy, the most important of which was The Machine That Kills Bad People *(1952) directed by Rossellini.*

for going back home since even her contract with Goldwyn had come to an end, decided to try her luck in Italy. Tall, blonde, with naughty dark eyes set in an angel's face, she featured in *Follie per l'opera*, (1948) *(Mad About Opera)*, as Margaret, a Covent Garden employee who tries to steal young Gina Lollobrigida's boyfriend, Aroldo Tieri. The movie wasn't bad. The following year, she was offered a contract by Michele Scarella for three more films.

Beautiful, elegant but a bit cold, she liked to present herself as an upper-class femme fatale. Very often she was cast in cruel roles, or at the best, as a mistress compulsively after other women's husbands. She did, however, get the chance to play other kinds of roles too, such as Lilly in *Miss Italia* (1950) directed by Duilio Coletti. A box-office smash, it is a story in which the protagonist heroically sacrifices herself in a mad automobile race, clearing the way for a triumphant Lollo.

The Dowling sisters were the first to go to Italy and form the "foreign legion" of Cinecittà. Above: Doris Dowling alongside Jacques Sernas in Cuori sul mare *(1950). Below: Constance Dowling with Mino Doro in* Miss Italia *(1950).*

The Dowling Sisters

In the summer of 1947, Italians received with satisfaction the important announcement that their country would receive economic aid from the United States: the famous Marshall Plan. In that same summer, twenty-four-year-old Constance Dowling, or Connie, arrived from America. Gregory Ratoff had promised to give her a part in *Cagliostro* (1947) *(Black Magic)*, but in the end nothing actually materialized.

Connie, who had no reason whatsoever

Constance had a sister, Doris, two years older than her, who had had some luck in Hollywood, and had managed to feature as supporting actress in one of Billy Wilder's masterpieces, *The Lost Weekend* (1945). Like her sister, Doris headed for Italy and once there, seemed to find success quite easily. The young director, Giuseppe De Santis, a keen admirer of American movies, engaged her to play the main character in *Riso amaro*, (1948) *(Bitter Rice)*, a movie which was to leave a deep mark on the history of Italian mores. Nevertheless, it isn't Doris who makes that "mark," but an Italian actress making her debut who steals the scene: Silvana Mangano, Italy's first post-war sex-symbol, "the most beautiful bosom in Europe," the newspapers claim. Doris, instead, is petit and delicately elegant: rivalry with the impressive newcomer, Silvana Mangano, is an unfair challenge.

Doris' name appears before Silvana Mangano's in the opening credits, but in the scene when Silvana's full-bodied column-like legs rise out of the waters of the plantation rice paddies, the poor American actress is inevitably uptstaged. *Bitter Rice* is her Waterloo; she drops from main character to second lead. If you look at her carefully, you will notice a sad look in her eyes, a look that doesn't belong solely to the character but is also her own.

In Rome, the Dowlings lived in a luxury hotel. As good sisters they would have liked to have played in a film together, but were never given a chance. Doris seemed doomed to wicked roles: in *Alina*, (1950) she is a nasty French woman who tries to steal Amedeo Nazzari from his wife, Gina Lollobrigida.

Connie also played these kinds of parts, in particular in *La città dolente*, (1949) *(City of*

Pain), a difficult anti-Communist film in which she is a communist militant.

Foreign actresses nearly always played cruel parts in Italian movies: they stole husbands, carried out secret plots, deceived and spied, and corrupted young honest men. They indirectly served the purpose of enhancing moral virtues embodied in the juicy, brawny and healthy Mediterranean beauty. Although Italian men were easily excited by the exotic type of beauty that the foreign actresses offered, Italian movies were in fact morally very conservative. Constance and Doris Dowling were victims of this attitude towards their kind of beauty. The wicked characters they played didn't let audiences identify themselves with the actresses. In the end, this jeopardized their appeal and was the main reason why the popularity of foreign actresses in general did not endure in the hearts of Italians.

However, the grim image of the Dowlings was also due to the unfulfilled love of writer Cesare Pavese for Constance. Giuseppe De Santis asked Pavese to participate as an advisor while making *Bitter Rice* and it was thus that Pavese met and fell deeply in love with Connie. He continued to visit the set during the shooting. Giuseppe De Santis recalled Constance, "She was terribly beautiful. In a certain way, she was like the great star who would be born some years later, Marilyn Monroe. Constance shared with the famous sex symbol great erotic freedom, also great candor… She would never have made any difference (she never had) between Cesare Pavese, a cameraman, or a willing actor if she had the chance…"

Cesare Pavese loved her and wrote poems to her. Connie was "heart beat, shivers, long lasting sighs," a passion of "love and death." Constance allowed photographers to take pictures of them together in Cervinia. But their affair was short-lived. Constance Dowling didn't want to develop a relationship that was already becoming too oppressive for her. Cesare Pavese, poet of the "habit of living," was forty-two years old when he committed suicide in a hotel room in Turin. Director Riccardo Freda recalled the tragic event in a harsh way, "The Dowling sisters could break down for anything except the death of Cesare Pavese. Constance never actually cared about Pavese. There was a great distance between them: she was a conventional woman, beautiful, cheerful and superficial."

Cesare Pavese died in 1950, the same year in which the Dowlings left Italy. They later appeared in only a few American movies. From a professional point of view, the most enduring actress of the two was Doris, whose name could still be seen in some television productions of the eighties.

Tamara Lees

One of the foreigners to become most popular in the Italian movies was the Viennese Tamara Mappleback, stage name Tamara Lees, the daughter of a Russian actress and an English diplomat.

After some attempts at breaking into the movies in Great Britain, she moved to Italy to act in *Il Falco rosso* [The red falcon] (1949), a historic adventure movie in which she is an innocent young woman victim of kidnappers. However, the success of *Vita da cani* (1950) *(It's a Dog's Life)* was the turning point in her career in Italy. A melodrama about the entertainment world, Tamara is a poor working girl who becomes a dancer and marries a rich industrialist. However, one day she sees her former fiancé again and, realizing that she has wasted her life, commits suicide. It is a magnificent role in a box-office smash and puts Tamara on the road to fame.

In her first year in Italy, Tamara appears in many movies, notably *Totò sceicco* [Sheik Totò] (1950), where she is Antinea, the icy queen of Atlantis, ready to be consumed in the passionate flames of Totò's love... With long, loose hair flowing over her bare shoulders, Tamara is very much a Hollywood Antinea, Veronica Lake-style. Her glance can freeze your blood.

In *Canzone di primavera* [Spring song] (1950), Lees is a vamp, a foreign lady who comes between Leonardo Cortese and his sweet little girlfriend Delia Scala, spoiling their cosy little romance. This is only the first in a series of roles as a marriage-wrecking seductress that come her way. Her "wickedness" reaches its high point in *La tratta delle bianche* (1952) *(Frustrations)* where Tamara – in a role enriched with homosexual overtones – is involved in a criminal organization that aims at perverting innocent young girls. Among her victims is even fresh Sofia Lazzaro, the future Sophia Loren.

Cold and reserved, Tamara had snow-white skin and jet-black hair, big eyes and high eyebrows, a tiny wicked nose, and a protruding mouth. She was very good at wearing a grim look that suggested someone capable of the most awful deceitfulness, and, because of this, was increasingly cast as a wicked and unscrupulous female.

Eduardo De Filippo, who had a weakness for angular beauties, gave her the part of Titina's antagonist in *Filumena Marturano* (1951), the movie version of a comedy by

Tamara Lees is perfect in the part of the wicked woman, such as in **Frustrations** *(1952).*

The other side of Tamara Lees, the romantic, anxious, and intense wife of hero Amedeo Nazzari in **Romanticismo** *(1951).*

the same name. Tamara possessed a solid artistic background and, as soon as the opportunity presented itself, she showed herself a fine actress. She attained great fame. Even the advertising industry showed interest in her: her image was identified with the Lux beauty soap ad, the soap used "by nine out of ten stars."

A woman of taste and culture, Tamara wanted to reinvest her profits and begin producing her own films, which would also have given her more freedom in choosing her roles. She wanted to break away from the cliché parts that Italian cinema had always imposed upon her. In 1951 Lees also co-wrote, with journalist Lucio Varisco, the screenplay of *Il grande incubo* [The great nightmare] a film that was never produced.

The role of marriage-wrecker which she acted in so many of her movies, from *Ti ho sempre amato* [I have always loved you] to *Perdonami!* [Forgive me!] and then again in *Terra straniera* [Foreign soil] and *Noi peccatori* [We sinners], seemed to pursue her even in real life. In 1953, when she was already very successful and preparing to re-marry, this time to director of production Fulvio Vergari, Tamara received a court summons. The Sicilian soubrette Pina Carli, Fulvio Vergari's ex-fiancée was accusing her literally of being "a husband-stealer in the movies and this time also in real life." The clash between Tamara Lees and Pina Carli was just the kind of copy journalists loved and their columns gushed with news of broken hearts, false promises, menacing phone calls, physical and verbal blows, attorneys, accusations and counter-accusations. Despite the fiasco, Tamara married Vergari just the same, but it didn't last long... perhaps some black magic by Pina Carli?

Yvonne Sanson

Just like Tamara Lees, Yvonne Sanson also seemed to be a true man-eater, but unlike Lees who often acted out of evil intentions, Sanson never embodied dishonest femininity. If Tamara's Nordic looks represented wickedness and deception, the Mediterranean Yvonne was more motherly than anything else.

The Mediterranean stock in Yvonne's blood came from her half-Russian half-French father and her half-Turkish half-Polish mother: an ethnic cocktail which resulted in a goddess-like, buxom, and slightly cowlike beauty. Yvonne Sanson would become probably the "most Italian" of the foreign actresses who landed in the world of Italian cinema: she corresponded perfectly to the local type of beauty. Her round face gushing with honesty, her eyes, like fountains of good intention.

Yvonne had a high forehead, thick lips, and a hint of a double chin. Her majestic curves seemed more suited to motherhood than to seduction. Housecoats suited her far better than evening gowns. Though perhaps a bit overweight, she was always considered a splendid object of desire.

Yvonne's struggle with those extra kilos was reported in detail in the gossip columns. And yet, she was gorgeous, radiant. Her beauty ennobled the myth of conjugal love, which was often treated with derision on the screen. Perhaps it was precisely this quality that led to her enormous popularity.

The women she portrayed were always either consumed by passion or shame; the result of a father's cruelty, an unfaithful husband, or ungrateful children. Suffering was her vocation.

Sanson's most brilliant successes were her performances in *Catene* [Chains] (1949) and *Tormento* [Torment] (1950), fiercely passionate dramas in the style of director Raffaello Matarazzo, the Luchino Visconti of the poor. She appeared in eight films of particular dramatic intensity under his capable and, at the time, still unknown direction. Hers was the role of the simple woman who searches to fulfill a dream of quiet marital bliss, only attainable after much suffering. The Italian audience shed floods of tears for her (as her producers rubbed their hands gleefully).

In the passionate melos by director Matarazzo, which carried Yvonne to the top of the Italian Olympus, she inevitably co-starred with Amedeo Nazzari, indisputably the most ideal partner for her. They were brought together in at least nine movies (seven of them directed by Matarazzo), and seemed to have a monopoly on box-office hits in the fifties. Yvonne and Amedeo were perfect for each other: he was as paternal as she was maternal; he was tender and honest, she was tricky but only in love; he had large strong shoulders to lean on, she was as heavy-breasted as a nanny; he was the real Italian father and she, the real mother. They were two statues in flesh and blood just waiting for destiny's trials and tribulations.

Even off the screen, Yvonne was known to be a wonderful woman, a hard worker, economical. Her four puppies were the innocent companions that lived with her in a house on the outskirts of Rome built with the savings of her first early years in movies.

Yvonne took no part in the *dolce vita* of the Roman socialites. An actress by vocation, a housewife by instinct, she preferred the solitude of her home to jet-set parties and galas. Like Tamara Lees, Sanson also had some vague projects to produce her own films, hoping in this way to have a freer hand in choosing her roles. Nevertheless, her filmography certainly left little to be desired, for it abounded in dramatic portrayals. To her, the movies were essentially pure drama.

Despite this, the lighter side of her image also deserves mention, such as that of the little flirt alongside comic actors like Totò in *L'imperatore di Capri* [The emperor of Capri] (1949), Walter Chiari in *L'inafferrabile 12* (1950) *(Double Trouble)*, Nino Taranto in *La moglie è uguale per tutti* [Wives are the same for everyone] (1955).

Yvonne had a vast repertoire: she was brilliant in historical movies like *Il cappotto* (1952) *(The Overcoat)* and also epic movies such as *Nerone e Messalina* [Nero and Messalina] (1953), with her truly classic beauty. She had the ironic wit vital for very sophisticated comedy such as *La bella mugnaia* (1955) *(The Miller's Wife);* and she was also very good at character roles as in *La diga sul Pacifico* (1957) *(This Angry Age)* and *Anima nera* [Black soul] (1962). In short, she was an extraordinarily versatile actress and she literally dominated the Italian movie scene of the fifties.

Her reign lasted about a decade and began to wane at the beginning of the sixties. So unjustly underestimated by the critics (who never forgave her for obtaining her major successes in director Matarazzo's mistreated melos) Yvonne Sanson – together with Sophia Loren and Gina Lollobrigida – still remains one of the greatest interpreters of the dreams, aspirations, and sensibilities of postwar Italy.

Kerima

This beautiful girl from Algeria was someone who really believed in the silver screen and its myths. First launched by director Carol Reed in *The Outcast of the Islands* (1951), it would be Italy to offer her the most important role of her life. Although she never uttered a word in Reed's movie, her performance did not fail to attract the interest of some of the most prestigious directors in Italian cinema such as Roberto Rossellini and Michelangelo Antonioni. It was Alberto Lattuada, however, who would eventually direct her in the decisive *La lupa* (1953) *(The Vixen* or *The Wolf)*, when he took over from Clemente Fracassi.

Kerima, who had already tried the patience of the Legion of Decency with her first appearance in *The Outcast of the Islands* as a superbly lustful female creature, was again a sublime sexual object. She became known as "the desert rose": pitch-black hair, deep eyes, a wild beauty, almost transgressive. In real life, however, she was not exactly a desert nomad; her father was a wealthy French industrialist operating in Algeria. In *The Vixen*, Kerima acts a very intense role, originally intended for Anna

Kerima, with Ettore Manni in the movie The Vixen *(1953), perfectly portrays an aggressive and sensual southern woman.*

Yvonne Sanson, here with Amedeo Nazzari and Aldo Nicodemi, became popular after the war in tearjerker melos such as Catene *(1949).*

Magnani. The twenty-five-year-old Algerian actress transforms herself quite easily into a lustful forty-year-old provincial woman reputed for her lack of morals. Kerima's aging is absolutely necessary for this portrayal since she has a daughter in the film, Marichia (played by another foreign actress, Swedish Mary Britt) also old enough to be seduced. Kerima's performance of the ravenous female is magnificent, she is aggressive, sexy, a true she-wolf with a wild animalistic erotic power that pervades the film from beginning to end. It was bound to be a success, and offers came flooding in. Director Raffaello Matarazzo directed Kerima in *La nave delle donne maledette* [The ship of the accursed women] (1953), in which she plays the part of a rebel. Kerima almost always portrayed women of great passion. In *Cavalleria rusticana* (1953) *(Fatal Desire)* she is Lola, in *Tam Tam Mayumbe* (1955) she is a hot-blooded native girl and and her moving love scene with Marcello Mastroianni is unforgettable.

Her only attempt at comedy was *Io sono la primula rossa* [I am the red primrose] (1954) alongside Italian comedian Renato Rascel. However, the mediocre results proved that she was much better suited to the role of a creature of wild desire. In the fifties, Kerima was a popular personality of Rome's sophisticated set. Italy became her second home. In fact, it was precisely in the ancient city hall of Rome, that she married Greek actor Alexis Revides much to the delight of the nosy gossip columns. Kerima's star would continue to shine brightly until the end of the decade.

Belgian Catherine Spaak found excellent opportunities in Italy to prove herself as an actress.

Catherine Spaak

The most famous nymphet of the Italian cinema was certainly Catherine Spaak. The daughter of the great screenwriter Charles Spaak, Catherine was only fifteen when Alberto Lattuada – a close family friend and regular guest at the Spaak's residence – offered her the leading role in his movie *I dolci inganni* [Sweet deceptions] (1960).

Tall and slender, with eyes like those of a Persian cat, a sassy little face, Catherine Spaak holds the screen all by herself for eight minutes as the movie opens. Nude under a bedsheet she recalls not very innocent nocturnal fantasies and dreams. A little girl's face with a woman's body, she portrays Francesca, an upper middle-class student who lives love with the seriousness of an adult. Her ingenuity is exquisite, her innocence provocative.

Spaak's performance immediately met with tremendous success. In Italy she made film after film, such as *Il carro armato dell'8 settembre* [The armored tank of September 8] (1960) directed by Gianni Puccini; *La voglia matta* (1962) *(Crazy Desire* or *This Crazy Urge)* by Luciano Salce; *La noia* (1963) *(The Empty Canvas)* by director Damiano Damiani; *Il sorpasso* (1962) *(The Easy Life)* by Dino Risi; and *La parmigiana* [Woman from Parma] (1963) by Antonio Pietrangeli. *La parmigiana* and *The Easy Life* were the two films which best revealed her personality. In *La parmigiana*, considered her most important movie, she plays Dora, a beautiful and idle young orphan girl who leaves her small hometown in the northern region of Romagna to explore the joys of life in the city. However, the many trials and tribulations she gaily experiences will come to a tragic end.

Between 1960 and 1965, Catherine Spaak and other cinema nymphets were considered important models by Italian teenage girls. In the streets and in discos, it wasn't unusual to see a group of fifteen-year-olds dressed in the same clothes, wearing the same hair styles and make-up as the heroines of *Les Adolescents* [Adolescents] and *Labbra rosse (Red Lips)*.

Nevertheless, if the popularity of most of these nymphets was short-lived, Catherine Spaak's, however, was long and happy.

Possessing the refinement and culture so lacking in her counterparts, Catherine Spaak outlived the brief Lolita interval, thanks to a strong personality. As the years went by, she up-dated her image, becoming an elegant bourgeois woman. Nevertheless, she always kept that special aura of sensuality created by her natural innocence and angelic femininity reminiscent of childhood.

SOCIAL PROTEST

At the beginning of the sixties a carefree mood prevailed in an Italy still euphoric from its economic boom.

The summer of '66 was marked by the "shake," a dance imported from the anglo-saxons. Crazed young people were shaking everywhere and anytime to the new rhythm, a vaguely psychedelic expression of a new urge for freedom. For this younger generation, the world was much too stiff and formal, and even on Italy's affluent façade of the so-called "economic miracle," small cracks were starting to appear. Not everything that shines is gold, as they say, even if Fiat was exporting its new jewel, the 124 sedan worldwide, and as a result was opening a factory in Togliattigrad in the USSR. The Christian Democratic party, which had been ruling Italy over the entire postwar period, was veering to the left. Prime Minister Aldo Moro invented the center-left, a new government formula which resulted in an alliance with the Socialists. The working class was starting to make itself felt. Workers were no longer willing to be excluded from the distribution of the nation's wealth.

In Italy, as in France, a fringe group of intellectuals supported Communist third-world guerillas in their struggles against conservative regimes. Che Guevara was a hero. Milanese publisher Giacomo Feltrinelli traveled to La Paz, Bolivia, to witness the trial against French writer Regis Debray, accused of collaborating with the anti-governmental guerillas. Feltrinelli was arrested and expelled. Then, he was killed while preparing a terrorist attack.

Terrorist attacks particularly along high tension trusses where Feltrinelli had also met his death, were increasing. Police were killed or badly injured. Restless uncertainty was shuddering through Italian society, though many preferred to ignore it. Bloodshed even reached the Sanremo Italian song festival, one of the pillars of popular culture. On January 27, 1967 singer-songwriter Luigi Tenco shot himself: his song, *Ciao amore ciao* [Bye love bye], steeped in life's suffering, had been rejected by the festival jury. The suicide left its traces of blood on the last haven of carefree fun. The act was also a cry of protest by an artist who represented a "cultured" tradition of Italian music against a debilitating musical regimen. It hit the music industry in the guts.

New ideas for the future were brewing in the universities. In November 1967 many of them were occupied by the students. Even the Catholic University in Milan was not spared.

Orderly assemblies in the classrooms. Megaphones and long beards. The fathers of these young people were Marx and Lenin. But, above all, Mao Tse Tung because – as a paradoxically menacing slogan warned – "China is here."

The patron saint of the revolution was philosopher Herbert Marcuse, leader of the Berkeley protests a few years earlier. The charismatic leader of the Italian rebels was Mario Capanna. The student demonstrators marched through the cities. They staked out the glamorous soirées before the famous La Scala in Milan and threw rotten eggs at high-society ladies in furs. They cursed the modern consumer society. They were the war babies.

The situation exploded during the first months of '68 with police intervention to clear the occupied universities: in January, at the Catholic University of Milan, in March at the School of Architecture in Rome, where open fighting occurred. The students reacted to the police's blows by firing pistols and machine guns snatched from the police. Raised fists. Molotovs against tear gas. Overturned police cars burning in the streets. Hundreds of people were injured. The student movement continued to gain momentum and spread to the high schools. Even junior high school students joined in. Extremist groups were striving for utter chaos.

From France news arrived that encouraged the Italian youths to keep fighting: it was May '68 and Paris had risen up, the Sorbonne students were fighting in the streets of the Latin quarter. The echo of the Parisian revolutionary song, *Joli Mai*, resounded like a cry of destiny. Something epoch-making was happening. At the end of the summer, the protest movement even involved the Venice Film Festival.

The students joined forces with the workers. If 1968 was the year of the students movement, 1969 would be the year of workers protest. In Italy it was the beginning of a "long hot autumn" of workers' demands for higher wages and not only general rebellion against "the masters." Factories were occupied. The battlecry was freedom. Power to the workers. As a reaction to the leftist pressure, some extreme-right groups provoked a series of bloody bomb attacks. Italian society, just as the French, seemed to be bracing itself for an imminent revolution. Old myths crumbled. Governments were shaken. Everything was put into question. A violent fearful whirlwind of ideas, hopes, projects, slogans, utopias.

THE SEXUAL REVOLUTION

The Italian woman felt split between a conservative Catholic culture, strongly branded into her flesh and her mind, and a frenetic desire for freedom that was a sign of the times. Censorship was still very severe. A risqué dress worn by Gina Lollobrigida in the movie *Bambole!* (or *Four Kinds of Love*) provoked a veritable scandal. And in November 1966, Lollo, still one of the living myths of Cinecittà, was sentenced to two months in prison for offense against public decency. She managed to be released thanks to a 1967 amnesty. Italy still remained attached to its Catholic roots: sins lay in waiting around every corner, but for every sinner there was the possibility of forgiveness. But only if he or she repented. Sins and repentance were the two perverse poles of

Italian morality, and, of course, even on the screen.

The same attitude was applied to sexual morality as well: it was possible to sin (and repent), but not to talk about sex. Younger generations would not tolerate this hypocrisy any longer. The newsletter, *La Zanzara*, published by a high school in Milan, sparked off a judicial and political "case" which even went to Parliament. Three seventeen-year-olds, Marco Sassano, Claudia Beltramo and Marco De Poli, had conducted a survey among their classmates about love, sexual education, premarital sex, and the pill. They were taken to court along with their headmaster. According to an old ruling under Fascist law which was still in force, they underwent a physical examination. Pietro Nenni, the Italian Socialist party leader, wrote to the father of one of the youths: "There are still a lot of laws to be done away with."

In the meantime, a parliamentary commission voted for a bill which was meant to legalize divorce in Italy. It was considered blasphemy in the country of the Papacy.

The girls of the student movement were adopting an unkempt new look refusing to go to the hairdresser's and they now wore glasses without feeling ashamed. The boldest of them had long messy hair and blue-jeans with oversized turtle-neck pullovers, heavy overcoats and, sometimes, a red scarf. Curves were definitely out.

The fashion was unisex clothes, to destroy any differences between men and women: this was one of the young girls' objectives in their movement's struggle. Even so, many of them still wore smart good-girl suits. Knee-high boots were the latest fad, and made them look like soldiers ready for their battle against the Establishment. However, in reality, men still by far out-numbered women when it came to fighting in the streets and piazzas.

Cigarettes dangling from girls' lips were an offense to parents. Smoking, which until the fifties had been a man's privilege, or else, part of the image of the prostitute, was now spreading among lower middle-class girls. Many of them didn't even know how to light up. They soon learned. Smoking was a highly visible sign of rebellion yet caused very few feelings of guilt. The sexual revolution, however, seemed much more difficult to bring about in very Catholic Italy: it would remain a myth, existing more in words than in action.

Nevertheless, images of the nude female body became more and more common, especially in hackneyed men's magazines, but

Gina Lollobrigida, in the episode Monsignor Cupid *from the movie* Bambole! *or in Great Britain,* Four Kinds of Love *(1965), ran into trouble with Italian censors.*

Sylva Koscina between Guido Mannari and Giorgio Tavaroli in He and She *(1969) launches almost-total nude scenes in Italian cinema.*

also in publications by well-known contributors. *Playboy* and *Playmen* became a symbol of the general protest. The identity of nude models, once concealed, was now revealed. Tamara Baroni, Miss Cinema 1968, posed in an infinite variety of nude photos and her images were not only limited to the private pages of men's magazines. Nymphet Stefania Sandrelli appeared with only her hands protecting her tiny teenage breasts. Both Luigi Tenco and Gino Paoli, the two tortured songwriters of the age, fell madly in love with her (Gino Paoli, just as Luigi Tenco, shot himself, in the heart, and survived).

There was a feverish longing for transgression in the air. Sex was becoming a means, like any other, to liberation even if women were not the leaders of the change. Sylva Koscina, in 1969, performed almost completely nude in Mauro Bolognini's movie *L'assoluto naturale (He and She)* and from there bounced onto the pages of *Playboy* and *Caballero*. The movie was confiscated, prosecuted and subsequently absolved from the accusation that it was obscene, with the explanation: "The common meaning of decency in the last years has undergone considerable change, particularly in cinema, and consequently the average person can accept without moral reaction, public demonstrations of sexuality which only a few years ago would never have been conceivable."

Bigoted Catholic Italy had a morbid curiosity for the first nudist colonies, often English or German. In the movie *Il sole sulla pelle* (1971) *(Sun on the Skin)* Ornella Muti, a student in the bloom of youth visits a nudist colony with her classmates as if it were a zoo, and they are left speechless at the sight of the naked bodies. Finally, a police squad rushes to the spot to arrest the entire "disgraceful" lot.

In the meantime, the movie industry was creating a new kind of woman. After the sunny but chaste eroticism of the well-endowed *maggiorata* of the fifties, counterparts of the Italian economic boom, the new goddesses of eroticism were perverse and malicious exhibitionists. References to sex became obsessive. After the triumph of the bust, which had, at the time, nevertheless been based upon the impossibility of actually exposing the nipples, the time was now ripe for total nudes, which, in fact, took millimetrical care to hide the genitals. Already-existing taboos were a drawback. The vulva fixed an invisible limit for decency in the movies, though it was suggested in the exclamatory eyes of the male characters of many erotic comedies. The feminists loved to produce the triangular shape of it by joining thumbs and forefingers with their hands as they marched through the cities, brandishing the symbol as if it were a weapon. They warned the masculine phallocrats, "Be careful, be careful, the witches are back…"

Little by little, movie audiences began to catch a glimpse of a nipple here, and even some pubic hair there – still very little in comparision to the eighties. The most important change was this general desire to challenge the rules. And this was very clearly expressed by billboards, film titles, trailers. Erotic expectations that were hardly ever fulfilled in fact. Yet this illicit attitude created

161

What was the difference between the "endowed" maggiorata Sophia Loren of the fifties, and the eighties maggiorata, Francesca Dellera?

an exciting atmosphere between men and women. Conservatives just shook their heads in dismay.

There were more and more movie producers who deliberately set out to create scandal. The exotic melodrama *Bora Bora* (1968) was set in a Polynesian paradise which became the background for perversions more psychological than sexual. Before being confiscated, the film cashed two billion lire – as much as the other box-office smash that same year, *C'era una volta il West (Once Upon a Time in the West...)*. Silvana Mangano strips, one petal at a time, in *Teorema*, also in 1968. An androgynous Jane Fonda acts in the erotic *Barbarella*, the same year. And also Isabella, the Duchess of the Devils, an adult cartoon character, goes on screen. Titles which a few years earlier would have provoked the intervention of the vice squad were now advertised everywhere, such as *Scusi facciamo l'amore? (Listen, Let's Make Love)* and *Scusi lei conosce il sesso?* [Excuse me, do you know about sex?], both in 1968. Then, there were films such as *Eva la venere selvaggia* [Eve, the wild Venus]; *Gungala la pantera nuda* [Gungala the nude panther]; *Luana la figlia della foresta vergine* [Luana daughter of the virgin forest]; *Il dolce corpo di Deborah* [Deborah's soft body]; *Tarzana sesso selvaggio* [Wild sex Tarzana]; *Dove vai tutta nuda?* [Where are you going all nude?]; *Il diario segreto di una minorenne* [Secret diary of a

minor], all belonging to the hot years 1968-69. Censorship, which was still very severe, cut here and there and everywhere. A third of the movies released were "Prohibited to minors under 18." Nevertheless, the common catch phrase in Italian society was now, "It is forbidden to forbid."

Sex meteor Olinka Berova makes her sensational debut in *Lucrezia* (1968), then acts in *Le calde notti di Poppea* [Poppea's hot nights] (1969). And then there is Marisa Solinas, Italian cinema's "pocket Venus" who takes something off with every step she takes. Even Romeo and Juliet are in bed in Zeffirelli's blockbuster. Florinda Bolkan makes love to two men at once (Tony Musante and Lino Capolicchio) in *Metti una sera a cena* [Sit an evening down to dinner] (1969) with a sinful atmosphere so thick you can cut it with a knife. Tinto Brass shoots *Nerosubianco* [Black-on-white] (1969) with "Eros" plastered across the bill. Helmut Berger disguises himself as Lili Marlene in *La caduta degli dei* (1969)*(The Damned)*. In *La donna invisibile* [The invisible woman], Giovanna Ralli kisses the lips of Carla Gravina, Geronimo Meynier's ex-girlfriend, now a public sinner because of her love affair with Gian Maria Volonté, a married man. Sapphic suggestions here and there. In reality, however, on the screens it was all smoke and no fire. Nevertheless, smoke signals could be seen for miles around.

Lisa Gastoni

When Lisa Gastoni became an aunt, Italian movies turned the page. Upon the release of *Grazie zia* (1968) [Thank you auntie], it did not strike audiences as an epoch-making movie, but it in fact eventually left a deep mark on the history of Italian mores. A neurotic militant boy seduces his aunt and plunges her into a series of ardent love games. Incest and fatal passions. A slick but cruel recipe: eros plus rebellion. We were not very far from the time (almost twenty years before) when Giuseppe De Santis had launched a sexy Silvana Mangano in *Riso amaro* (1949) *(Bitter Rice)* with another lucky formula which marked an epoch. In that case Silvana Mangano's outrageous beauty exploded against a Communist milieu and social realism made sure that the "bad" Vittorio Gassman and "good" Raf Vallone were clearly defined.

In *Grazie zia,* the erotic suggestions of aunt Lisa Gastoni suggest a framework of anarchic nihilism. The social setting, instead of the poor conditions of the postwar period, is the well-off new middle class. Aunt Lea is a liberal doctor, and her terrible nephew Alvise, a spoiled brat. Sexual harassment gives way to incest. If the family represented the essential foundation of society, then here (according to *enfant terrible* director Salvatore Samperi, with whom Marco Bellocchio shared the title of "the angry young man" of Italian cinema) the incest served to undermine society at its very foundations – transgressing sacred family relations. So incest, which had rarely been seen on Italian screens, became a popular subject. The theme recurred in *La caduta degli dei* (1969) *(The Damned)* between mother and son, and in *Addio fratello crudele* [Good-bye cruel brother] (1971) between brother and sister. And Lea Massari, as a mother, would yield to her son Benoit Ferreux, but only for a didactic-liberating purpose, in the film *Le souffle au coeur* (1971) *(Murmur of the Heart)* by Louis Malle. Incest and rebellious ideology clearly went hand in hand.

The sexual and ideological rebellion presented in *Grazie zia* is expressed through thirty-three-year-old Lisa Gastoni's body who belongs to the past more than to the future. She has a floridness which is sensually lit by the first signs of aging. She is full-bodied, mature, slightly flabby in her fine underwear, with long black hair inevitably messed up. Clearly a sexual object. Between her and Lou Castel, (survivor of *I pugni in tasca* (1965) *(Fist in the Pocket)*, there is only an age difference of eight years. The generation gap is highlighted by the boy's rebellious attitude, who, according to the script, is only seventeen. In short, he is a minor. It is a provocative situation which makes the incest, of which the aunt is at the same time victim and agent, all the more deplorable.

Grazie zia makes Lisa Gastoni's popularity soar, but she doesn't manage to become a truly big star, possibly due to her age. Director Alberto Lattuada, the reputed alchemist of Italian stardom, commented at the time, "She needs to be angry to express all her capacities as an actress." However he fails to rouse her adequately in the upper-crust setting of *L'amica* [The girlfriend] (1969), in which she is a betrayed wife who wants to get her revenge on life. During the movie, she tries to seduce the son of her nasty friend (Elsa Martinelli). Her majestic beauty continues to couple with adolescent boys.

Hers is a "cerebral" kind of eroticism. The strength of her sensuality comes from the contrast between her upper-class face, somewhat motherly, and her eyes that light up with sudden lust. Lisa Gastoni, as Claretta Petacci in *Mussolini ultimo atto* (1974) *(Last Days of Mussolini)*, is the alternative to the usual Lolita-type roles in Italian cinema: she gives value to feminine maturity, full-bodied thighs, the first shadows of heaviness on her hips, the appeal of maturity. From *Grazie zia* on, she becomes even more "motherly" with a lustful scent of incest. Her relations are nearly always physical and directed to younger men like in *Amore amaro* [Bitter love] (1974), where she is a widow in the arms of a young man who works in a drycleaners. Conventional relationships are not frequent in her seventies movies. In *Labbra di lurido blu* [Lips of lurid blue] (1975) she is the nymphomaniac wife of a homosexually inclined Corrado Pani.

Lisa Gastoni added to this

Lisa Gastoni's erotic appeal in the "scandalous" movie **Grazie zia** *(1968).*

morbid sensuality her talent as an actress which was universally recognized, with the awarding of the Nastro d'Argento for *Svegliati e uccidi* [Wake up and kill] (1967). Her sex appeal suited artistic *cinema d'autore* films. Jerzy Kawalerowicz, for example, gave her a very serious role, the female lead in *Maddalena* (1972), a tormented movie that treated the subject of the Catholic idea of sin. The sinner Maddalena leaves her husband to participate in orgies, becomes an alcoholic and pursues her desperate attraction to a young priest, who is tortured by doubts of his own. The desire for a spiritual rebirth overwhelms her. But not only. Repentance and seduction go together, and are almost an obsession.

Maddalena was the greatest film performance by Lisa Gastoni, but also the last important film in a declining career. It was a decade after *Grazie zia* that she was again directed by Samperi in *Scandalo* [Scandal] (1976), a movie set against a historical backdrop in France, that tried to revive the essence of that earlier success. Gastoni is a provincial pharmacist who becomes love-crazed for a young shop assistant. Again as usual, the movie presents the psychological submission of a mature woman to lustful young love. And in the end, it worked.

To leave the movies, however, was not a traumatic experience for a woman who had never felt part of that world. Kawalerowicz called her "the alien."

Lisa Gastoni, the temptress in Grazie zia *(1968).*

Laura Antonelli

The real sex symbol of the seventies was still Laura Antonelli who in those years was the most favorite fantasy of young Italian men's dreams, beginning with the cult movie *Malizia* (1973) *(Malicious)*. In the corridors of all-boys schools her name was whispered, with transgressive, intimate and disturbing insinuations.

With her fixed stare, soft voice, prominent forehead, and gentle but aloof smile, Laura Antonelli's incredibly expressive eyes communicated a deep goodness. She spoke very little. Her erotic recipe was submission and melancholy. She was perfect for the parts of maids, waitresses, housekeepers. She was the image of submissiveness, never objecting to her role as an object of pleasure: she let herself be touched, fondled, looked at and used in any way. As a female object she had a predilection for languid poses. Like a silent movie actress, she found herself at ease in the art-deco setting of *La divina creatura* (1975) *(The Divine Nymph)*. In a decade obsessed by completely nude scenes, Laura Antonelli also blithely undressed constantly and with complete ease. She was at her best in her nude scenes.

Her magnificent body lent itself well to the lustful psychological games, so dear to *enfant terrible* Salvatore Samperi, which were based on domination and the pleasure of submission. His characters were the most outrageous figures of desire that the Italian movies would ever invent.

Native of Pola, a town in the Istrian region in northeastern Italy (just as Alida Valli was), Laura Antonelli was born on November 28, 1945 (though biographers have sometimes erroneously reported 1946). A refugee from Istria, from a poor family, she moved to sunny Naples and graduated from the Istituto Superiore di Educazione Fisica (a professional school for physical education teachers). There she met actor Mario Marenco, at the time an obscure architect, and following her boyfriend to Rome, became a physical education teacher at the fine arts high school on Via di Ripetta.

She got into movies after stints as a model, actress in photoplay magazines such as *Caballero*, and TV ads. Her body didn't leave any doubts: she was definitely bound for success. Antonelli made her debut on the screens before the age of twenty in a parody spy story with Franco Franchi and Ciccio Ingrassia, *Le spie vengono dal semifreddo* (1966) *(Dr. Goldfoot and the Girl Bombs)*. She shows the same perverse innocence and hypnotic eyes of the early Brigitte Bardot, though stiller and more passive, due to her terrible shyness — which she overcomes with her tremendous determination — when it comes to undressing. Her femininity is the kind to be devoured with the eyes in a cinematic panorama especially made for peeping Toms. "I don't think it's

Laura Antonelli, object of men's desires in **Il malato immaginario** *(1979).*

shameful to be naked," explained the actress, "the human body is the truest expression of the beauty of nature."

Laura Antonelli dove straight into the tunnel of exciting erotic movies being made everywhere. Necklines were bursting, bras were stripped off, garters flew. Panties were inexorably removed. In *Malicious*, Alessandro Momo even takes them off from Antonelli at lunch, maneuvering under the table with trembling sweaty hands, while she is sitting with her fiancé Turi Ferro and other unsuspecting guests, among whom the parish priest Pino Caruso. Morbid exhibitionism becomes her trademark. She meets Jean-Paul Belmondo on the set of *Les mariés de l'an II* (1971) *(The Scoundrel)* by Rappeneau. Together they play in *Docteur Popaul* (1972) (*Scoundrel in White*) by Claude Chabrol. Halfway through the seventies she moved into the big house in Paris where Jean-Paul was living with his three children. A great love story, though Laura was often forced to travel the world over looking for her Jean-Paul... he would always remain a bit of a scoundrel.

It was precisely during this period that she enjoyed her greatest successes, the most famous being *Malicious*. Salvatore Samperi, the new prophet of artistic erotism, engaged Laura Antonelli (after Mariangela Melato's refusal it was rumored) in the place of Lisa Gastoni and elaborately reworked the same theme: the erotic games of a precocious boy with a very womanly woman. This time there's no rebellion, no black and white, no social backdrop. She is the perfect maid who replaces the deceased mother in a middle-class Sicilian family. All the men in the family want her body, even the youngest (Alessandro Momo) who discovers his first sexual anxieties.

Vittorio Storaro plays with color, light and

shadow, especially in the crucial scene when the young boy follows nude Antonelli in the dark house, and suddenly, with a flashlight first pointed directly into her eyes, reveals her gradually in a play of light and darkness. Laura's body emerges in an outline from the shadows. Seen and unseen. Hide and seek. A high point of cinematographic erotism of the seventies.

For Laura Antonelli it is a tremendous success. Images that force themselves upon the collective imagination. One in particular: we see her at the top of a ladder to take a book from a shelf, the boy below, with his eyes fixed under her skirt. A bit mother, a bit maid, also a sweetheart, an object of pleasure, she represented and exalted the taboos of the Italian male regarding female sensuality.

Although she was undeniably a sex object, Antonelli managed to avoid giving way to the second-rate erotic comedies of the mid-seventies. On the contrary, she demanded the best directors and only appeared in big budget movies of the genre. She continued working for Samperi appearing in, for example, *Peccato veniale* [Venial sin] (1974), where she again co-starred with the lewd sixteen-year-old Alessandro Momo and was again deflowered by him. She was also the protagonist of *L'innocente* (1976) (*The Innocent*), Luchino Visconti's swansong who confessed to her, "You remind me of my mother."

Laura was not only a sex object. Over the years she developed her acting technique, which was subdued but spontaneous. In the episodic movie *Sessomatto* [Mad sex] (1973), Dino Risi teaches her comedy, though her inert beauty is better in morbid characterizations, above all women from other periods. Seventeenth-century necklines suited her full breasts. Patroni Griffi, Mauro

Bolognini, Tonino Cervi liked using her in refined historical pictures.

A very ambitious one was *La divina creatura* (*The Divine Nymph*), an erotic melodrama set against the backdrop of Fascist Italy, in which sexuality became a complex psychological game. Like Lisa Gastoni, Laura Antonelli too had a special gift for psychologically wicked deeds and expressed them with her magnificent body in forms of mental erotism.

As the years went by, she became less static, less passive. In *La gabbia* [The cage] (1985) she deliberately seeks scandal with her role as a lady of prey, with flashes of pure madness. She kidnaps her ex-lover Tony Musante, chains him to the bed, and makes love to him, wounding him, taking care of him, feeding him. All with her daughter as an accomplice. The usual psychological acrobatics. But the role of a tigress doesn't suit her acting which is slightly wooden and mute.

Though she has never had any inhibitions, she does refuse erotic film director Tinto Brass' offer to play the protagonist in his *La chiave* (1983) *(The Key)*. It seemed cheap sex to her. She didn't want to ruin her image as a high-class erotic actress. In 1981 she signed a contract with *Penthouse*. In the Italian edition of the for-men-only magazine she replied to readers in an erotic advice column. She signed her suggestions "donna Malizia."

In the meantime, on the screen what worked best for her was a combination of literature (from Molière to D'Annunzio) and sudden "sinful" flashbacks. Renaissance necklines in *La venexiana* [The Venetian] (1986) show off her generous bust. She naturally was more decent on TV, where Mauro Bolognini directed her in an adaption of Alberto Moravia's novel *Gli indifferenti* [The indifferent]. Her beauty had become a literary one.

In her love life, Belmondo's star shone for almost a decade. It ended in 1984 when she got engaged to Dino Risi, nine years younger than her. This was the same age difference between her and Alessandro Momo in *Malicious*. There were rumors: "So it *is* true Antonelli has a weakness for young boys…" She confessed, "I always feel like a mother to my men." Then came the turn of just-twenty-year-old shopowner Gianni Dedeu, of gynecologist Riccardo Agostini, and after him, of interior decorator Andrea D'Aloja. Nevertheless, the man who would mark her life significantly would be the fascinating Neapolitan producer Ciro Ippolito, forty years old, with his blue eyes and premature gray hair.

She met him in the second half of the eighties, when the chances of success were becoming slimmer and slimmer and she was starting to experience the bitter taste of her decline. Even if she had once asserted that she needed "no protector" in the movie world, now – over forty – she joined up with this bold and unscrupulous producer. But what really was brought about by the connection between Ciro Ippolito and Antonelli was actually one of her judicial misfortunes. In 1991 Laura Antonelli was arrested by the police who found thirty-six grams of cocaine in her house in Cerveteri (just north of Rome). She spent a few days in a cell at the Rebibbia prison in Rome, and when brought before the judge she defended herself by accusing Ciro Ippolito, by then her ex-boyfriend, "He always brought me cocaine. It was his way of keeping me bound to him."

Laura Antonelli had just finished shooting *Malizia 2000* [Malicious 2000] (1991), sequel of the film which had made her famous in distant 1973. The ex-maid, now respectable wife of Turi Ferro, manages to bewitch a sixteen-year-old boy who goes mad over her. Exactly what had happened twenty years before to Alessandro Momo. Not very convincing. It was a pathetic attempt to make a comeback, and everyone judged it a failure.

The only reason the press gave any coverage at all to *Malizia 2000* was that the actress was suing producer Silvio Clementelli for administering an anti-wrinkle product to her which after a few months was now slowly disfiguring her face. To make her look younger she had been injected with a substance that was now causing a delayed allergic reaction. Photos of Laura Antonelli's deformed face, swollen lips and eyes, appeared in all the papers. She looked like a monster.

A few months later, her name was again in the papers when she announced that she had donated her house in Cerveteri (where the cocaine had been found) to the religious charity organization Caritas as a shelter for the homeless. Some said it was just a publicity stunt, a desperate attempt to get into the papers again. And so this was the wretched end of the story of one of the seventies' greatest myths: Laura Antonelli, who had built her fame on being "malicious."

Laura Antonelli and Terence Stamp in **The Divine Nymph** *(1975).*

Ornella Muti

The eyes of a Lolita, the body of a mermaid. A tiny waist, torpedo breasts, slightly pudgy little hands. A tiny, pretty, freckled nose. Full lips. A wide mouth which would keep opening in childish smiles, up to forty and over. Long black lashes, large doe eyes of clear aquamarine, almond shaped, a small head like a cat's.

Ornella Muti, whose name was invented by Damiano Damiani, Francesca Romana Rivelli's first director (not to be confused with Luisa Rivelli), was born in Rome on March 9, 1956. Why "Muti" (which in Italian means "silent")? Probably because of that still, inert look, like a beautiful little statue. She would deny this, saying that Damiani had been inspired by the name of the theater actress Eleonora Muti.

The first roles she played were girls from the south of Italy. Though she had the build of a girl from the South, the shape of her eyes suggested a Slavic or Nordic influence. Like Silvana Mangano whose sensuality was born out of a contrast between northern blood (an English mother) and Mediterranean (a Roman father), she was the ideal mix of dissonant ethnic origins. Sensuality and idleness, shades of Estonia and those of the Mediterranean. In one of her very first movies, *Il sole nella pelle* (1971) *(Sun on the Skin)* her face has the androgynous Scandinavian beauty of Tazdius in *Morte a Venezia (Death in Venice)* which Luchino Visconti was shooting that same year.

Her mother was Estonian and Ornella would use her maiden name, Krause, when she wanted to go unrecognized. Her father was a sharp Neapolitan journalist who died when Ornella was only twelve. When Ornella used to tell him she wanted to be a ballet dancer her father warned, "Women in show business are all hookers."

Her sister, who was betrothed to one of the sons of the President of the Republic, Giovanni Leone, was a photoplay actress. This was a road which even Ornella Muti would take for a while, at the very beginning of her career. They went together to do the screen test for the main character in *La moglie più bella* [The most beautiful wife] (1970) and Damiano Damiani was struck by the amazing photogenic quality of this fourteen-year-old schoolgirl. "Just one test was enough to see she had something special in her eyes," the director recalled. She was perfect for the role of Franca Viola, the Sicilian girl whose story all the nation had followed in the press. Kidnapped and raped by a *picciotto* (a young thug, in dialect), her aggressor had rebelled against the die-hard traditions of Sicilian culture by refusing to marry her. Franca Viola courageously reports him to the police and creates a scandal, becoming the first true symbol of the feminist movement in Italy.

Ornella Muti with her bewitching eyes, naughty smile, and body of a mermaid.

Thanks also to the taps Damiani gave her on the set while shooting the movie to wake her from her sluggishness, Ornella Muti was a success. She left the institute where she was studying, and became a star of photoplay magazines; then posed for *Playboy* wearing nothing more than her long tresses. She was coupled with Alessio Orano, (her raper in *La moglie più bella*), in several movies as well as in private life. He had the good looks of a photoplay hero, with his deep eyes and a rebel black forelock. In *Sun on the Skin* they bathe nude in the sea off the coast of Circeo (though the closing credits specify that a double has appeared in all of Ornella Muti's nude scenes). In handsome Alessio, who was ten years older, she found a guide, a protector, a companion, a new daddy. In 1974 they married, without any wedding celebration. Just the two of them, alone with their witnesses, at the City Hall in Rome.

Ornella had just given birth to a beautiful baby girl called Naike (the name of an Indian chief killed at Wounded Knee), from another man, however, and whose identity she would never reveal. Alessio open-heartedly recognized the child as his own. But this did not help salvage their marriage which would end very soon after. Later, many years after the end of their marriage, Ornella tried to bring an action against the legitimacy of this paternity.

Ornella nevertheless had another more influential patron, the producer Achille Manzotti, who slowly created a special place for her in Italian cinema by means of star vehicles he custom styled to accomodate for her weak acting skills. Manzotti's friend, a financier from Bergamo, Federico Facchinetti, became the most important figure in her sentimental life.

Life was lived at top speed for Muti. At twelve she had lost her father, at fourteen she had already made her first movie, and at fifteen left school. At seventeen she had had her first child. At eighteen, she was already married. At twenty, she had reached stardom and was an idol both in Italy and Spain, where she had also made many movies. But she was still a child, with long silky doll's hair falling down to her hips and a flawless porcelain complexion. Under her fragility, young energy, but wild.

Nearly all her early roles played on this look: a child's heart (and face) in a woman's body. And to highlight the perverse side of this fact, her partners in these films were often much older, fatherly lovers or fatherly husbands, like Ugo Tognazzi in *Romanzo popolare* [Popular novel] or Gabriele Ferzetti in *Appassionata* [Passionate], both made in 1974. Exactly the opposite of what happened to Laura Antonelli, or "auntie" Lisa Gastoni.

It was on the set of *Romanzo popolare* that Ornella Muti realized she was pregnant with Naike. Maternal instinct would work for her as an antidote against the movie world which gave her fame and fortune but treated her badly in her intimate life. For long years, Muti remained the "plastic mermaid" or even worse, "the little potato with blue eyes." Her efforts as an actress were constantly torn to pieces, more or less up to *Io e mia sorella* (1987) [Me and my sister]. The critics said she was photogenic but empty. Too beautiful to also be very talented. Her diction was too Roman. Hardly any voice. So, almost grudgingly, she dedicated herself to her family.

Ornella Muti reversed her image and became the actress who didn't want to give up the joys of family life for her career ("Babies smell so good"). To the rare journalists she accepted interviews from, she showed herself like a hen with her brood of chicks, surrounded by diapers and baby bottles. She often appeared on the set followed by a court of toddlers, nannies and maids. And of course, her new partner. A tribe which followed her everywhere even into the jungle of *Cronaca di una morte annunciata* (1987) *(Chronicle of a Death Foretold)* or to the mountains of Utah for *Aspetta primavera Bandini* (1990) *(Wait Until Spring, Bandini!)*. "I'm a full-time mother," she admitted. She didn't worry about showing her pregnancy in close-ups. In *Il futuro è donna* (1984) *(The Future is Woman)* she proudly holds out her big swollen tummy like a trophy and colors it with suggestive lesbian erotism. Nevertheless, Ornella Muti was the highest-paid Italian actress of the time and was obsessed by the fear that her children might be kidnapped.

Ornella, who said she was a practicing Catholic and who embodied the male dream of an object-woman, showed a special feeling for the most transgressive of the Italian directors, Marco Ferreri. She made three movies with him, *L'ultima donna* [The last woman] (1976), *Storie di ordinaria follia* [Story of ordinary madness] (1981), and *Il futuro è donna (The Future is Woman)*.

In 1977, on the set of *La stanza del Vescovo* [The bishop's room] Ornella met the love of her life, Federico Facchinetti, the unscrupulous financier. Like Alessio Orano he had a mesh of hair falling over his forehead and was ten years older. Another father figure. Their love story would be long and intense. Two children, a wedding (though this comes much later, on 25 June 1988, when their relationship is already on the rocks), a lot of different homes. Facchinetti, who had many financial misadventures, was forced to flee abroad when he was charged with clandestine exporting of capital. He was also pursued by his creditors. Out of love, Ornella resigned herself to living outside Italy, in Switzerland, and in 1980, she moved to the States for five years and set up house in Beverly Hills. She came to her beloved Federico's rescue many times to cover his debts until in 1994 – after his separation from Muti – he was arrested for fraudulent bankruptcy and criminal conspiracy.

Ornella Muti had actually gone to the States with the cast of *Flash Gordon* (1980) in which she had only had a small role, but had decided to stay when Facchinetti couldn't return to Italy. During her five years there, from 1980 to 1985, she appeared in the all-American production with Klaus Kinski, *Love and Money* (1981), a movie which even she called "awful." It was during this American exile that she gave birth to her second child, in a clinic in Los Angeles.

Co-starring with Adriano Celentano, Ornella was a box-office success, first with *Il bisbetico domato* [Taming of the rogue] (1980) and immediately after, with *Innamorato pazzo* [Wildly in love] (1981). She is the child-woman who seduces the batty super-macho. The usual gossipers imagine an affair between the two stars. Later, new proof is released about this adventure with Celentano: secret photos, naughty backstage talk, above all photocopies of the passionate love letters (with lots of grammatical mistakes) written by Ornella to her Adriano. It was a doubly bad show, not only because of the passionate tone of the letters, but also the mistakes. They had been entrusted to the safe-keeping of her best friend and personal photographer, Vincenzino Falsaperla, who filed a complaint against unknown persons for "theft."

During the end of the eighties and beginning of the nineties Ornella Muti, who up to this point had received everything from her career but the appreciation of the critics, sought to establish herself as a serious artist by entrusting herself to important directors: Schloendorff, Maselli, Citti, Nuti, Rosi, besides Marco Ferreri. She also looked to the security offered by literary masterpieces by such great writers as Proust, Garcia Marquez, Bukowski, Cocteau, John Fante. She was after virtuosity. On the set of *Tutta colpa del paradiso* [All the fault of paradise] (1985) in an Alpine refuge high up in the mountains she recites a six-minute monologue after which the entire troupe in the middle of the scene breaks out into applause. She was determined to be a serious actress.

Her first part to be truly appreciated by the critics was actually the one she played in *Io e mia sorella*. Carlo Verdone, a popular Roman actor and director, succeeded in giving her performance the force she had always been missing in her image as the passive woman and actress only to be admired.

However, her promotion to the status of "serious actress" came with *Codice privato* [Private code] (1988), an intimate story in which Ornella Muti was on the screen alone from the very first frame to the last. Actually, the whole movie was just one long close-up, like in Hitchcock's legendary *Rope* (1948). But here on the screen there is only Ornella, with her open and slightly fragile expressiveness, abandoned in a large split-level loft lined with books and the belongings of her absent lover. At the Venice Film Festival the film was successful and Ornella received the Premio Pasinetti award. A new feeling for an actress who had up to then always been used to only harsh criticism.

When her fifteen-year story of love and debts ended with Federico Facchinetti, Ornella had an irresistible need for change. She could no longer bear the little-girl look that had so tenaciously followed her right up to the threshold of the age of forty. She finally cut her famous long hair, the locks she had so stubbornly refused to trim for years and which made her look like a little girl. In *Nessuno è perfetto* [No one is perfect] (1981) she simply hid them under a rubber cap. Her new companion was François Goize, a young French assistant director, she had met while shooting *Il conte Max* [Count Max] (1991) on location in Paris. He was eleven years younger than Ornella and his loving photos of her were in all the papers.

"Sometimes, there are young girls or old women who stop to kiss me on the street," she said after her fortieth birthday. In 1994 a survey by the magazine *Class* says she is "still the most beautiful woman in Italy." Whereas her seventies success partner, Laura Antonelli is reduced to a monster with the terrible alchemy used on her to make *Malizia 2000*, Ornella Muti is still the most beautiful woman in the kingdom. Of course Ornella Muti was ten years younger than Laura Antonelli and therefore it was normal her beauty be longer-lived, but it was also due to a healthier more stable lifestyle, a genuine love of her home, and a supreme disdain for the world of cinema.

In 1995 Ornella Muti was named Commendatore of the Italian Republic (a State honor) and received this award from Irene Pivetti, President of the Chamber. She was now part of the nation's history. A monument to beauty. Only a statue in her honor was missing, but she received even this too very soon after. Indeed, the architects of a social housing complex built in Mappano, in the surrounding countryside of Turin, embellished one of their medieval-style buildings with towers, arches, columns and a marble statue of the Italian movie diva, Ornella Muti.

Ornella Muti's Hollywood image in the comedy Oscar *(1991).*

THE FEMINISTS

Stefania Sandrelli
[see also p. 96]

It wasn't only because of the ultra-feminist movie *Io sono mia* [I am mine] (1978) that Stefania Sandrelli became the best interpreter of feminism in the seventies. It was also her independent air of a girl (and afterwards a woman) who was used to counting only on her own resources, without a lover-patron, and despite a poor education which didn't go any further than secondary school. For despite her thousand feminine wiles and blandishments on the screen she had always been a feminist, "even if I was never actively involved in any kind of movement."

In the first years of the seventies, the nice grown-up girl with cunning eyes and childish teeth turned into a foxy kind of lady, while the gossip magazines tried to catch up with her many love affairs (among the victims: Luigi Tenco, Gino Paoli, Robin Philips, Mario Ceroli, Umberto Balsam, etc.).

At the striking of the prophetic hour of '68, Stefania Sandrelli was by then one of the queens of Italian cinema. Yet she was stubbornly anti-star, incapable of being chic, harbored no intellectual ambitions, and was as honest as a good plate of soup. Her greatest ambition was to collect perfume bottles ("if I hadn't become an actress, I'd probably have opened a perfume shop").

Bernardo Bertolucci fit her into the cast of two epoch-making movies, *Partner* (1968) and *Il conformista* (1970) *(The Conformist)*, and later even in the vast fresco *Novecento* (1979) *(1900)*. However, the best roles to suit her personality were comic ones like Tiburzia da Pellocce in *Brancaleone alle crociate* [Brancaleone in the Crusades] (1970) and, above all, terrible Mariarosa, Dustin Hoffman's wife, in *Alfredo Alfredo* (1972). Here she meets up again with Pietro Germi her Pygmalion from the past, who has become even more misogynist with the passing of the years. This Mariarosa is sort of a "queen bee" who, after having conquered her unfortunate husband with fresh-faced innocence, torments him mercilessly until she obtains a much-desired divorce. A scene that will go down in the history of cinema is Mariarosa's first orgasm, which takes place on a train, punctuated by her animal cries as she grabs at the emergency brake.

While her little daughter Amanda was growing up (she was going to become an actress, too), born from the shattered relationship with songwriter Gino Paoli, Stefania Sandrelli married the playboy Nicky Pende, son of a famous scholar of medicine and important figure of Roman *dolce vita* nightlife. For two years Sandrelli left the movies. She gave birth to little Vito, openly declaring that she wanted to dedicate full time to being a wife and mother.

Greatly in demand by producers, she matured magnificently. Besides her natural photogenic qualities she was a fine actress and embodied the best of Italian movies in the seventies. One of the most intense roles of her career was the portrayal of Luciana, in the masterpiece by Ettore Scola *C'eravamo tanto amati* (1974) *(We All Loved Each Other So Much)*, a thirty-year chronicle of Italian history and the aspirations of three friends, whose dreams revolve around the innocent femininity of a provincial girl. Luciana, who comes to Rome to become an actress, resigns herself to a different destiny, lets herself be swept away by love, and confronts the hardships of life. There is tremendous dignity and tenderness in this character that Stefania portrays with an emotional precision that seems to go back way before the seventies, to a very distant past.

Ettore Scola directed her again in *La terrazza* [The terrace] (1981), for which she

Stefania Sandrelli: from a mischievous and falsely innocent young girl to a sexually mature woman.

was awarded the Italian Silver Ribbon award, and in *La famiglia* [The family] (1987).

She was also much appreciated in France, where she interpreted important movies like *Les magiciens* [Magicians] (1975) by Claude Chabrol, *Police Python 357* (1976) by Alain Corneau, *Le voyage de noces* [The honeymoon] (1976) by Nadine Trintignant and *Le maître nageur* (1978) [The lifeguard] by Jean-Louis Trintignant. Poor Trintignant had such a terrible crush on her that he couldn't hide his feelings from his wife Nadine. "He wrote me such an extraordinary letter, so absolute, that every time I get a little depressed I read it over again," Sandrelli would say.

Time didn't seem to pass for Stefania. Between the end of the seventies and the beginning of the eighties she also discovered a new dimension as an erotic woman-object, starting with *L'ingorgo* (1979) [The jam] by Luigi Comencini, *La disobbeddienza* [Disobedience] (1981), from a novel by Alberto Moravia, up to her explosive and outrageous performance in *La chiave* (1983) *(The Key)* by director Tinto Brass, the manifesto of a new kind of erotism with no taboos, which was further confirmed by the hot nude scenes in *Lo specchio* [The mirror] and in *L'attenzione* [Attention] (1985).

Even though close to forty, Stefania Sandrelli made a big change and, from the fresh-faced girl of Italian comedy she used to be, she became the queen of the cinematic brothels created by Tinto Brass. Alberto Moravia was quite right when, at the time of the making of *Sedotta e abbandonata* (1964) *(Seduced and Abandoned)*, he called her "someone who just by walking exudes sex."

The Key, from the Japanese novel by Junichiro Tanizaki, is a movie that exudes scandal. It tells the story of the erotic duel between two lovers who try to avoid boredom and physical decay. To play this role Stefania puts on a little weight. Above all, she shows breasts and buttocks generously despite the first signs of aging and some wrinkles. Sex and exhaustion (just like Lisa Gastoni in *Grazie zia*): this is the dynamite cocktail of *The Key*. "Of course trying on costumes couldn't have been done anywhere else but in a lingerie shop, one called Treppiedi in Rome. I stripped nude for Tinto Brass and his wife Tinta: it seemed to me the easiest way to tell him 'this is what I look like, so do what you have to do'…"

The Key was confiscated for nine days and banned from the Venice Film Festival while in Piazza Ducale, with thousands of onlooking tourists, a noisy demonstration was organized: half-naked girls brandishing giant polystyrene keys.

Her "forbidden trilogy" *(The Key, Una donna allo specchio* [A woman in the mirror]

and *L'attenzione)* would remain for a long time Italian box-office smashes. And would even start to imprison her in a hackneyed erotic image she didn't actually deserve. And so she refused the tremendous sum offered to her to play *Miranda*, the movie which would launch Serena Grandi as the new Tinto Brass sex star. "I had to try so hard to get rid of that burden and I wanted to free myself from the squalid scripts people kept sending me." Stefania finally turned the page with the chaste role Ettore Scola gave her in *La famiglia* [The family].

Her new partner in the eighties was Giovanni Soldati, the son of the famous writer and director, Mario Soldati. Also a movie director himself (she had met him in 1979 on the set of *1900)*, he directed her in *L'attenzione* in which for the very first time Stefania and her daughter Amanda appear together, and in *La sposa americana* [American bride] (1986). Unexpectedly, this was the beginning of a new golden age for Stefania Sandrelli, now forty years old, during which the actress was making three or four movies a year – quite impressive for any actress!

Stefania Sandrelli alternated between parts as the uninhibited woman, to roles as a concerned, loving, and sometimes cumbersome mother, as in Mignon Has Left *(1988).*

Having reached an age where all her other counterparts were just trying to survive in the movies, Stefania Sandrelli was living a second (or perhaps even third) youth. She co-starred and starred in a great many movies, directed by old lions and new emerging talent, always meeting with great success. She appeared in the inspiring *Speriamo che sia femmina* (1986) *(Let's Hope It's a Girl)*, in Francesca Archibugi's lucky debut *Mignon è partita* (1988) *(Mignon Has Left)*, in the box-office smash *Il piccolo diavolo* [Little devil] (1988), in the Italian film by Margarete Von Trotta *L'africana* [The African woman] (1990), in the all-star cast of *Lo zio indegno* [The unworthy uncle] (1989), and alongside the mythic figures of Giancarlo Giannini and Vittorio Gassman in the ancient Rome of *Secondo Ponzio Pilato* [According to Pontius Pilatus] (1987). Then, there were the TV movies. In other words, she appeared everywhere, either as mother or lover. And there were also rumors of her aspirations as a director (though this never materialized).

But what was the secret of so much wonderful energy? Perhaps it was that innocent girlish air, or else her reckless courage, maybe it was her slight perverseness which still gave her that sensuality. Or it could have been that magic young circle in which she lived, so protected; her strange little family comprised of little Vito, her daughter Amanda (married to the young actor Blas Roca Rey), who actually looked more like Sandrelli's younger sister, and her companion, Giovanni Soldati, seven years younger than her.

Looking back on her career as an actress we can't help feeling a slight shiver of excitement considering the longevity and intensity of it, which never seemed so remarkable while it was unfolding, but now can be appreciated in all its splendor. A philosophy of taking one step at a time, slowly but surely, but always in the best direction. A great actress even if at the last minute Meryl Streep was chosen over her as the protagonist of *The Bridges of Madison County* (1955).

The out-and-out feminist Eleonora Giorgi had no objections to appearing nude in **Disposta a tutto** *(1977).*

Eleonora Giorgi

Ornella Muti's main rival in Rome, especially regarding her status as a sex symbol, was Eleonora Giorgi, who in the first years of the seventies became famous for her preaching of free sex, mainly in movies such as *Storia di una monaca di clausura* (1973) *(Diary of a Cloistered Nun)*, *Conviene far bene l'amore* [You should make love well] (1975) and *Disposta a tutto* [Ready for anything] (1977). This ethereal languid slow blonde, with her blue eyes, a funny mouth like Totò's, a hint of Hungarian blood running through her veins, lectured on beach nudism and raised hell in the papers by declaring to reporters, "Bras? I never wear one."

T-shirts and blue-jeans were her uniform. Well-scrubbed face without the slightest trace of make-up, Eleonora Giorgi flung herself into the muddy waters of erotic movies in the first years of the seventies. "I'm ambitious," she would confess later. To enter the biz she first exploited her Lolita look, thus seducing the Italian movie industry dominated at the time by "over-forties" who saw in Eleonora infinite perverse possibilities.

Born in Rome on October 21, 1955, she grew up in a big family with seven children headed by a father who gave her the taste of

freedom early in life. When she was fifteen she left home to go and live with her boyfriend, a medical student. She started earning money as a model and got her first important role in the movie *La sbandata* [The crush] (1974).

In the first years of her career, Eleonora was the starlet "ready for anything" as the title of one of her erotic melos advertised. Avid novice, seducer of middle-aged dentists, an accomplice in incest. In *Appassionata* [Passionate] (1974) she goes beyond all limits with Ornella Muti, also as young as she is. Years later she would describe her secret disgust in playing these roles. Her only escape was to go for joy rides on her brand-new Honda 750.

In 1977 she spoke openly in an interview with the brilliant Italian journalist Enzo Biagi. It was a program on erotic movie starlets with Eleonora Giorgi, "Cicciolina" Ilona Staller and the then unknown Ines Pellegrini. Eleonora lamented. She didn't want to stay an X-rated star all her life, she really expected much more from cinema. She related the disappointment and bitterness of her chaotic experiences as a "sex object." A bit clumsily she showed off her cultural leanings. She even cited Nietzsche, but it was quite obvious this was not really her. Enzo Biagi remembered her as a little girl with a lot of confused ideas and recalled, "She spoke like a girl full of preconceived ideas that she had heard somewhere but not understood."

More beautiful than talented, she was disliked by many of her counterparts. They envied her, even hated her for being so lucky. Her lucky number had a name: Angelo Rizzoli. Rizzoli belonged to one of the most influential families in Italy, with a large financial holding company and successful activities in publishing and cinema. She met him one spring evening in 1978 and it was love at first sight. Twenty-four hours later Eleonora was living with him in his house on Via Veneto. He was thirty-four. "He was a lonely man, shut up in his ivory tower."

Poor Eleonora Giorgi! She spent the rest of her youth swearing that she hadn't married him for his money or out of ambition or interest, but only out of love. No one would ever believe her.

The quality of her life improved and at the same time the directors who worked with her too, in movies that then all bore the Rizzoli stamp: Franco Brusati, Damiano Damiani, Liliana Cavani, Alberto Lattuada (later replaced by Nino Manfredi in *Nudo di donna* [Woman nude] in 1981). Their love-nest was the princely Roman residence, Villa Medici. Butlers, gardeners, cooks, bodyguards, drivers, vintage automobiles, secretaries, lackeys. Beneath these shows of a brilliant fortune, however, the financial empire of the Rizzolis was falling apart quickly.

Angelo and Eleonora married secretly without their respective families, since the Rizzolis greatly disapproved of Angelo's choice. At the wedding, bodyguards took pictures of the bride and groom and a secretary carried the bride's bouquet. One of the witnesses was Bruno Tassan Din, Rizzoli's administrator and the real brain behind the publishing group, someone who would play an important role during the agony of its downfall.

The years Eleonora spent by Angelo Rizzoli's side were also those that witnessed the fall of the major Italian publishing group. Rizzoli was arrested three times and remained for a long period in prison. In 1981 his connection with a secret Masonic lodge, the famous P2 was discovered. Occult powers, obscure movements of capital, suspect bankruptcies. His name was linked to Licio Gelli, to names of bankrupt companies and political plotters. Some say, though, that Angelo Rizzoli was just a scapegoat.

In 1980, Andrea junior was born, their one and only son. Because of the pregnancy, Giorgi had to refuse a part in a movie being undertaken by Liliana Cavani, though she would have the chance to work with the director two years later in *Oltre la porta* [Beyond the door] (1982), which she herself would call "hard porn."

Even when working with top directors Eleonora still persisted with her nude scenes and perverse and evil image. These were still her weapons as an actress. In *Nudo di donna* she played the double role of middle-class wife and prostitute. She gave her best performance opposite Mariangela Melato in *Dimenticare Venezia*, (1979) *(Forget Venice)*, when Brusati wove a sapphic relationship between the two women against a fine Bergmanian backdrop. The movie, which of course was produced by Rizzoli and backed by huge promotion, won an Oscar nomination. Yet *Forget Venice*, a collective movie, could not truly be considered a star vehicle.

Eleonora found some personal satisfaction in a comedy by Carlo Verdone *Borotalco* [Talcum powder] (1982), where she was finally allowed to be herself. Playing a bookseller in blue-jeans and T-shirt, she brilliantly conveys the simplicity of the fresh-faced girl. "Too little to win the Oscar or the Silver Ribbon" the usual detractors whispered.

While she flirted with *cinema d'autore* movies, Eleonora still frequently took plunges into vulgarity and bad taste agreeing to appear in films by storytellers Castellano and Pipolo which nevertheless satisfied the box-office. Yet the low comedies such as *Mani di velluto* [Velvet hands] (1979), *Mia moglie è una strega* [My wife is a witch] (1980), *Grand Hotel Excelsior* (1982), kept Eleonora's reputation high, she was almost a big star.
"I like being a clown" she explained.
Co-starring with Renato Pozzetto she was the typical brilliant commercial comedy actress,

flighty and light, rarely pleasant but not all that offensive. It was a shame she never managed to shed her standard role of "the master's wife" which Silvana Mangano could play with so much more class in her movies with De Laurentis.

At her best Eleonora can be compared to Ornella Muti, without ever really succeeding in taking her place. The press built up a real rivalry between them, as in the good old days of Sophia Loren and Gina Lollobrigida. But now stardom was in its lean years. Eleonora was just in time to see the sun set on a great dynasty. Then, even her marriage was overturned by the events. When she divorced there was more malicious talk: those who had said that Eleonora had married Rizzoli for his money, now pointed out that she was getting rid of him because he was in trouble.

After the separation, her popularity plunged. In the summer of 1983 she appeared as special guest on a TV variety show, *Sotto le stelle* [Beneath the stars], and for four episodes she imitated movie myths: Marilyn Monroe, Marlene Dietrich, Brigitte Bardot and Rita Hayworth. The last flashes. When a movie star starts performing on TV shows it means she's already finished.

The movies completely forgot her. Her name disappeared from the papers. In February 1986 her house was searched. There was talk of drug dealing. When it turned out she was only a user, this still didn't do much for her image, already so precarious. She found some consolation in the arms of a popular photoplay star, Massimo Ciavarro, one of the "beautiful men" of the eighties. Her last chance to appear in a film of any note was offered to her by Carlo Verdone in *Compagni di scuola* [Schoolmates] (1988). Then for Eleonora began the crossing of the real desert.

Mariangela Melato

"Ugly but smart" that's what they used to say about her at the beginning of her career, when she appeared like a circling albatros in Lena Wertmüller's productions. Time has now erased these negative comments and what remains today is the mark of a great actress, one capable of cinema, theater, TV, cabaret and even variety. The Italian Glenn Close. A complete performer with an intellectual air. "Only because I'm no idiot" she says.

The daughter of a dressmaker mother and police officer father, she was born in Milan on September 19, 1945. Poor, sickly and not very good-looking, she had two brothers and a sister. She soon began dreaming of becoming an actress, like her almost-homonym Maria Melato who had acted Luigi Pirandello's masterpieces in the twenties.

Mariangela began studying drama, attending the Accademia (the most important national drama school) and working as a window decorator at the department store Rinascente in the meantime. She was an unconventional girl for the times. A small nervous body, thin nose, big and slightly bulging green eyes, a lost stare, dyed hair (sometimes even green!) much to mom and dad's despair.

She frequented the "Giamaica", an artists' rendezvous in the Brera neighborhood of Milan, and met painters, sculptors, directors, writers, journalists such as Migneco, or Squarzina and Buzzati.

Trained in the hard school of theater (extra bit parts, minor roles, even prompter or costume maker, if necessary) fame awaited her in the mid-sixties when Luchino Visconti gave her the leading part in the film *La monaca di Monza* [The nun of Monza]. She became a Juliette Greco of the poor who worked with all

Two rebel feminists, Eleonora Giorgi and Mariangela Melato, were hailed by spectators and critics for their convincing performance, even as lesbians, in **To Forget Venice** *(1979).*

the stage directors of the Italian theater scene, but most of all Luca Ronconi. As the first American astronaut set foot on the moon, she was acting in a mythical production of *Orlando Furioso* in Milan, in the Piazza Duomo.

The movies discovered her only at the beginning of the seventies, when Mariangela left Milan for Rome. Playing a young teacher in *Per grazia ricevuta* [Thank goodness passed] (1971), Melato was also being considered for the lead role in *Malizia (Malicious).* It seemed she in fact refused the role, much to Laura Antonelli's gratitude. At last she found the road to fame thanks to Elio Petri, who directed her in *La classe operaia va in Paradiso* [The working class goes to paradise] (1971) where she is hairdresser Lidia, the partner of workaholic laborer Gian Maria Volonté.

Amidst factories, striking workers, and red flags, Mariangela Melato also appeared in *Mimì metallurgico ferito dell'onore* (1972) [Mimì metalworker of wounded honor], and this film would give birth to the famous enduring collaboration with Giancarlo Giannini. Even Mimì was a metalworker, like Volonté. Mariangela was beginning to embody the working class beauty with its beginnings of socialist revolution. In *Mimì metallurgico* she's a Trotsky anarchist. Wertmüller, who practically makes her into her muse (she would appear four times in the director's movies), continued to cast her as an anarchist in *Film d'amore e d'anarchia* (1973) (*Love and Anarchy*). In *L'albero di Guernica* [Tree of Guernica] (1975), she is a peasant republican. In *Caro Michele* (1976) Mario Monicelli gave her the role (refused by Laura Antonelli) of a young returning rebel of '68.

In a movie world where the norm was brainless women wiggling in bed, Mariangela's "alternative" femininity was strengthened. She rarely played the wife, as she did in *Lo chiameremo Andrea* [We'll call him Andrea] (1972), but rather friend, lover, mistress. Unable to be a slave to convention, she lived on free love, often with married men (with Volonté in *La classe operaia* [The working class] and Giannini in *Mimì metallurgico).* She's a whore in *Love and Anarchy* and a lesbian in *Dimenticare Venezia* (1979) (*Forget Venice*).

Described as "ugly" by people who had a conventional middle-class idea of feminine beauty, Mariangela was in fact absolutely fascinating and created her cinematic beauty through sensitivity and gentleness unequalled by any actress. The scene of metalworker Mimì falling in love with Trotskyist Fiore is still one of the most touching in the Italian cinema of the seventies. Unlike Ornella Muti or Eleonora Giorgi who were lovely fawns for close-ups, madonnas to admire for the perfection of their faces, Mariangela Melato played in heavily spoken roles. Her character portrayals in northern dialect (Milanese or Bolognese) were full of rich interpretation. She was the one to

turn Italian cinema away from the hackneyed Roman drawl. After having made a myth of the working-class Mariangela, Lina Wertmüller had fun in doing just the opposite in *Travolti da un insolito destino in un azzurro mare di agosto* (1974) (*Swept Away…by an Unusual Destiny in the Blue Sea of August*) where she was entrusted the role of a high-class snob opposite the usual Giancarlo Giannini who, for his part, continued to play a poor man. (On the set, Mariangela was injured and Lina Wertmüller fought tooth and nail against the producer who wanted to substitute her with Glenda Jackson). In *Notte d'estate* [Summer night] (1986), however, Giannini would appear as a tycoon who kidnaps a poor unfortunate soul, exactly the opposite of *Swept Away…* These films were the confirmation of Mariangela's extreme flexibility as an actress. With Giancarlo Giannini she appeared in the comedy *Bello mio, bellezza mia* [Handsome mine, beautiful mine] (1982), but without the extraordinary and grotesque disguises invented by Lina Wertmüller.

Melato became the muse of those filmmakers fighting against the banality of the mainstream. She won an important place in the political Italian movie movement which was at its peak in the mid-seventies. Her talent and her special aggressive look were used, by both Petri and Wertmüller, as a vehicle of grotesque satire and violent protest. Here her wild creativity, unconventional femininity with her hooked nose and protruding eyes, were all the more precious.

Mariangela succeeded Monica Vitti to the throne as the queen of women comedians. Co-starring with Giancarlo Giannini, she became the representative of the new Italian comedy abroad, its ambassadress. As harsh as Goldie Hawn, as atypical as Meryl Streep, as histrionic as Glenn Close, Mariangela was riding on the crest of her wave of popularity. Lina Wertmüller's movies were acclaimed in the United States. The nomination for an Oscar for *Forget Venice* crowned her international

Mariangela Melato's talent is best revealed in films directed by Lina Wertmüller.

success. Between the end of the seventies and the beginning of the eighties Melato was ready to make the big leap into American cinema.

Ridley Scott gave her a screen test for *Alien* and the role was lost by a hair's breadth to Sigourney Weaver. Excellent also was her screen test for Alan Pakula's *Sophie's Choice*, though this time Meryl Streep ran away with it. Mariangela would have been perfect for both of these roles. Dino De Laurentis encouraged her to give American life a try, which she did. She also attended intensive diction courses. Unfortunately, the only movie she would have to show for all these efforts would be *So Fine* (1981), which she considered a disaster. Moreover, to make this awful comedy she had been obliged to refuse to play *Macbeth* on stage with Vittorio Gassman. This was the last straw for her. An anti-star, stubbornly single, totally uninterested in marriage, Mariangela was detached from the middle-class values of her counterparts and lived a love story that lasted nine years with the anti-conformist entertainer Renzo Arbore. In the mid-eighties there was gossip of a romance with actor-singer Giorgio Gaber, her frequent partner on the stage. She denied this and built a wall of silence around her private life.

She was the great black sheep of Italian show biz. A big question mark. In 1985 she refused an interesting offer from the RAI Italian television network to host the most popular talk show in Italy, "Domenica In" as a replacement for the nation's TV star Pippo Baudo. She also declined another substitution on air for the famous entertainer Raffaella Carrà. She instead accepted to perform as a ballerina in the TV show *Al Paradise* in the role of a music hall singer in the TV movie by Sandro Bolchi *Lulù* (1986), where she sings, dances and even feigns a strip-tease.

Florinda Bolkan

A face with a wild kind of beauty, severe, with bony features, a bit masculine, with the body of a tall and lanky fashion model.

A cascade of pitch black hair over skin the color of ebony. Cheekbones as high as an Indian's. Her beauty was glamorous, arrogant, bold. A fine woman, a cosmopolitan myth, a high society jet-setter more than actress, Florinda was one of the seven wonders of the world between the end of the sixties and the beginning of the seventies.

This 1968 Venus was also admired by the feminists because of her strength, she was a winner with guts, and certainly didn't need any man to help her get through life. However, she was too aristocratic to mix with the masses. On the screen she was the icy lady of luxury; beautiful, distant, and a snob. And yet she came from one of the poorest countries on earth, and was born in Uruburetama, a city in the state of Céara, in northeastern Brazil, on the borders of Amazonia. She was born on February 5, 1941. "We Brazilians are proud of having mixed blood. In all of us there is some Portuguese, some Italian, a bit of German, mixed with our Indian blood." In her family there were four sisters, all very beautiful. When she was a little girl, Florinda moved with her family to Rio de Janeiro. Her father was the writer and poet, Soares Bulcao (pronounced *Bolkan*), who also went into politics. Elected as a deputy, he was one of the first to fight for the preservation of the Amazonian forest. However, he died when he was still young, forcing the four Bulcao sisters to start working at an early age.

Florinda went from one job to another from clerk to secretary, then hostess on the

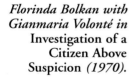

Florinda Bolkan with Gianmaria Volonté in **Investigation of a Citizen Above Suspicion** *(1970).*

Brazilian airline Varig. "I traveled back and forth preaching about how beautiful my country was and how comfortable its flights were," she says.

Finally, a picture of Florinda was chosen for a poster in Varig's advertising campaign in Europe. In Italy, France, Germany, Great Britain, on the streets or in magazines, there was beautiful Florinda telling you, "I am Brazil." She didn't go unnoticed.

In 1963 Florinda married the mature playboy Francis Forbes, an extremely short-lived relationship. She moved to Paris, went to the Sorbonne in the years immediately before the general protest of the sixties. She traveled around the world becoming an international socialite. In the mid-sixties, before getting into movies, she was already a very talked-about woman, almost as much as Jacqueline Kennedy. She attended the most exclusive salons. Then in Ischia, she met Luchino Visconti.

Fascinated by her androgynous and wild beauty, Visconti gave her a three-day screen test in 1967 and offered her the part as Olga, Helmut Berger's lover, in *La caduta degli dei* (1969) *(The Damned)*, a mixture of lewdness, corruption and a melancholic sense of beauty, where the men are transvestites of Lili Marlene and the women have hearts of stone.

However, it was Venetian countess Marina Cicogna, the go-getter producer and owner of Euro International Film, who would actually launch Florinda, putting her on contract and, between 1968 and 1971, sponsoring a series of star vehicles specially designed for her friend, from *Metti una sera a cena* [Sit an evening down to dinner] (1969) to *Indagine su un cittadino al di sopra di ogni sospetto* (1970) *(Investigation of a Citizen above Suspicion)*. There were rumors that Marina Cicogna – a romantic and decadent personage – had made Florinda her lover as well as her protégé. "She is still my best friend and my manager" explained the Brazilian actress in 1983. In an interview of the same year, the journalist Catherine Spaak (for the June 28, 1983 issue of the weekly *Amica)*, questioned her incessantly, without mentioning any names, about what she thought of bi-sexuality: "What does it mean for a woman to love another woman?"

With Helmut Berger, Florinda embodied the bi-sexual myth of angels. Her cold beauty exuded a scent of scandal. She made other people's marriages tremble (Liz Taylor and Richard Burton's); she made love with two men at once *(Metti una sera a cena);* she flirted with women. For her, movies were only a wonderful life accident. "After having seen *Metti una sera a cena* I understood I wasn't Eleonora Duse" she would say when she was over forty, with her movie career a thing of the past.

Her greatest performance was given in *Anonimo veneziano* (1970) *(The Anonymous Venetian)*, meant to be the Italian answer to the romantic tearjerker *Love Story* of the same year. Her fate was once again linked with Venice: her high-class looks mingled with the decadent beauty of the city. The very handsome Tony Musante is a musician condemned to die of an incurable disease. Florinda is his wife, though they are separated, who has made a new life elsewhere. They meet again, one dark autumn in Venice, return to the places where they had once known happiness, and make love for the last time. Fate, catharsis and eternal love (in Italy divorce has only just been legalized).

On the screen, hidden behind her flamboyant beauty, her acting was slightly frigid. A star by vocation, an actress purely by chance, the peak of Bolkan's career lasted five years with movies produced by Marina Cicogna and directed by the élite of Italian "progressive" cinema intelligentsia: Visconti, Petri, Patroni Griffi, Vittorio De Sica, Giannetti, Mingozzi, Salerno. Then the quick plunge into B-movie status.

She left Italy, her adopted movie homeland, after *Una breve vacanza* [A brief vacation] (1973) and moved to London. She traveled the world, squandering the money and prestige earned during the golden years. She bragged about having learnt to pilot planes and wrote a book of poems, published in Brazil at the beginning of the eighties. She appeared in the popular TV movie *La piovra* [The giant squid] as a Sicilian aristocrat (Olga Camastra), the widow of a notable, sent to prison by Commissioner of the Police, again Michele Placido, because of dealings with the mafia.

In 1992 Florinda published a recipe book in Italy, "Invitation To Try My Favorite Recipes," just in case one evening, at dinner, you feel like following some suggestions from Florinda Bolkan…

Androgynous and ambiguous Florinda Bolkan in Metti una sera a cena *(1969). Here, with Lino Capolicchio.*

Dalila Di Lazzaro

Ice-cold eyes, a just-out-of-bed lioness' mane, triangular face, long thin hands, Dalila Di Lazzaro was the sporty feminist who almost always wore pants. She had a thin sinewy body fit for a high jump champion. Very few curves and tiny breasts. She had winning eyes though, very deep. And that was it. Nervous, a bit stiff, coldish, expressionless, she belonged to that group of physical actresses, former models, who broke into the movies only because they were photogenic.

Her avid movie-going father decided to call her Dalila after seeing the movie *Samson and Delilah* on the day she was born and was completely overwhelmed by Hedy Lamarr's enthralling beauty in the film. Dalila was born into her well-off family from Udine in northern Italy on January 29, 1953. Her father, Attilio Di Lazzaro, a big man nearly two meters tall, had been a boxer in France. As a heavyweight in the thirties he had even challenged Primo Carnera (who was also from the same region of Friuli in northern Italy). Dalila's father had invested his money wisely and when he gave up boxing he joined the police force in his hometown of Udine.

Dalila was a naughty little girl and was expelled from school before even graduating from junior high school. She started working as a hairdresser in a shop owned by her family. At fifteen she got married and had a baby. Her marriage, to a student still studying for his degree, lasted five years.

As a model she appeared in ads for brandy, beauty soap, and stockings. At twenty she left for the United States and fell in with Andy Warhol's entourage. "I was a page in his

Splendid Dalila Di Lazzaro's intensely cold gaze.

court, a sort of Alice in Wonderland," she remembered. She got a part in the movie *Il mostro è in tavola... barone Frankenstein* [The monster is served... baron Frankenstein] co-starring Joe Dallesandro and produced by Carlo Ponti, who had a weakness for Dalila.

It was rumored that she was Ponti's new favorite (maybe his lover too) and he called her the new Sophia Loren. Together with Italy's Sophia she acted in the movie *La pupa del gangster* [The gangster's baby] (1975). "You will be the Greta Garbo of the eighties" Ponti predicted to her. He was perhaps a little too optimistic.

Nevertheless, in the second half of the seventies, Dalila Di Lazzaro was one of the most popular budding actresses in Italy. Only Ornella Muti and Laura Antonelli could outshine her. She was discovered by the talent scout of blossoming beauties, Alberto Lattuada, who had her undress for audiences in *Oh, Serafina!* (1976), an exciting title role in which she plays an heiress who renounces her inheritance to live a life close to nature. The kind industrialist Renato Pozzetto finds her locked up in an asylum and falls in love with her. Dalila shocks the well-brought-up middle-class public as she sits down to lunch with her breasts totally exposed. She is a modern woman, outrageous and uninhibited, who refuses to accept social convention. Luigi Comencini, a great admirer of Di Lazzaro enhanced this feminist image by giving her a part in the cast of his weird thriller *Il gatto* [The cat] (1977), and then the role of a militant mother during the days of youth social protest in *Voltati Eugenio* [Turn around Eugenio] (1980). Refusing to seriously assume any maternal responsibility she declares, "I sleep with whomever I like and whenever I like." A mother by pure chance, she wears jeans, pullovers and tennis shoes, smokes, has an abortion, and demonstrates to slogans such as, "You repressed male pigs, go masturbate in the loo."

After being involved in a plane accident in Jamaica, she swore she would never board a plane again in her life and, in fact, while shooting the French movie *Trois hommes à abattre* (1980), she made the trip Rome-Paris every week by car (then, in the eighties she was obliged to accept a role as an air hostess in the TV series, *International Airport*). Dalila still stuck to her casual look of pants and T-shirts playing Alain Delon's mistress. The beautiful Delon paid homage to her by quipping, "You have the most beautiful ass in the world."

Despite this distinction, and roles in a few important movies, Dalila didn't really hit it big. While Ornella Muti's star was shining brighter and brighter, Di Lazzaro's seemed to be on the wane. Perhaps it was her fear of flying or wrong choices, or the lack of a protective sponsor. She liked to call herself "a

lazy country girl." In fact, even at the peak of her career she made very few movies. She apparently rejected two roles as a James Bond girl in Roger Moore's 007 films. In *Never Say Never Again* (1983) her character (the gorgeous Domino) went to the still unknown Kim Basinger. "I didn't accept since it meant going to Bulgaria and staying away from my son for six months," she explained in an interview.

In 1984, she tried to launch herself as a singer and recorded the album entitled "Extra Love," but her heart really wasn't in it. During the same period she played the lead in one of the first Italian experiments in high definition movies, *Oniricon,* a seven-minute short in which she was the victim of an obsession which became reality.

Nevertheless, by the mid-eighties Dalila Di Lazzaro, as the dismal headmistress of a boarding school in the film *Phenomena* (1985) *(Creepers),* was quickly disappearing from the screens. "They keep offering me obscene scripts" she complained. She started spending money out of her own pocket to buy original material hoping to organize a production on her own, but in vain. Luckily there was TV and parts for her in TV films and series.

She had always been a lazy actress, even slightly apathetic. Moreover, she could afford to take a lot of breaks since she also had a second occupation as a fashion designer for a small company. She mainly designed ceremonial and evening gowns and was also a fashion photographer.

Death suddenly came into her life when her cherished son Cristian was killed in a motorcycle accident on May 19, 1991. He was twenty-two years old. This tragic event again put Dalila on the front page of newspapers of the time, when she immediately began the difficult attempts to have another child. It was rumored that she intended to go to Brussels to be artificially inseminated by donations from the three men she had loved the most in her life (her divorced ex-husband Franco Coccetta, Just Jaeckin, the director of *Emanuelle,* and Fabrizio Messina) deliberately choosing not to know which one of them would actually be the father.

After giving up this idea, she started a legal battle to adopt a child. For, under Italian law, Dalila could not apply for adoption since she was single. She made an appeal to the Constitutional Court which was rejected in 1994, though it paved the way for a possible new law. If single women are one day allowed to adopt children in Italy, this will largely be thanks to Dalila's efforts.

And her movie career? Di Lazzaro wrote screenplays and dreamed of making her own movie based on a story about two women much like *Thelma and Louise.* She would have liked Ornella Muti to co-star with her. In the meantime she consoled herself with bread-and-butter TV movies. The sensational magazine *Novella 2000* revealed her love affair with prince Roffredo Gaetani Lovatelli, famous for having challenged amateur boxer Mickey Rourke in the ring.

THROUGH THE KEYHOLE

When women started undressing, the Revolution was drawing near. In the beginning of the seventies an army of buttocks and bare breasts invaded the Italian movie screens, exalting the voyeurism of Latin males. A true barbarian invasion, comparable to the descent of the Visigoths or the Huns against which, in vain, the Church's voice now railed, threatening ex-communication, condemning through every means at its disposal.

Of course, however, not all buttocks were equal. There were those suitable for "artistic" movies, considered politically acceptable and viewed in respectful silence by audiences of experimental cinema. This cinema bore the official left-wing stamp of approval (the battle against movie censorship was then raging in Parliament and progressive intellectuals were speaking up in defense of "artistic" nudes in the name of authors' freedom of expression). And then, there were the politically indifferent bottoms, the B-movie ones, exposed in mediocre low-budget, quickly-thrown-together productions that flooded the screens of second and third-run theaters on the outskirts of town, and which were viewed amidst whistling, booing, hooting, by an audience that ran the gamut from beefy thugs, jailbirds, soldiers on permission, to embarrassed young boys, truck drivers, or ordinary voyeurs. Whatever the case may be, millions of young men in the sex-phobic and sex-bigoted Italy of the seventies, owed the basics of their sexual education to Barbara Bouchet, Edwige Fenech, Gloria Guida and Femi Benussi.

So, as feminists over megaphones shouted, "Hung-up males go masturbate in the bathroom," a new generation of starlets who specialized in commercial erotic comedies came into its own. They were extremely physical and prolific actresses like Barbara Bouchet, Edwige Fenech, Gloria Guida, Femi Benussi, ex-singer Carmen Villani, Karin Schubert, Marina Malfatti, who rose to stardom overnight, though this recognition might only be in B-movies replete with locker-room humor.

Very often, titles suggested sex-packed scenes galore that the film, the public discovered, did not contain at all. Italian erotic comedy was definitely soft – all words and no action. But wasn't the game of desire, in fact, just that? To promise, to allow just a glimpse, a light touch, sometimes without ever intending to go an inch further?

Alfredo Pea peeps through a keyhole at Edwige Fenech as she undresses in L'insegnante *(1975).*

Edwige Fenech

The titles of Edwige Fenech's films were the most imaginative and risqué Italians had ever witnessed in cinema and which went something like: The Young Woman with the Long, Long Thighs, Big Ubalda Nude and Hot, Gorgeous Antonia First a Nun Then a Demon, The Inconsolable Widow Thanks All Her Consolers... all made during the two-year period 1972-1973. Cunning tongue-twister titles, appetizing plays on words, proded the imaginations and whetted the appetites of male audiences everywhere. In the end, though, it all seemed to amount to little more than a flash of nude flesh under the shower. Lots of flying panties, slips and garters. A few exposed breasts with a large dose of hard breathing.

Nevertheless, in the seventies Edwige Fenech continued to hold the throne as queen of Italian sex movies. Unforgettable female characters were associated with her cunning she-cat personality: the policewoman in such movies as *La poliziotta fa carriera* [The policewoman makes a career] (1976), *La poliziotta della squadra buoncostume* [The vice-squad policewoman] (1979), *La poliziotta a New York* (1981) [The New York policewoman]; the woman soldier in *La soldatessa alla visita militare* [The woman soldier at military inspection] (1977), *La soldatessa alle grandi manovre* [The woman soldier in big manoeuvres] (1978); the schoolteacher in *L'insegnante va in collegio* [Teacher goes to college], *L'insegnante viene a casa* [Teacher comes home] both made in (1978), and finally, the doctor in *La dottoressa del distretto militare* [The woman doctor at military recruiting] (1976). Cheerful little ladies thrown to lewd swinish toughies; at times to nerdy soldiers, at others, to thick-headed students, or even batty riot police, a grotesque Keystone Cops world where Edwige was at home in her roles as a willing and available woman. The concept of sex highlighted in her movies was always quite showy but inoffensive. Lots of naughty things but excusable, as confirmed by the censors who only prohibited them to minors under fourteen. With her sphinx-like smile, she let you peek, desire, but very rarely touch.

Fenech had the delicate oval face of a Renaissance Venus, elegant breasts, feline movements. Her glance was limpid, her eyes gorgeous, something almost oriental about her manner, a fine nose. Also that "international" accent, as Totò called it, with its slightly French tone, suited her image well.

She was born on December 24, 1948 in Bona (now Annaba) in Algeria. The Sfeneks were a well-off family of *pieds-noirs*, that is, Europeans born in North Africa. Her mother was from Sicily but of Venetian origin, her father, a Maltese with a bit of Scottish and a

bit of Czech blood in him too. A real melting pot enriched with the colors, sounds and fragrances of Algeria.

At the tender age of nine Edwige joined the ballet of Annaba. When the revolution broke out in Algeria, the Sfeneks first moved to Tunisia, then to France, settling in Nice. Edwige was a very beautiful and precocious young lady. At fifteen she was already modelling, at seventeen was crowned Miss France, at eighteen had moved to Italy where she got married, and at nineteen was divorced.

Italy became her second home, in some ways even her first, since it was the country that brought her success. After her first appearances on screen, she became the muse as well as companion of a young screenwriter linked to the golden age of mythological movies, Luciano Martino, who at the time was very active in producing low-budget movies. The Martinos, Gennaro Righelli's offspring (the director of the first legendary Italian talkie, *La canzone dell'amore* [Love song], were a family of moviemakers: Luciano's youngest brother, Sergio, had already started a fairly successful career as a film director.

Edwige Fenech is the uncontested queen of the pseudo-sexy Italian comedy of the 1970s.

It was Luciano and Sergio who launched beautiful Edwige into orbit, writing, directing and producing her movies. They invented those lustful titles brimming with fun and desire such as the infamous "Big Ubalda..." The family business took off. These small productions, shot in three weeks, with an approximate cost of 100-150,000,000 lire, cashed in billions. The gimmick was all in the sensational titles and the misleading provocative publicity.

In only two or three years, between 1972 and 1975, Edwige (along with her contemporary Barbara Bouchet) became the living myth of suburban movie theaters. Unlike Barbara Bouchet, she concentrated on putting out great quantities of films, working within the small structure of a family-run and artisanal production company. Edwige also had a son to take care of, Edwin, from a relationship with a French actor (whose identity the actress always refused to reveal) and who lived in Nice, with Edwige's parents. Though she was a militant fighter in the trench battles of Cinecittà studios, at the same time Edwige insisted that she was a conservative, and resided in the fashionable Roman neighborhood of Villa Ada, publicly asserting her staunch anti-feminist convictions.

At the end of the seventies Fenech attempted to escape the B-movies at the origin of her successful career. She played a dual role in *Dottor Jekyll e gentile signora* [Doctor Jekyll and the nice lady] (1979), then the desperate part of a wretched creature in ancient Galilee, a little bit of a hooker, a little bit of a pauper, in *Il ladrone* [The thief] (1980). She was now directed by more well-known directors such as Steno, Festa Campanile, even Dino Risi and Alberto Sordi. Nevertheless, she still was not above accepting roles in sexy Italian-style comedies and declared in a 1979 interview, "I'll go on stripping just as long as my body lets me get away with it."

But it was not only a question of her body. At the beginning of the eighties Italian-style sex comedy was already considered pretty corny. The production companies of B-movies seemed to be in trouble. It was time to set one's sights on new horizons, and TV was now the answer. Edwige gathered her forces and made the leap into the new medium as TV entertainer and showgirl.

In Italian TV showbiz, you had no chance without the help of influential patrons. Edwige, who had always been clever at choosing the right partners at the right time, found a new up-to-date eighties love, Luca Cordero di Montezemolo, a young manager connected to the Fiat group, a holding that controlled the most important companies of that decade: Cinzano, the Soccer World Championship, the soccer home team of the Agnelli family, the "Juventus," and even Ferrari. He was truly more than a good match

and it was difficult to ascertain just how important her status as a "highly placed lady" counted in her success in television.

Sexy comedy didn't suit her new image anymore and in 1982 Edwige refused Tinto Brass' offer to play in the super-erotic movie *La chiave (The Key)* — a part which he offered to a good half of the actresses in Italy before ending up with all-rounder Stefania Sandrelli. Fenech also declined the final outbursts of radical-chic erotism by Salvatore Samperi.

As a lady, nothing was too ambitious for her. She designed clothes and presented her collections to the upper-crust Milanese society. She took up stage drama as the protagonist of *D'amore si muore* [One can die of love], first played on the screen by Silvana Mangano. And more. She wanted to be a top executive like her Montezemolo. And, since no one wanted to risk refusing the demands of a high-society lady, she soon set up her own production company for the RAI (Immagine e Cinema, its plush offices located in the high-class Roman suburb of Parioli). In 1992 she produced a series for Raiuno (Italy's state-owned Channel 1) which she asked Sergio Martino, Luciano's brother, to direct. The tables had turned: now she was the boss giving orders to her ex-director Sergio Martino.

She dreamed of producing movies by famous directors, had a project with Lina Wertmüller in mind, had plans to release blockbusters equal to those of Arnon Milchan, the producer of *Pretty Woman*. She was part of Italy's business élite. Only the rich and beautiful were welcome to her gorgeous villa in Capri.

Shy, attached to traditional family values, but extremely ambitious, Edwige Fenech was the starlet of Italian sex comedy who grew old the most gracefully. In fact, as time went by she seemed to grow even more radiant. Reserved, beautiful, slender, witty, fashionable. Her smile was still enchanting...the miraculous alchemy of power.

Barbara Bouchet

The liveliest starlet of Italian erotic comedy was an actress of German extraction, with an American professional background. A tiny mouth, two naughty little eyes, a foreign accent, and, of course, long thick golden tresses. Her cute cunning little face wasn't really very special. She wasn't particularly photogenic, nor terribly beautiful, nor exceptionally talented either, despite coming from a family in the movie business.

Among these bawdy starlets Barbara Bouchet is the one who undresses the least, but her body is the most well known, though the most inaccessible. In the seventies, her nude scenes are on everybody's mind, but have a mythic quality, often since in her films, other actresses strip in her place and when the scene simply cannot do without a shot of that highly desired bottom, here comes another actress stand-in (though always discreetly). Barbara Bouchet depended heavily on foxy glances and winks given generously in a rather childish way, almost clownlike. Nevertheless, men fell for them just the same.

She was the queen of the erotic movie genre, the one who most openly demanded the title of "sophisticated lady," also because of her Hollywood background, which put her a notch above her rivals. In addition, Barbara married a minor film producer, Luigi Borghese, who tried his best to clean up his wife's cinematic image, creating specially for her in the early eighties more respectable comedies such as: *Per favore occupati d'Amelia* [Please, take care of Amelia] (1981), *Se tutto va bene siamo rovinati* [If all goes well we've had it] (1984), and *Tutti possono arricchire tranne i poveri* [Everyone can get rich except the poor] (1976).

Barbara Bouchet was born in mid-August in the year 1944 in Reichenburg, in Nazi Germany, to a family in the movie business. Her father was a cameraman, her mother an actress from Alsace. At the end of the fifties her family emigrated to the United States where Barbara studied acting, won a few beauty contests and got her start in several small parts in excellent films such as *In Harm's Way* (1965) by Otto Preminger, as Kirk Douglas' flirtatious wife who dies during the tragic attack on Pearl Harbor. In *Sweet Charity* (1969) Bob Fosse makes her into a snobbish starlet. Finally, in *Casino Royal* (1967), directed by John Huston and several other directors, she plays the legendary Moneypenny, the secret agent's multi-talented secretary.

Nevertheless, it was in Italy that Bouchet found her paradise. She arrived at the end of the sixties with that somewhat exotic flair only Hollywood could bestow and was an immediate success. Five movies in 1970, six in 1971, and eight in 1972. In a few months she was the darling of low-budget Italian movie productions everywhere. Why? National production was churning out B-movies at an incredible rate. And, though Bouchet was an actress who was professional, pretty, and could boast a more-than-respectable acting pedigree, she decided to accept these low-calibre offers to take over the Italian market. She even accepted risqué parts her counterparts refused out of modesty such as *Una cavalla tutta nuda* [The totally nude mare] (1972), a collection of fourteenth-century tales with an erotic twist, in which Barbara Bouchet plays the lead part. Leopoldo Trieste, a rather dim-witted farmer, lets himself be tricked by the mercenary, Don Backy, who convinces the poor man that he can turn his beautiful young wife, Barbara Bouchet, into a mare. And presto! Here we find our fair Barbara in a stable completely nude among fodder, barrels, and horses. She

even goes down on all fours, stark naked, as she contentedly nibbles on some straw. Censors cut the most outrageous scenes, but a few men's magazines got hold of the stills and they were published, much to their readers' delight.

Barbara even undresses in detective movies. In *Milano calibro 9* [Milan calibre 9] (1972) she appears in a nightclub scene wearing a completely transparent two-piece suit and then totally nude in bed with Gastone Moschin.

Only towards 1975 does she start to worry about her cinematic respectability, accepting parts in such films as *Per le antiche scale (Down the Ancient Staircase)* and comedies like *L'anatra all'arancia (Duck in Orange Sauce), Come perdere una moglie e trovare un'amante* [How to lose a wife and find a mistress] (1978), *Liquirizia* [Liquorice] (1979), *Sono fotogenico* [I'm photogenic] (1980). In 1981, at thirty-seven, she said good-bye to the Italian movie world with a final appearance in *Spaghetti a mezzanotte* [Spaghetti at midnight]. She would continue to capitalize on the myth of her beauty and body which had brought her such fortune. She discovered the big business of aerobics, opening her own gym in the chic Roman suburb of Parioli, and devoted herself to teaching well-off Italian ladies how to be beautiful and seductive even after forty.

Above: *Barbara Bouchet's erotic appeal in the disturbing* Down the Ancient Staircase *(1975).*
Below: *Deliciously nude, Bouchet plays at being uninhibited and teases Ugo Tognazzi's manly appetite in* Duck in Orange Sauce *(1975).*

Gloria Guida

Poised between childish candor and lustful sensuality, Gloria Guida was the turbo-engine girl. Many of the titles of her movies were puns based on this ambiguity of her blossoming teenage image. She made her debut in *La ragazzina* [The young girl] (1974), then appeared in the movies *La minorenne* [The minor] also in 1974, *La ragazza alla pari* [Au pair girl] (1976), and *La novizia* [The novice] (1975), following *Quell'età maliziosa* [That malicious age] (1975). She was the answer to Barbara Bouchet's full-blown femininity, the schoolgirl of *La liceale* [The high school girl] of 1975, *La liceale nella classe dei ripetenti* [The high school girl in the class of repeaters], *La liceale seduce i professori* [The high school girl seduces her teachers], and *La liceale, il diavolo e l'acquasanta* [The high school girl, the devil and holy water], all made in the two-year period 1978-79.

In her there was the typical sunny sensuality of women from the north-central region of Italy called Emilia. She was the tomato sauce-flavored Viking: big shiny eyes, a natural kind of beauty, quite ordinary in fact, like a salesgirl.

Her sex appeal didn't consist of the sophisticated pep of a Barbara Bouchet or the French accent of an Edwige Fenech. The secret was a naughty bold little girl playing at sex: a provocative femininity, even sometimes a little vulgar, and this was precisely what the male population of Gloria Guida's fans were looking for at the peak of her short-lived career, that lasted from 1974 to 1980.

Born on November 19, 1955 in Merano, from Bolognese parents, Gloria grew up sharing the same enthusiasm as the other girls of her age for pop tunes.

She was launched by Silvio Amadio and Mario Imperoli, two cunning old devils of the B-movie scene. Her world was that of very low-budget productions, with their

beaches, sunbathing, blue-jeans, bare breasts galore, showers and bubble baths. While Barbara Bouchet and Edwige Fenech play the parts of flirtatious wives, Gloria Guida has absolutely no intention of getting married. She is always going to be the eternal schoolgirl on her bench. She remains in high school until twenty and even twenty-five, much like Irasema Dilian of the Fascist "white telephone" period, with the difference that Guida lets everyone in class touch her bottom, especially that old devil Lino Banfi.

A gossip magazine reported that Gloria Guida even came to orgasm filming her love scenes. The easy mythology of the seventies. "Sex is already so unimportant to me in real life, imagine what it means to me on the set," she would say in a 1976 interview. However, her face did have an animal-like sensuality, like a lizard's, lustful in a natural way. A dirty mouth half smudged with sex, half with jam. A kinky animal, halfway between a child and a hooker: a seventies Lolita. And this look would make her famous.

In everyday life she was very far from the girl who shows off this freakish sexy-child image on the screen. "I can't wait for Sundays to go home to Mom," she confessed, with nothing more on her mind than tortelli and ravioli. Unlike many of her counterparts, Gloria Guida wasn't terribly ambitious at all, which probably explains her very short career, with no lining up for TV parts or metamorphosis into a high society lady.

And thus in 1982, after only eight years in the movies, she took her leave. In the last seasons of her short career she finally did get to act in more than just B-movies, and enjoyed appearing in more challenging productions such as *Bollenti spiriti* [Boiling spirits] (1981) directed by Giorgio Capitani and *Sesso e volentieri* [Sex and volunteers] (1982) by Dino Risi. In these movies she co-stars with Johnny Dorelli, her almost constant partner (even in real life) since 1980, on screen and on stage. In fact, they actually met on stage, performing together in the musical comedy *Accendiamo la lampada* [Let's switch on the lights] at the Sistina Theater, the Roman temple of musicals, where Gloria got the chance to show what a complete performer she was, acting, dancing, and singing. They would experience everything together: movies, TV series, variety, radio programs. And, of course, eventually a child. Everyone considered them the perfect couple. On April 11, 1984 Gloria Guida gave birth to a baby girl, Guendalina. This was the third child for Johnny Dorelli who had also had children with two other women, the stars Lauretta Masiero and Catherine Spaak. When he started going gray, though, even Johnny Dorelli was seduced by the firm body of the "high school girl."

THE GIANTESSES

Here come the new *maggiorate*, generously endowed daughters of the eighties, the decade which signalled a new Italian pride in another swelling economic boom, more pervasive than that of the sixties. Everyone spent, consumed, invested, corrupted. Above all, expanded. For Italy, the sky was the limit. As the sailboat "Azzurra" flashed over the waves, billions were spent in preparation for the World Soccer Games (the ones managed by Edwige Fenech's boyfriend Luca Di Montezemolo), and new stadiums were built, old highways became superhighways bigger and better than ever. The new female myths also had to reflect this larger-than-life greatness, excessiveness. Like Loren and Lollo, their measurements were overpowering and represented the sexual appetites of giants during a period of almost nightmarish economic well-being.

They were known as Lory De Santo, Carmen Russo, Serena Grandi, Francesca Dellera, Deborah Caprioglio, with such close runners-up as Claudia Koll, and the ultra-Mediterranean beauty Maria Grazia Cucinotta. The TV screen gave audiences Pamela Prati, Alba Parietti, Valeria Marini (launched in the movies by Bigas Luna, the Spanish Tinto Brass). To describe them as "exuberant" would have been an understatement. Breasts like zeppelins, inflated lips, the smack of silicone everywhere.

There was also the new TV beauty Italians were discovering on the American-style programs of Silvio Berlusconi's networks which were rapidly sweeping away the old-fashioned modesty of the RAI chorus girls, with flouncing busts squeezed into impossible microscopic bras. Fast food seduction. A new kind of turkey-woman was all the rage, hypertrophic, inflated to what seemed dangerously close to the bursting point.

These stars were impossible to fit into the narrow spaces of reality. Their beauty was so dazzling they became abstract symbols, unimaginable in the roles of ordinary women. They were exclusively dream girls. It was no accident that many of them were discovered by that woman dreamer par excellence Tinto Brass, who, in his cinematic-sex laboratory, was busy experimenting with new models of transgression.

Serena Grandi or the return of the pin-up **maggiorata.**

Serena Grandi

Here was someone who literally moaned sex. Her vital statistics were those of a pure-bred *maggiorata* in all her glory. Roaringly erotic, small, penetrating eyes, heart-shaped little mouth, curly hair, the vocation of an Italian geisha, a wasplike waist, thighs like giant sausages, breasts pumped up with Lambrusco wine to quench her thirsty lovers. Her sexuality was like a Mother's Day celebration.

Serena's uniform: garters and a bathrobe. Panties? Almost never, as in the movie that set her in orbit, *Miranda* (1985). For her mind-boggling curves, Tinto Brass moves the story of Goldoni's tavern girl to Romagna in the forties, amidst boogie-woogie and mambo, raising the ghost of Silvana Mangano.

Born in Bologna on March 23, 1958, Serena Grandi was the daughter of a housewife and a steadfastly uncorruptible police marshal. He could never be persuaded to see the films that had made his daughter famous. Her mother, on the other hand, had always nurtured a secret dream: as a girl she had been stopped in the street by Pietro Germi and was offered a screen test for *Il ferroviere (Man of Iron)* (1956), but being too shy, she had refused and regretted it all her life.

The Grandi family spent their winters in Bologna, but in the summer they moved to Fellini's Rimini where the splendors of the Grand Hotel and the myth of Gradisca were still alive. Serena was a tomboy: "I often had very short hair and up to the age of three I stomped around the beach in the nude since my mother never dressed me in a bathing suit. From three until nine I only wore swimming shorts. In those days I was one of the boys." To be like her policeman father, Serena played with guns.

Physically precocious, at ten she was 5'8". At eleven she already wore a cup C. "My first contact

Serena Grandi, even as an impetuous common girl is still provocatively sexy.

with the movie world? In cinema toilets where I made love, since when you were fifteen in those days there was never anywhere else to go." These were the declarations made by Serena Grandi (and later denied) in the first interviews she gave after becoming a box-office success.

In 1980 Serena left Bologna for Rome to seek her fortune after several years working in a medical laboratory. (The image of her ample *maggiorata* body wrapped in a white medic's uniform conjures up the medical roles played by Edwige Fenech). She wanted to act, sing, and dance, exploit her deluxe chassis and undiscovered talents. Her torturous road to success passed through radio and commercial television. Serena also worked in theater, minor parts with Antonella Steni, a few lines for 47,000 lire a night. She found minuscule parts in low-budget films like *Teste di quoio* [Leather heads] (1981), *Sturmtruppen 2* (1982), and *Malamore* (1982) where she made love with a dwarf. Her "Thousand-and-One-Nights" body looked good on the slick, for-men-only magazine covers and risqué calendars. She became "Miss Fast Food" on the Berlusconi TV variety show *Drive In*. Strapless bras and traditional lingerie, memories of the fifties and echoes of the "big" *maggiorata* women. One evening she had to fill in for music hall singer Carmen Russo. Her appearance didn't go unnoticed.

In early 1983 the starlet was the talk of the town because of her affair with singer Gianni Morandi, a veteran of the sixties, on the crest of a new comeback.

Having emerged from anonymity, Serena took her gorgeous body on a summer tour of Italian discos with her Serena Grandi Show. But it took Tinto Brass to transform her into a real star in the film *Miranda*. The Venetian director had spotted Serena Grandi while preparing a movie whose production was later postponed based on Mario Soldati's book *Lettere da Capri* [Letters from Capri] (which would become *Capriccio*, a star vehicle for the future diva Francesca Dellera). "I chose her," Brass explained, "because she was a woman with big, healthy appetites. She liked to drink, eat, look and touch, but also to be touched and sniffed. For her, lovemaking was a big feast." *Miranda* was not only the title role, but it was also a myth of the new erotic cinema. Brass, master of the erotic, was continuing in the wake of his scandalous cult movie *La chiave* (1983) *(The Key)*. He wanted women of giant sexuality: inflated breasts, generous hips, and large legs spread wide – provocative and scandalous images against an elegant soft-core setting.

To make *Miranda*, Serena voluntarily gained sixteen pounds, almost as much as Robert De Niro in *Raging Bull* (1980)! Miranda, the innkeeper, in a very free adaptation from Goldoni's masterpiece, runs a country establishment where men from all walks of life stop in, attracted by the exciting "merchandise" of its owner. It is wartime and her husband Gino has been sent to the front. While waiting for his return, the good hostess skillfully runs the family business juggling bills, bank drafts and bed sheets, in a hullaballoo of riotious sex. Serena puts a disarming vulgarity into play, a kind of merry wickedness. Her exchanges with the consul (played by Franco Interlenghi) invariably wind up with her hands in his pants. She is billed "More Wicked than Trucula Bon Bon," the star of the famous nightclub Crazy Horse.

The films of Brass were contemplative and sly, not without subtle refinement and ferocious irony. Disdained by the critics, the film was a tremendous box-office success and the almost unknown Serena Grandi was suddenly a celebrity. The newspapers announced the return of the voluptuous *maggiorata*.

She exploited the sex myth that Brass had invented for her and called herself a superwoman in search of a superman: "Someone who has economic and physical power too, like a Berlusconi, a Montezemolo, a De Benedetti if they are also super-sexed. I know there are only a few around, and I have had those few. I call them 'champions' since they have been able to meet my superwoman needs." Exactly like the innkeeper Miranda, she boasted of her exceptional sexual prowess. "The bed is my natural habitat, just as Berlusconi's is the Board of Directors conference room. I would love to have a bed in the form of a boxing ring and hold at least one match there daily," she declared. In an interview with the women's weekly *Novella 2000* she talked about a night she had spent in bed with two boxers. "It was a contest of physical endurance. In the end, I wore them out." Serena deliberately sought scandal, as if to confirm the provocative success of *Miranda*. One year later she would deny it all. "I was just starting out. I needed to punch the public in the stomach and make them notice me. But it was all untrue." And she did a complete about-face. In 1986 in Rimini she married Beppe Ercole, the well-known Roman antique dealer and ex-playboy of the Rome *dolce vita* scene.

But Serena's strong point was still her sexy performances, above all her legendary bust which was insured for a billion lire. "It costs me ten million a year out of my own pocket," the actress sighed. The glories of a diva had its ups and downs. One admirer sent her a telegram and swore he was ready to come to Rome from Piedmont on foot for her. But unfortunately the roles that Grandi played after *Miranda*, added nothing new to her myth. She shot a disappointing movie version of Italo Svevo's novel *Senilità* [Senility] entitled *Desiderando Giulia* [Desiring Giulia] (1986). She entrusted herself to Gianfranco Minigozzi in the impossible attempt at an artistic erotic film, *L'iniziazione* [The initiation] (1986). She tread the path of the erotic thriller with *Le foto di Gioia* [Joy's photos] (1987). She even had a go at a film with that experienced and still successful old lion Dino Risi.

Grandi separated from her husband in 1993 (they had had a child, Eduardo, in 1990). The ex-playboy Beppe Ercole was jealous of his wife in erotic movies, a banal scenario. Serena would go down in movie history as the showiest monument to the greatness of the Italy of the eighties, as strident as she was futile, the embodiment of Eros.

Francesca Dellera

Tinto Brass created Serena Grandi from nothing, gave her life and set her loose in the world. On the second day, after he had rested, he took another handful of clay and fashioned Francesca Dellera.

After *Miranda*, Tinto Brass invented another sex queen for his movie *Capriccio* (*Letters From Capri*), a twenty-one-year-old from Latina, an upcoming fashion model discovered in a Parioli disco by the producer Giovanni Bertolucci. "I never accepted to pose nude when I was a photomodel," Francesca explained, "but the quality of the film, Tinto Brass' charisma, and the team spirit on the set, relieved all my anxieties." She was called the "new Serena Grandi." For the very optimistic she was "the new Ava Gardner." She accepted the comparison with Gardner, but rejected the one with Grandi: "We have nothing in common, not even my little fingernail! I don't even find her sexy." Furthermore, Francesca Dellera was nine years younger than Serena Grandi and felt that she belonged to the younger generation. She put a lot of emphasis on "*We girls* of today...".

Twenty-one, long, long legs on imperative high heels, a tiny waist, a model's gait, and heavy thighs just made for black stockings; a bust of normal proportions but protuberant, held high without the help of a bra. She had an oval face, an infantile voice, a straight nose and a large, impudent mouth, fleshy lips, exaggeratedly swollen (with silicone retouching, said the malicious). All the marks of an, excessive, bombastic, slightly rhetorical beauty.

Her vital statistics were not the mind-boggling ones of a Serena Grandi. But Francesca Dellera bore the mark of the divas of the past: the way she posed, the way she

Another "ultra" Italian **maggiorata,** *Francesca Dellera, the fetish actress of directors such as Tinto Brass and Marco Ferreri. With Sergio Castellitto in* **La carne** *(1991).*

walked, her enigmatic smile, her disdainful mouth – something grandiose that put her in supernatural contact with such timeless greats as Francesca Bertini and Sophia Loren whose press agent, Enrico Lucherini, she shared.

Born on October 2, 1966 in Rome, her real name was Francesca Cervellera. While growing up in Latina with her housewife-mother, her sister, and chartered-accountant father, her father went through a mystic crisis and turned to Buddhism. He left Latina, traveling extensively in India and becoming a follower of the Indian guru Sri Baba. (In 1991 in *La carne* [Flesh], Francesca played the role of a follower of the Indian guru Sri Nanda).

In high school all the boys were madly in love with her. Francesca left Latina and went to Rome to work as a model. She participated in promotional campaigns for Coca-Cola, Stefanel, Revlon and many other companies. She got her start in movies as a look-alike for Kelly Le Brock, famous for an imitation of Marilyn Monroe in *The Woman in Red* in 1984 in *Grandi magazzini (Department stores)*. But her acting debut was confirmed by appearances on the pages of photoplay magazines (just like Sophia Loren). Under the stage name Francesca Lisi La Dellera, she appeared on the cover of the monthly issue of *Darling* as the heroine of the photoplay *Ritorno a Villa dei Gelsi* [Return to the Gelsi villa]. Her hair was blonde and she did not yet have those enormous lips which would be the trademark of her sex appeal.

According to informed sources, Francesca still slept with her stuffed teddy bear while

shooting the super-erotic film *Capriccio* (1987). Glued in her diary, a simple school notebook, were two picture cards: one of Snoopy, and the other of Tom and Jerry. Francesca had her young age going for her. Brass provocatively kept lowering the age of his nymphs: he went from the "old hen" Stefania Sandrelli in *The Key*, to the bursting twenty-seven-year-old Serena Grandi in *Miranda,* and, finally, to the twenty-one-year-old Francesca Dellera and her erect little breasts in *Capriccio.* From soap to sexy artistic cinema was not as big a leap as it may seem. Tinto Brass continued to pursue a deluxe and slick type of eroticism that recalled the esthetic standards of high-class advertising. *Capriccio* was a great box-office hit. Dellera became the new queen of eroticism and was asked to participate in TV discussions on seduction on the program *Nove settimane e mezzo* (1986) [9 ½ Weeks] on television's Canale 5.

But Francesca's fiancé, Hubertus Van Doren, a Dutch millionaire known as the "tulip king," didn't like *Capriccio.* He had renamed a precious new hybrid flower after his beloved Francesca. Shaken by her appearance as a sex symbol, he left her. Dellera's love life lived up to that of all famous divas and was a regular topic in popular weeklies. There was talk that she and Gianni Boncompagni were in love, that he had often shown up on the set of *Capriccio* laden with spectacular bouquets of red roses. On her list of supposed lovers there was also the Neapolitan producer Ciro Ippolito, the singer Prince, Emanuele Filiberto (the scion of the house of Savoy and would-be heir to the Italian throne), the American model Zane O'Donnell, the irresistibly handsome Christophe Lambert, and even Silvio Berlusconi.

There can be no doubt that Francesca Dellera, with her retro style, was an actress that Berlusconi liked very much. For Canale 5 she first made *La romana* [The Roman woman] (a remake of Zampa's movie), then *La bugiarda* [The liar] (a remake of Comencini's), interpreting roles that had first been played by the two celebrated beauties, Gina Lollobrigida and Catherine Spaak. In the television version of *La romana* (1988), Gina Lollobrigida, then in her sixties, played the role of her mother. On and off the set there were violent explosions, quarrels, temper tantrums in the best traditions of film stardom. Lollo went on the attack, "I saw Dellera in *Capriccio* and it's better if I don't say what I thought of it. In *La romana,* the live sound take was impossible because of her inexperience and it was her fault that I had to re-dub a part that I had acted with such intensity as to suffer physically from it." Francesca Dellera retaliated: "I hope I don't grow old like Lollo who continues to pretend to be a young girl and can't manage to get on with her life."

Her voice brought Francesca Dellera a lot of criticism for its rather petulant tone and lack of inflection. She consoled herself with advertising stints. In 1989 she made a big ad for the Italiana Petrol company for which she got paid the exaggerated figure of 950 million lire (more than Lollobrigida from Moulinex blenders or Ornella Muti from Lux beauty soap). Directed by Maurizio Nichetti she imitated the cartoon temptress Jessica Rabbit driving a cartoon automobile in the movie *Who Framed Roger Rabbit?* (1988).

Francesca continued to recycle movie history. She made up like Ava Gardner. Her Jessica Rabbit imitation was in itself an imitation of the vamps of the forties. Dellera was a living fossil of film stardom. Like the mastodonic billboards of Anita Ekberg in the episode *Temptation of Dr. Antonio* in *Boccaccio '70* (1962), Francesca Dellera appeared almost completely nude in gigantic billboards along Italian motorways, while drivers went careering out of control, hypnotized by her Lepel lingerie.

But her stardom as a femme fatale also brought her some unpleasantness. Dellera became the favorite target of Cinzia Leone who did caricatures of her on TV and made Francesca furious. Marco Ferreri joked with Dellera's myth, making her the protagonist of *La carne* [Flesh] where the beautiful woman-object is literally devoured by her lover Sergio Castellitto (who keeps her corpse in the fridge between champagne and cans of tuna – a great sex orgy that concludes in a very symbolic meal).

A success at the Cannes Film Festival, *La carne* opened the doors of French cinema to Dellera. Francesca moved to Paris, threw herself into the much gossiped-about love affair with Christophe Lambert and made *L'ours en peluche* [The stuffed teddy bear] (1993) with Alain Delon. In the film, she plays a wayward lawless young girl, who falls in love with a much older man, a doctor, who is still extremely appealing.

Strangely enough, though Dellera only made a few films, she still stayed on the crest of the wave: she was one of those rare actresses who didn't even need cinema to be a big star. In a 1993 survey by the magazine *Fashion* on European sex symbols, Francesca Dellera and Claudia Cardinale were given first place. According to another survey in December 1994, Dellera and Ornella Muti were the only Italian stars cited. In 1995 Francesca's picture appeared on the cover of the German weekly *Stern* (a still from the movie *La romana*) to illustrate a feature article on prostitution. Francesca was not at all offended. She was very aware of the value of publicity.

Maria Grazia Cucinotta

What a destiny! Her father was a post-office clerk, her sister and brother were too. And she, after having begun a successful career as a fashion model, married a very special post office employee – Massimo Troisi, Pablo Neruda's "postman." And she became famous.

This was the story of Maria Grazia Cucinotta, the Sicilian beauty from Messina, and now the new ambassadress of Mediterranean beauty subsequent to the American success of *Il postino* (1995) *(The Postman)*, with its Oscar nomination for best picture. Dark featured as a mussel shell, a body of top-model perfection, tall, svelte, a kind of black flamingo. A fleshy mouth of the kind that gives birth to obsessions, tapered hands, determined eyes – in short, a photogenic thoroughbred. She is compared to Sophia Loren with whom she shares the same explosive beauty.

At fifteen she left Messina with only a few coins in her pocket to join her brother Tonino – ten years her senior – in Brescia, and tried her luck on the runways of Milanese fashion shows, a cruel world in which, as she would later comment, "You either break through like Cindy Crawford, or you feel no more than a clothes hanger." Eventually she rose from the ranks of the ordinary models and worked the

Maria Grazia Cucinotta is the latest sexy discovery of Italian movies.

world over, traveling as far as China. But by modelling standards, she was actually too shapely. "My bust was too big. I was even going to have it reduced just to be able to keep on working in Milan," Maria Grazia remembers.

She got into Italian TV as an MC's assistant on some quite well-known shows. On the extremely popular Saturday night program *Fantastico,* she appeared together with Nathalie, who would be Massimo Troisi's girlfriend at the time of *The Postman.* Maria Grazia also had a role as a lovely statue in *Indietro tutta,* the off-beat show created by Renzo Arbore where she was an odalisque. And thus was born the myth of Cucinotta's Mediterranean beauty. She began getting small parts in modest films such as *Vacanze di Natale 90* [Christmas vacation 90].

But her face became famous even before her name through TV commercials. She made about fifty of them for big companies not only in Italy but also abroad where she became the symbol of Mediterranean loveliness. She was even coupled with Gérard Dépardieu in a commercial directed by Ridley Scott. She advertised Barilla pasta for the international market and played a fiery, impetuous young woman who, during an argument with her fiancé, is calmed down by Depardieu brandishing a plate of spaghetti.

Cucinotta was truly an actress of the nineties. Contrary to what had normally happened in the past, it was now the movies that capitalized on the popularity of stars in television commercials and shows. Her face was famous, her name still unknown. But when news spread that Massimo Troisi had

chosen her for the female lead in *The Postman,* her name was on everyone's lips. He called her "a little bundle of nerves" because of her fears and anxieties on the set.

Bitter but intense, Cucinotta (a cacophonous name and a mouthful, in the same way as the name Lollobrigida) conquered the public in her role as the tavern-owner Beatrice, a reserved islander, closed and proud, who is won over by the poetic innocence of the postman created by Troisi. Italians were fascinated by her overwhelmingly photogenic beauty and, when *The Postman* was announced among the five movies nominated for an Oscar, Americans too discovered the power of Maria Grazia Cucinotta.

Offers began to pour in. She was a photo-play actress in Leonardo Pieraccioni's first film *I laureati* [The graduates]. In *El dia de la bestia* [The day of the beast] by the transgressive Spanish director Alex de la Iglesia, Cucinotta was even a platinum blonde. But Maurizio Ponzi turned her back into a Mediterranean-type in *Italiani* [Italians], where the poor Cucinotta must give birth to a child in a train compartment. In 1995 she was one of the most popular Italian actresses in both movies and television. But her acting career is still too young to draw any conclusions today. Will she be the star of the year 2000? Two things remain from her career as a fashion model: her wonderful friendship with Giorgio Armani, with whom she is still bound under exclusive contract, and her miraculous photogenic quality that keeps her even more present on magazine covers than on the screen.

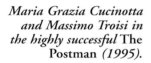

Maria Grazia Cucinotta and Massimo Troisi in the highly successful **The Postman** *(1995).*

REIGNING LADIES OF CINECITTÀ

The end of the sixties and early seventies, with its revolutionary charge of general dissent, feminism, student uprisings and armed struggles, seemed unable to touch the intangible charisma of some screen stars. Many others, however, were swept away by the revolutionary changes in tastes and styles and slowly disappeared from the screens, only to be glimpsed fleetingly in B-movies or an occasional minor role on TV.

Nothing lasts forever. The years passed, wrinkles began taking their toll on the most flawless beauties of Cinecittà. But whether out of self-pity or blind vanity, some of the stars could not bring themselves to play the mother roles or character parts then offered to them. Thus Rossi Drago, Schiaffino, Lollobrigida, Franca Marzi, and Gianna Maria Canale preferred to say good-bye to the set as did the "unfortunate but lovely girls" Allasio, De Luca and Panaro. Not all had the serenity necessary to express themselves in their new status as mature women. The great Alida Valli was one of the few with the courage to appear, considerably uglied, first in *Berlinguer ti voglio bene* [Berlinguer I love you] (1977), and then in *Sogni mostruosamente proibiti* [Dreams monstruously forbidden] (1982). She accepted roles as a mother and even as a grandmother in films such as *La bocca* [Mouth] (1991). Sandra Milo simply wouldn't give up, and was often a favorite topic of gossip for her appearances as a television entertainer or her presumed love affair with a South American president.

Valentina Cortese appeared less and less in films, but in 1973 seized the exceptional opportunity to act in François Truffaut's *Day for Night* as an unforgettable Séverine, an absent-minded actress at the end of her career (a cruel autobiographical note) who, once on the set, forgets all her lines. It was a role so intensely felt and movingly interpreted that it brought her very close to a first Oscar. Nominated, she lost by a hair's breadth to Ingrid Bergman for the role in *Murder on the Orient Express* (1974). Upon receiving the statuette, Bergman paid public tribute to her Italian counterpart saying, "Valentina, this prize should be yours."

Neither did Lea Masari fear the passing of the years. In *Murmur of the Heart* (1971) Louis Malle gives her a beautiful role as a vigilant, over-anxious mother, though with an animal sensuality capable of awakening her adolescent son's first sexual feelings. Besides incest, she is also quite willing to appear wrinkled as parchment in *Viaggio d'amore* [Voyage of love] (1990), a road movie for the

Two glorious Italian stars of the past.
Above: *Alida Valli in* **La bocca** *(1987).* **Below:** *Valentina Cortese in the famous film by Truffaut,* **Day for Night** *(1973).*

Lea Massari and Omar Sharif in Viaggio d'amore *(1990).*

elderly, as she embarks on a search for bygone days along the Adriatic coast.

Every now and then Giovanna Ralli and Rossana Podestà indulged in small and discreet appearances such as in *C'eravamo tanti amati (We All Loved Each Other So Much)* (1974) or *Segreti, segreti* [Secrets, secrets] (1985). In France, Antonella Lualdi found the recognition she was sometimes denied at home (her daughter Antonellina's star was now, however, twinkling timidly in the background). Sylva Koscina continued a shaky career in some quite popular TV films. Lea Padovani divided her time between the theater, TV, and rare appearances on the screen, as in the movie *Ehrengard* (1982). Lucia Bosè, on rare occasions, abandoned her golden cage in Madrid when a movie happened to tickle her fancy, such as *Violanta* (1977). Caterina Boratto still continued to appear, quite chubby but with her perpetually rosy complexion, in film parts in both TV and theater such as *Primo amore* [First love] (1978) and *Claretta* (1984). Giulietta Masina made a surprise appearance in *Ginger and Fred* (1986), though she was but a nostalgic caricature of herself. Even the great queen, Anna Magnani, could no longer find roles equal to her fame in the early seventies, except for some television parts created by Alfredo Giannetti. Rosanna Schiaffino chose to retire in pampered luxury by the side of her second husband, the industrialist Falck. Carla Gravina pursued a career in Parliament and the stage, leaving the fascination of the set behind her. Nevertheless, other actresses continued to fly high in the industry's skies and held their thrones as the reigning ladies of Cinecittà: Silvana Mangano, Monica Vitti, Claudia Cardinale, Sophia Loren, and Virna Lisi.

Silvana Mangano
[see also p. 74]

Silvana Mangano's total strip-tease in *Teorema* (1968) not only scandalized the Board of Censors but even many of her fans already shaken by their idol's incestuous embraces shared with Franco Citti in *Edipo re* (1967) *(Oedipus Rex)*. These were two "sins" that the sublime Signora De Laurentis would not easily let director Pier Paolo Pasolini live down for a long time. Pasolini wrote her a famous letter to dissipate doubts and bad feelings. Then, almost as if to make amends, he offered her a symbolic part – that of the Virgin Mary in the final scene of *The Decameron* (1971). The Madonna appears to the painter Giotto – played by Pasolini himself – working on the frescos in the church of Santa Chiara in Naples. It is a mystical vision, sacred and asexual, exactly as the maternal Mangano in her dreams wanted to appear to eradicate that hated sex-symbol image.

But besides sainthood in the bosom of a family, Silvana Mangano also dreamed of supreme elegance. Thus, it was perfect to return to the Visconti world that she had already known in the biographical episode of *The Witches* (1976). Tremendous publicity announced the reunion of the "Great Lady of Italian Cinema" and the aristocratic Visconti for the production *Morte a Venezia* (1971) *(Death in Venice)*. It was a role of extreme sensitivity, the mother of Tadzio. Tadzio, the image of disembodied seduction and highest inaccessible beauty. ("You remind me so much of my mother," says Luchino to Silvana, for whom motherhood was the only acceptable mode of femininity.) Dressed in Piero Tosi's early nineteenth-century costumes, Silvana Mangano walks as if on clouds – light and ethereal, transparent and unreal, unapproachable in the noble fascination of a great lady that she emanates. For Visconti, she is an aristocratic Venus who leads and highlights the true object of seduction, Tadzio, the ephebus. It is a restrained and ancillary role, yet absolutely unforgettable.

In 1971, a year of grace for the actress, Mangano worked with her affectionate friend (and silent and tireless suitor) Alberto Sordi again in a deliciously eccentric movie directed by Luigi Comencini, *Lo scopone scientifico* (1972) *(The Scientific Card Player)* one of the last sparks of the great comic tradition, which plays a bristling Bette Davis and leathery Joseph Cotten opposite the two Roman stars. Mangano is a crumpled cleaning woman, wife of a ragseller, with five children to fend for. Every year, punctually, the poor couple take up a challenge to play cards against a rich couple, and every year the poor wretches lose. Sordi and Mangano once again demonstrate their rapport as a comic team unequalled, with the exception perhaps, of Marcello Mastroianni and Sophia Loren. For Mangano it was also a spectacular occasion to break out of the bubble of elegance in which she was kept prisoner.

Before a new encounter with Visconti to play another role of a woman of luxury – that of Cosima von Bülow in the spectacular *Ludwig* (1972) – Silvana gets side-tracked in a totally wrong production: *D'amore si muore* [One dies from love] (1972), based on a play by her friend Giuseppe Patroni Griffi. Of all the cast of this complete disaster, only Silvana manages a good performance, though she is asked to portray a cliché upper middle-class lady, cold and forbidding, almost a caricature of herself. To be taken far more seriously was the character Cosima, created by Visconti, and once again costumed by designer Tosi: a scandalously pushy adulteress, she is composer Richard Wagner's mistress and accomplice in a plan to extort money out of the mentally disturbed king of Bavaria. Unfortunately the strength of Cosima's role, as of all the others in the film, is lost in the meanderings of an endless plot that is completely drowned in its own fascination with history.

Visconti and Tosi once again gave Silvana the touch of elegance in a modern version of an aristocratic lady in *Gruppo di famiglia in un interno* (1974) *(Conversation Piece)*. This disdainful woman was an unusual role for Silvana, a mother with amorous aspirations surrounded by a brood of restless children and morphine-addicted gigolos. Out of respect for Visconti, Silvana accepted the part of a character with whom she had absolutely no affinity, the role being very far from her reserved nature and image of concerned mother.

Then for many years there was total silence. Silvana left Italy to take up a quiet family life in the United States with husband Dino De Laurentis who had set up a new production company there. In 1981 their only son, Federico, heir to the reins of the family, died in an airplane crash. This tragedy triggered off a long period of depression in Mangano's life, aggravated by the failure of her marriage with Dino. Alone, Silvana fell seriously ill and began a long, painful plunge to death. Her daughter Raffaella, now a producer, convinced her to return to the screen with an appearance in the science-fiction world of *Dune* (1948). Here, the beautiful ex-rice picker is unrecognizable, reduced to a shadow of herself, in the part of an oedipal high priestess, Mother Ramallo. Two years later, having left America for good, she went to Madrid to live in a house next to her youngest daughter Francesca.

Surprisingly Mangano returned to the screen in *Dark Eyes* (1987) partnered by a magnificent Marcello Mastroianni. Pale and emaciated, close to death, Silvana drew on her last energies to interpret the part of a magnetic provincial lady. By now the incurable illness within her had reached her lungs. She succumbed to it in December 1989. Her ashes rest in a New York cemetery beside the tomb of her beloved son Federico who, like his mother, seemed to look upon the merry-go-round of the movie world with utter detachment.

Silvana Mangano in **Conversation Piece** *(1974).*

Monica Vitti

[see also p. 82]

At the beginning of the seventies, Monica Vitti was the uncontested queen of Italian comedy, a genre, however, which was already beginning its decline. After the international success of *The Girl With a Pistol* (1968), Monica inherited Silvana Mangano's place as Alberto Sordi's partner, who also directed her in many films during the five-year period from 1969 to 1973, from *Amore mio aiutami* (1969) *(Help Me, Darling)* to *Polvere di stelle* [Stardust] (1973) and with whom she would team up again ten years later in the melancholy *Io so che tu sai che io so* [I know that you know that I know] (1982).

Becoming number one on the Italian comedy scene, Vitti had other male comedy stars as partners such as Vittorio Gassman, Ugo Tognazzi, and Nino Manfredi, and became recognized for her comic vitality and perfect sense of timing. She was the only actress who could match (and sometimes even steal scenes from) these giants of comedy.

While many of her sister actresses were undressing on movie sets or for the pages of men's magazines, Vitti was reticent about sex and would not appear in the nude, considering herself too serious an actress. Her only concession to the pseudo-erotic taste was to be seen in a slip, in bed, sometimes alone or with her partner of the moment. Her films were nevertheless full of beds and alcoves (her autobiography is called *Il letto è una rosa* [Bed Is a Rose], the title taken from an old song). It was there that her brilliant amorous triangles took place, but always very discreetly. In *Dramma della gelosia* (1970) *(The Motive Was Jealousy)*, Monica actually finds herself in bed with two men – Marcello Mastroianni and Giancarlo Giannini. Even when there was no bed, however, there was always a love triangle. Thus in *Help Me, Darling* Vitti portrays a typical bourgeois wife who goes on a cruise and falls in love with a serious professor, Silvano Tranguilli. In *Polvere di stelle,* she temporarily abandons her partner for the flattery of John Philip Law, an American sailor. In *L'anatra all'arancia* (1975) *(Duck in Orange Sauce)* she responds to the love of a stranger, betraying her very bourgeois husband who is also having an illicit affair. In *Amori miei* (1978) *(My Loves)* she even goes so far as to change her name in order to share bed and affection with two men equitably, Johnny Dorelli and Enrico Maria Salerno, neither of whom, of course, knows about the other.

The actress' real love life continued to go hand in hand with her career, a sign of fragility seeking protection. And it may not be coincidental that two of her lovers were image makers – after her relationship with Antonioni's photographer Carlo De Palma came another photographer, Roberto Russo, who directed her in *Flirt* (1983) and *Francesca è mia* [Francesca is mine] (1986), two modest films that enjoyed little public appeal.

The great comedien, Monica Vitti, refused to accept that comedies were going out of style. She continued to pursue a dream of the frivolous upper middle-class world, pet subject of playwrights Aldo Debenedetti and Jacques Deval, the warhorses of the movies of the thirties, revived in a suicidal way in the eighties with such films as *L'altra metà del cielo* [Other half of the sky] (1977), *Non ti consoco più, amore* [I don't know you anymore my love] (1980), or *Tango della gelosia* [Tango of jealousy] (1981) and *Scusa se è poco* [Sorry if it's not enough] (1982), very far from the tastes of the modern public. As a result, the myth of Vitti paled and withered. Even her attempt to return to drama, when she was entrusted to her first Pygmalion, Michelangelo Antonioni, resulted in a tremendous flop: *Il mistero di Oberwald* (1980) *(The Mystery of Oberwald)* was a tormented mistake of a film which conceded too much to electronics and nothing to the heart.

During those years, Vitti was only offered three mother roles: one, in the episode *Mamma* directed by Dino Risi (one of twelve episodes of the film *Noi donne siamo fatte così* [We women are like that] (1971); the second, a brief appearance in Luis Bunuel's *Le fantome de la liberté* (1974) *(The Phantom of Liberty)* and finally, the mother of a drug-addict daughter in the controversial *Io so che tu sai che io so* (1982). If other actresses of

Monica Vitti and Alberto Sordi in **Io so che tu sai che io so** *(1982).*

her generation accepted mother roles gladly, this was a luxury which Monica Vitti could do without. Ill-advised, probably over-worshipped, Vitti stubbornly insisted on parts as lover, wife, and leading lady, even at the price of her credibility. This was a professional choice in the style of an old-fashioned diva and one feels that behind it lay an understandable feminine affectation, but also a lack of healthy objectivity from which her coherence as an actress could have benefited. And then, better to pass over in silence her unfortunate attempt as film director of *Scandolo segreto* [Secret scandal] (1990), a collection of errors and stylistic failures.

One positive note in the last decade has been Monica's return to the stage – received enthusiastically by the critics and especially by the public – she turned Neil Simon's comedy *The Odd Couple* into a fanstastic success. Vitti and Rosella Falk act a female version of the play which outdoes the original male version as played on stage and screen by Jack Lemmon and Walter Matthau.

Other than her commitments as an actress, Monica Vitti has dedicated herself in recent times almost full time to being a "godmother" to talented young filmmakers. As presenter of a television program entirely devoted to cinema (*Passione mia*), she works as a talent scout presenting short subjects by young directors, many of whom have subsequently shown themselves to indeed have promising futures. Among these are Stefano Reali, Francesca Archibugi, Graziano Diana, and Sandro Bencivenni. Hyperactive, readily available, omnipresent, she appears at all the important social events, art shows, previews, festivals, but also continues to leave her mark on TV, radio and in bookshop windows, having produced another autobiography, *Sette sottane* [Seven petticoats], after her first book, *Il letto è una rosa*.

Claudia Cardinale

[see also p. 80]

They call her "the most fascinating grandmother of today's cinema" and Claudia Cardinale's post '68 period still holds great riches for this actress in the prime of her beauty, sollicited by such giants in Italy and abroad as Comencini, Damiani, Bolognini, Zampa, Skolimowski, Herzog, and Marco Ferreri.

In the early seventies she left her Pygmalion-husband Franco Cristaldi and entered the world of her new companion, the director Pasquale Squitieri. From the making of *I guappi* [The Louts] (1974) onwards, Cardinale was an almost fixed member of the cast of all his films,

sometimes in quite marginal roles that were nevertheless a precious addition to productions which boasted very little else that was precious, though many were well made and with occasional touches of social commitment.

Though capable of excellent performances in many of her films, big and small, Cardinale suffered from type-casting that did little to enhance her image as an actress. Mauro Bolognini created a fine part for her as the lead in *Libera amore mio* [Free, my love] (1975). Unfortunately the material, treated conventionally, irritated the public that deserted the theaters.

Little by little, Claudia Cardinale's image faded even if her appearances at art show openings and festivals showed a radiant woman accompanied by her companion and children.

Between 1984-87 Claudia returned to the top with two extremely dramatic mother roles, both of them set in Fascist Italy. One was the role of the fragile Claretta Petacci, the Duce's mistress in *Claretta*, and the other, the one Luigi Comencini offered her in his filming of *La storia* (*History*). At the Venice Film Festival *Claretta* was hooted, boycotted, and accused of shameful superficiality. But Claudia Cardinale escaped unscathed from the polemics thanks to her moving interpretation for which she was awarded the Premio Pasinetti and soon after, the Nastro d'Argento. The next year Claudia acted in *La storia* (1987), a role this time seen from the other side, as the schoolteacher Ida Ramado, persecuted because she is a Jew, and above all because she is the daughter of an anarchist. Cardinale didn't turn up her nose at mother roles either, nor those even more threatening to her image. She knew how to appear aged, dim, worn when the script called for it. Deeply moving was her portrayal of the character in *Atto di dolore* (1990) [Act of pain], her last film for Squitieri. (A few years later, their love affair ended when rumors began circulating of Cardinale's relationship with then French Prime Minister Jacques Chirac.)

While waiting for more challenging dramatic roles to come her way, Cardinale allowed herself a bit of fun playing the part of a devilish Roberto Benigni's mother in *Il figlio della pantera nera (Son of the Pink Panther)* (1994).

Claudia Cardinale did not disdain accepting roles as a mother, as in the intense La storia *(1987). Here, with Fiorenzo Fiorentini.*

Virna Lisi

[see also p. 90]

She was the loveliest of the international cinema's sixty-year-olds. Virna Lisi passed through the seventies without letting the feminist battles either infect her nor trample her down.

Having set aside Hollywood dreams (she had no ambitions of being a new Grace Kelly or a mediocre Marilyn Monroe), the blonde Virna Lisi had already given her baby-doll image a forceful new twist at the end of the sixties in *Tenderly* (1968) where she played a non-conformist girl suffocated by her mother. Here Virna gave previously unimaginable evidence of being a fine actress, flexible and protean, and ready to pull out her claws, especially when she was in the hands of an able director. Her perfect face, its enviable profile, her dazzling smile, her supreme serenity, all risked typing her as a beautiful and icy bourgeois woman, like the character she played in *Roma bene* [Respectable Rome] (1971).

In the second half of the seventies, Virna Lisi gave another new turn to her career, appearing dull and dry as Elizabeth Nietzsche in *Al di là del bene e del male* (1977) *(Beyond Good and Evil)*, for which she won her first Nastro d'Argento award as supporting actress and evoked the praise of critics. Lisi was presented as the "rediscovered actress," even if

Almost unrecognizable, Virna Lisi gives a memorable performance in La reine Margot *(1994).*

producers insisted on offering her old-fashioned parts as middle-class ladies too elegant to be in step with the times. What saved her was her devil-may-care attitude and her courage to appear tired and worn. Thus, for her interpretation in *Ernesto* (1978), she again won critical praise. Her popularity rose thanks to Alberto Lattuada's film *La cicala* [Chatterbox] (1980) where she had the opporunity of playing a coarse variety-show singer and for which took home the David di Donatello award for best female actress. It was a great triumph for an actress considered as typed in elegant middle-class roles. No one would have bet on her success in the role of a sluttish singer – the kind of role that had made Anna Magnani famous. This was the only scabrous role in her elegant career.

In 1983 Lisi made a surprise appearance in one of Carlo Vanzina's vacation films, *Sapore di mare* [Taste of the sea], which triggered off "operation nostalgia." She plays the part of a mother watching her son's trials and tribulations in love. A charming quip ends the film: "The difference between us and our children? None. Only that our hearts used to beat harder." A line that melts the hearts of fifty-year-olds in the audience.

In the eighties Virna Lisi became the official *mamma* of TV movies, the omnipresent middle-class housewife of the little screen. But, like Claudia Cardinale, Virna Lisi didn't mind the traces of age on her face. And these traces were of more interest to the movies than they were to television. In *Buon Natale, Buon Anno* [Happy Christmas, Happy New Year] (1989) Lisi interprets the part of a separated wife who is gripped by nostalgia for her husband and rediscovers passion by meeting him secretly amidst lies and subterfuges. This role won her the Nastro d'Argento award for best actress. But this success was nothing compared to the triumph she enjoyed at Cannes in 1994 when, playing on the opponent's field, she beat the French cinema "in its own court" in the person of the young and lovely Isabelle Adjani, her counterpart in the spectacular *La reine Margot* [Queen Margot]. It was Virna who was awarded the prize for best actress that many had predicted would be Adjani's. Ugly, old, and even repellent, Virna Lisi dishes up a Catherine de' Medici who is a true monster of grit and nastiness. With the heavy make-up applied by Kuno Schlegelmich, Virna is practically unrecognizable. She resembles another queen, Elizabeth I of England, whom Bette Davis brought to the screen twice. But Davis was always dressed in red, whereas costume designer Moidele Bickel thinks up a shiny-black look for Virna Lisi.

Sanctified by this international triumph, Virna Lisi returned home and, more wrinkled than ever, played the part of a grandmother in *Va dove ti porta il cuore* [Go where your heart takes you] (1995) based on the bestseller by the Trieste writer Susanna Tamaro. In this film, Olga, a woman who is gravely ill, feels that her end is near and writes her life story in a diary, a tale of mute rancor.

The wrinkles made Lisi more beautiful than ever and also brought her luck. But above all, behind the aged face, one glimpsed the intelligence of an actress who, instead of futilely hiding from the inevitable, knew how to confront the passing of time with dignity and wisdom. And also, with the serenity of a bourgeois woman who had always preferred to keep to herself, in the comfort of her gilded actress' world, sheltered from gossip, scuffles, and revolt.

Sophia Loren
[see also p. 111]

A decade elapsed between the sunny, impulsive, fiery, and beautiful farm girl of *C'era una volta* (1967) *(More Than a Miracle)* and the shabby drudge of a housewife in *Un giorno particolare* (1977) *(A Special Day)*. An intense and terrible decade for Italy, but Sophia Loren – despite a series of insipid little movies that added nothing to her reputation – continued to be Italy's ambassadress of beauty to the world.

Sophia remained unscathed by her misadventures with the Italian tax authorities. Even after spending forty days in a Caserta jail, the polls showed her to still be the actress Italians loved best. The queen, splendid and resplendent, gave no hint of an intention to abdicate from her throne. After 1986, Loren acted beside such stars as Richard Burton, Peter O'Toole, Richard Harris, and Jean Gabin. But it was only with her chosen partner, Marcello Mastroianni, that she again reached the luster of her best moments. Ettore Scola in *A Special Day* created a great and moving character for her, a woman injured in her innermost being by the brutal course of history. Not since the days of *Two Women* had audiences had the chance to admire so real an interpretation of hers, closed in the microcosm of authentic everyday suffering and acted with such sincere rapture. This film was the beginning of Sophia's step-by-step ascent. She won the Nastro d'Argento and David di Donatello prizes.

Was this a new Loren being born at the dawn of the eighties? So it seemed. But her family, her age, and above all a series of television movies removed her from the world of cinema. She told her own life story in a hammy Canadian television production entitled *Sophia, Her Own Story* (1980) where she could only play her own mother, Romilda Villani. She was a big hit in *The Fortunate Pilgrim* (1986) when she acted the part of a mother who takes up the fight against the

drug pushers slowly killing her addicted son. It was based on a novel by Mario Puzo and directed by Stuart Cooper. The television audience also enjoyed *Sabato, domenica e lunedì* (*Saturday, Sunday and Monday*), Eduardo De Filippo's play, in a version skillfully directed by Lina Wertmüller. Here Loren finally regains her Neapolitan brilliance. The one mistake in this period – a mistake in which the excellent director Dino Risi joined her – was a TV remake of *Two Women* (1988).

Paradoxically, the nineties were kinder to her, bringing her recognition and postponing her farewell to acting. In 1991 Sophia won the Caesar and was sanctified with an Oscar for her career. Gregory Peck, who had been her partner in *Arabesque*, consigned the precious statuette to the actress whom he termed "one of the movie world's most precious treasures."

Beautiful and sexy Sophia Loren in La pupa del gangster *(1975).*

Right: *Sophia Loren, as beautiful and fascinating as ever, in her latest movie* Grumpier Old Men *(1995). With Walter Matthau.* Below: *Loren, the neglected wife in* A Special Day *(1977).*

In 1992 French President François Mitterand honored her with the medal of the Legion of Honor. But these awards did not signal the end of her career. In 1994, the splendid sixty-year-old announced her sensational return to the screen: Robert Altman wanted her together with Marcello Mastroianni again for his caustic *Ready-to-Wear*, a comedy which unfortunately was not entirely successful. A rare and unexpected flop in Altman's career, it was nevertheless viewed worldwide by millions of flocking spectators. Sophia, however, emerged a winner, ironic and sensual. The newspapers talked most of all about her new version of the famous strip-tease in *Ieri, oggi e domani (Yesterday, Today and Tomorrow)* redone after thirty years, with, however, a wry variation: the aching and ailing Marcello falls asleep during the exciting spectacle. What? Is Sophia no longer sexy? On the contrary, Loren is still very beautiful, and while press and TV hold her up as an example of the evergreen woman, excellent offers and opportunities continue flooding in. Here she is willing and ready again in *Grumpier Old Men* (1995) playing opposite that odd couple Jack Lemmon and Walter Matthau – a great success in America (but much less so back home).

In interviews Sophia says that she is proud to be Italian, and especially to be Neapolitan. Perhaps it is from the most secret roots of her Mediterranean soul that this actress, a living monument to feminine seduction, continues to draw her vitality.

THE EMIGRANTS

The Italian cinema of the early nineties was very poor in female roles and the few offered were almost completely monopolized by the fair-haired Margherita Buy, a turn-of-the-century Assia Noris, an actress so Italian that she was utterly unknown abroad. The younger generation of Italian actresses, therefore, were forced to seek opportunities outside Italy, in neighboring France, or Spain, Germany, and Portugal, further away too, even across the ocean.

The new women of Italian cinema were wandering stars, partly out of necessity, partly out of choice, but also because this younger generation spoke foreign languages. The enigmatic Laura Morante kept one foot in Italy and one in France, until she finally moved definitively beyond the Alps. Anna Galiena too, who was launched, in fact, in a French film, *The Hairdresser's Husband* (1990) by Patrice Leconte, had a house and her husband in Montparnasse. Valeria Golino, despite her neorealistic first films in ultra-proletarian roles, flirted unabashedly with Hollywood. Francesca Neri had her base in the Spain of Bigas Luna and Carlos Saura (though she dreamt of Kevin Costner). The excellent Chiara Caselli made a big leap in quality thanks to *My Own Private Idaho* (1991) by the independent American Gus Van Sant, but also worked with Costa-Gavras and did screen tests for Adrian Lyne and Quentin Tarantino. Better chances abroad were found too by Francesca Prandi, the atypical beauty popular with the Portuguese, and Isabella Ferrari.

The only actress to travel in the opposite direction was Carol Alt, who immigrated successfully to Italy where she found work and fame as an actress in the popular fairy-tale films of the Vanzina brothers, though she too was a starlet who lived out of a suitcase.

Carol Alt

The Barbie doll of Italian cinema, Carol Alt, an American actress, was the muse of the Vanzina brothers' fairy-tale world and their school of cinema; films deeply rooted in the culture of photoplay magazines and which were raking in millions at the box office.

Big blue eyes of the type completely foreign to Italian women, a sweet Snow White smile, baby-doll features, a good 5'10" and less than 120 pounds – all this was Carol Alt whom the photographer Oliviero Toscani called "a broom-stick beauty." Ethereal and unreal, she embodied the sugar-sweetness of the pleasure-seeking Italy of the eighties with its beauty cult, obsession with power, and awareness of the omnipotence of corruption. Among Carol Alt's friends there was Gianni De Michelis, the powerful socialist, second only to Bettino Craxi.

A vegetarian, abstemious, with an iron military discipline in her sweetness (to such a point that she always kept her personal acting coach, Sharon Madden, on the set with her), Carol Alt was born in Long Island in December 1960. Her mother was an office worker and her father, fire chief of the South Bronx, had formerly been a military officer. She was later engaged to a West Point cadet and studied law thanks to a military scholarship, but both the engagement and her studies fell to pieces. At eighteen, Carol ran away to become a fashion model. In a drug store, she met Richard Avedon, the famous photographer. He found her too chubby and advised her, "The raw material is

Carol Alt, an American at Cinecittà.

there, come back when you're thirty pounds thinner." Carol went on a strict diet and got that stringbean silhouette audiences know so well today. Rumors were that she suffered from anorexia; this was categorically denied.

In 1979 Carol Alt got a great start in a brilliant modelling career as one of the girls of the agency Elite, one of New York's biggest. Very soon she was wildly in demand (the Wilhelmine Agency vainly tried stealing her from Elite) and was earning up to $25,000 a day.

In the life story of this Grace Kelly of the eighties there was a deeply romantic fairy tale. She was already a top model when she met Ronnie Gersham, an ice hockey hero at a crucial period in his life: because of a serious accident during one of his games, he was threatened with paralysis. Carol nursed him lovingly for two years, refusing all work that would take her away from New York. The ex-captain of the New York Rangers recovered, went back to his career in hockey and married Carol. Today Gersham runs a large pollution clean-up company and is practically a multi-millionaire. (Apparently Carol had a weakness for sports heroes since another story leaked out of a past love affair with the racing driver Ayrton Senna).

There were almost always fabulous sums of money in the happy endings of Carol Alt's fairy tales, on and off the screen. Too lovely for any tale of ordinary squalor, she seemed to glide above the ground of common mortals. And her film debut already reflected this mood when she appeared in *Via Montenapoleon* (1987), with her parallel life in Milan's elegant society, a sugary fashion show of fatuity. Carlo Vanzina had already wanted her in his previous film, *Sotto il vestito niente* [Under her dress, nothing] (1985) set in the fashion world, but Carol had one of her rare commitments in theater, the musical *Sweet Charity* in America, directed by Bob Fosse. (Which was not exactly a triumph for her.)

Carol Alt put the trademark of her sweetness on Carlo Vanzina's comedies, almost all of them realized with the participation of Reteitalia, the production branch of Silvio Berlusconi's Fininvest company. A sensation was created by the cinematic biography of aristocrat Marina Lante della Rovere (later Mrs. Ripa di Meana), *I miei primi quarant'anni* (1987) *(My First Forty Years)*, an account of postwar Italy as seen by the jet-set woman who spends her life between alcoves and salons, obsessively pursued by blue-bloods, industrial tycoons, oil men, politicians and powerful journalists. Then there's the nostalgia of the *dolce vita* of the sixties: Via Veneto and environs. Carol also acted in the sequel to this successful comic strip of a film, *La più bella del reame* (1989) *(The Fairest One of All)* whose title tells all.

In *Bye Bye Baby* (1988) Carol is first a married woman and later, after divorce, the secret mistress of the wealthy Luca Barbareschi. (Some sensational weeklies hinted of a true affair between them in real life too.) In *Miliardi* [Billions] (1990) she plays the black sheep in a family of industrial tycoons. In *Treno di panna* [Train of cream] (1988) she is a busy American who meets the penniless Sergio Rubini in a chic Italian language school. In short, Carol Alt celebrated the lavish splendors of an American-style jet-set femininity which was also quite close to television soap opera.

Star of movies and television productions of light entertainment, Carol Alt had occasionally tried to oppose her stereotype of a "beauty without substance" and to offer herself for dramatic roles, as in the TV movie *Il vizio di vivere* [The vice to live] (1989) directed by the veteran Dino Risi. In this true story taken from the autobiography of Rosanna Benzi, she plays the dramatic part of a gravely ill girl who must live in an iron lung. To find herself deprived of her body would seem to be quite a challenge for such a "physical" actress. Nevertheless, this was not the role for which Carol Alt would most be remembered.

Valeria Golino wins her medals as an actress thanks to Storia d'amore *(1986).*

Valeria Golino

A tiny body, deep gaze from beautiful eyes somewhere between green and gray, her voice a little low, small hands with short nails like a little girl's, with a casual style and a weakness for knapsacks. A cascade of untamed dark curls that she twists with her fingers into knots like a high-school girl during a lesson, and the large melancholy eyes of a little girl who has had to grow up too soon. This was Valeria Golino, the only Italian actress who appeared in Hollywood films between the end of the eighties and the beginning of the nineties; as Tom Cruise's fiancée in *Rain Man* (1988), Gary (Beethoven) Oldman's lover in *Beloved Immortal* (1995), and as the nutty psychiatrist in *Hot Shots*. She was also in the cast of *Indian Runner* (1991), *Red Wind*, *Four Rooms*, *Leaving Las Vegas* and other films. She had a house in West Hollywood and another in Rome on the noisy piazza Campo de' Fiori where she lived with her boyfriend, Fabrizio Bentivoglio. For Americans she became a familiar face, not yet a true star, because she hadn't yet had the part that could truly do it. But she came close to finding it: she was supposed to be the lead in *Pretty Woman*. Julia Roberts beat her by a nose in the race for the part.

Half-Greek, half-Italian, Valeria Golino was born in Naples on October 22, 1966. Her mother, a Greek painter, later separated from her father, a professor of Greek studies and a journalist. Among her childhood memories was a house with a view from which to admire the island of Capri. Her family was one of artists and writers and Valeria's brother, Alessandro, was a sax player.

Valeria spent her adolescence moving between Capri, Naples and Athens. Unfortunately she was struck down with a grave form of scoliosis. Neither exercise nor a cast would help. She underwent a complicated surgical operation in Chicago. The resulting large scar that runs like a braid all the way down her backbone is glimpsed in a shot in *Storia d'amore* [Love story] (1986).

Almost out of spite, she was determined to be a model – even an actress. Her uncle, Enzo Golino, then managing editor and today vice director of the weekly *L'Espresso* contacted Lina Wertmüller about his niece's ambitions. After returning from a trip to Los Angeles to make a commercial, Wertmüller had fifteen-year-old Valeria do a screen test, in which she was asked to recite a monologue from *The Taming of the Shrew*. She got a part as Ugo Tognazzi's daughter in the movie *Scherzo del destino* (1983) *(A Joke of Destiny Lying in Wait Around the Corner Like a Street Bandit).*

Bitten by the acting bug, Valeria left high school and set up house in Rome. Her mentor and companion, Peter Del Monte, introduced her to jazz and also good movies at cinema

Valeria Golino with Charlie Sheen in **Hot Shots!** *(1991) a mad Hollywood comedy.*

clubs. He was to launch her as the heroine in *Piccoli fuochi* [Small fires] (1985), where she plays the part of a baby-sitter who becomes the object of a child's inordinate thirst for love.

A leading actress right from the start, Valeria impressed the public and critics with her efficacious and natural expressiveness. Paradoxically, she, who was so middle class, made her mark in playing poor or completely destitute girls: a drug addict in *Figlio mio infinitamente caro...* [My son, infinitely dear] (1985) and a working class girl from the outskirts in *Storia d'amore*, a proletarian drama in which Francesco Maselli offers her the type of role which consecrates an actress, up to and including a suicide ending.

It was the triumph of a proletarian eros based on sleeveless T-shirts and thread-bare working boots which fascinated the Venice Film Festival. Though it was virtually her debut, Valeria Golino was awarded the prestigious prize for best actress, beating the tough international competition.

Golino built her career on this interpretation and immediately wiped out the stereotype of a working-class beauty by appearing in *Gli occhiali d'oro* [Gold glasses] (1987) where she is an opportunistic Jewish girl in Ferrara at the end of the thirties. But she refused the part Mauro Bolognini offered her in *La venexiana* [Woman from Venice] (1986).

It was pure chance that took Valeria Golino

to Hollywood, but it was thanks to her abilities that she stayed there. Overseas, she made her debut in a children's fairy tale, *Pee Wee's Big Adventure* (1985), a movie too American to be released in Europe. Renamed "Gina" in honor of Lollobrigida, Golino plays a trapeze artist who gives a long, long kiss to Pee Wee Herman, alias Paul Reubens, the eternal kid, idol of American teenagers. The kiss lasts three minutes and seems endless. For reasons of "decency" Paramount cuts half of it. "But make no mistake," Valeria declared, "it's still a hell of a good kiss." In order to shoot this film the very young actress missed the luscious tit-bit of a part that Francesco Maselli had cooked up for her in *Codice privato* [Private code] (1988). It was swallowed whole by that girl-of-all-trades Ornella Muti.

But Valeria created a sensation in America. It was said that her innocent little face had conquered Paul Reubens (the famous Pee Wee) and even Tom Cruise himself, who insisted on having her act with him in *Rain Man.* To make the part appropriate for her, Tom Cruise's girlfriend is changed into a European girl (Susanna) who does not share her American boyfriend's way of behaving nor thinking. Valeria Golino calls on all her warm animal talent, updating it with a bit of Actor's Studio passion. The *New York Times* went wild over this doe-eyed Neapolitan girl. The Americans even adored that deep husky voice that back home had not been particularly successful. There were whispers that beautiful Tom Cruise was also pushing for a part for her in *Born on the Fourth of July*, but Oliver Stone was reticent.

Timothy Dalton was also said to be among Valeria's conquests, her partner on the set of Axel Corti's *La Putain du roi* [The king's whore] (1990) for which the Neapolitan actress received the very respectable fee of 600 million lire. The film, in which Valeria plays a sublime courtesan, was hailed at Cannes but misunderstood by the public. The cash registers, however, soon went ting-a-ling for *Hot Shots* and its sequel. The bouncy love story of the virgin psychiatrist, Valeria Golino, and the repentant top gun Charlie Sheen repeats in parody form the most popular moments of movie history from *The Lady and the Tramp* to *Rocky*. Valeria sings, dances, flirts, kisses, prances around in a beautiful elegant wardrobe.

Not too many years had passed since her role as an ultra-proletarian in *Storia d'amore*, but Valeria had shown that she was a true actress who had her sights set high. During the 1988 Oscar ceremony she was seated between Cher and Michael Douglas, just like a real international star. The cinema world in which Valeria moved was stateless just like her own half-Greek, half-Italian roots. Capable of acting in English, she often found herself among international casts like that of *Torrents*

of Spring (1989). Too bad that the Italian public had no great liking for her, possibly because she stubbornly insisted on developing her career outside Italy, possibly because off the set she had never worked to make herself popular, or perhaps because of that strange dark and croaky voice of hers so out of keeping with her pretty face. When she was dubbed "behind her back" in *Paura e amore* [Fear and love] (1988) by Von Trotta, Valeria got very angry: "I didn't deserve that," she protested.

But her main goal still remained Hollywood where the European director Agniezska Holland directed her in *Red Wind*, a Chandler mystery with Danny Glover playing detective Marlowe. Golino appears in a pink negligé with oriental slippers and a boa of ostrich plumes. "A slut from the forties, a little vulgar and a little innocent," the actress commented.

Salvatores gave her a fine part as an adventuress in the pseudo-Mexican movie *Puerto Escondido* (1992). The ironic vein in the director's personality, which already emerged in the two-part *Hot Shots* was confirmed in one of the four tales of *Four Rooms* where Valeria Golino makes a lovely sorceress alongside the witch Madonna. Behind the disarming innocence of this Neapolitan girl lay an extraordinary, unexpected malleability. The mark of real acting talent.

Laura Morante

She was known as "the Black Madonna of Italian films." With her severe beauty, distant and introverted, never banal, Laura Morante became in the eighties the most radical of anti-divas, the muse of directors who made no concessions for the commonplace, directors like Giuseppe Bertolucci, Gianni Amelio, Nanni Moretti, Joao César Monteiro, and Alain Tanner.

The pensive face of a romantic heroine, icy femininity, jet-black hair often gathered at the nape, a soft but intransigent mouth, an elegant oval face and swan-like neck. One of Modigliani's creatures. Large, intense eyes, nervous legs, a dancer's gait. In a panorama of femininity dominated by flouncing top models with silicone-injected lips, someone like Laura Morante was rare indeed.

Born on August 21, 1956 at Santa Fiora near the town of Grosseto to a very big family, the sixth of eight children, three girls and five boys, Laura was the child of a housewife and a criminal lawyer with a passion for drama. Above all, however, she was the niece of the writer Elsa Morante. Perhaps this family tie accounted in part for the intellectual halo she was given and the fact that she was destined for artistic *cinema d'autore*. For the time being, however, Laura was breathing the dust of dance studios and little avant garde theaters.

When she finished secondary school she got a scholarship and moved to Rome to fulfill her childhood dream: to become a classical ballet dancer. She then went from classical to modern dance. Then, as an actress she began to move in the circles of experimental theaters – the so-called underground "cellar" theaters. "In 1977 I was working with the Danzatori Scalzi group when Carmelo Bene asked our teacher, Patrizia Cerroni, if any of us knew how to dance on her toes. He needed a ballerina for his Parisian show S.A.D.E." Thus, going with Bene, with whom she would also work in *Richard III*, Laura Morante abandoned dance for acting. "The theater had always fascinated me, so much so that at seventeen I directed a piece written by my father," she explained. Her companion, Daniele Costantini, was also a man of the theater (and occasionally a film director) and later became the father of her first child, Eugenia, born in 1981.

Laura Morante got her start in films with the role of a drug addict in Giuseppe Bertolucci's hyper-realistic movie *Oggetti smarriti* [Lost objects] (1980). Immediately afterwards, Bernardo Bertolucci cast her in *La tragedia di un uomo ridicolo* (1981) *(The Tragedy of a Ridiculous Man)*. But it is Nanni Moretti who truly launches her, first in *Sogni d'oro* [Dreams of gold] (1981), then in *Bianca* (1984) which remains the decisive film in Morante's career. "I had an old friendship with Nanni Moretti harking back to my days in avant garde theater and he often came to see our shows."

A misogynist like Michele Apichella, the autobiographical hero of his film, Nanni Moretti found in Laura Morante the perfect model of femininity, a dream woman, who miraculously was saved from all the sentimental banalities of a consumerist epoch. The schoolteacher Bianca succeeds in the impossible enterprise of seducing (and actually kissing) Michele Apicella. The Calvanistic Nanni Moretti considered Laura Morante the ideal actress, one reason being her lack of determination to succeed, which was an all-too-common defect among women in Italian movie circles. "He says that I never fight for a close-up. But he doesn't know why I don't. The fact is that I am proud and that often I do not feel sure about my acting. Therefore I prefer to remain in the background."

Terribly shy, fatalistic, quarrelsome, Laura was a pathologically insecure actress who instead of planning her career, let herself drift with the current, tasting her roles sip by sip. "I could continue acting or I could quit. Certainly I would have to face the problem of making a living for myself. I don't know how to do anything else." Her detractors accused her of an absent, cold attitude. They said she

didn't even seem to be an actress. But this, in her eyes, was probably a compliment.

After the success of *Bianca*, Laura Morante was well known throughout Europe. She bounced like a ball from Switzerland, France, Spain, and Portugal where she worked with the brilliant Monteiro. In Spain she plays the duchess of Alba in a film on Goya. The Swiss Alain Tanner entrusts a fine role to her in *La vallée fantôme* [The phantom valley] (1987) where she plays the muse of Trintignant as a movie director in a crisis. Important directors created the roles of enigmatic women for her, one who lived outside the bounds of ordinary life. Mario Monicelli gave her an important role in *Le due vite di Mattia Pascal* [The two lives of Mattia Pascal] (1985). Salvatores, no less a misogynist than Nanni Moretti, placed her at the center of a lively love triangle in *Turné* (1990), creating one of the rare well-rounded female characters in his films for her.

After *Colpo al cuore* (1982) *(Blow to the Heart)* and *Turné* her Italian film appearances became ever less frequent. Little by little, France became Laura Morante's second home. She acted in films by Bruno Gantillon, Alain Klarer, Elie Chouraqui, and José Pinheiro. She was in the cast of *Affaire Dreyfus* [The Dreyfus case] that Yves Boisset prepared for French television. At Cannes in 1994 her all-French movie *Il faut pas rire de bonheur* [You mustn't laugh out of happiness] directed by Guillaume Nicloux was presented out of competition.

At the end of the eighties Morante also

Intellectual actress Laura Morante found more opportunities in France than in Italy.

went to live in France in order to be close to the man she had married in 1987, George Claisse, actor and scriptwriter. They moved to a small village forty kilometers from Paris with little Eugenia (the child of her previous union with the director Daniele Costantini) and their second child, Agnese, born in 1988.

Morante returned to Italy sporadically for a few TV movies (when she plays Anita in Luigi Magni's *Garibaldi* and Giuseppina Strepponi in Mauro Bolognini's *Casa Ricordi*) and some theater appearances. Even then, she worked with filmmakers such as Mario Monicelli who gave her the role of Madame de Tourvel in a stage version of *Dangerous Liaisons*. Meanwhile she dreamed of Tarkovski and Iosseliani. She worked hard at writing screenplays, none of which ever reached completion, mainly out of disinterest. Her appearances in Italian films became rarer and rarer. Occasionally she worked with Peter Del Monte or Paolo Virzi. She dreamed of comic roles, practically impossible for her to get with her reputation as the great melancholy actress. She dreamed of shooting a film in black and white. She dreamed of a cinema which no longer existed.

Francesca Neri

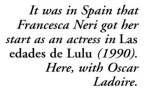

It was in Spain that Francesca Neri got her start as an actress in **Las edades de Lulu** *(1990). Here, with Oscar Ladoire.*

Together with the Neapolitan Iaia Forte, Francesca Neri was the only gifted actress to come out of the Centro Sperimentale di Cinematografia in the post '68 period. She had auburn, almost frankly red hair brightened up with henna, a very light complexion, never tanned, something child-like in her glance. She was nevertheless proud like all Istrian women in general, and her sister-Istrian, Alida Valli, in particular (who was also a child of the Centro Sperimentale).

Large high breasts and a tense body with long, slender legs. Her eyes, small, luminous, dry and very blue. But in bad weather they turned gray. They resembled Hugo Pratt's Nordic women. She had a suffering and apathetic air – the typical complicated young woman, fascinating but a little passive, à la Catherine Deneuve. Timid and fragile, given to sudden angry outbursts ("I am someone who shouts a lot"), suffering from insomnia and dark torments ("I feel the need to find a true faith") which led her to the psychoanalyst's couch. Her angelic sensuality would have conquered Alfred Hitchcock. In the eighties and early nineties Francesca Neri had the right face to express fragility, neuroses, and the emotional tangles of the new generation.

Istrian and Apulian blood ran in her veins. She was born in 1964 in Trent in a family raised on irredentism and nationalism. Daughter of an agronomist, she led a Heidi-like childhood amidst woods and gardens thanks to daddy Claudio. But the most important figure in her childhood was grandmother Maria, opera singer in her soul, though usher and cashier by profession in the single movie house in a village near Pola.

Not wanting to go to university in Trent, after high school Francesca joined her brother who was studying economy and commerce in Rome. She wanted to get a degree in the

history of cinema, but in the capital she took acting lessons, first from Fersen and finally at the Centro Sperimentale. She and her classmates shot *Il grande Blek* [The big Blek] (1987), a film about their generation produced by the young Domenico Procacci who would become her boyfriend. She did not seem destined for a great career.

But at the Cannes Festival in 1989 she got her big break. She was at the festival with her boyfriend Domenico Procacci who was looking for buyers for Giuseppe Piccioni's movie *Il grande Blek*. Just as they were leaving, news came that Bigas Luna was desperately looking for an actress to take over for Angela Molina in *Las edades de Lulù* (1990). Just ten days before shooting, Molina had told them to all go to hell, defining the film "pornographic." Francesca Neri put down her suitcase went for a screen test and got the part. It was the lead, the title role. "Suddenly I found myself on the set with my wrists bound and hanging from the ceiling with gay guys in leather exhibiting themselves in front of me in violent erotic rituals," Francesca Neri remembered. The film smacks of scandal and makes news. Interviews and magazine covers abound for Lulu. Francesca's popularity began to soar even before the movie was released, but her parents refused to see it. In the small town of Trent people talked of nothing else: Francesca, from a conservative family that had always voted for the right-wing Almirante, appeared fully nude in the movie, enjoying the delights of sex with the help of a battery-powered vibrator. Scandalous!

Despite the extreme images, *Las edades de Lulù* is not pornography at all. Bigas Luna, drawing from the novel by Almudena Grandes, recounts the sexual curiosity of young girls and at the same time examines the sentimental education of a woman from her fifteenth to her thirtieth year. The voyage of this sweet Madrilenian girl through the realm of vice and sin reveals a Francesca Neri who is perfect – measured, haughty, sensitive. It seems to be the unexpected discovery of a new talent. Certainly for a girl like her it was something of a trauma to see herself advertised all over the front pages as a sex symbol. Francesca didn't like the role of a sexual animal and shuddered at the idea of being associated with the starlets in Tinto Brass's "harem."

She said she didn't like the way she looked and insisted that her legs were "ugly, too thin and maybe bowlegged as well." She refused to pose for the kind of risqué photos Francesca Dellera delighted in and continued to wear loose clothes that hid her curves. "I'm too shy to go dressed in that way." And yet Luciano Manuzzi, the director of *Sabato italiano* [Italian Saturday] (1992), gave her the part of a strip-tease dancer hired to undress for a party of twelve-year-olds.

Massimo Troisi was the one to go against this sex-symbol image when he gave her the part of Cecilia in the Rohmer-like comedy *Pensavo fosse amore e invece era una calesse* [I thought it was love but instead it was a carriage] (1991). Cecilia is the unfaithful fiancé of Troisi who, just before the wedding, leaves him, dismissing him over the front-door intercom, with a nonchalant, "…but let's keep in touch," which becomes the catch-phrase of the kids of the new generation.

Having reached the peak of success by now, Francesca also acted in films by other "bigs" in the business: Carlo Verdone directed her in *Al lupo, al lupo* [Wolf, wolf] (1992) and Gabriele Salvatores in *Sud* [South] (1993). But the relationship she formed with Troisi was much more profound. The intimate style inspired by Rohmer that Troisi tried out in *Pensavo fosse amore…* was much closer to Francesca's heart devoted to sentimental comedy. In fact, the Neapolitan director became one of Francesca Neri's trusted counsels: "A very possessive advisor," the actress stated. "He made me say no to every movie. We read the scripts together and he always said no. He was extremely exacting. He even made me reject *Puerto Escondido*, which I am still a little sorry about."

Her first role as a mother came from Carlo Carlei in *La corsa dell'innocente* (1992) *(The Flight of the Innocent)*, a fiasco in Italy but a success in America. Francesca flew there to shoot a film based on a comic strip by Simon and Kirby, *Captain America*.

Carlos Saura offered her a fine role in a film about a circus rider's vengeance in *Despara!* [Shoot anyone who passes!] (1993), but the movie turned out to be an absolute disaster. Given the cold shoulder at the Venice Film Festival, the public too ignored it and Francesca Neri suffered from its failure. It was the beginning of a long period of crisis which coincided with her break-up with Domenico Procacci, full of tears and upheavals. "It ended when I wanted to get out of movies and for him cinema was the most important thing in life, even more important than me. We hurt each other…" Francesca related.

Another reason she was inactive was her contract option binding her to Kevin Costner. In the hope of getting a part in the huge production, *Waterworld* (1995), Francesca refused too many movies and risked being forgotten by her public. For two long years she was off the set. She went into an intense program of Jungian psychoanalysis (three times a week, with "telephone therapy" during the time she was away in Spain shooting *Despara!*). In the end Kevin Costner was a disappointment. "It was all his fault and my aspirations to greatness. I deluded myself in thinking I could get a part in *Waterworld* with him. I went to London to perfect my English,

I accepted a three-year option, I prepared for the part. Then I went to Los Angeles and they rejected me in 48 hours."

Suspended between international ambitions (we find her again in the Italian-Swiss production *Bankomatt* with Bruno Ganz) and the fragility of an image which had not yet been confirmed, Francesca Neri ran the risk of becoming an unfulfilled promise.

Anna Galiena

The most beloved hairdresser of moviegoers in recent times is named Anna Galiena. It was not only Jean Rochefort whom she stunned in Patrice Leconte's *The Hairdresser's Husband* (1990), but audiences all over the world that acknowledged the charm and talent of this Italian actress who grew up just off Broadway and was discovered by the French movies. For her, too, the saying goes, "No one is a prophet in his own country."

Hers was a classical and languid beauty, an authoritative kind of femininity, politically committed, with that pinch of mystery and sexiness. Long wavy chestnut hair, always in movement and that sometimes she allowed to fall over her face. Fleshy lips, a wide, sensuous mouth, a smile that sparked fires, eyebrows dark and well marked above two deep blue eyes shining ardently: Anna Galiena was certainly not the girl-next-door in jeans à la Margherita Buy. She was the clamorously feminine woman, run through with deep veins of spirituality. She would have appealed to Truffaut who loved women

Anna Galiena's radiant smile.

like Fanny Ardant.

Anna Galiena was born in Rome on December 22, 1954 to a middle-class family in the respectable quarter of San Giovanni. As a child, in class plays she was always given the role of the Madonna. She was already beautiful then. At eleven, when she was already a shapely little woman, a trusted "family friend" raped her. The little creature did not even understand what had happened, but she felt betrayed and abused. Courageously she overcame the trauma and it would strengthen her human qualities in later life. Furthermore she grew up in an enlightened liberal family.

She enrolled in political science at the university specializing in international relations with the hope that this would be the way to satisfy her lust for travel. But she didn't last long at the university. Involved in a production of *Waiting for Godot* in Messina, she realized that destiny was taking her to the stage. She flew across the Atlantic. In Toronto she was the presenter of a TV program in Italian. In New York she worked as a waitress (after first working in a factory that produced military supplies), and in the evenings she studied at the Actor's Studio. She and Francesca De Sapio were the only Italians to become members of the Studio. She read Beckett and flirted with Shakespeare. She acted for free in the little theaters off Broadway before getting a chance on the prestigious stage of the Public Theater with Michael Moriarty (in *Uncle Vanya*), Christopher Walken and Ellen Burstyn. She played Juliet in *Romeo and Juliet* (1978), then Nina in Chekov's *The Seagull* (1980). With the American Shakespeare Company she acted in *Richard III*. Among her directors on the stage there was even the seventy-five-year-old Elia Kazan who directed her in an unforgettable *Orestes*. Anna Galiena even found a husband, John, in New York, but their marriage was not all roses.

She returned home in 1984, a dark year for Italian cinema. Cinecittà only offered her bit parts in *Mosca addio* (1987), *Willy Signori e vengo da lontano* [Willy Signori and I come from afar] (1989). Fortunately she found other admirers in Paris such as Yves Boisset, Jacques Rouffio, and Edouard Molinaro. Then the wonderful role created by Patrice Leconte came her way: Mathilde, the men's hairdresser, who accepts the powerful declaration of love from her customer Jean Rochefort. To play the part of Mathilde, Galiena gains fifteen pounds since Leconte thinks she's too thin. And above all, she must take lessons from a real barber ("Now I'm the one who cuts my nieces' and nephews' hair in the family"). But her masterful performance was most of all made up of silences, glances, pauses, slow gestures, and locks of hair falling over her face. This romantic character was contained entirely in the expressiveness of her body, her fragility and emotional honesty. In order not to see love fade, Mathilde prefers to end her life by throwing herself into the stormy sea. "When you stop loving me, swear that you won't pretend," Mathilde implores Jean Rochefort.

In the same year, 1990, Anna Galiena went to Spain to shoot another important movie, *La viuda du capitan Estrada* [Captain Estrada's widow] by the talented young José Luis Cuerda, which again helped to enrich her image as an unconventional actress. Everyone was singing the praises of Anna Galiena, even in Italy, but most of her films continued to be French (or, at least, non-Italian). Thus in France she found her second homeland, and also motivated by a great love, she settled down there to raise a family in Montparnasse with the blond French distributor Philippe Langlet whom she wed on December 21, 1992. The ceremony was extremely intimate, very much like Mathilde's in *The Hairdresser's Husband*.

Anna Galiena's career took her from France to Spain to Germany and elsewhere. She was a complete actress, extraordinary, who could act without an accent in Italian, English, French and Spanish. She would even speak Ladina, the Medieval Scottish tongue, in *Being Human* (1992), interpreting one of the film's five episodes with Robin Williams as a partner. Italy was only one stop (and not one of the most frequent) on her cinematographic wanderings around Europe. And theatrical. Galiena did not forget her beginnings in the theater and often returned to the stage. She played the part of a transvestite in Jean Genet's *The Balcony* at the Odéon Theater in Paris. In Italy she performed at the Spoleto Festival and also in Genoa. In 1994, in Avignon, Anna Galiena was the first woman anywhere in the world to be allowed to act in a Japanese No theater company (by tradition strictly male), directed by Hiroshi Teshigara, the director of the unforgettable movie, *Woman in the Dunes* (1954).

A singular honor was bestowed upon her in 1991 when she was chosen to be "godmother" of the Venice Film Festival. On the filmed title of the Festival she appears draped in an all-gold dress designed by Romeo Gigli and with enormous shining earrings ("like Venetian lanterns," Anna recalled), the living symbol of the magical city on the lagoon.

International cinema continued to shower Anna Galiena with offers. She worked with André Dussolier in *L'écrivain publique* [The scribe]. In *Veille canaille* [Old rascal] she partnered Michel Serrault.

Spain's Bigas Luna, who had a weakness for Italian beauties, gave her the role of a prostitute-mother in *Jamòn, jamòn* (1992). Anna accepted the role of the destitute woman who, to feed her children, picks up men in a trucker's bar. But Anna refuses to

take off her clothes. Not that she lacks the courage. In Bob Swaim's hammy adventure *Atlantide* (1992) she dresses up like a man.

Italy continued to ignore her disgracefully. In *Il grande cocomero* [The big watemelon] (1993) she played a secondary part as a mother of an epileptic little girl under treatment by a doctor played by Castellitto. More substantial are the parts she plays in *Senza pelle* [Skinless] (1994) by Alessandro D'Alatri (a movie for which she wins the Globo d'Oro and Grolla d'Oro prizes) and in Daniele Lucchetti's *La scuola*. In both of these films she plays a married woman who is the object of an impossible love. In *Senza pelle* it is Kim Rossi Stuart, a raving psychopath, who is in love with her and writes her febrile poems and love letters. In *La scuola* it is the turn of the clumsy professor Silvio Orlando. For the Italian cinema Anna Galiena was a woman out of reach, too beautiful and too fascinating to be approached. In fact, the petty bourgeois dimensions of the Italian comedy were far too constricting. Nevertheless, in both *Senza pelle* and *La scuola*, Anna Galiena managed to build credible female characters who combined firmness, tenderness, and sincere wonder.

The love story of *La scuola* is a very delicate and fragile one in which a very measured Galiena plays a character who is entirely self-contained, who never betrays herself, but suffers, is joyous, and is set afire by mysterious merriment fed by secret feelings. Just like Mathilde in *The Hairdresser's Husband*, this role will remain indelibly associated with her forever.

At the stratospheric heights reached by her beauty and talent, Anna Galiena was a monument of cinematic womanhood. Too lovely and too sensationally gifted for the impoverished Italian cinema of the eighties and nineties, she necessarily turned to the international scene where audiences continue to admire her in great works such as *Mario e il mago* [Mario and the wizard] (1995) by Brandauer and, above all in the very fine *Trois vies et une seule mort* [Three lives, only one death] (1996) of Raul Ruiz.

Anna Galiena as the splendid heroine in The Hairdresser's Husband *(1990). Here, with Jean Rochefort.*

Chiara Caselli

A round, impertinent, scheming little face, with deep-set, mischievous eyes, childish hands, the air of an effeminate young boy, hair almost always cut short, Chiara Caselli sometimes plays at being a male. Which was why Francesco Nuti gave her the part of Lucignolo (alias Lucy Light) in his film *Occhiopinocchio* (1994).

Born on May 17, 1967 in Bologna, daughter of a doctor and an English teacher, her adolescence was not a happy one. At a very early age she drifted into a marriage that proved very short-lived. Her acting experience began on the stage of the Teatro Stabile di Bolzano. Immediately afterwards she played the Teatro Belli in Rome in *Play it again Sam* with Antonio Salines. In Germany she did a TV series in 39 episodes, *Il nido* [The nest] performing in German.

Chiara Caselli's first years of career were very hard as a young actress with a guttural "*r*" which long hours of diction exercises helped her to correct, just in time for her movie debut. Francesco Maselli, who cast her in *Il segreto* [The secret] (1990), threatened to have her dubbed because of that guttural "*r*" which was so out of character. Just to avoid the shame of being dubbed, Chiara subjected herself to intense diction exercises. She may look like a little girl, but she has an iron will. The *New York Times* called her "a paradoxical combination of porcelain and steel." Childlike fragility and icy eyes are the key to her beauty.

Her little-girl quality also had an erotic aspect of unimaginable intensity. In most of her films, Chiara Caselli appears nude in torrid love scenes. Gus Van Sant films a sexual marathon in the long embraces of *My Own Private Idaho* (1991). In the arms of her boyfriend, Keanu Reeves, Chiara makes love with inexhaustible rage, animated by a subterranean force, as if trying to cancel her childlike look. In *Al di là delle nuvole* [Beyond the clouds] (1995) her love scenes with Peter Weller (his face between her legs) are pervaded by painful violence. And yet Chiara Caselli has nothing to do with the new queens of cinematic sex nor with Tinto Brass' big babes. Hers is an intimate eroticism strongly tied to the childlike innocence of her face. The lively eyes, small nose, thin lips (negation of the silicone protuberances of the post-*maggiorata* women), the slender, flexible body not at all striking, make her into a marvelous sexual creature, since she is so unpredictable. Her seductiveness, which is mostly mental, is interwoven with the most secret male fantasies, the most unpronounceable ones.

Her horizons were those of artistic cinema (from the Taviani brothers to Costa-Gavras, from Maselli to Peter Del Monte) that took the most subtle roads to seduction. Her presence gave density and warmth to Liliana Cavani's *Dove siete? Io sono qui* [Where are you? I'm here] (1993) where she plays the part of a deaf mute. Chiara, always scrupulously professional, dedicated much time to learning sign language for the film and for this role she won the Nastro d'Argento and Grolla d'Oro prizes.

The success of *My Own Private Idaho* opened the doors of Hollywood to her. Adrian Lyne gave her a screen test for *Indecent Proposal* and Quentin Tarantino for *Pulp Fiction*, but neither produced positive results. Still, her rendezvous with the major studios seemed only to be a matter of time.

It was she who was honored to walk in Alida Valli's footsteps in the French remake of *Senso* [Sense] directed by Gérard Vergez. Here she plays the part of the ultra-romantic Countess Serpieri, twenty-one years old and married to an aged count played by Jean-Pierre Aumont. "I married him to gain social position, but also out of affection. When he falls ill and goes into coma, I bring up the past and confess to the tormented relation that had bound me five years before to a much-loved and desired Austrian official, the actor Werner Schreyer."

In France Chiara Caselli also shot *L'année de l'eveil* [The year of the awakening]. Like Anna Galiena she found admirers abroad, but at home too she had rich opportunities to show what she could do, such as in *Sabato italiano* [Italian Saturday] (1992), *Zuppa di pesce* [Fish soup] (1992), and *Storie d'amore con crampi* [Love story with cramps] (1995). Unfortunately few people have seen *La domenica specialmente* [Especially Sunday] (1991) which is still one of her finest interpretations. Directed by Marco Tullio Giordana she reveals herself to be a mature and vibrant actress in the role of a girl who lets her mother-in-law spy on her as she makes love with her husband. Another morbid and difficult part that confirmed her image as an unlikely storyteller of desire.

Italy's Chiara Caselli is on her way to becoming an international star.

FILMOGRAPHY

ALLASIO MARISA
1952 Gli eroi della domenica by M. Camerini.
1953 Perdonami by M. Costa.
1954 Cuore di mamma by L. Capuano.
Ballata tragica by L. Capuano.
1955 Le diciottenni by M. Mattoli.
Ragazze d'oggi by L. Zampa.
1956 War and Peace by K. Vidor.
Maruzzella by L. Capuano.
Le schiave di Cartagine by G. Brignone.
Poor but Handsome (Poveri ma belli) by D. Risi.
1957 Susanna tutta panna by Steno [S. Vanzina].
Irresistible (Belle ma povere) by D. Risi.
Marisa la civetta by M. Bolognini.
The Seven Hills of Rome by R. Rowland and M. Russo.
1958 Carmela è una bambola by G. Puccini.
Venice, the Moon and You by D. Risi.
Camping by F. Zeffirelli.
Nacht, wie Gott sie schuf by H. Schott-Schoeninger.

ALT CAROL
1987 Via Montenapoleone by C. Vanzina.
My First 40 Years (I miei primi 40 anni) by C. Vanzina.
1988 Bye Bye Baby by E. Oldoini.
Treno di panna by A. De Carlo.
1989 Mortacci by S. Citti.
La più bella del Reame by C. Ferrario.
1990 Un piede in Paradiso by E.B. Clucher [E. Barboni].
Miliardi by C. Vanzina.
1991 Un orso chiamato Arturo by S. Martino.
1993 Anni '90 – parte II by E. Oldoini.

ANTONELLI LAURA
1965 Le sedicenni by L. Petrini.
1966 Dr. Goldfoot and the Girl Bomb (Le spie vengono dal semifreddo) by M. Bava.
1968 La rivoluzione sessuale by R. Ghione.
1969 Detective Belli (Un detective) by R. Guerrieri.
L'arcangelo by G. Capitani.
Venus im Pelz by M. Dillmann [M. Dallamano].
1970 Gradiva by G. Albertazzi.
A Man Called Sledge (Sledge) by G. Gentili and V. Morrow.
1971 Incontro d'amore (Bali) by U. Liberatore and P. Heusch.
Il merlo maschio by P. Festa Campanile.
Sans mobile apparent by Ph. Labro.
The Scoundrel (Les mariés de l'an II) by J.P. Rappeneau.
1972 All'onorevole piacciono le donne by L. Fulci.
Scoundrel in White (Docteur Popaul) by C. Chabrol.
1973 Malicious (Malizia) by S. Samperi.
Sessomatto by D. Risi.
1974 Peccato veniale by S. Samperi.
Histoire de l'eil by P. Longchamps.
Mio Dio, come sono caduta in basso! by L. Comencini.
1975 The Divine Nymph (Divina creatura) by A. Patroni Griffi.
1976 The Innocent (L'innocente) by L. Visconti.
1977 Black Journal (Gran bollito) by M. Bolognini.
Wifemistress (Mogliamante) by M. Vicario.
1979 Letti selvaggi (epis. Un pomeriggio noiosetto; Una donna d'affari) by L. Zampa.
Il malato immaginario by T. Cervi.
1980 Mi faccio la barca by S. Corbucci.
1981 Passione d'amore by E. Scola.
Il turno by T. Cervi.
Casta e pura by S. Samperi.
1982 Porca vacca by P. Festa Campanile.
Sesso e volentieri (epis. La nuova Marisa, Crociera d'amore, L'avventura, La principessa e il cameriere) by D. Risi.

Viuuulentemente mia by C. Vanzina.
1984 Tranches de vie (epis. Une nuit inoubliable) by F. Leterrier.
1985 La gabbia by G. Patroni Griffi.
1986 Grandi Magazzini by F. Castellano and Pipolo [G. Moccia].
1987 Rimini Rimini by S. Corbucci.
Roba da ricchi by S. Corbucci.
1990 L'avaro by T. Cervi.
1991 Malizia 2000 by S. Samperi.

BARBARA PAOLA
1935 Campo di maggio by G. Forzano.
1936 Amazzoni bianche by G. Righelli.
L'antenato by G. Brignone.
1937 Questi ragazzi by M. Mattoli.
Eravamo sette sorelle by N. Malasomma.
1938 Per uomini soli by G. Brignone.
Orgoglio by M. Elter.
L'albergo degli assenti by R. Matarazzo.
Lotte nell'ombra by D.M. Gambino.
1939 Follie del secolo by A. Palermi.
Napoli che non muore by A. Palermi.
1940 Il ponte dei sospiri by M. Bonnard.
La granduchessa si diverte by G. Gentilomo.
La peccatrice by A. Palermi.
1941 Il bravo di Venezia by C. Campogalliani.
The King's Jester (Il re si diverte) by M. Bonnard.
Turbine by C. Mastrocinque.
Confessione by F. Calzavara.
1942 Rossini by M. Bonnard.
Quarta pagina by N. Manzari.
1943 Fiebre by P. Zeglio.
Accadde a Damasco by J. Lopez Rubio and P. Zeglio.
La danza del fuoco by G.C. Simonelli.
1944 Noche fantastica by L. Marquina.
1945 Su ultima noche by C. Arevalo.
Leyenda de feria by J. De Orduna.
1946 La prodiga by R. Gil.
Audencia publica by F. Rey.
1947 La nao capitana by F. Rey.
Tres espejos by I. Vajda.
La monaca di Monza by R. Pacini.
1948 I cavalieri dalla maschera nera / I beati Paoli by P. Mercanti.
Campo bravo by P. Lazaga Sabatè.
1949 Por el Gran Premio di P. Caron.
El sotano by J. De Mayora.
Torna a Napoli / Simme 'e Napule, paisà by D.M. Gambino.
1950 La figlia del mendicante by C. Campogalliani.
1952 Eran trecento / La spigolatrice di Sapri by G.P. Callegari.
I figli non si vendono by M. Bonnard.
La figlia del diavolo by P. Zeglio.
1953 La cavallina storna by G. Morelli.
Nerone e Messalina by P. Zeglio.
Capitan Fantasma by P. Zeglio.
1954 Sua Altezza ha detto: no! by M. Basaglia.
1955 Il coraggio by D. Paolella.
1956 Storia di una minorenne by P. Costa.
1960 Call Girls of Rome (I piaceri del sabato notte) by D. D'Anza.
1961 Le sette sfide by P. Zeglio.
1963 Il segno del Coyote by M. Caiano.
1964 Ride and Kil (Cavalca e uccidi) by J.L. Mallorqui [J.L. Borau].
1965 Have Another Bier (Des pissenlits par la racine) by G. Lautner.
Two Gunmen (Los rurales de Texas) by A. Greepy [P. Zeglio].
I quattro inesorabili by P. Zeglio.
Ménage all'italiana by F. indovina.
1966 El diablo también llora by J.A. Nieves Conde.
1968 Killer adios by P. Zeglio.
1969 The Appointment by S. Lumet.
1970 A Man Called Sledge (Sledge) by G. Gentili and V. Morrow.
La banda de los tres crisantemos by S. McCoY [I. F. Iquino].
1975 Irene, Irene by P. Del Monte.
1978 Scherzi da prete by P.F. Pingitore.

BENETTI ADRIANA
1941 Do You Like Women? (Teresa Venerdì) by V. De Sica.
1942 Avanti c'è posto by M. Bonnard.
Four Steps in the Clouds (Quattro passi fra le nuvole) by A. Blasetti.
C'è sempre un ma! by L. Zampa.
1943 Gente dell'aria by E. Pratelli.
Tempesta sul golfo by G. Righelli.
Quartieri alti by M. Soldati,
Les petites du quai au fleurs by M. Allégret.
1945 Il sole di Montecassino by G.M. Scotese.
1946 Torna... a Sorrento by C.L. Bragaglia.
O sole mio by G. Gentilomo.
1947 Inquietudine by V. Carpignano.
Uno tra la folla by E. Cerlesi and P. Tellini.
Furia (Furia) by G. Alessandrini.
Tombolo, paradiso nero by G. Ferroni.
1948 Manù il contrabbandiere by L. De Caro.
1949 Llegada de noche by J.A. Nieves Conde.
Neutralidad by E.F. Ardavin.
1950 La mujer de nadie by G. Delgras.
Gli ultimi giorni di Pompei by P. Moffa and M. L'Herbier.
47 morto che parla by C.L. Bragaglia.
1951 Donde comenzian los pantanos by A. Ber Ciani.
1952 Las aguas bajan turbas by H. del Carril.
1954 Le due orfanelle by G. Gentilomo.
1955 Le diciottenni by M. Mattoli.
1957 A vent'anni è sempre festa by V. Duse.

BERTI MARINA
1941 La fuggitiva by P. Ballerini.
Divieto di sosta by M. Albani.
1943 Giacomo l'idealista by A. Lattuada.
La valle del diavolo by M. Mattoli.
La primadonna by I. Perilli.
Storia di una capinera by G. Righelli.
La donna della montagna by R. Castellani.
1944 La porta del cielo by V. De Sica.
1945 I dieci comandamenti (epis. Non desiderare la roba d'altri) by G.W. Chili.
1946 Il fantasma della morte by J. Glavany [G. Guarino].
Il testimone by P. Germi.
Notte di tempesta by G. Franciolini.
1947 Preludio d'amore by G. Paolucci.
Sinfonia fatale by V. Stoloff.
1948 The Earth Cries Out (Il grido della terra) by D. Coletti.
1949 Prince of Foxes by H. King.
Vespro siciliano by G. Pàstina.
1950 Il cielo è rosso by C. Gora.
1951 Quo Vadis? by M. LeRoy.
Il sentiero dell'odio by S. Grieco.
Il capitano nero by A. Pozzetti and G. Ansoldi.
Up Front by A. Hall.
Deported by R. Siodmak.
1952 The Queen of Sheba (La regina di Saba) by P. Francisci.
Carne inquieta by S. Prestifilippo.
Amore rosso by A. Vergano.
La colpa di una madre by C. Duse.
1953 Ai margini della metropoli by C. Lizzani.
Febbre di vivere by C. Gora.
1954 Casta Diva by C. Gallone.
Abdullah the Great by G. Ratoff.
Operazione mitra by G. Cristallini.
1955 I cavalieri della Regina by J. Lerner.
Faccia da mascalzone by R. Andreassi and L. Comfort.
Il canto dell'emigrante by A. Forzano.
1956 Marie-Antoinette, reine de France by J. Delannoy.
1858 Il cavaliere dalla spada nera by L. Kish.
1959 Ben Hur by W. Wyler.
1960 Un eroe del nostro tempo by S. Capogna.
1961 Madame (Madame Sans-Gêne) by Christian-Jaque.
1962 Jessica (id.) by J. Negulesco.
Damon and Pythias / The Tyrant of

Syracuse (in G.B.) (Il tiranno di Siracusa) by C. Bernhardt.
Swordsman of Siena (La congiura dei Dieci) by B. Bandini and E. Périer.
1963 Cleopatra by J.L. Mankiewicz.
1964 Le conseguenze by S. Capogna.
Monsieur by J.P. Le Chanois.
1965 Made in Italy (id.) by N. Loy.
1966 Angel for Satan (Un angelo per Satana) by C. Mastrocinque.
1967 The Strangers Returns (Un uomo, un cavallo, una pistola) by L. Vance [L. Vanzi].
Qualcuno ha tradito by F. Shannon [F. Prosperi].
1968 Temptation by L. Benvenuti.
1969 If It's Tuesday, This Must Be Belgium by M. Stuart.
Le avventure di Ulisse by F. Rossi.
1970 Cran d'arrêt by Y. Boisset.
Strada senza uscita / Dead End by G. Palmieri.
La califfa by A. Bevilacqua.
1971 Tre nel Mille by F. Indovina.
1973 Buona parte di Paolina by N. Rossati.
1974 Il pianeta Venere by E. Tattoli.
La polizia chiede aiuto by M. Dallamano.
1975 Night Train (L'ultimo treno della notte) by A. Lado.
The Divine Nymph (Divina creatura) by M. Bolognini.
1976 Don Milani by A. Angeli.
Moses (Mosè) by G. De Bosio.
Garofano rosso by L. Faccini.
1977 Jesus of Mazareth by F. Zeffirelli.
Una spirale di nebbia by E. Visconti.
1985 Il pentito by P. Squitieri.
1986 L'ultima mazurka by G. Bettetini.
1988 La posta in gioco by S. Nasca.
1991 Ostinato destino by G. Albano.

BERTINI FRANCESCA
(only the talkies)
1931 La femme d'une nuit by M. L'Herbier.
1934 Odette by J. Houssin e G. Zambon.
1943 Dora, la espia by R. Matarazzo.
1956 A sud niente di nuovo by G.C. Simonelli.
1975 Una ragazza di Praga by S. Pastore.
1976 1900 (Novecento) by B. Bertolucci.

BOLKAN FLORINDA
1968 Candy by Ch. Marquand.
1969 Una ragazza piuttosto complicata by D. Damiani.
The Damned (La caduta degli dei) by L. Visconti.
Detective Belli (Un detective) by R. Guerrieri.
Le voleur de crimes by N. Marquand Trintignant.
Machine Gun McCain (Gli intoccabili) by G. Montaldo
Metti, una sera a cena by G. Patroni Griffi.
1970 Investigation of a Citizen Above Suspicion (Indagine su un cittadino al di sopra di ogni sospetto) by E. Petri.
...e venne il giorno dei limoni neri by C. Bazzoni.
The Anonymous Venetian (Anonimo veneziano) by E.M. Salerno.
The Last Valley by J. Clavell.
1971 Lizard in a Woman's Sky (Una lucertola con la pelle di donna) by L. Fulci.
Romance (Incontro) by P. Schivazappa.
Una stagione all'inferno by N. Risi.
1972 The Master Touch – A Man to Respect (in G.B.) (Un uomo da rispettare) by M. Lupo.
Non si sevizia un paperino by L. Fulci.
Le droit d'aimer by E. Le Hung.
1973 Cari genitori by E.M. Salerno.
Una breve vacanza by V. De Sica.
1974 Le mouton enragé by M. Deville.
Flavia, la monaca musulmana by G. Mingozzi.
1975 Le orme by L. Bazzoni.
Royal Flesh by R. Lester.
The Day That Shook the World / Assassination (in G.B.) (Atentat u Sarajevo) by V. Bulajic.

210

Il ponte dei sospiri by P. Pierotti.
Il treno del sabato by V. Sala.

CARDINALE CLAUDIA
1958 Goha by J. Baratier.
Bid Deal on Madonna Street / Persons Unknown (in G.B.) (I soliti ignoti) by M. Monicelli.
Tre straniere a Roma by C. Gora.
1959 La prima notte by A. Cavalcanti
Fiasco in Milan (Audace colpo dei soliti ignoti) by N. Loy.
Il magistrato by L. Zampa.
The Facts of Murder / A Sordid Affair (G.B.) (Un maledetto imbroglio) by P. Germi.
Upstairs and Downstairs by R. Thomas.
1960 Vento del Sud by P. Provenzale.
The Battle of Austerlitz (Austerlitz) by A. Gance.
Rocco and His Brothers (Rocco e i suoi fratelli) by L. Visconti.
Bell'Antonio (Il bell'Antonio) by M. Bolognini.
I delfini by F. Maselli.
1961 The Girl with a Suitcase (La ragazza con la valigia) by V. Zurlini.
Les lions sont lachés by H. Verneuil.
La Viaccia (id.) / The Love Makers (in G.B.) (La viaccia) by M. Bolognini.
1962 Senilità (id.) by M. Bolognini.
Cartouche (id.) / Swords of Blood (in G.B.) (Cartouche) by Ph. de Broca.
1963 The Leopard (Il gattopardo) by L. Visconti.
Bebo's Girl (La ragazza di Bube) by L. Comencini.
8 1/2 (id.) / Eight and a Half (G.B.) (8 1/2) by F. Fellini.
1964 The Pink Panther by B. Edwards.
Circus World by H. Hathaway.
Time of Indifference (Gli indifferenti) by F. Maselli.
The Magnificent Cuckold (Il magnifico cornuto) by A. Pietrangeli.
1965 Blindflod by Ph. Dunne.
Sandra / Of a Thousand Delights (G.B.) (Vaghe stelle dell'Orsa) by L. Visconti.
1966 Lost Command by M. Robson.
The Professionals by R. Brooks.
Sex Quartet (Le fate – epis. Fata Armenia) by M. Monicelli.
1967 Una rosa per tutti by F. Rossi.
Don't Make Waves by A. Mackendrick.
1968 The Day of the Owl (Il giorno della civetta) by D. Damiani.
The Hell with Heroes by J. Sargent.
A Fine Pair (Ruba al prossimo tuo…) di F. Maselli.
Once Upon a Time in the West (C'era una volta il West) by S. Leone.
1969 The Red Tent (Krāsnaja palátka) by M. Kalatazov.
Nell'anno del Signore by L. Magni.
Certain, Very Certain, as a Matter of Fact… Probable (Certo, certissimo… anzi probabile) by M. Fondato.
1970 The Adventures of Gerard by J. Skolimowsky.
1971 The 21 Carat Snatch (Popsy Pop) by J. Herman.
Bello onesto emigrato Australia sposerebbe compaesana illibata by L. Zampa.
The Legend of Frenchie King (Les pétroleuses) by Christian-Jaque.
1972 Papal Audience (L'udienza) by M. Ferreri.
Hit Man (La Scoumoune) by J. Giovanni.
1973 Fury (il giorno del furore) by A. Calenda.
1974 I guappi by P. Squitieri.
Conversation Piece (Gruppo di famiglia in un interno) by L. Visconti.
1975 Midnight Pleasure (A mezzanotte va la ronda del piacere) by M. Fondato.
Libera, amore mio! by M. Bolognini.
Lucky Girls (Qui comincia l'avventura) by C. Di Palma.
1976 Il comune senso del pudore by A. Sordi.
1977 Jesus of Nazareth (Gesù di Nazareth) by F. Zeffirelli.
Goodbye & Amen (id.) by D. Damiani.
La part du feu by E. Périer.
Il prefetto di ferro by P. Squitieri.
1978 The Gun (L'arma) by P. Squitieri.

Corleone by P. Squitieri.
The Girl in Blue Velvet by A. Bridges.
1979 Escape to Athena by J. Pan Cosmatos.
1980 Si salvi chi vuole by R. Faenza.
The Salamander by P. Zimmer.
1981 La pelle by L. Cavani.
Fitzcarraldo by W. Herzog.
1982 The Gift (Le cadeau) by M. Lang.
Le ruffian by J. Giovanni.
1984 Henry IV (Enrico IV) by M. Bellocchio.
Claretta by P. Squitieri.
L'été prochain by N. Trintignant.
1985 La donna delle meraviglie by A. Bevilacqua.
1987 History (La storia) by L. Comencini.
1988 A Man in Love by D. Kurys.
Blu elettrico by E. Gaeng [D. Thermes].
1989 The French Revolution by R. Enrico and R.T. Heffron.
Hiver 54 l'abbé Pierre by D. Amar.
1990 Atto di dolore by P. Squitieri.
1991 588 Rue Paradis by H. Verneuil.
1993 Son on the Pink Panther by B. Edwards.
1994 Elles ne pensent qu'à ça by Ch. Dubreuil.

CARMI VERA
1940 Addio giovinezza! by F.M. Poggioli.
1941 L'amore canta by F.M. Poggioli.
Un marito per il mese d'aprile by G.C. Simonelli.
Il cavaliere senza nome by F. Cerio.
Villa da vendere by F. Cerio.
1942 La fortuna viene dal cielo by A. Ráthonyi.
Una volta alla settimana by A. Ráthonyi.
Redenzione by M. Albani.
Happy Days (Giorni felici) by G. Franciolini.
Labbra serrate by M. Mattoli.
1943 Due cuori fra le belve by G.C. Simonelli.
Anything for a Song (Ho tanta voglia di cantare) by M. Mattoli.
La vispa Teresa by M. Mattoli.
Il fidanzato di mia moglie by C.L. Bragaglia.
La signora in nero by N. Malasomma.
1944 Finalmente sì by L. Kish.
07… tassì by A. D'Aversa.
Circo equestre Za-Bum (epis. Galop finale al circo) by M. Mattoli.
1945 I dieci comandamenti (epis. Onora il padre e la madre) di G.W. Chili.
Le miserie del signor Travet by M. Soldati.
1946 O sole mio (id.) by G. Gentilomo.
Addio, mia bella Napoli by M. Bonnard.
Le modelle di via Margutta by G.M. Scotese.
1947 Tempesta d'anime by G. Gentilomo.
Come persi la guerra by C. Borghesio.
Trepidazione by T. Frenguelli.
Natale al campo 119 by P. Francisci.
1948 Il fiacre n° 13 (1° epis. Delitto – 2° epis. Castigo) by M. Mattoli.
Sono io l'assassino by R. Bianchi Montero.
L'isola di Montecristo by M. Sequi.
1950 Una domenica d'agosto by L. Emmer.
Le due sorelle by M. Volpe.
1951 Buon viaggio, pover'uomo by G. Pàstina.
Milano miliardaria by M. Girolami, M. Marchesi and V. Metz.
Anema e core by M. Mattoli.
1952 Penne nere by O. Biancoli.
1953 La cieca di Sorrento by G. Gentilomo.
Agenzia matrimoniale by G. Pàstina.
La figlia del reggimento by G. von Bolvary and T. Covaz.
Ti ho sempre amato! by M. Costa.
1954 In amore si pecca in due by V. Cottafavi.
Passione by M. Calandri.
Appassionatamente by G. Gentilomo.
Tradita by M. Bonnard.
Trieste, cantico d'amore by M. Calandri.
Ho pianto per te! by G. Rippo.
1955 Friends for Life (Amici per la pelle) by F. Rossi.
La ladra by M. Bonnard.
Prigionieri del male by M. Costa.

1956 Mai ti scorderò by G. Guarino.
I miliardari by G. Malatesta.

CASELLI CHIARA
1990 Il segreto by F. Maselli.
L'année de l'eveil by G. Corbiau.
Tracce di vita amorosa by P. Del Monte.
1991 Segno di fuoco by N. Bizzarri.
La domenica specialmente (epis. La neve sul fuoco by M.T. Giordana).
My Own Private Idaho by G. Van Sant.
1992 Italian Saturday (Sabato italiano) by L. Manuzzi.
Zuppa di pesce by F. Infascelli.
Senso by G. Vergez.
Nero by G. Soldi.
1993 The Little Apocalypse (La petite Apocalypse) by Costa Gavras.
Floréal (Fiorile) by P. e V. Taviani.
Dove siete? Io sono qui by L. Cavani.
1994 Occhiopinocchio by F. Nuti.
1995 Storie d'amore con i crampi by P. Quartullo.
Al di là delle nuvole (epis. Non mi cercare) by M. Antonioni.
1996 Oui by A. Jardin.

CEGANI ELISA
1935 Aldebaran by A. Blasetti.
1936 Ma non è una cosa seria by M. Camerini.
Cavalleria by G. Alessandrini.
1937 Countess of Parma (Contessa di Parma) by A. Blasetti.
1938 Napoli d'altri tempi by A. Palermi.
Ettore Fieramosca by A. Blasetti.
1939 Retroscena by A. Blasetti.
1941 The Iron Crown (La corona di ferro) by A. Blasetti.
1942 La cena delle beffe by A. Blasetti.
Gioco pericoloso by N. Malasomma.
1943 Gente dell'aria by E. Pratelli.
Harlem by C. Gallone.
Nessuno torna indietro by A. Blasetti.
1945 I dieci comandamenti (epis. Non mentire!) by G.W. Chili.
1946 A Day in the Life (Un giorno nella vita) by A. Blasetti.
1948 Eleonora Duse by F.W. Ratti.
1949 Fabiola (id.) by A. Blasetti.
1950 Le château de verre by R. Clément.
1952 La prigioniera della torre di fuoco by G.W. Chili.
Time Gone By / Infidelity (in G.B.) (Altri tempi) by A. Blasetti.
Pride, Love and Suspicion by A. Blasetti.
La nemica by G. Bianchi.
1953 Luxury Girls (Fanciulle di lusso) by B. Vorhaus.
Canzone appassionata by G.C. Simonelli.
1954 Amarti è il mio peccato by S. Grieco.
Nel gorgo del peccato by V. Cottafavi.
Casa Ricordi by C. Gallone.
Graziella by G. Bianchi.
Anatomy of Love / A Slice of Life (in G.B.) (Tempi nostri) by A. Blasetti.
Una donna libera by V. Cottafavi.
Il vetturale del Moncenisio by G. Brignone.
1955 Nana (id.) by Christian-Jaque.
Lucky to Be a Woman (La fortuna di essere donna) by A. Blasetti.
1957 The Doll That Took the Town (La donna del giorno) by F. Maselli.
Amore e chiacchiere by A. Blasetti.
1958 Al servizio dell'imperatore by C. Canaille and E. Anton.
1959 Ciao, ciao bambina by S. Grieco.
1961 Constantine and the Cross / Constantin the Great (in G.B.) (Costantino il Grande) by L. De Felice.
Il giudizio universale by V. De Sica.
1962 La monaca di Monza by C. Gallone.
The Reluctant Saint by E. Dmytryk.
Escapade in Florence by S. Previn.
Giacobbe ed Esaù by M. Landi.
1963 Perseus Against the Monster (Perseo l'invincibile) by A. De Martino.
1964 Liolà by A. Blasetti.
Saul e David by M. Baldi.
1966 Io, io, io… e gli altri by A. Blasetti.
1968 The Killer Likes Candy (Un killer per Sua Maestà) by R. Owens [F. Chentrens].
1969 Simón Bolivar by A. Blasetti.

The Sicilian Clan (Le clan des Siciliens) by H. Verneuil.
1973 La rosa rossa by F. Giraldi.
1976 Languidi baci, perfide carezze by A. Angeli.
1977 Beyond Good and Evil (Al di là del bene e del male) by L. Cavani.
1982 Domani si balla! by M. Nichetti.

CORTESE VALENTINA
1941 L'orizzonte dipinto by G. Salvini.
Il bravo di Venezia by C. Campogalliani.
First Love (Primo amore) by C. Gallone.
1942 La cena delle beffe by A. Blasetti.
Una Signora dell'Ovest (id.) by C. Koch.
La regina di Navarra by C. Gallone.
Soltanto un bacio by G.C. Simonelli.
Orizzonte di sangue by G. Righelli.
Happy Days (Giorni felici) by G. Franciolini.
Quarta pagina by N. Manzari.
1943 Quattro ragazze sognano by G. Giannini.
Nessuno torna indietro by A. Blasetti.
Chi l'ha visto? by G. Alessandrini.
1945 I dieci comandamenti (epis. Non bestemmiare) by G.W. Chili.
A Yank in Rome (Un americano in vacanza) by L. Zampa.
1946 Roma città libera / La notte porta consiglio by M. Pagliero.
1947 Bullet for Stefano (Il Passatore) by D. Coletti.
Les miserables (I miserabili) by R. Freda.
Il corriere del re by G. Righelli.
1948 The Wandering Jew (L'ebreo errante) by G. Alessandrini. Crossroads of Passions (Gli uomini sono nemici) by E. Giannini and H. Calef.
1949 Black Magic by G. Ratoff.
Thieves' Highway by J. Dassin.
Malaya / East of the Rising Sun (in G.B.) by R. Thorpe.
The Glass Mountain by H. Cass.
1950 Unwanted Women (Donne senza nome) di G. von Radványi.
1951 Shadow of the Eagle (La rivale dell'imperatrice) by S. Salkow and J. Comin.
House on Telegraph Hill by R. Wise.
1952 The Secret People by T. Dickinson.
1953 Lulù by F. Cerchio.
La passeggiata by R. Rascel.
1954 Angels of Darkness / Forbidden Women (in G.B.) (Donne proibite) by G. Amato.
Il matrimonio by A. Petrucci.
Cartouche / Le avventure di Cartouche) by S. Sekely and G. Vernuccio.
The Barefoot Contessa by J.L. Mankiewicz.
Avanzi di galera by V. Cottafavi.
1955 Il conte Aquila by G. Salvini.
Adriana Lecouvreur by G. Salvini.
The Girl Friends (Le amiche) by M. Antonioni.
1956 Magic Fire by W. Dieterle.
Faccia da mascalzone by R. Andreassi and L. Comfort.
Calabuch by L. G. Berlanga.
1977 Kean, genio e sregolatezza by V. Gassman.
Dimentica il mio passato by P. Zeglio.
1958 Amore e guai by A. Dorigo.
Amore a prima vista by F. Rossi.
1961 Barabbas (Barabba) by R. Fleischer.
1962 Square of Violence (Nasije na tragu) by L. Bercovici.
Axel Munthe (Le livre de San Michele) by G. Capitani and R. Jugert.
1963 The Evil Eye (La ragazza che sapeva troppo) by M. Bava.
1964 The Visit (Der Besuch) by B. Wicki.
1965 The Possessed (La donna del lago) by L. Bazzoni and F. Rossellini.
Juliet of the Spirits (Giulietta degli spiriti) by F. Fellini.
1966 Le soleil noir by D. de la Patellière.
1968 The Legend of Lylah Clare by R. Aldrich.
Listen, Let's Make Love (Scusi facciamo l'amore?) by V. Caprioli.
1969 Toh, è morta la nonna! by M. Monicelli.
The Secret of Santa Vittoria by S. Kramer.
1970 Le bateau sur l'herbe by G. Brach.

211

First Love (Erste Liebe) by M. Schell.
1971 L'iguana dalla lingua di fuoco by R. Pareto [R. Freda].
Give Her the Moon (Les caprices de Marie) by Ph. de Broca.
Madly by R. Kahane.
1972 Imputazione di omicidio per uno studente by M. Bolognini.
Brother Sun, Sister Moon (Fratello Sole, sorella Luna) by F. Zeffirelli.
The Assassination of Trotsky by J. Losey.
1973 Day for Night (La nuit américaine) by F. Truffaut.
1974 Il bacio by M. Lanfranchi.
La grande trouille by P. Grunstein.
Appassionata by G. Calderone.
Amore mio non farmi male by V. Sindoni.
1975 Son tornate a fiorire le rose by V. Sindoni.
La chair de l'orchidée by P. Chéreau.
Il cav. Costante Nicosia demoniaco, ovvero Dracula in Brianza by L. Fulci.
Kidnap Syndicate (La città sconvolta: caccia spietata ai rapitori) by F. Di Leo.
1976 Gli amici di Nick Hezard by F. Di Leo.
Le grand escogriffe by C. Pinoteau.
1977 Jesus of Nazareth by F. Zeffirelli.
Widow's Nest (Nido de viudas) by T. Navarro.
1978 Tanto va la gatta al lardo… (epis. Tanto va la gatta al lardo – Amore coniugale) by M. Aleandri.
1979 Un'ombra nell'ombra by P. Carpi.
1980 When Time Ran Out by J. Goldstone.
1987 Via Montenapoleone by C. Vanzina.
Tango blu by A. Bevilacqua.
1989 The Adventures of the Baron of Munchausen by T. Gilliam.
1992 La Ferdinanda by R. Horn.
1994 Sparrow (Storia di una capinera) by F. Zeffirelli.

CUCINOTTA MARIA GRAZIA
1990 Vacanze di Natale 90 by E. Oldoini.
Viaggio d'amore by O. Fabbri.
1993 Abbronzatissimi 2 – Un anno dopo by B. Gaburro.
Alto rischio by M. Steel [S. Massi].
1994 The Postman (Il postino) bu M. Radford.
1995 I laureati by L. Pieraccioni.
El dia de la bestia by A. de la Iglesia.
Il decisionista by M. Cappelloni.
Italiani by M. Ponzi.

DELLA CORTE BIANCA
1938 Per uomini soli by G. Brignone.
1939 Ball at the Castle (Ballo al castello) by M. Neufeld.
Assenza ingiustificata by M. Neufeld.
1940 Dopo divorzieremo by N. Malasomma.
Addio, giovinezza! by F.M. Poggioli.
1941 Il pozzo dei miracoli by G. Righelli.
L'attore scomparso by L. Zampa.
Schoolgirls Diary (Ore 9 lezione di chimica) by M. Mattoli.
First Love (Primo amore) by C. Gallone.
1942 Count of Monte-Cristo (Le comte de Monte-Cristo) by R. Vernay.

DELLERA FRANCESCA
1986 Grandi magazzini by F. Castellano and Pipolo [G. Moccia].
1987 Letters from Capri (Capriccio) by T. Brass.
1991 Roba da ricchi by S. Corbucci.
La carne by M. Ferreri.
1994 L'ours en peluche by J. Deray.

DEL POGGIO CARLA
1940 Maddalena… zero in condotta by V. De Sica.
1941 La bocca sulla strada by R. Roberti.
La scuola dei timidi by C.L. Bragaglia.
1942 Un garibaldino al convento by V. De Sica.
C'è sempre un ma! by L. Zampa.
Violette nei capelli by C.L. Bragaglia.
Signorinette by L. Zampa.
1943 Incontri di notte by N. Malasomma.
1944 Tre ragazze cercano marito by D. Coletti.
1946 L'angelo e il diavolo by M. Camerini.
The Bandit (il bandito) by A. Lattuada.
Umanità by J. Salvatori.
1947 Tragic Hunt / The Tragic Pursuit (in

G.B.) (Caccia tragica) by G. De Santis.
1948 Lost Youth (Gioventù perduta) by P. Germi.
Without Pity (Senza pietà) by A. Lattuada.
1949 The Mill on the River (Il mulino del Po) by A. Lattuada.
1950 Cavalcata d'eroi by M. Costa.
Lights of Variety (Luci del varietà) by A. Lattuada and F. Fellini.
Sigillo rosso by F. Calzavara.
1951 Il sentiero dell'odio by S. Grieco.
The Ungrateful Heart (Core 'ngrato) by G. Brignone.
1952 Les loups chassent la nuit by B. Borderie.
Tormento del passato by M. Bonnard.
It Happened in Rome / Rome Eleven O'Clock (in G.B.) (Roma ore 11) by G. De Santis.
Melodie immortali / Mascagni by G. Gentilomo.
1953 Dangerous Woman (Bufere) by G. Brignone.
1954 Cose da pazzi by G.W. Pabst.
Les révoltes de Lomanach by R. Pottier.
Le secret d'Hélène Marimon by H. Calef.
1956 The Wanderers (I girovaghi) by H. Fregonese.

DE LUCA LORELLA
1955 The Swindler (Il bidone) by F. Fellini.
1956 Poor but Handsome (Poveri ma belli) by D. Risi.
Orlando e i paladini di Francia by P. Francisci.
1957 Sette canzoni per sette sorelle by M. Girolami.
Padri e figli by M. Monicelli.
Mysteries of Paris (I misteri di Parigi) by F. Cerchio.
Gente felice by M. Loy.
L'ultima violenza by R. Matarazzo.
Irresistible (Belle ma povere) (id.) by D. Risi.
Il medico e lo stregone by M. Monicelli.
1958 El hombre del paraguas blanco di J.R. Marchent.
Napoli, sole mio by G.C. Simonelli.
Dinanzi a noi il cielo by R. Savarese.
Domenica è sempre domenica by C. Mastrocinque.
È permesso, maresciallo? by C.L. Bragaglia.
Love on the Riviera / Girls for the Summer (in G.B.) (Racconti d'estate) by G. Franciolini.
Don Vesuvio by S. Marcellini.
1959 Sign of the Gladiator (Nel segno di Roma) by G. Brignone.
Poveri milionari by D. Risi.
First Love (Primo amore) by M. Camerini.
Ciao, ciao, bambina! by S. Grieco.
La duchessa di Santa Lucia by R. Bianchi Montero.
Costa azzurra by V. Sala.
Agosto, donne mie non vi conosco by G. Malatesta.
Quanto sei bella Roma by M. Girolami.
1960 Il principe fusto by M. Arena.
Caccia al marito by M. Girolami.
1961 Bellezze sulla spiaggia by R. Guerrieri [M. Girolami].
1962 Taras Bulba, il cosacco by F. Baldi.
La notte dell'Innominato by L. Demar [L. De Marchi].
1963 Charge of the Black Lanciers (I lancieri neri) by G. Gentilomo.
The Shortes Day (Il giorno più corto) by S. Corbucci.
Scorching Sands (Shéhérazade) by P. Gaspard-Huit.
1965 Una voglia da morire by D. Tessari.
A Pistol for Ringo (Una pistola para Ringo) by D. Tessari.
The Return of Ringo (El retorno de Ringo) by D. Tessari.
1966 Kiss kiss… bang bang by D. Tessari.
1967 Per amore… per magia by D. Tessari.
1971 Una farfalla con le ali insanguinate by D. Tessari.
1974 Three Tough Days (Uomini duri) by D. Tessari.
1976 La Madama by D. Tessari.
1978 L'alba dei falsi dei by D. Tessari.

1993 Bonus Malus by V. Zagarrio.

DENIS MARIA
1932 La telefonista by N. Malasomma.
1933 Piccola mia by E. De Liguoro.
Treno popolare by R. Matarazzo.
Non c'è bisogno di danaro by A. Palermi.
Il signore desidera? by G. Righelli.
1934 L'impiegata di papà by A. Blasetti.
1860 / i mille di Garibaldi by A. Blasetti.
Villafranca by G. Forzano.
Paraninfo by A. Palermi.
Seconda B by G. Alessandrini.
1935 "Fiat Voluntas Dei" by A. Palermi.
Lorenzino de' Medici by G. Brignone.
Re burlone by E. Guazzoni.
1936 Re di denari by E. Guazzoni.
Joe il rosso by R. Matarazzo.
Ballerine by R. Matarazzo.
1937 Countess of Parma (Contessa di Parma) by A. Blasetti.
I due misantropi by A. Palermi.
Lasciate ogni speranza by G. Righelli.
Napoli d'altri tempi by A. Palermi.
1938 L'ultima nemica by U. Barbaro.
Partire by A. Palermi.
Hanno rapito un uomo by G. Righelli.
Le due madri by A. Palermi.
1939 Chi sei tu? by A. Palermi.
Belle o brutte si sposan tutte by C.L. Bragaglia.
Il documento by M. Camerini.
1940 Abbandono by M. Mattoli.
L'assedio dell'Alcazar by A. Genina.
Fortuna by M. Neufeld.
Pazza di gioia by C.L. Bragaglia.
Addio giovinezza! by F.M. Poggioli.
1941 La compagnia della teppa by C. D'Errico.
L'amore canta by F.M. Poggioli.
Sissignora by F.M. Poggioli.
1942 I sette peccati by L. Kish.
Le due orfanelle by G. Gallone.
La maestrina by G. Bianchi.
1943 Canal Grande by A. Di Robilant.
La vie de Bohème by M. L'Herbier.
Nessuno torna indietro by A. Blasetti.
1946 Malìa by G. Amato.
1947 Cronaca nera by G. Bianchi.
Cuatro mujeres by A. Del Amo Algara.
1948 La danse de mort by M. Cravenne.
Nada by E. Neville.
Private Angelo by P. Ustinov.
1949 La fiamma che non si spegne by V. Cottafavi.
1954 Anatomy of Love / A Slice of Life (Tempi nostri – epis. Scusi ma…) by A. Blasetti.

DI LAZZARO DALILA
1974 Il bestione by S. Corbucci.
Andy Warhol's Frankenstein / Flesh for Frankenstein (in G.B.) (Il mostro è in tavola… barone Frankenstein) by A. Dawson [A. Margheriti] and P. Morrissey.
1975 La pupa del gangster by G. Capitani.
L'ultimo treno della notte by A. Lado.
1976 Oh, Serafina! by A. Lattuada.
L'Italia s'è rotta by Steno [S. Vanzina].
1977 Il gatto by L. Comencini.
La ragazza dal pigiama giallo by F. Mogherini.
Tre tigri contro tre tigri (epis. 2°) by Steno [S. Vanzina] and S. Corbucci.
1979 Un dramma borghese by F. Vancini.
1980 Trois hommes à abattre by J. Déray.
Voltati Eugenio by L. Comencini.
Stark System by A. Balducci.
Il bandito dagli occhi azzurri by A. Giannetti.
1981 Quando la coppia scoppia by Steno [S. Vanzina].
Prima che sia troppo presto by E. Decaro.
Miss Right by P. Williams.
1982 Una di troppo by P. Tosini.
1984 Tutti dentro by A. Sordi.
1985 Creepers (Phenomena) by D. Argento.
1989 Spogliando Valeria by B. Gaburro.
1990 Paganini by K. Kinski.
Diceria dell'untore by B. Cino.
1991 Strepitosamente… flop by P.F. Campanella.
1992 Rose rosse per una squillo by A. Barney.

DILIAN IRASEMA
1940 Ecco la felicità by M. L'Herbier.
Maddalena… zero in condotta by V. De Sica.
1941 Do You Like Women? (Teresa Venerdì) by V. De Sica.
Schoolgirl's Diary (Ore 9 lezione di chimica) by M. Mattoli.
1942 I sette peccati by L. Kish.
Malombra by M. Soldati.
Violette nei capelli by C.L. Bragaglia.
La principessa del sogno by M.T. Ricci and R. Savarese.
1943 Fuga a due voci by C.L. Bragaglia.
1946 Un drama nuevo by J. De Orduña.
Cuando llegue la noche by J. Kish.
Cero en conducta by F. Otzoup [F. Ozep].
The Black Eagle (Aquila nera) by R. Freda.
1947 The Captain's Daughter (La figlia del capitano) by M. Camerini.
Il corriere del re by G. Righelli.
1949 39 cartas de amor by F. Rovira Beleta.
Il vedovo allegro by M. Camerini.
1950 Unwanted Women (Donne senza nome) by G. von Radványi.
Né de père inconnu by M. Cloche.
Muchachas de uniforme by A.B. Crevenna.
1951 Angélica / Un dia de lluvia by A.B. Crevenna.
1952 La mujer que tu quieras by E. Gomez Muriel.
Paraiso robado by J. Bracho.
1953 Wuthering Heights (Cumbras burrascosas) by L. Buñuel.
La cobarde by J. Bracho.
Las infieles by A. Galindo.
Un minudo de bondad by E. Gomez Muriel.
1954 La desconocida by C. Urueta.
Historia de un abrigo de mink by E. Gomez Muriel.
Dos mundos y un amor by A.B. Crevenna.
1955 Pablo y Carolina by M. De La Serma.
Primavera en el corazon by R. Rodriguez.
1956 Y si ella volviera by V. Orona.
1957 La estrella del Rey by D. Maiuri and L.M. Delgado.
La ausente by J. Bracho.
1958 Fruto prohibido by A.B. Crevenna.
La muralla by L. Lucia Mingarro.

DOWLING CONSTANCE
1944 Knickerbocker Holiday by H.J. Brown.
1945 Up in Arms by E. Nugent.
1946 The Black Angel by R.W. Neil.
Blackie and the Law by D. Ross Lederman.
The Well-Goomed Bride by S. Lanfield.
1947 The Flame by J.H. Auer.
Blind Spot by R. Gordon.
1948 Follie per l'opera by M. Costa.
1949 Addio Mimì by C. Gallone.
City of Pain (La città dolente) by M. Bonnard.
Una voce nel tuo cuore by A. D'Aversa.
1950 Duel Without Honor (Duello senza onore) by C. Mastrocinque.
Miss Italy (Miss Italia) by D. Coletti.
La strada finisce sul fiume by L. Capuano.
1954 Gog by H.L. Strock.

DOWLING DORIS
1945 The Lost Weekend by B. Wilder.
1946 The Blue Dahlia by G. Marshall.
1949 Bitter Rice (Riso amaro) by G. De Santis.
1950 Cuori sul mare by G. Bianchi.
Alina by G. Pàstina.
1952 Othello by O. Welles.
1956 Running Target by M.R. weinstein.
1958 The Party Crashers by B. Girard.
Wink of an Eye by W. Jones.

DURANTI DORIS
1935 Aldebaran by A. Blasetti.
The Golden Arrow (Freccia d'oro) by P. Ballerini and C. D'Errico.
Il serpente a sonagli by R. Matarazzo.
Ginevra degli Almieri by G. Brignone.
1936 La gondola delle chimere by A. Genina.

Vivere! by G. Brignone.
Amazzoni bianche by G. Righelli.
The White Squadron (Squadrone bianco) by A. Genina.
1937 Sentinelle di bronzo by R. Marcellini.
1938 Sotto la croce del Sud by G. Brignone.
1939 Diamanti by C. D'Errico.
Cavalleria rusticana by A. Palermi.
1940 È sbarcato un marinaio by P. Ballerini.
Ricchezza senza domani by F.M. Poggioli.
Il cavaliere di Kruja by C. Campogalliani.
La figlia del Corsaro Verde by E. Guazzoni.
1941 The King's Jester (Il re si diverte) by M. Bonnard.
1942 Capitan Tempesta by C. D'Errico.
Il leone di Damasco by C. D'Errico.
Giarabub by G. Alessandrini.
Carmela (id.) by F. Calzavara.
Tragica notte by M. Soldati.
La contessa Castiglione by F. Calzavara.
1943 Calafuria by F. Calzavara.
Nessuno torna indietro by A. Blasetti.
1944 Resurrezione by F. Calzavara.
Rosalba by F. Cerio and M. Calandri.
1950 Estrella de manhã by O. Marquès De Oliveira.
Il voto by M. Bonnard.
1951 The Counterfeiters (I falsari) by F. Rossi.
1952 Clandestino a Trieste by G. Salvini.
A fil di spada by C.L. Bragaglia.
Tragico ritorno by P.L. Faraldo.
Pentimento by E. Di Gianni.
La storia del fornaretto di Venezia by G. Solito.
La muta di Portici by G. Ansoldi.
The Moment of Truth (Le minute de verité) by J. Delannoy.
1953 Vuelo 971 by R. Salvia.
François il contrabbandiere by G. Parolini.
1975 The Divine Nymph (Divina creatura) by G. Patroni Griffi.

EKBERG ANITA
1952 The Mississippi Gambler by R. Maté.
1953 Abbott and Costello go to Mars by Ch. Lamont.
The Golden Blade by N.H. Juran.
1955 Blood Alley by W.A. Wellman.
Artists and Models by F. Tashlin.
1956 Man in the Vault by A.V. McLaglen.
Hollywood or Bust by F. Tashlin.
War and Peace by K. Vidor.
Back from Eternity by J. Farrow.
1957 Zarak by T. Young.
Valerie by G. Oswald.
Pickup Alley / Interpol (in G.B.) by J. Gilling.
1958 Paris Holiday by G. Oswald.
The Screaming Mimi by G. Oswald.
The Man Inside by J. Gilling.
1959 Sign of the Gladiator (Nel segno di Roma) by G. Brignone.
1960 La Dolce Vita / The Sweet Life (in G.B.) (La dolce vita) by F. Fellini.
Dam on the Yellow River (Apocalisse sul fiume giallo) by R. Merusi.
Little Girls and High Finance / The Call Girl Business (in G.B.) (Anonima cocottes) by C. Mastrocinque.
Le tre eccetera del colonnello by C. Boisset.
1961 Behind Closed Doors (A porte chiuse) by D. Risi.
The Mongols (I mongoli) by L. Savona and A. De Toth.
1962 Boccaccio '70 – epis. The Temptation of Dr. Antonio (Boccaccio '70 – epis. Le tentazioni del dottor Antonio) by F. Fellini.
1963 Call Me Bwana by G. Douglas.
Four for Texas by R. Aldrich.
1964 Bianco, rosso, giallo, rosa (epis. L'incastro) by M. Mida.
1965 Who Wants to Sleep? – epis. Lolita (Das Liebeskarussel – epis. Lolita) by A. von Ambesser.
The Alphabet Murders by F. Tashlin.
1966 Way, Way Out by G. Douglas.
Scusi, lei è favorevole o contrario? by A. Sordi.
Come imparai ad amare le donne by L. Salce.
1967 The Cobra (Il Cobra) by M. Sequi.

Woman Seven Times (epis. Neve) by V. De Sica.
The Glass Sphinx (La sfinge d'oro) by L. Scattini.
1968 Cronica de un atraco by J.J. Balcázar.
Standin for a Killing by S. Pink.
1969 Malenka, the Vampire (Malenka) by A. De Ossorio.
If Is Tuesday, This Must Be Belgium by M. Stuart.
Death Knocks Twice (Blonde Köder für der Mürder) by H. Phillip.
1970 Il debito coniugale by F. Prosperi.
The Clowns (I clowns) by F. Fellini.
Il divorzio by R. Guerrieri.
Quella chiara notte d'ottobre by M. Franciosa.
1972 Casa d'appuntamento by F. Lyons Morris [F. Merighi].
1974 Valley of the Widows (Das Tal der Tanzenden Witwen) by V. Vogeler.
1978 The Mud by M. Vajda.
1979 Suor omicidi by G. Berruti.
1982 Cicciabomba by U. Lenzi.
1986 La dolce pelle di Angela by A. White [A. Bianchi].
1987 Intervista by F. Fellini.
1991 Il conte Max by Ch. De Sica.
Cattive ragazze by M. Ripa di Meana.
1992 Ambrogio by W. Labate.
1993 The Red Dwarf by Y. Le Moine.
1996 Bambola di B. Luna.

FENECH EDWIGE
1967 Toutes folles de lui by N. Carbonnaux.
1968 Sexy Susan Sins Again (Frau Wirtin hat auch einen Grafen) by F. Antel [F. Legrand].
Il figlio di Aquila Nera by J. Reed [G. Malatesta].
Samoa, regina della giungla by J. Reed [G. Malatesta].
Der Mann mit dem goldenen Pinsel by F. Marischka.
1969 Top Sensation by O. Alessi.
Play the Game or Leave the Bead (Die Nackte Bovary) by H. Schott-Schöbinger.
Komm Liebe Maid und Macha by J. Zachar.
Alle Kätschen Naschen gerb by J. Zachar.
Madame und ihre Nichte by E. Schroeder.
Testa o croce by P. Pierotti.
1970 Cinque bambole per la luna d'agosto by M. Bava.
Le Mans – Scorciatoia per l'inferno by R. Kean [O. Civirani].
Don Franco e don Ciccio nell'anno della contestazione by M. Girolami.
Satiricosissimo by M. Laurenti.
1971 Lo strano vizio della signora Wardh by S. Martino.
Deserto di fuoco by R. Merusi.
Le calde notti di Don Giovanni by A. Bradley [A. Brescia].
1972 Quel gran pezzo dell'Ubalda tutta nuda e tutta calda by M. Laurenti.
Quando le donne si chiamavano Madonne by A. Grimaldi.
Il tuo vizio è una stanza chiusa e solo io ne ho la chiave by S. Martino.
La Bella Antonia, prima monica e poi dimonia by M. Laurenti.
Tutti i colori del buio by S. Martino.
1973 La vedova inconsolabile ringrazia quanti la consolarono by M. Laurenti.
Anna, quel particolare piacere by G. Carnimeo.
Giovannona coscialunga disonorata con onore by S. Martino.
Il suo nome faceva tremare… Interpol in allarme by M. Lupo.
Fuori uno sotto un altro, arriva il Passatore by A. Ascot [G. Carnimeo].
1974 La signora gioca bene a scopa? by G. Carnimeo.
Innocenza e turbamento by M. Dallamano.
1975 Grazie nonna by F. Martinelli [M. Girolami].
L'insegnante by N. Cicero.
Il vizio di famiglia by M. Laurenti.
1976 La poliziotta fa cariera by M.M. Tarantini.
La pretora by L. Fulci.
Cattivi pensieri by U. Tognazzi.
La dottoressa del distretto militare by

N. Cicero.
40 gradi all'ombra del lenzuolo (epis. La cavallona) by S. Martino.
1977 Taxi Girl by M.M. Tarantini.
La vergine, il toro e il capricorno by L. Martino.
La soldatessa alla visita militare by N. Cicero.
1978 L'insegnante va in collegio by M. Laurenti.
L'insegnante viene a casa by M.M. Tarantini.
Il grande attacco by U. Lenzi.
La soldatessa alle grandi manovre by N. Cicero.
Amori miei by Steno [S. Vanzina].
1979 La poliziotta della squadra del buoncostume by M.M. Tarantini.
La patata bollente by Steno [S. Vanzina].
Dottor Jekyll e gentile signora by Steno [S. Vanzina].
1980 Sono fotogenico by D. Risi.
Il ladrone by P. Festa Campanile.
Io e Caterina by A. Sordi.
La moglie in vacanza… l'amante in città by S. Martino.
Zucchero, miele e peperoncino by S. Martino.
1981 Il ficcanaso by B. Corbucci.
Cornetti alla crema by S. Martino.
Asso by F. Castellano and Pipolo [G. Moccia].
La poliziotta a New York by M.M. Tarantini
Tais-toi quand tu parles by Ph. Clair.
1982 Ricchi, ricchissimi… praticamente in mutande by S. Martino.
Il paramedico by S. Nasca.
1984 Vacanze in America by C. Vanzina.
1988 Un delitto poco comune by R. Deodato.

FERIDA LUISA
1935 The Golden Arrow (Freccia d'oro) by P. Ballerini and C. D'Errico.
Re burlone by E. Guazzoni.
1936 L'ambasciatore by B. Negroni.
I due sergenti by E. Guazzoni.
Amazzoni bianche by G. Righelli.
Il grande silenzio by G. Zannini.
Lo smemorato by G. Righelli.
1937 La fossa degli angeli by C.L. Bragaglia.
I fratelli Castiglioni by C. D'Errico.
I tre desideri by K. Gerron.
Il conte di Bréchard by M. Bonnard.
1938 L'argine by C. D'Errico.
Tutta la vita in una notte by C. D'Errico.
Il suo destino by E. Guazzoni.
1939 Stella del mare by C. D'Errico.
Animali pazzi by C.L. Bragaglia.
Il segreto di Villa Paradiso by D.M. Gambino.
1940 An Adventure of Salvator Rosa (Un'avventura di Salvator Rosa) by A. Blasetti.
La fanciulla di Portici by M. Bonnard.
1941 The Iron Crown (La corona di ferro) by A. Blasetti.
Nozze di sangue by G. Alessandrini.
Amore imperiale by A. Wolkoff.
La cena delle beffe by A. Blasetti.
1942 Fari nella nebbia by G. Franciolini.
L'ultimo addio by F. Cerio.
Orizzonte di sangue by G. Righelli.
La bella addormentata by L. Chiarini.
Fedora (id.) by C. Mastrocinque.
Il figlio del Corsaro Rosso by M. Elter.
Gelosia by F.M. Poggioli.
1943 Harlem by C. Gallone.
Tristi amori by C. Gallone.
1944 La locandiera by L. Chiarini.
1945 Un fatto di cronaca by P. Ballerini.

FERRERO ANNA MARIA
1950 Il cielo è rosso by C. Gora.
1951 The Forbidden Christ (Il Cristo proibito) by C. Malaparte.
Lorenzaccio by R. Pacini.
Tomorrow is Another Day (Domani è un altro giorno) by L. Moguy.
Il conte di Sant'Elmo by G. Brignone.
Le due verità by A. Leonviola.
1952 Lo sai che i papaveri… by V. Marchesi and V. Metz.
Ragazze da marito by E. De Filippo.
Canzoni di mezzo secolo (epis. Oi Mari) by D. Paolella.
1953 I vinti (epis. italiano) by M. Antonioni.
Febbre di vivere by C. Gora.

The Unfaithfuls (Le infedeli) by Steno and M. Monicelli.
Luxury Girls (Fanciulle di lusso) by B. Vorhaus.
Siamo tutti inquilini by M. Mattoli.
Napoletani a Milano by E. De Filippo.
Giuseppe Verdi by R. Matarazzo.
Villa Borghese (id.) (epis. Pi-greco) by G. Franciolini.
1954 Chronicle of a Poor Lovers (Cronache di poveri amanti) by C. Lizzani.
Una parigina a Roma by E. Kobler.
Guai ai vinti by R. Matarazzo.
1955 Totò e Carolina by M. Monicelli.
Il falco d'oro by C.L. Bragaglia.
Canzoni di tutta Italia by D. Paolella.
The Widow (La vedova X) by L. Milestone.
La rivale by A.G. Majano.
1956 War and Peace (Guerra e pace) by K. Vidor.
The Violent Patriot (Giovanni dalle Bande Nere) by S. Grieco.
Suprema confessione by S. Corbucci.
1957 Kean, genio e sregolatezza by V. Gassman.
1958 Desert Warrior / The Son of the Sheik (in G.B.) (Los amantes del desierto) by F. Cerchio and G. Vernuccio.
Captain Falcon, Adventurer (Capitan Fuoco) by C. Campogalliani.
1959 Le sorprese dell'amore by L. Comencini.
La notte brava (id.) by M. Bolognini.
1960 L'impiegato by G. Puccini.
Gastone by M. Bonnard.
Austerlitz / The Battle of Austerlitz (in G.B.) (Austerlitz) by A. Gance.
I delfini by F. Maselli.
Love and Larceny (Il mattatore) by D. Risi.
The Hunchback of Rome (Il gobbo) by C. Lizzani.
1961 Un giorno da leoni by N. Loy.
L'oro di Roma by C. Lizzani.
Le capitane Fracasse by P. Gaspard-Huit.
1962 Una domenica d'estate by G. Petroni.
1963 Un marito in condominio by A. Dorigo.
1964 Controsesso (epis. Cocaina di domenica by F. Rossi).

GALIENA ANNA
1986 Puro cashmere by B. Proietti.
1987 L'estate sta finendo by B. Cortini.
Mosca, addio by M. Bolognini.
Mr. Rorret by F. Wertzel.
1988 Laggiù nella giungla by S. Reali.
1989 Willy Signori e vengo da lontano by F. Nuti.
La travestie by Y. Boisset.
L'argent by J. Rouffio.
Les grandes familles by E. Molinaro.
La fée carabine by Y. Boisset.
1990 The Hairdresser's Husband (Le mari de la coiffeuse) by P. Lecomte.
Giorni felici a Clichy (Jours tranquilles à Clichry) by C. Chabrol.
La viuda du Capitan Estrada by J.L. Cuerda.
1991 Atlantide by B. Swaim.
Jamón, Jamón by B. Luna.
Vieille canaille by G. Jourd'hui.
1992 Il grande cocomero by F. Archibugi.
Being Human by B. Forsyth.
L'écrivain public by J.F. Amiguet.
1993 Mario and the Magicien by K.M. Brandauer.
1994 Senza pelle by A. D'Alatri.
Prima le donne e i bambini by S. Joxe.
1995 La scuola by D. Luchetti.
Vite a termine by G. Soldati.
1996 Trois vies et une seule mort by R. Ruiz.
Cervellini fritti impanati di M. Zaccaro.
The Leading Man by J. Duigan.
Les caprices d'un fleuve by B. Giraudeau.
Tre by Ch. De Sica.

GASTONI LISA
1954 You Know What the Sailors Are by K. Annakin.
Dance Little Lady by V. Guest.
Beautiful Stranger / Twist of Face (in USA) by D. Miller.
The Runaway Bus by V. Guest.
Doctor in the House by R. Thomas.

213

1955 Man of the Moment by J. Paddy Carstairs.
They Who Dare by L. Milestone.
1956 Face in the Night / Menace in the Night (in USA) by L. Comfort.
Dust and Gold by S. Guillermin.
Josephine and Men by R. Boulting.
1957 The Baby and the Battleship by Jay Lewis.
Three Men in a Boat by K. Annakin.
Suspended Alibi by A. Shaughnessy.
Man from Tangier / Thunder over Tangier (in USA) by L. Comfort.
Blue Murder at St. Trinian's by F. Launder.
Second Fiddle by M. Elbvey.
The Strange Awakening by M. Tully.
1958 The Truth About Women by M. Box.
Chain of Events by G. Thomas.
Hello London by S. Smith.
Family Doctor / RX Murder (in USA) by D. Twist.
Intent to Kill by J. Cardiff.
1959 The Treasure of Santa Teresa / Long Distance (in USA) by A. Rakoff.
Wrong Number by V. Sewell.
1960 Visa to Canton / Passport to China (in USA) by M. Carreras.
1961 The Breaking Point by L. Comfort.
Hell Below Deep (Le avventure di Mary Read) by U. Lenzi.
1962 Tharus figlio di Attila by R. Bianchi Montero.
Duello nella Sila by U. Lenzi.
Eve by J. Losey.
Eighteen in the Sun (Diciottenni al sole) by C. Mastrocinque.
1963 RO.GO.PA.G. (epis. Il pollo ruspante by U. Gregoretti).
The Four Musketeers (I quattro moschettieri) di C.L. Bragaglia.
Il monaco di Monza by S. Corbucci.
Gidget Goes to Rome by P. Wendkos.
Dungeons of Venice (Il vendicatore mascherato / I piombi di Venezia) by P. Mercanti.
1964 Le roi du village by H. Gruel.
I maniaci by L. Fulci.
The Three Avengers (Gli invincibili tre) by G. Parolini.
The Seven Vipers (Le sette vipere) by R. Polselli.
Crimine a due by R. Freemont [. Ferrara].
L'ultimo gladiatore by U. Lenzi.
1965 I tre centurioni by R. Mauri.
The Myth (La violenza e l'amore) by A. Sala.
1966 The Deadly Diaphanoids (I diafanoidi vengono da Marte) by A.M. Dawson [A. Margheriti].
Wild, Wild Planet / War of the Planets (in G.B.) (I criminali della Galassia) by A.M. Dawson [A. Margheriti].
The Man Who Laughs / The Man with the Golden Mask (in G.B.) (L'uomo che ride) by S. Corbucci.
Night of Violence (Le notti della violenza) by R. Mauri.
Svegliati e uccidi by C. Lizzani.
1968 Grazie, zia by S. Samperi.
I sette fratelli Cervi by G. Puccini.
La pecora nera by L. Salce.
1969 L'amica by A. Lattuada.
1970 L'invasion by Y. Allégret.
1972 Maddalena by J. Kawalerowicz.
1973 Seduction (La seduzione) by F. Di Leo.
1974 Last Days of Mussolini (Mussolini ultimo atto) by C. Lizzani.
Amore amaro by F. Vancini.
1975 Labbra di lurido blu by G. Petroni.
1976 Scandalo by S. Samperi.
1978 L'immoralità by M. Pirri.

GIOI VIVI
1936 Ma non è una cosa seria by M. Camerini.
1937 Il signor Max by M. Camerini.
1939 Bionda sotto chiave by C. Mastrocinque.
Frenesia by M. Bonnard.
Mille chilometri al minuto by M. Neufeld.
1940 Alessandro, sei grande! by C.L. Bragaglia.
Vento di milioni by D. Falconi.
Cento lettere d'amore by M. Neufeld.
Rose scarlatte by V. De Sica and G. Amato.

Dopo divorzieremo by N. Malasomma.
La canzone rubata by M. Neufeld.
1941 Il pozzo dei miracoli by G. Righelli.
L'attore scomparso by L. Zampa.
L'amante segreta by C. Gallone.
First Love (Primo amore) by C. Gallone.
1942 Giungla by N. Malasomma.
Sette anni di felicità by R.L. Savarese.
Bengasi by A. Genina.
1943 Lascia cantare il cuore by R.L. Savarese.
Harlem (id.) by C. Gallone.
Cortocircuito by A. Gentilomo.
Piazza San Sepolcro / Cronache di due secoli by G. Forzano.
1944 Service de nuit by J. Faurez and B.L. Randone.
1945 La casa senza tempo by A. Della Sabbia [A. Forzano].
Tutta la città canta by R. Freda.
1946 Il marito povero by G. Amato.
1947 Tragic Hunt / The Tragic Pursuit (in G.B.) (Caccia tragica) by G. De Santis.
1949 The Earth Cries Out (Il grido della terra) by D. Coletti.
1950 Cielo così by F. Cerchio.
Unwanted Women (Donne senza nome) By G. von Radvanyi.
La porteuse de pain by M. Cloche.
1951 Senza bandiera by L. De Felice.
1956 Rice Girls (La risaia) by R. Matarazzo.
1963 Il processo di Verona by C. Lizzani.
1967 Dio non paga il sabato by A. Anton [T. Boccia].
1974 Il baco da seta by M. Sequi.

GIORGI ELEONORA
1973 Diary of a Cloistered Nun (Storia di una monaca di clausura) by D. Paolella.
1974 La sbandata by A. Malfatti.
Il bacio by M. Lanfranchi.
Appassionata by G.L. Calderone.
Alla mia cara mamma nel giorno del suo compleanno by L. Salce.
1975 Conviene far bene l'amore by P. Festa Campanile.
1976 L'ultima volta by A. Lado.
Liberi armati pericolosi by R. Guerrieri.
Cuore di cane by A. Lattuada.
L'Agnese va a morire by G. Montaldo.
1977 Disposta a tutto by G. Stegani.
Una spirale di nebbia by E. Visconti.
1978 Suggestionata by A. Rizzo.
6.000 km. di paura by A. Thomas [B. Albertini].
1979 Forget Venice (Dimenticare Venezia) by F. Brusati.
Un uomo in ginocchio by D. Damiani.
Mani di velluto by F. Castellano and Pipolo [G. Moccia].
1980 Inferno (id.) by D. Argento.
Mia moglie è una strega by F. Castellano and Pipolo [G. Moccia].
1981 Nudo di donna by N. Manfredi.
1982 Borotalco by C. Verdone.
Grand Hotel Excelsior by F. Castellano and Pipolo [G. Moccia].
Oltre la porta by L. Cavani.
1983 Mani di fata by Steno [S. Vanzina].
Sapore di mare 2 – Un anno dopo by B. Cortini.
1984 Vediamoci chiaro by L. Salce.
1986 Giovanni senzapensieri by M. Colli.
1988 Il Volpone by M. Ponzi.
Compagni di scuola by C. Verdone.

GOLINO VALERIA
1983 A Joke of Destiny Lying in Wait Around the Corner Like a Street Bandit (Scherzo del destino in agguato dietro l'angolo come un brigante da strada) by L. Wertmüller.
Blind Date by N. Mastorakis.
1985 Figlio mio, infinitamente caro by V. Orsini.
Piccoli fuochi by P. Del Monte.
1986 Dumb Dicks (Asilo di polizia) by F. Ottoni.
Storia d'amore by F. Maselli.
1987 Gli occhiali d'oro by G. Montaldo.
Dernier été à Tanger by A. Arcady.
1988 Paura e amore by M. von Trotta.
Big Top Pee-Wee by R. Kleiser.
1989 Rain Man by B. Levinson.
Torrents of Spring (Acque di primavera) by J. Skolimowsky.
Il y a des jours et des lunes by C. Lelouch.

1990 The King's Whore (La putain du roi) by A. Corti.
Tracce di vita amorosa by P. Del Monte.
1991 Hot Shots! by J. Abrahams.
The Indian Runner by S. Penn.
1992 Year of the Gun by J. Frankenheimer.
Puerto Escondido by G. Salvatores.
1993 Hot Shots! 2 by J. Abrahams.
Clean Slate by M. Jackson.
1994 Come due coccodrilli by G. Campiotti.
La strage del gallo by A. Panzis.
1995 Immortal Beloved by B. Rose.
Leaving Las Vegas by M. Figgs.
Four Rooms (epis. Strange Brew by A. Anderson).
Red Wind by A. Holland.
1996 EsCoriandoli by A. Rezza.

GRANDI SERENA
1980 Tranquille donne di campagna by C. De Molinis [C. Giorgi].
The Grim Reaper (Antropophagus) by J. d'Amato [A. Massaccesi].
1981 Teste di quoio by G. Capitani.
1982 Pierino colpisce ancora by M. Girolami.
Pierino la peste alla riscossa by U. Lenzi.
Sturmtruppen 2 / Tutti al fronte by S. Samperi.
Malamore by E. Visconti.
1985 Miranda by T. Brass.
1986 La signora della notte by P. Schivazappa.
Desiderando Giulia by A. Barzini.
L'iniziazione by G. Mingozi.
1987 Rimini Rimini by S. Corbucci.
Le foto di Gioia by L. Bava.
Teresa by D. Risi.
Roba da ricchi by S. Corbucci.
1989 L'insegnante di violoncello by L. Webber [M. Girolami].
1990 In nome del popolo sovrano by L. Magni.
1992 Centro storico by R. Giannarelli.
Saint Tropez, Saint Tropez by F. Castellano and Pipolo [G. Moccia].
1993 Graffiante desiderio by S. Martino.
1994 Delitto passionale by F. Mogherini.
1995 La strana storia di Olga "O" by A. Bonifacio.

GRAVINA CARLA
1957 Guendalina by A. Lattuada.
Amore e chiacchiere by A. Blasetti.
1958 Big Deal on Madonna Street / Persons Unknown (in G.B.) (I soliti ignoti) by M. Monicelli.
Anche l'inferno trema / Un'ora per vivere by P. Regnoli.
1959 Policarpo, ufficiale di scrittura by M. Soldati.
First Love (Primo amore) by M. Camerini.
Esterina by C. Lizzani.
1960 Five Branded Women (Jovanka e le altre) by M. Ritt.
Everybody Go Home! (Tutti a casa) by L. Comencini.
1961 Scano boa by R. Dall'Ara.
Un giorno da leoni by N. Loy.
1966 A Bullet for the General (Quien sabe?) by D. Damiani.
1968 Banditi a Milano by C. Lizzani.
I sette fratelli Cervi by G. Puccini.
1969 The Lady of Monza (La monaca di Monza) by E. Visconti.
Cuore di mamma by S. Samperi.
La donna invisibile by P. Spinola.
Sierra Maestra by A, Giannarelli.
1971 Sans mobile apparent by Ph. Labro.
1972 Alfredo, Alfredo (id.) by P. Germi.
Il tema di Marco by M. Antonelli.
Il caso Pisciotta by E. Visconti.
1973 The Inheritor (L'héritier) by Ph. Labro.
The Bit Player (Salut l'artiste) by Y. Robert.
Tony Arzenta by D. Tessari.
1974 The Tempter (L'Anticristo) by A. De Martino.
And Now My Love (Toute une vie) by C. Lelouch.
Il gioco della verità by M. Massa.
1976 Comme un boomerang by J. Giovanni.
1980 La terrazza by E. Scola.
1993 Il lungo silenzio by M. von Trotta.

GUIDA GLORIA
1974 La ragazzina by M. Imperoli.
La minorenne by S. Amadio.
1975 Quell'età maliziosa by S. Amadio.
Blue Jeans by M. Imperoli.
La liceale by M.M. Tarantini.
Il gatto mammone by N. Cicero.
La novizia by P.G. Ferretti.
Peccati di gioventù by S. Amadio.
1976 Il solco di pesca by M. Liverani.
L'affittacamere by M. Laurenti.
La ragazza alla pari by M. Guerrini.
Il medico e la studentessa by S. Amadio.
Scandalo in famiglia / Grazie zio by M. Andrei.
1977 Maschio latino... cercasi by G. Narzisi.
Orazi e Curiazi 3-2 by G. Mariuzzo.
1978 The Secrets of the Bermuda Triangle (El Triángulo de las Bermudas) by R. Cardona jr.
La liceale nella classe dei ripetenti by M. Laurenti.
Avere vent'anni by F. Di Leo.
Travolto dagli affetti familiari by M. Severino.
1979 L'infermiera di notte by M. Laurenti.
La liceale seduce i professori by M. Laurenti.
La liceale, il diavolo e l'acquasanta by N. Cicero.
1980 Fico d'India by Steno [Stefano Vanzina].
1981 Bollenti spiriti by G. Capitani.
1982 La casa stregata by B. Corbucci.
Sesso e volentieri (epis. Domenica In, Radio Taxi, Rasoio all'antica, Armanda e il violinista, Luna di miele) by D. Risi.

JACOBINI MARIA
1930 Perché no? by A. Palermi.
1931 La Scala by G. Righelli.
Stella del cinema by M. Almirante.
Patatrac by G. Righelli.
1934 Paraninfo by A. Palermi.
1937 Gli uomini non sono ingrati by G. Brignone.
1938 Chi è più felice di me by G. Brignone.
Giuseppe Verdi by C. Gallone.
1939 Le educande di Saint-Cyr by G. Righelli.
1940 Eternal Melodies (Melodie eterne) by C. Gallone.
Cento lettere d'amore by M. Neufeld.
1941 L'attore scomparso by L. Zampa.
1942 La signorina by I. Kish.
Via delle cinque lune by L. Chiarini.
Signorinette by L. Zampa.
1943 La danza del fuoco by G.C. Simonelli.
Tempesta sul golfo by G. Righelli.
La donna della montagna by R. Castellani.

KERIMA
1951 The Outcast of the Islands by C. Reed.
1953 The Vixen (La lupa) by A. Lattuada.
La nave delle donne maledette by R. Matarazzo.
Fatal Desire (Cavalleria rusticana) by C. Gallone.
1954 Io sono la Primula Rossa by G.C. Simonelli.
1955 Native Drums / Tom Toms of Mayumba (in G.B.) (Tam Tam Mayumbe) by G.G. Napolitano.
1956 Kiss of Fire (Goubbiah) by R. Darène.
1957 The Quiet American by J.L. Mankiewicz.
1958 La rivolta dei gladiatori by V. Cottafavi.
1959 Il mondo dei miracoli by L. Capuano.
La notte del grande assalto by G.M. Scotese.
1962 Jessica (id.) by J. Negulesco and O. Palella.

KOSCINA SYLVA
1955 Siamo uomini o caporali? by C. Mastrocinque.
1956 THe Railroad Man / Man of Iron (in G.B.) (Il ferroviere) by P. Germi.
Michael Strogoff (Michel Strogoff) by C. Gallone.
1957 I fidanzati della morte by S. Marcellini.
Guendalina by A. Lattuada.
Femmine tre volte by Steno [S. Vanzina].
Oh, Sabella (La nonna Sabella) by D. Risi.

Le naif aux quarante enfants by P. Agostini.
The Mighty Invaders / The Mighty Crusaders (in G.B.) (La Gerusalemme liberata) by C.L. Bragaglia.
Non sono più guaglione by D. Paolella.
1958 Giovani mariti by M. Bolognini.
Ladro lui, ladra lei by L. Zampa.
Mogli pericolose by L. Comencini.
Hercules (Le fatiche di Ercole) by P. Francisci.
La nipote Sabella by G. Bianchi.
Totò a Parigi by C. Mastrocinque.
Totò nella luna by Steno [S. Vanzina].
Quando gli angeli piangono by M. Girolami.
Love on the Riviera / Girls for the Summer (in G.B.) (Racconti d'estate) by G. Franciolini.
1959 Poveri milionari by D. Risi.
Le sorprese dell'amore by L. Comencini.
Hercules Unchained (Ercole e la regina di Lidia) by P. Francisci.
La cambiale by C. Mastrocinque.
Hard Times for Vampires / Uncle Was a Vampire (in G.B.) (Tempi duri per i vampiri) by Steno [S. Vanzina].
Le confidant de ces dames by J. Boyer.
1960 Genitori in blue-jeans by C. Mastrocinque.
Love, the Italian Way (Femmine di lusso) by G. Bianchi.
I piaceri dello scapolo by G. Petroni.
Siege of Syracuse (L'assedio di Siracusa) by P. Francisci.
Hercules Pills (Le pillole di Ercole) by L. Salce.
Trapped by Fear (Les distractions) by J. Dupont.
Ravissante by R. Lamoureux.
Mariti in pericolo by M. Morassi.
Il vigile by L. Zampa.
1961 Il sicario by D. Damiani.
Mani in alto by G. Bianchi.
1962 Jessica (id.) by J. Negulesco and O. Palella.
Girl Game (Copacabana Palace) by Steno [S. Vanzina].
Swordsman of Siena (La congiura dei Dieci) by B. Bandini and E. Perier.
Le massaggiatrici by L. Fulci.
Le masque de fer by H. Decoin.
1963 The Three Fables of Love – epis. The Hare and the Turtle (Le quatre vérités – epis. Le lièvre et la tortue by A. Blasetti).
La salamandre d'or by M. Régamey.
Agent 8 3/4 / Hot Enough for June (in G.B.) by R. Thomas.
Il fornaretto di Venezia by D. Tessari.
The Little Nuns (Le monachine) by L. Salce.
Cyrano et D'Artagnan by A. Gance.
L'appartement des filles by M. Deville.
1964 Love in 4 Dimensions – epis. Love and Life (Amore in quattro dimensioni – epis. Amore e vita by J. Romain).
Let's Talk About Women (Se permettete, parliamo di donne) by E. Scola.
Una storia di notte by L. Petrini.
Love and Marriage – epis. Saturday, July 18 (L'idea fissa epis. Sabato 18 luglio by G. Puccini).
Cadavere per signora by M. Mattoli.
Judex (id.) by G. Franju.
1965 Juliet of the Spirits (Giuletta degli spiriti) by F. Fellini.
That Man in Instanbul (Estambul 65) by A. Isasi Isasmendi.
I soldi (epis. Pirulicchio) by G. Puccini.
Made in Italy (id. – epis. Colpo di fulmine) by N. Loy.
Le grain de sable by P. Kast.
Thrilling (epis. L'autostrada del sole by C. Lizzani).
The Dictator's Guns / Guns for the Dictator (L'arme à gauche) by C. Sautet.
The Double Bed (Lit à deux places – epis. Un monsieur de passage by F. Dupont-Midy).
The Dreamer (Il morbidone) by M. Franciosa.
1966 Io, io, io... e gli altri by A. Blasetti.
Monkey Money (Monnaie de singe) by Y. Robert.
Baraka sur X-13 by E. Lawson [S. Siano] and M. Cloche.
Carré des dames pour un as by J. Poitrenaud.
Deadler then the Male by R. Thomas.
1967 Johnny Banco (id.) by Y. Allégret.
Three Bites of the Apple by A. Ganzer.
The Secret War of Harry Frigg by J. Smight.
1968 A Lovely Way to Die by D. Lowell Rich.
I protagonisti by M. Fondato.
Fight for Rome (Kampf um Rom – 1° Teil) by R. Siodmak.
1969 Justine / Justine and Juliet (in G.B.) (Marquis de Sade: Justine) by J. Franco.
Vedo nudo by D. Risi.
He and She (L'assoluto naturale) by M. Bolognini.
Battle of the Neretva (Bitka na Neretvi) by V. Bulajic.
1970 La modification by M. Worms.
Hornets' Nest by Ph. Karlson.
La colomba non deve volare by S. Garrone,
Vertige pour un tueur by J.P. Desagnat.
Ninì Tirabusciò, la donna che inventò la mossa by M. Fondato.
1971 Mazzabubù... quante corna stanno quaggiù? by M. Laurenti.
Homo eroticus by M. Vicario.
Les jambes en l'air by J. Dewever.
Il sesso del diavolo / Trittico by O. Brazzi.
1972 Boccaccio by B. Corbucci.
Historia de una trahición by J.A. Nieves Conde.
Uccidere in silenzio by G. Rolando.
Beati i ricchi by S. Samperi.
Crimes of the Black Cat (Sette scialli di seta gialla) by S. Pastore.
Confessions of a Sex Maniac (Rivelazioni di un maniaco sessuale al capo della Squadra Mobile) by R. Bianchi Montero.
The Italian Connection / Manhunt in Milan (in G.B.) (La mala ordina) by F. Di Leo.
No deseáras la mujer del vecino by F. Merino.
1973 Il tuo piacere è il mio by C. Racca.
1974 Delitto d'autore by A. Green [M. Sabatini].
1975 The House of Exorcism (La casa dell'esorcismo) by M. Bava.
Il cav. Costante Nicosia demoniaco, ovvero Dracula in Brianza by L. Fulci.
Un par de zapatos del 32 by R. Romero Marchent.
Las correrias del vizconde Arnau by J. Cole Espona.
1977 Some Like It Cool / The Rise and Rise of Casanova (in G.B.) (Casanova & Co.) by F. Legrand.
1980 Sunday Lovers – epis. Rome (Les séducteurs – epis. Le carnet d'Armando by D. Risi).
1981 Asso by F. Castellano and Pipolo [G. Moccia].
1983 Mani di fata by Steno [S. Vanzina].
Questo e quello (epis. Quello col basco rosso) by S. Corbucci.
1987 Rimini, Rimini by S. Corbucci.
1992 Ricky & Barabba by Ch. De Sica.
C'è Kim Novak al telefono by E. Roseo.

LEES TAMARA
1947 While the Sun Shines by A. Asquith.
Bond Street by G. Parry.
1949 The Gay Lady by B. Desmond Hurst.
Il falco rosso by C.L. Bragaglia.
1950 Quel bandito sono io by M. Soldati.
It's a Dog's Life (Vita da cani) by Steno and M. Monicelli.
Totò sceicco by M. Mattoli.
1951 Canzone di primavera by M. Costa.
Romanticismo by C. Fracassi.
Filumena Marturano by E. De Filippo.
Tizio, Caio e Sempronio by V. Metz, M. Marchesi and A. Pozzetti.
Verginità by L. De Mitri.
Bellezze a Capri by A. Bianchi.
La città si difende by P. Germi.
1952 Il lupo della frontiera by E. Anton and P. Scanziani.
È arrivato l'accordatore by D. Coletti.
Le meravigliose avventure di Guerrin Meschino by P. Francisci.
Frustrations (La tratta delle bianche) by L. Comencini.
Il tallone di Achille by M. Amendola and R. Maccari.
Il segreto delle tre punte by C.L. Bragaglia.
Il moschettiere fantasma by W. French [M. Calandri].
1953 Perdonami! by M. Costa.
Noi peccatori by G. Brignone.
Frine, cortigiana d'Oriente by M. Bonnard.
Anna, perdonami! by T. Boccia.
Balocchi e profumi by F.M. De Bernardi and N. Montillo.
Ti ho sempre amato! by M. Costa.
1954 Terra straniera by S. Corbucci.
La Castiglione by G. Combret.
Il tiranno del Garda by I. Ferronetti.
I cavalieri della regina by J. Lerner.
Queen of Babylon (La cortigiana di Babilonia) by C.L. Bragaglia.
Addio, Napoli! by R. Bianchi Montero.
1955 Beautiful but Dangerous (La donna più bella del mondo) by R.Z. Leonard.
Incatenata dal destino by E. Di Gianni.
Torna, piccina mia! by C. Campogalliani.
Canzoni di tutta Italia by D. Paolella.
1956 Lo spadaccino misterioso by S. Grieco.
Serenata al vento by L. De Marchi.
1957 Ho amato una duva by L. De Marchi.
Orizzonte infuocato by R. Bianchi Montero.
Tre straniere a Roma by C. Gora.
1959 Le imprese di una spada leggendaria / Mantelli e spade insanguinate / Le quattro spade by N. Juran and F. McDonald.
Agosto, donne mie non vi conosco by G. Malatesta.
1961 Una spada nell'ombra by L. Capuano.

LISI VIRNA
1953 ...e Napoli canta! by A. Grottini.
1954 La corda d'acciaio by C. Borghesio.
Desiderio 'e sole by G. Pàstina.
Lettera napoletana by G. Pàstina.
Il vetturale del Moncenisio by G. Brignone.
Il cardinale Lambertini by G. Pàstina.
Piccola santa by R. Bianchi Montero.
Addio, Napoli! by R. Bianchi Montero.
1955 Luna nuova by L. Capuano.
La rossa by L. Capuano.
Les hussards by A. Joffé.
Le diciottenni by M. Mattoli.
1957 The Doll That Took the Town (La donna del giorno) by F. Maselli.
Il conte di Matera by L. Capuano.
1959 Lost Souls / Lost Lives (in G.B.) (Vite perdute) by A. Bianchi and R. Mauri.
Il padrone delle ferriere by A.G. Majano.
Il mondo dei miracoli by L. Capuano.
Caterina Sforza, leonessa di Romagna by G.W. Chili.
1960 Un militare e mezzo by Steno [S. Vanzina].
1961 Sua Eccellenza si fermò a mangiare by M. Mattoli.
Cinque marines per cento ragazze by M. Mattoli.
Duel of the Titans (Romolo e Remo) by S. Corbucci.
1962 Eva (id.) by J. Losey.
1963 The Shortes Day (Il giorno più corto) by S. Corbucci.
Don't Tempt the Devil (Les bonnes causes) by Christian-Jaque.
1964 The Black Tulip (La tulipe noir) by Christian-Jaque.
Coplan Agent-005 (Coplan prend de risques) by M. Labro.
How To Murder Your Wife by R. Quine.
1965 The Possessed (La donna del lago) by L. Bazzoni and F. Rossellini.
Bambole! / Four Kinds of Love (in G.B.) – epis. The Telephone Call (Le bambole – epis. La telefonata by D. Risi).
Oggi, domani e dopodomani (epis. L'ora di punta by E. De Filippo).
Casanova '70 (id.) by M. Monicelli.
A Maiden for a Prince / A Virgin for the Prince (in G.B.) (Una vergine per il principe) by P. Festa Camnpanile.
Made in Italy (id. – epis. Creatura indifesa) by N. Loy.
1966 Assault on a Queen by J. Donohue.
The Birds, the Bees and the Italians (Signori e Signori) by P. Germi.
Not With My Wife, You Don't by N. Pamama.
1967 The Girl and the General (La ragazza e il generale) by P. Festa Campanile.
Arabella (id.) by M. Bolognini.
Anyone Can Play (Le dolci signore) by L. Zampa.
The 25th Hour (La vingt-cinquième heure) by H. Verneuil.
1968 Better a Widow (Meglio vedova) by D. Tessari.
The Girl Who Couldn't Say No (Tenderly) by F. Brusati.
Lo smemorato by L. Salce.
1969 The Secret of Santa Vittoria by S. Kramer.
The Christmas Tree (L'arbre de Noël) by T. Young.
If It's Tuesday, This Must Be Belgium by M. Stuart.
1970 Le temps des loups by S. Gobbi.
Giochi particolari by F. Indovina.
1971 A Strange Love Affair (Un beau monstre) by S. Gobbi.
Roma bene by C. Lizzani.
The Statue by R. Amateau.
1972 Bluebeard (Barbablù) by L. Sacripanti and E. Dmytryk.
Lesgalets d'Etretat by S. Gobbi.
1973 The Serpent (Le serpent) by H. Verneuil.
White Fang (Zanna Bianca) by L. Fulci.
1974 Challenge to White Fang (Il ritorno di Zanna Bianca) by L. Fulci.
1977 Beyond Good and Evil (Al di là del bene e del male) by L. Cavani.
Cocktails for Three by B. Izzard.
1979 Ernesto (id.) by S. Samperi.
1980 La cicala by A. Lattuada.
1981 Bugie bianche by S. Rolla.
1982 Miss Right by P. Williams.
1983 Sapore di mare by C. Vanzina.
1984 Amarsi un po' by C. Vanzina.
1989 Buon Natale, Buon Anno by L. Comencini.
1994 La reine Margot by P. Chéreau.
1995 Và dove ti porta il cuore by C. Comencini.

LOLLOBRIGIDA GINA
1946 The Black Eagle (Aquila Nera) by R. Freda.
Lucia di Lammermoor by P. Ballerini.
1947 Il segreto di Don Giovanni by C. Mastrocinque.
Flesh Will Surrender (Il delitto di Giovanni Episcopo) by A. Lattuada.
L'elisir d'amore by M. Costa.
A Man About the House by L. Arliss and G. Amato.
1948 Mad About Opera (Follie per l'opera) by M. Costa.
Loves of a Clown (I pagliacci) by M. Costa.
1949 The Bride Couldn't Wait (La sposa non può attenndere / Anselmo ha fretta) by G. Franciolini.
Children of Change (Campane a martello) by L. Zampa.
1950 Miss Italy (Miss Italia) by D. Coletti.
Alina by G. Pàstina.
It's a Dog's Life (Vita da cani) by Steno and M. Monicelli.
The White Line (Cuori senza frontiere) by L. Zampa.
1951 A Tale of Five Women / A Tale of Five Cities (in G.B.) (Passaporto per l'Oriente – 2° epis. "Rome" by R. Marcellini).
La città si difende by P. Germi.
The Young Caruso (Enrico Caruso, leggenda di una voce) by G. Gentilomo.
Amor non ho! però... però... by G. Bianchi.
Achtung! Banditi by C. Lizzani.
1952 Fanfan the Tulip (Fanfan la Tulipe) by Christian-Jaque.
Wife for a Night (Moglie per una notte) by M. Camerini.
Time Gone By / Infidelity (in G.B.) [epis. Phryne] (Altri tempi – epis. Il processo di Frine) by A. Blasetti.
Night Beauties (Les Belles-de-nuit) by R. Clair.
1953 The Unfaithfuls (Le infedeli) by Steno and M. Monicelli.
The Wayward Wife (La provinciale) by

M. Soldati.
Bread, Love and Dreams (Pane, amore e fantasia) by L. Comencini.
1954 Crossed Swords (Il maestro di Don Giovanni) by M. Krims and V. Vassarotti.
Beat the Devil by J. Huston.
Flesh and the Woman / Card of Fate (Le grand jeu) by R. Siodmak.
Woman of Rome (La romana) by L. Zampa.
Frisky / Bread, Love and Jealousy (in G.B.) (Pane, amore e gelosia) by L. Comencini.
1955 Beautiful But Dangerous (La donna più bella del mondo) by R.Z. Leonard.
1956 Trapeze by C. Reed.
The Hunchback of Notre Dame (Notre Dame de Paris) by J. Delannoy.
1958 Fast and Sexy / Anne of Brooklyn (in G.B.) (Anna di Brooklyn) by R. Denham and C. Lastricati.
1959 Where the Hot Wind Blows (La loi) by J. Dassin.
Never So Few by J. Sturges.
Solomon and Sheba by K. Vidor.
1961 Go Naked in the World by R. MacDougall.
Come September by R. Mulligan.
1962 She Got What She Asked For (La bellezza di Ippolita) by G. Zagni.
Imperial Venus (Venere imperiale) by J. Delannoy.
1963 Mare matto by R. Castellani.
1964 Woman of Straw by B. Dearden.
Strange Bedfellows by M. Frank.
1965 Bambole! / Four Kinds of Love (in G.B.) – epis. Monsignor Cupid (Le bambole – epis. Monsignor Cupido by M. Bolognini.
1966 Io, io, io… e gli altri by A. Blasetti.
Les Sultans by J. Delannoy.
Le piacevoli notti by A. Crispino and L. Lucignani.
Hotel Paradiso by P. Glenville.
1967 The Young Rebel / Cervantes (in G.B.) (Cervantes) by V. Sherman.
1968 A Curious Way of Love (La morte ha fatto l'uovo) by G. Questi.
The Private Navy of Sgt. O'Farrell by F. Tashlin.
Buona sera Mrs. Campbell by M. Frank.
1969 Stuntman by M. Baldi.
Un bellissimo novembre by M. Bolognini.
1971 Bad Man's River (El hombre de Rio Maslo) by E. Martin.
1972 Le avventure di Pinocchio by L. Comencini.
King, Queen, Knave (König, Dame, Bube) by J. Skolimowski.
1974 The Lonely Woman (No encontré rosas para mi madre) by F. Rovira Beleta.

LOREDANA
1939 Grandi magazzini by M. Camerini.
Il carnevale di Venezia by G. Adami and G. Gentilomo.
1940 La nascita di Salomè by J. Choux.
Scandalo per bene by E. Pratelli.
Ecco la radio! by G. Gentilomo.
1941 L'elisir d'amore by A. Palermi.
Idillio a Budapest by G. Ansoldi and G. Varriale.
The King's Jester (Il re si diverte) by M. Bonnard.
La sonnambula by P. Ballerini.
1942 Il figlio del Corsaro Rosso by M. Elter.
Gli ultimi filibustieri by M. Elter.
La signorina by L. Kish.
Musica proibita by C. Campogalliani.
1943 Gioco d'azzardo by P. Bassi.
Dente per dente by M. Elter.
Storia di una capinera by G. Righelli.
La fornarina by E. Guazzoni.
1946 La gondola del diavolo by C. Campogalliani.
1948 Rocambole by J. de Baroncelli.
La revanche de Baccara by J. de Baroncelli.
1949 Emigrantes by A. Fabrizi.

LOREN SOPHIA
1950 Cuori sul mare by G. Bianchi.
Quo Vadis by M. LeRoy.
Lights of Variety (Luci del varietà) by A. Lattuada and F. Fellini.
Il voto by M. Bonnard.

Bluebeard's Seven Wives (Le sei mogli di Barbablù) by C.L. Bragaglia.
Tototarzan by M. Mattoli.
1951 Milano miliardaria by V. Metz, M. Marchesi and M. Girolami.
Il mago per forza by V. Metz, M. Marchesi and M. Girolami.
Io sono il Capataz by G.C. Simonelli.
Il padrone del vapore by M. Mattoli.
Era lui… sì! sì! by V. Metz and M. Marchesi.
Brief Rapture (Lebbra bianca) by E. Trapani.
Anna (id.) by A. Lattuada.
1952 È arrivato l'accordatore by D. Coletti.
The Dream of Zorro (Il sogno di Zorro) by M. Soldati.
Frustrations / Girls Marked Danger (in G.B.) (La tratta delle bianche) by L. Comencini.
La Favorita by C. Barlacci.
1953 Africa Under the Seas / Woman of the Red Sea (in G.B.) (Africa sotto i mari) by G. Roccardi.
Aida (id.) by C. Fracassi.
Ci troviamo in galleria by M. Bolognini.
La domenica della buona gente by A.G. Majano.
1954 A Day in Court (Un giorno in pretura) by Steno [S. Vanzina].
Il paese dei campanelli by J. Boyer.
Two Nights with Cleopatra (Due notti con Cleopatra) by M. Mattoli.
Miseria e nobiltà by M. Mattoli.
Pellegrini d'amore by A. Forzano.
Attila the Hun (Attila) by P. Francisci.
Neapolitan Fantasy (Carosello napoletano) by E. Giannini.
Anatomy of Love – epis. The Camera) / A Slice of Life (in G.B.) (Tempi nostri – epis. La macchina fotografica) by A. Blasetti.
Too Bad She's Bad (Peccato che sia una canaglia) by A. Blasetti.
Gold of Naples – epis. Pizzas on Credit or The Ring) (L'oro di Napoli – epis. Pizze a credito) by V. De Sica.
Woman of the River (La donna del fiume) by M. Soldati.
1955 The Sign of Venus (Il segno di Venere) by D. Risi.
The Miller's Wife (La bella mugnaia) by M. Camerini.
Scandal in Sorrento (Pane, amore e…) by D. Risi.
Lucky to Be a Woman (La fortuna di essere donna) by A. Blasetti.
1957 The Pride and the Passion by S. Kramer.
Boy on a Dolphin by J. Negulesco.
Legend of the Lost by H. Hathaway.
1958 Desire Under the Elms by Delbert Mann.
Houseboat by M. Shavelson.
The Key by C. Reed.
Black Orchid by M. Ritt.
1959 That Kind of Woman of S. Lumet.
1960 Heller in Pink Tights by G. Cukor.
It Started in Naples by M. Shavelson.
A Breath of Scandal by M. Curtiz.
The Millionairess by A. Asquith.
1961 Two Women (La ciociara) by V. De Sica.
El Cid by A. Mann.
Madame (Madame Sans-Gêne) by Christian-Jaque.
1962 Boccaccio '70 – epis. The Raffle (id. – epis. La riffa by V. De Sica.
Five Miles to Midnight (Le couteau dans la plaie) by A. Litvak.
The Condemned of Altona (I sequestrati di Altona) by V. De Sica.
1963 Yesterday, Today and Tomorrow (Ieri, oggi e domani) by V. De Sica.
1964 The Fall of the Roman Empire by A. Mann.
Marriage Italian Style (Matrimonio all'italiana) by V. De Sica.
1965 The Great Spy Mission (in U.S.A.) / Operation Crossbow by M. Anderson.
Lady L by P. Ustinov.
Judith by Daniel Mann.
1966 Arabesque by S. Donen.
A Countess from Hong Kong by Ch. Chaplin.
1967 More Than a Miracle / Cinderella, Italian Style (C'era una volta) by F. Rosi.
Ghosts, Italian Style (Questi fantasmi)

by R. Castellani.
1970 Sunflower (I girasoli) by V. De Sica.
The Priest's Wife (La moglie del prete) by D. Risi.
1971 Lady Liberty (La mortadella) by M. Monicelli.
1972 White Sister (Bianco, rosso e…) by A. Lattuada.
Man of La Mancha by A. Hiller.
1974 The Voyage (Il viaggio) by V. De Sica.
The Verdict (Verdict) by A. Cayatte.
1975 La pupa del gangster by G. Capitani.
1976 Cassandra Crossing by G. Pan Cosmatos.
Angela by B. Sagal.
1977 A Special Day (Una giornata particolare) by E. Scola.
1978 Brass Target by J. Hough.
Blood Feud (Fatto di sangue fra due uomini per causa di una vedova) by L. Wertmüller.
1979 Firepower by M. Winner.
1985 Aurora (Qualcosa di biondo) by M. Ponzi.
1994 Ready to Wear/ Prêt-à-Porter by R. Altman.
1995 Grumpier Old Men by H. Deutch.

LOTTI MARIELLA
1938 Jeanne Doré by M. Bonnard.
1939 Io, suo padre by M. Bonnard.
Il socio invisibile by R. Roberti.
1940 Il ponte dei sospiri by M. Bonnard.
Kean by G. Brignone.
Il signore della taverna by A. Palermi.
L'ispettore Vargas by G. Franciolini.
La figlia del Corsaro Verde by E. Guazzoni.
1941 Il cavaliere senza nome by F. Cerio.
I mariti (Tempesta d'anime) by C. Mastrocinque.
Marco Visconti by M. Bonnard.
Il vetturale del San Gottardo by H. Hinrich and I. Illuminati.
1942 Fari nella nebbia by G. Franciolini.
Turbamento by G. Brignone.
La Gorgona by G. Brignone.
Acque di primavera by N. Malasomma.
Mater dolorosa by G. Gentilomo.
1943 Quelli della montagna by A. Vergano.
Silenzio, si gira! by C. Campogalliani.
Nessuno torna indietro by A. Blasetti.
La freccia nel fianco by A. Lattuada.
1944 Il fiore sotto gli occhi by G. Brignone.
Squadriglia bianca by J. Sava.
1945 I dieci comandamenti (epis. Ricordati di santificare le feste) by G.W. Chili.
Canzone eterna (Canto, ma sottovoce) by G. Brignone.
1946 A Day in the Life (Un giorno nella vita) by A. Blasetti.
Malacarne / Oltraggio all'amore by P. Mercanti and G. Zucca.
1947 Il cavaliere del sogno by C. Mastrocinque.
La fumeria d'oppio by R. Matarazzo.
Le avventure di Pinocchio by G. Guardone.
I fratelli Karamazoff by G. Gentilomo.
1948 Arrivederci papà by C. Mastrocinque.
1949 The Pirates of Capri (I pirati di Capri) by E.G. Ulmer and G.M. Scotese.
Il principe ribelle by P. Mercanti.
1950 Guarany by R. Freda.
Twelve Hours to Live (È più facile che un cammello…) by L. Zampa.
1951 Il diavolo in convento by N. Malasomma.
Gli innocenti pagano by L. Capuano.
1952 Il capitano di Venezia by G. Puccini.
La donna che inventò l'amore by F. Cerio.
Nez de cuir, gentilhomme d'amour by Y. Allégret.
La storia del fornaretto di Venezia by G. Solito.
Solo per te Lucia by F. Rossi.
A Town on Trial (Processo alla città) by L. Zampa.
1953 Carmen proibita by G.M. Scotese.

LUALDI ANTONELLA
1949 Prince of Foxes by H. King.
Signorinella by M. Mattoli.
1950 Canzoni per le strade by M. Landi.
Twelve Hours to Live (È più facile che un cammello…) by L. Zampa.
1951 Abbiamo vinto by R.A. Stemmle.

Miracolo a Viggiù by L.M. Giachino.
Ha fatto 13! by C. Manzoni.
L'ultima sentenza by M. Bonnard.
1952 I due segeti by C.A. Chiesa.
È arrivato l'accordatore by R. Freda.
The Overcoat (Il cappotto) by A. Lattuada.
Cani e gatti by L. De Mitri.
Three Forbidden Stories (Tre storie proibite) by A. Genina.
Il romanzo della mia vita by L. De Felice.
I figli non si vendono by M. Bonnard.
Adorables créatures by Christian-Jaque.
1953 La cieca di Sorrento by G. Gentilomo.
Canzoni, canzoni, canzoni (epis. Signorinella) by D. Paolella.
La figlia del reggimento by G. von Bolvary and T. Covaz.
Perdonami! by M. Costa.
Gli uomini, chemascalzoni! by G. Pellegrini.
1954 Cronache di poveri amanti by C. Lizzani.
Amori di mezzo secolo (epis. Napoli 1943 by R. Rossellini).
Pietà per chi cade by M. Costa.
Avanzi di galera by V. Cottafavi.
Papà Pacifico by G. Brignone.
Casta diva by C. Gallone.
Scarlet and Black (Le rouge et le noir) by C. Autant-Lara.
1955 Non c'è amore più grande by G. Bianchi.
Le signorine dello 04 by G. Franciolini.
Gli innamorati by M. Bolognini.
Andrea Chénier by C. Fracassi.
1956 Altair by L. De Mitri.
I giorni più belli by M. Mattoli.
1957 Il cielo brucia by G. Masini.
Padri e figli by M. Monicelli.
Méfiez-vous fillettes by Y. Allégret.
La Ceniciente y Ernesto by P.L. Ramirez.
1958 Mon coquin de père by G. Lacombe.
Polikuschka by C. Gallone.
End of Desire (Une vie) by A. Astruc.
Giovani mariti by M. Bolognini.
1959 Délit de fuite by B. Borderie.
La notte brava (id.) by M. Bolognini.
Web of Passion (A double tour) by C. Chabrol.
Match contre la mort by C. Bernard-Aubert.
J'irai cracher sur vos tombes by M. Gast.
1960 Via Margutta by M. Camerini.
A Summer Date (Appuntamento a Ischia) by M. Mattoli.
I delfini by F. Maselli.
1961 The Mongols (I mongoli) by L. Savona and A. De Toth.
1962 My Son, the Hero / Sons of Thunder (in G.B.) (Arrivano i Titani) by D. Tessari.
Sesto senso (epis. Il gusto) by S. Ubezio.
Disorder (Il disordine) by F. Brusati.
1963 Hong Kong, un addio by G.L. Polidoro.
The Shortest Day (Il giorno più corto) by S. Corbucci.
Gli imbroglioni by L. Fulci.
Il figlio del circo by S. Grieco.
1964 Amore mio by R. Matarazzo.
I cento cavalieri by V. Cottafavi.
Let's Talk About Women (Se permettete, parliamo di donne) by E. Scola.
Sexy Party (Delitto allo specchio) by J. Josipovici and A. Molteni.
Le repas des fauves by Christian-Jaque.
1965 Su e giù (epis. Il marito d'agosto) by M. Guerrini.
1966 Die schlacht im Teutoburger Wald by F. Baldwin [P. Baldi].
The Sea Pirate / The Fighting Corsair (in G.B.) (El Tigre de los siete mares) by S. Bergonzelli.
Tormenta sobre El Pacifico by S. Bergonzelli.
How to Seduce a Playboy (Bel Ami 2000 oder Wie verführt man einen playboy?) by \M. Pfleghar.
1968 Columna by M. Dragan.
Ragan by L. Lelli.
1970 Un caso di coscienza by G. Grimaldi.
1974 Vincent, François, Paul… et les autres by C. Sautet!
1975 I giorni della chimera by F. Corona.

1976 La legge violenta della squadra anticrimine by S. Massi.
1978 Non sparate sui bambini by G. Crea.
1980 Mafia: una legge che non perdona by B. Ghisais [R. Girometti].
1986 Una spina nel cuore by A. Lattuada.
1990 Diritto di vivere by S. Arquilla.
1992 Per amore o per amicizia by P. Poeti.
L'urlo della verità by S. Massi.
Tutti gli uomini di Sara by G. Tescari.
1994 Nefertiti by G. Gilles.

MAGNANI ANNA
1934 The Blind Woman of Sorrento (La cieca di Sorrento) by N. Malasomma.
Tempo massimo by M. Mattoli.
1935 Quei due by G. Righelli.
1936 Cavalleria by G. Alessandrini.
Trenta secondi d'amore by M. Bonnard.
1938 La principessa Tarakanowa by F. Ozep and M. Soldati.
1940 Una lampada alla finestra by G. Talamo.
1941 La fuggitiva by P. Ballerini.
Do You Like Women? (Teresa Venerdì) by V. De Sica.
1942 La fortuna viene dal cielo by A. Ráthonyi.
Finalmente soli by G. Gentilomo.
1943 L'avventura di Annabella by L. Menardi.
Campo de' Fiori by M. Bonnard.
La vita è bella by C.L. Bragaglia.
L'ultima carrozzella by M. Mattoli.
Gli assi della risata (epis. Il mio pallone) by G. Brignone and R. Bianchi Montero.
1944 Il fiore sotto gli occhi by G. Brignone.
Quartetto pazzo by G. Salvini.
1945 Open City (Roma città aperta) by R. Rossellini.
Abbasso la miseria by G. Righelli.
1946 Peddlin' in Society / Down with Riches! (Abbasso la ricchezza) by G. Righelli.
Un uomo ritorna by M. Neufeld.
The Bandit (Il bandito) by A. Lattuada.
Before Him All Rome Trembled (Avanti a lui tremava tutta Roma) by C. Gallone.
1947 Angelina (L'onorevole Angelina) by L. Zampa.
1948 Lo sconosciuto di San Marino by M. Waszynsky.
Assunta Spina by M. Mattoli.
Ways of Love – 1° epis. The Human Voice; 2° epis. The Miracle (L'Amore – 1ª epis. Una voce umana; 2° epis. Il miracolo) by R. Rossellini.
The Street has Many Dreams (Molti sogni per le strade) by M. Camerini.
1950 Volcano (Vulcano) by W. Dieterle.
1951 Bellissima by L. Visconti.
1952 Camicie rosse (id.) by G. Alessandrini.
The Golden Coach (La carrozza d'oro) by J. Renoir.
1953 We, the Women – epis. Anna Magnani (Siamo donne – epis. Anna Magnani) by L. Visconti.
1955 The Rose Tattoo by Daniel Mann.
1956 The Awakening / The Last Temptation (in G.B.) (Suor Letizia) by M. Camerini.
1957 Wild is the Wind by G. Cukor.
1959 And the Wild, Wild Women / Caged (in G.B.) (Nella città l'inferno) by R. Castellani.
1960 The Fugitive Kind by S. Lumet.
The Passionate Thief (Risate di gioia) by M. Monicelli.
1962 Mamma Roma (id.) by P.P. Pasolini.
1963 Le magot de Josepha by C. Autant-Lara.
1965 Made in Italy (id. epis. La traversata) by N. Loy.
1969 The Secret of Santa Vittoria by S. Kramer.
1971 …Correva l'anno di grazia 1870 by A. Giannetti.
1972 Fellini's Roma (Roma) by F. Fellini.

MANGANO SILVANA
1947 L'elisir d'amore by M. Costa.
Flesh Will Surrender (Il delitto di Giovanni Episcopo) by A. Lattuada.
1948 Gli uomini sono nemici by H. Calef and E. Giannini.
Mad About Opera (Follie per l'opera) by M. Costa.

1949 Black Magic by G. Ratoff.
Bitter Rice (Riso amaro) by G. De Santis.
The Wolf of the Sila (Il lupo della Sila) by D. Coletti.
1950 Il brigante Musolino by M. Camerini.
1951 Anna (id.) by A. Lattuada.
1954 Ulysses (Ulisse) by M. Camerini.
Mambo by R. Rossen.
Gold of Naples – epis. Theresa (L'oro di Napoli – epis. Teresa) by V. De Sica.
1957 Uomini e lupi by G. De Santis.
This Angry Age / The Sea Wall (in G.B.) (La diga sul Pacifico) by R. Clément.
1958 Tempest (La tempesta) by A. Lattuada.
1959 The Great War (La grande guerra) by M. Monicelli.
1960 Five Branded Women (Jovanka e le altre) by M. Ritt.
And Suddenly it's Murder / Killing in Monte Carlo (in G.B.) (Crimen) by M. Camerini.
1961 Il giudizio universale by V. De Sica.
Una vita difficile by D. Risi.
Barabbas (Barabba) by R. Fleischer.
1963 Il processo di Verona by C. Lizzani.
1964 The Flying Saucer (Il disco volante) by T. Brass.
La mia signora by M. Bolognini, T. Brass and L. Comencini.
1966 Io, io, io… e gli altri by A. Blasetti.
Scusi, lei è favorevole o contrario? by A. Sordi.
1967 Oedipus Rex (Edipo Re) by P.P. Pasolini.
The Witches (Le streghe) by M. Bolognini, V. De Sica, P.P. Pasolini, F. Rossi and L. Visconti.
1968 Theorem (Teorema) by P.P. Pasolini.
Capriccio all'italiana (epis. La bambinaia by M. Monicelli – Perché? by M. Bolognini – Viaggio di lavoro by P. Zac).
1971 The Decameron (Il Decameron) by P.P. Pasolini.
Scipione detto anche l'Africano by L. Magni.
Death in Venice (Morte a Venezia) by L. Visconti.
1972 D'amore si muore by C. Carunchio.
Ludwing (Ludwig) by L. Visconti.
The Scientific Card-Player (Lo scopone scientifico) by L. Comencini.
1974 Conversation Piece (Gruppo di famiglia in un interno) by L. Visconti.
1984 Dune by D. Lynch.
1987 Dark Eyes (Oci Ciornie) by N. Michalkov.

MARTINELLI ELSA
1954 Scarlet and Black (Le rouge et le noir) by C. Autant-Lara.
1955 The Indian Fighter by A. De Toth.
Rice Girls (La risaia) by R. Matarazzo.
1956 Donatella (id.) by M. Monicelli.
Four Girls in Town by J. Sher.
1957 Manuela by G. Hamilton.
1958 La mina by G. Bennati.
I battellieri del Volga by A. Genoino and V. Tourjansky.
1959 Ciao, ciao, bambina! by S. Grieco.
Costa azzurra by V. Sala.
La notte brava (id.) by M. Bolognini.
Tunisi Top Secret by P. Paolinelli and H. Leitner.
1960 Blood and Roses (Il sangue e la rosa) by R. Vadim.
Call Girls of Rome (I piaceri del sabato notte) by D. D'Anza.
Il carro armato dell'8 settembre by G. Puccini.
Un amore a Roma by D. Risi.
Captain Blood (Le capitan) by A. Hunebelle.
1961 La ménace by G. Oury.
1962 The Pigeon That Took Rome by M. Shavelson.
Hatari! by H. Hawks.
Pelle viva by G. Fina.
1963 The Trial (Le procès) by O. Welles.
The V.I.P.'s by A. Asquith.
Rampage by H. Hathaway and Ph. Karlson.
1964 De l'amour / All About Loving (in G.B.) (De l'amour) by J. Aurel.
1965 Marco the Magnificent (Le meravgliose avventure di Marco Polo / Lo scacchiere di Dio) by D. de la Patellière and

N. Howard.
L'or du Duc by J. Baratier and B. Toublanc-Michel.
The 10th Victinm (La decima vittima) by E. Petri.
Hail Mafia (Je vous salue, Mafia!) by R. Lévy.
Diamonds Are Brittle (Un milliard dans un billard) by N. Gessner.
1966 Come imparai ad amare le donne by L. Salce.
1967 The Oldest Profession – epis. Roman Nights (Le plus vieux métier du monde – epis Nuits romaines by M. Bolognini).
Qualcuno ha tradito by F. Shannon [F. Prosperi].
Maroc 7 by G. O'Hara.
Woman Seven Times (ep. Super Simone) by V. De Sica.
1968 The Belle Starr Story by N. Wich.
Manon 70 by J. Aurel.
Madigan's Millions (Un dollaro per 7 vigliacchi) by D. Ash [G. Gentili].
1969 Candy by Ch. Marquand.
If It's Tuesday, This Must Be Belgium by M. Stuart.
Maldonne by S. Gobbi.
Una sull'altra by L. Fulci.
L'amica by A. Lattuada.
The Road to Katmandu (Les chemins de Kathmandou) by A. Cayatte.
1970 OSS 117 prend des vacances by P. Kalfon.
1971 La part des lions by J. Larriaga.
La Araucana – Conquista de gigantes by J. Coll.
1976 Garofano rosso by L. Faccini.
1985 Sono un fenomeno paranormale by S. Corbucci.
1991 Once Upon a Crime by E. Lévy.

MARZI FRANCA
1943 Harlem by C. Gallone.
1946 Amanti in fuga by G. Gentilomo.
1947 Il segreto di Don Giovanni by C. Mastrocinque.
I due orfanelli by M. Mattoli.
Tombolo, paradiso nero by G. Ferroni.
1948 Mad About Opera (Follie per l'opera) by M. Costa.
Fifa e arena by M. Mattoli.
Una lettera all'alba by G. Bianchi.
L'isola di Montecristo by M. Sequi.
1949 Calamita d'oro by A. Fizzarotti.
The Pirates of Capri (I pirati di Capri) by G.M. Scotese and E.G. Ulmer.
La figlia del peccato by A. Ingegnero.
Totò le Mokò by C.L. Bragaglia.
Napoli eterna canzone by S. Siano.
A Night of Fame (Al diavolo la celebrità) by Steno and M. Monicelli.
1950 Il figlio di D'Artagnan by R. Freda.
Figaro qua… Figaro là by C.L. Bragaglia.
Devotion (L'edera) by A. Genina.
Ho sognato il Paradiso by G. Pàstina.
1951 Bellezze in bicicletta by C. Campogalliani.
Marakatumba… ma non è una rumba by E. Lozzi.
Arrivano i nostri by M. Mattoli.
Anema e core by M. Mattoli.
Amor non ho… però, però by G. Bianchi.
Milano miliardaria by V. Metz, M. Marchesi and M. Girolami.
La paura fa 90 by G.C. Simonelli.
Verginità by L. De Mitri.
Totò terzo uomo by M. Mattoli.
Lorenaccio by R. Pacini.
Tizio, Caio e Sempronio by V. Metz, M. Marchesi and A. Pozzetti.
La vendetta di Aquila Nera by R. Freda.
Santa Lucia luntana by A. Vergano.
Una bruna indiavolata by C.L. Bragaglia.
Carcerato by A. Zorri [A. Grottini].
Salvate mia figlia! by S. Corbucci.
Fuoco nero by S. Siano.
1952 Vendetta… sarda by M. Mattoli.
Ultimo perdono by R. Polselli.
Delitto al Luna Park by R. Polselli.
Maschera nera by F.W. Ratti.
Io, Amleto by G.C. Simonelli.
Eran trecento… / La spigolatrice di Sapri by G.P. Callegari.
Tragico ritorno by P.L. Faraldo.

Vedi Napoli… e poi muori! by R. Freda.
Non ho paura di vivere by F. Taglioni.
I morti non pagano tasse by S. Grieco.
A fil di spada by C.L. Bragaglia.
1953 La carovana del peccato by P. Mercanti.
La voce del sangue by P. Mercanti.
Lasciateci in pace by M. Girolami.
Canzoni a due voci by G. Vernuccio.
Il cavaliere di Maison Rouge by V. Cottafavi.
Cavallina storna by G. Morelli.
Riscatto by M. Girolami.
I piombi di Venezia by G.P. Callegari.
Rivalità / Medico condotto by G. Biagetti.
Fermi tutti… arrivo io! by S. Grieco.
1954 Canto per te by M. Girolami.
Monster of the Island (Il mostro dell'isola) by R. Bianchi Montero.
Il barcaiolo di Amalfi by M. Roli.
Il medico dei pazzi by M. Mattoli.
L'orfana del ghetto by C. Campogalliani.
1955 Ritrovarsi all'alba by A. Pizzi.
Suor Maria by L. Capuano.
La trovatella di Milano by G. Capitani.
1957 Nights of Cabiria (Le notti di Cabiria) by F. Fellini.
1958 Fortunella (id.) by E. De Filippo.
Love on the Riviera / Girl for the Summer (in G.B.) (Racconti d'estate) by G. Franciolini.
1959 Il raccomandato di ferro by M. Baldi.
1960 La contessa azzurra by C. Gora.
Gastone by M. Bonnard.
Totò, Fabrizi e i giovani d'oggi by M. Mattoli.
La garçonnière by G. De Santis.
1961 Psycosissimo by Steno [S. Vanzina].
Phantom Lovers (Fantasmi a Roma) by A. Pietrangeli.
1964 Le tardone (epis. Canto flamenco) by M. Girolami.
L'uomo che bruciò il suo cadavere by G. Vernuccio.
1966 Scusi, lei è favorevole o contrario? by A. Sordi.

MASINA GIULIETTA
1946 Paisan – 4 °epis. (Paisà – 4° epis.) by R. Rossellini.
1948 Without Pity (Senza pietà) by A. Lattuada.
1950 Lights of Variety (Luci del varietà) by A. Lattuada and F. Fellini.
1951 Behind Closed Shutters (Persiane chiuse) by L. Comencini.
Sette ore di guai by V. Metz and M. Marchesi.
Cameriera bella presenza offresi… by G. Pàstina.
1952 The Greatest Love (Europa '51) by R. Rossellini.
Il romanzo della mia vita by L. De Felice.
The White Sheik (Lo sceicco bianco) by F. Fellini.
Wanda la peccatrice by D. Coletti.
1953 Ai margini della metropoli by C. Lizzani.
Angels over Darkness / Forbidden Women (in G.B.) (Donne proibite) by G. Amato.
Via Padova, 46 by G. Bianchi.
1954 Cento anni d'amore – epis. Purification (id. – epis. Purificazione) by L. De Felice.
La Strada / The Road (in G.B.) (La strada) by F. Fellini.
1955 Buonanotte… avvocato! by G. Bianchi.
The Swindle (The Swindlers (in G.B.) (Il bidone) by F. Fellini.
1957 Nights of Cabiria (Le notti di Cabiria) by F. Fellini.
1958 Fortunella (id.) by E. De Filippo.
1959 And the Wild, Wild Women / Caged (in G.B.) (Nella città l'inferno) by R. Castellani.
Jons und Erdme by V. Vicas.
1960 Das Kunstseidene Mädchen by J. Duvivier.
1965 Juliet of the Spirits (Giulietta degli spiriti) by F. Fellini.
1966 Scusi, lei è favorevole o contrario? by A. Sordi.
1967 Non stuzzicate la zanzara by L. Wertmüller.

1969 The Madwoman of Chaillot by B. Forbes.
1986 Ginger & Fred (id.) by F. Fellini.
Frau Holle by J. Jakubisko.
1991 Aujourd'hui peut-être by J.L. Bertuccelli.

MASSARI LEA
1955 Forbidden (Proibito) by M. Monicelli.
1957 Dreams in a Drawer (I sogni nel cassetto) by R. Castellani.
1958 Auferstehung by R. Hansen.
1960 L'avventura / The Adventure (in G.B.) (L'avventura) by M. Antonioni.
From a Roman Balcony / A Day of Sin (in G.B.) (La giornata balorda) by M. Bolognini.
1961 The Colossus of Rhodes (Il colosso di Rodi) by S. Leone.
Morte di un bandito by G. Amato.
Una vita difficile by D. Risi.
I sogni muoiono all'alba by I. Montanelli.
1962 Paris Pick-up (La monte-charge) by M. Bluwal.
The Captive City (La città prigioniera) by J. Anthony.
The Four Days of Naples (Le quattro giornate di Napoli) by N. Loy.
1964 Llanto por un bandido by C. Saura.
L'insoumis by A. Cavalier.
1965 Le soldatesse by V. Zurlini.
Made in Italy (id. – epis. Ogni bel gioco…) by N. Loy.
1967 Il giardino delle delizie by S. Agosti.
1968 Lo voglio morto by P. Bianchini.
Volver a vivir by Mario Camus.
1970 The Things of Life (Les choses de la vie) by C. Sautet. Céleste by M. Gast.
1971 Senza via d'uscita by P. Sciumè.
Murmur of the Heart (Le souffle au coeur) by L. Malle.
1972 La course de li+vre a travers les champs by R. Clément.
La prima notte di quiete by V. Zurlini.
1973 L'impossibile object by J. Frankenheimer.
Le silencieux by C. Pinoteau.
La femme en bleu by M. Deville.
Le fils by P. Granier-Deferre.
1974 La main à couper by E. Périer.
Allonsanfàn by P. e V. Taviani.
1975 Night Caller (Peur sur la ville) by H. Verneuil.
1976 L'ordinateur des pompes funebres by G. Pirès.
Chi dice donna, dice donna (epis. Papà et maman) by T. Cervi.
La linea del fiume by A. Scavarda.
Violette et François by J. Rouffio.
1977 Antonio Gramsci – I giorni del carcere by L. Del Fra.
Repérages by M. Soutter.
Sale rêveur by J.M. Périer.
Les rendez-vous d'Anna by Ch. Akerman.
1979 Conmo un perro rabioso by A. Isasi Ismamendi.
Eboli (Cristo si è fermato a Eboli) by F. Rosi.
Le divorcement by P. Barouh.
1980 La flambeuse by R. Weinberg.
1983 Sarah by M. Dugowson.
1984 La septième cible by C. Pinoteau.
1985 Segreti segreti by G. Bertolucci.
1991 Viaggio d'amore by O. Fabbri.

MELATO MARIANGELA
1970 Basta guardarla by L. Salce.
Il prete sposato by M. Vicario.
Io non scappo… fuggo by F. Prosperi.
1971 Per grazia ricevuta by N. Manfredi.
La classe operaia va in paradiso by E. Petri.
Incontro by P. Schivazappa.
1972 Mimì metallurgico ferito nello'onore by L. Wertmüller.
La polizia ringrazia by Steno [S. Vanzina].
Lo chiameremo Andrea by V. De Sica.
Il generale dorme in piedi by F. Masaro.
La violenza: quinto potere by F. Vancini.
1973 Love and Anarchy (Film d'amore e d'anarchia: ovvero "Stamattina alle 10 in via dei Fiori nella nota casa di tolleranza…" by L. Wertmüller.
1974 La poliziotta by Steno [S. Vanzina].
Par le sang des autres by M. Simenon.

Nada (id.) by C. Chabrol.
Swept a Way… by on Unusual Destiny in the Blue Sea of August (Travolti da un insolito destino nell'azzurro mare di agosto) by L. Wertmüller.
Orlando furioso by L. Ronconi.
1975 Di che segno sei? (epis. "Aria") by S. Corbucci.
Attenti al buffone by A. Bevilacqua.
L'albero di Guernica by F. Arrabal.
Faccia di spia by Giuseppe Ferrara.
1976 Todo modo by E. Petri.
Caro Michele by M. Monicelli.
Moses (Mosè) by G. De Bosio.
1977 La presidentessa by L. Salce.
Casotto by S. Citti.
Il gatto by L. Comencini.
1978 Saxofone by R. Pozzetto.
1979 To Forget Venice (Dimenticare Venezia) by F. Brusati.
I giorni cantati by P. Pietrangeli.
1980 Oggetti smarriti by G. Bertolucci.
Il pap'occhio by R. Arbore.
Flash Gordon by M. Hodges.
1981 Aiutami a sognare by P. Avati.
So Fine by A. Bergman.
1982 Bello mio bellezza mia by S. Corbucci.
Domani si balla by M. Nichetti.
1983 Il buon soldato by F. Brusati.
The Windbreaker (Il petomane) by L. Salce.
1985 Segreti segreti bby G. Bertolucci.
Figlio mio, infinitamente caro… by V. Orsini.
1986 Notte d'estate con profilo greco, occhi a mandorla e odore di basilico by L. Wertmüller.
1989 Mortacci by S. Citti.
1992 La fine è nota by C. Comencini.

MERCADER MARIA
1936 Molinos de viento by R. Pi.
1939 L'étrange nuit de Noël by Y. Noé.
Il segreto inviolabile by J. Flechner de Gomàr.
1940 Marianela by B. Perojo.
Disillusion (La gerla di papà Martin) by M. Bonnard.
Una famiglia impossibile by C.L. Bragaglia.
El marido provisional by N. Malasomma.
1941 La forza bruta by C.L. Bragaglia.
Brivido by G. Gentilomo.
Il prigioniero di Santa Cruz by C.L. Bragaglia.
The King's Jester (Il re si diverte) by M. Bonnard.
L'attore scomparso by L. Zampa.
Due cuori sotto sequestro by C.L. Bragaglia.
1942 L'uomo venuto dal mare by R. De Ribon and B.L. Randone.
Finalmente soli by G. Gentilomo.
Se io fossi onesto by C.L. Bragaglia.
Un garibaldino al convento by V. De Sica.
La fanciulla dell'altra riva by P. Ballerini.
Musica proibita by C. Campogalliani.
1943 Buongiorno, Madrid by G.M. Cominetti and M. Neufeld.
La primadonna by I. Perilli.
Il treno crociato by C. Campogalliani.
Non sono superstizioso… ma! by C.L. Bragaglia.
I nostri sogni by V. Cottafavi.
La vita è bella by C.L. Bragaglia.
Nessuno torna indietro by A. Blasetti.
L'ippocampo by G.P. Rosmino.
1944 La porta del cielo by V. De Sica.
1945 Il canto della vita by C. Gallone.
1947 Natale al campo 119 by P. Francisci.
1948 Heart and Soul (Cuore) by D. Coletti.
Il cavaliere misterioso by R. Freda.
1952 Hello, Elephant (Buon giorno, elefante) by G. Franciolini.
1990 La casa del sorriso by M. Ferreri.
1991 Il conte Max by Ch. De Sica.

MERLINI ELSA
1931 Sunshine Susie (La segretaria privata) by G. Alessandrini.
1932 Una notte con te by E.W. Emo and F. Biancini.
Cercasi modella by W.W. Emo.
1933 Paprika by C. Boese.
Lisetta by C. Boese.
1934 Melodramma by R. Land and G.C. Simonelli.
1935 Ginevra degli Almieri by G. Brignone.

1936 Non ti conosco più by N. Malasomma.
Trenta secondi d'amore by M. Bonnard.
L'albero di Adamo by M. Bonnard-Amicizia by O. Biancoli.
1938 La dama bianca by M. Mattoli.
1939 Ai vostri ordini, signora! by M. Mattoli.
1941 L'ultimo ballo by C. Mastrocinque.
1942 La regina di Navarra by C. Gallone.
Gioco pericoloso by N. Malasomma.
1951 Cameriera bella presenza offresi…by G. Pàstina.
1955 The Last Five Minutes (Gli ultimi cinque minuti) by G. Amato.
I pappagalli by B. Paolinelli.
1958 Gambe d'oro by T. Vasile.

MILO SANDRA
1956 Lo scapolo by A. Pietrangeli.
Paris Does Strange Things / Elena and Men (in G.B.) (Eléna et les hommes) by J. Renoir.
Moglie e buoi… by L. De Mitri.
1957 Adventures of Arsene Lupin (Les aventures d'Arsène Lupin) by Jacques Becker.
La donna che venne dal mare by F. De Robertis.
1958 The Mirror Has Two Faces (Le miroir à deux faces) by A. Cayatte.
Totò nella luna by Steno [S. Vanzina].
1959 The Lost Souls / Lost Lives (in G.B.) (Vite perdute) by A. Bianchi and R. Mauri.
Herod the Great (Erode il Grande) by A. Genoino.
Le chemin des écoliers by M. Boisrond.
Un témoin dans la ville by E. Molinaro.
General Della Rovere (Il Generale della Rovere) by R. Rossellini.
The Green Mare / The Green Mare's Nest (in G.B.) (La jument verte) by C. Autant-Lara.
Match contre la mort by C. Bernard-Aubert.
1960 The Big Risk (Classe tous risques) by C. Sautet.
Love à la carte / Hungry for Love (in G.B.) (Adua e le compagne) by A. Pietrangeli.
1961 Phantom Lovers (Fantasmi a Roma) by A. Pietrangeli.
Gli scontenti by G. Lipartiti.
The Betrayer (Vanina Vanini) by R. Rossellini.
1963 La Visita (id.) by A. Pietrangeli.
The Shortest Day (Il giorno più corto) by S. Corbucci.
8 1/2 / Eight and a Half (in G.B.) (Otto e 1/2) by F. Fellini.
Méfiez vous, mesdames! by A. Hunebelle.
1964 Frenesia dell'estate by L. Zampa.
Le voci bianche by M. Franciosa and P. Festa Campanile.
Amori pericolosi (epis. Il generale by A. Giannetti).
La donna è una cosa meravigliosa (epis. Una donna dolce dolce by M. Bolognini).
Le belle famiglie (epis. Amare è un po' morire) by U. Gregoretti.
Relaxe-toi, chérie by J. Boyer.
1965 Male Companion (Un monsieur de compagnie) by Ph. de Broca.
Juliet of the Spirits (Giulietta degli spiriti) by F. Fellini.
L'ombrelone by D. Risi.
1966 Come imparai ad amare le donne by L. Salce.
1967 Per la notte pazza del coniggliaccio by A. Angeli.
Per amore… per magia by D. Tessari.
Bang Bang Kid by S. Prager by L. Lelli.
1968 T'ammazzo… raccomandati a Dio by O. Civirani.
1979 Tesoromio by G. Paradisi-Riavanti… marsch!… by L. Salce.
1982 Grog by F. Laudadio.
1984 Cenerentola 80 by R. Malenotti.
1995 Camerieri by L. Pompucci.

MIRANDA ISA
1933 Creature della notte by A.Palermi.
Il caso Haller by A. Blasetti.
1934 Il cardinale Lambertini by O. Bassi.
Tenebre by G. Brignone.

La signora di tutti by M. Ophüls.
Come le foglie by M. Camerini.
1935 Passaporto rosso by G. Brignone.
1936 Il diario di una donna amata by H. Kösterlitz [H. Koster].
Una donna fra due mondi by A.M. Rabenalt and G. Alessandrini.
Du bist mein Glück by K.H. Martin.
1937 Il fu Mattia Pascal by P. Chenal.
The Defeat of Hannibal (Scipione l'Africano) by C. Gallone.
Le mensonge de Nina Petrowna by V. Tourjansky.
1939 Hotel Imperial by R. Florey.
1940 Adventure in Diamonds by G. Fitzmaurice.
Senza cielo by A. Guarini.
1941 È caduta una donna by A. Guarini.
1942 Documento Z 3 by A. Guarini.
Malombra (id.) by M. Soldati.
Zazà by R. Castellani.
1943 La carne e l'anima by W. Strichewsky.
1945 My Widow and I (Lo sbaglio di essere vivo) by C.L. Bragaglia.
1947 L'aventure commence demain by R. Pottier.
1949 Beyond the Walls (Au delà des grilles) by R. Clément.
Patto col diavolo by L. Chiarini.
1950 La ronde by M. Ophüls.
1951 Cameriera bella presenza offresi… by G. Pàstina.
1952 Secret Conclave (Gli uomini non guardano il cielo) by U. Scarpelli.
The Seven Deadly Sins (epis. "Avarice" and "Anger") (Les sept péchés capitaux (epis. "Avarice" et "Colère" by E. De Filippo).
1953 We, the Women (epis. Isa Miranda) (Siamo donne (epis. Isa Miranda by L. Zampa).
1954 Avant le déluge by A. Cayatte.
Le secret d'Hélène Marimon by H. Calef.
Raspoutine by G. Combret.
1955 Summertime by D. Lean.
I pinguini ci guardano by G. Leoni.
Gli sbandati by F. Maselli.
1956 The Rommel's Treasure (Il tesoro di Rommel) by R. Marcellini.
1957 Arrivano i dollari by M. Costa.
Une manche et la belle by H. Verneuil.
I colpevoli by T. Vasile.
1959 Storie d'amore proibite by J. Audry.
1963 La corruzione by M. Bolognini.
The Empty Canvas (La noia) by D. Damiani.
1964 The Yellow Rolls-Royce (First Episode) by A. Asquith.
Hardi, Pardaillan! by B. Borderie.
Dog Eat Dog / When Strangers Meet (in G.B.) (Einer frisst den anderen) by R. Nazarro.
1966 Un mondo nuovo by V. De Sica.
The Great British Train Robbery (Die Gentlemen bitten zur Kassel) by J.F. Olden and C.P. Witt.
1067 Hell is Empty by J. Ainsworth and B. Knowles.
Una storia di notte by L. Petrini.
1968 The Shoes of the Fisherman by M. Anderson.
Caroline Chérie (id.) by D. de la Patellière.
1969 La donna a una dimensione by B. Baratti.
L'assoluto naturale by M. Bolognini.
1970 Within and Without (Un'estate con sentimento) by R. Scarsella.
Colpo rovente by P. Zuffi.
Dorian Gray (Il Dio chiamato Dorian) by M. Dallamano.
Roy Colt & Winchester Jack by M. Bava.
1971 Estado Civil: Martha by J.A. Nieves Conde.
Twitch of the Death Nerve / Bloodbath (in G.B.) (Ecologia del delitto) by M. Bava.
1972 Lo chiameremo Andrea by V. De Sica.
1974 The Night Porter (Il portiere di notte) by L. Cavani.
Le farò da padre by A. Lattuada.
1977 La lunga strada senza polvere by S. Tau.

MORANTE LAURA
1980 Oggetti smarriti by G. Bertolucci.
1981 The Tragedy of a Ridiculous Man (La tragedia di un uomo ridicolo) by B. Bertolucci.

Sogni d'oro by N. Moretti.
1982 Blow to the Heart (Colpire al cuore) by G. Amelio.
1983 Il momento dell'avventura by F. Rosati.
1984 Bianca by N. Moretti.
L'air du crime by A. Klarer.
1985 L'intruse by B. Gantillon.
Le due vite di Mattia Pascal by M. Monicelli.
1986 A flor do mar by J.C. Monteiro.
Man on Fire by E. Chouraqui.
1987 Luci lontane by A. Chiesa.
La vallée fantôme by A. Tanner.
1988 Un amore di donna by N. Risi.
1989 I ragazzi di via Panisperna by G. Amelio.
1990 Tracce di vita amorosa by P. Del Monte.
Le femme fardée by J. Pinheiro.
Turné by G. Salvatores.
Corps perdu by E. De Gregorio.
1991 La voix by P. Granier-Deferre.
Just avant l'orage by B. Herbulot.
1994 Io e il re by L. Gaudino.
1995 Ferie d'agosto by P. Virzì.
1996 Marianna Ucrìa by R. Faenza.

MUTI ORNELLA
1970 La moglie più bella by D. Damiani.
1971 Un posto ideale per uccidere by U. Lenzi.
Sun on the Skin (Il sole nella pelle) by G. Stefani.
1972 La casa de las palomas by C. Guerin Hill.
Experiencia prematrimonial by P. Maso.
Fiorina la vacca by V. De Sisti.
1973 Una chica y un señor by P. Maso.
Tutti figli di "Mammasantissima" di A. Caltabiano.
Le monache di Sant'Arcangelo by P. Dominici [D. Paolella].
Paolo il caldo by M. Vicario.
1974 Appassionata by G.L. Calderone.
Romanzo popolare by M. Monicelli.
Cebo para una adolescente by P. Lara.
1975 Un beso ante de asconderme by M. Camus.
Leonor (Léonor) by J. Buñuel.
1976 Come una rosa al naso by F. Rossi.
L'ultima donna by M. Ferreri.
La joven casada by M. Camus.
L'Agnese va a morire by G. Montaldo.
1977 Mort d'un pourri by G. Lautner.
La stanza del vescovo by D. Risi.
I nuovi mostri by M. Monicelli, D. Risi and E. Scola.
1978 Ritratto di borghesia in nero by T. Cervi.
Primo amore by D. Risi.
Eutanasia di un amore by E.M. Salerno.
1979 La vita è bella by G. Ciukraj.
Giallo napoletano by S. Corbucci.
1980 Il bisbetico domato by F. Castellano and Pipolo [G. Moccia].
Flash Gordon by M. Hodges.
1981 Innamorato pazzo by F. Castellano and Pipolo [G. Moccia].
Storie di ordinaria follia by M. Ferreri.
Love and Money by J. Toback.
Nessuno è perfetto by P. Festa Campanile.
1982 The Girl from Trieste (La ragazza di Trieste) by P. Festa Campanile.
1983 Bonnie e Clyde all'italiana by Steno [S. Vanzina].
Un povero ricco by P. Festa Campanile.
Un amour de Swann by V. Schlöndorff.
1984 The Future is Woman (Il futuro è donna) by M. Ferreri.
1985 Tutta colpa del Paradiso by F. Nuti.
1986 Grandi Magazzini by F. Castellano and Pipolo [G. Moccia].
Stregati by F. Nuti.
1987 Chronicle of a Death Foretold (Cronaca di una morte annunciata) by F. Rosi.
Io e mia sorella by C. Verdone.
Il frullo del passero by G. Mingozzi.
1988 Codice privato by F. Maselli.
1989 O' Re by L. Magni.
The Reasons of the Heart (Bandini) by D. Deruddere.
1990 Stasera a casa di Alice by C. Verdone.
Il viaggio di Capitan Fracassa by E. Scola.
1991 La domenica specialmente (epis. La

domenica specialmente by G. Bertolucci).
Oscar by J. Landis.
Once Upon a Crime by E. Lévy.
Il conte Max by Ch. De Sica.
Vacanze di Natale '91 by E. Oldoini.
1992 Non chiamarmi Omar by S. Staino.
1995 Benvenuta Tatiana by S. San Miguel.

NERI FRANCESCA
1986 Fuori scena by E. Muzii.
1988 Il grande blek by G. Piccioni.
1989 Bankomatt by V. Hermann.
Captain America by A. Pyun.
1990 Las edades de Lulù by B. Luna.
1991 Italian Sarturday (Sabato italiano) by L. Manuzzi.
Pensavo fosse amore invece era un calesse by M. Troisi.
1992 La corsa dell'innocente by C. Carlei.
Al lupo, al lupo! by C. Verdone.
1993 Despara! by C. Saura.
Sud by G. Salvatores.
1995 Ivo il tardivo by A. Benvenuti.
1996 La mia generazione by W. Labate.

NORIS ASSIA
1933 Tre uomini in frack by M. Bonnard.
La signorina dell'autobus by N. Malasomma.
1934 Giallo by M. Camerini.
La marcia nuziale by M. Bonnard.
1935 Quei due by G. Righelli.
Darò un milione by M. Camerini.
1936 Ma non è una cosa seria by M. Camerini.
Una donna fra due mondi by G. Alessandrini and A.M. Rabenalt.
L'uomo che sorride by M. Mattoli.
1937 Allegri masnadieri by M. Elter.
Il signor Max by M. Camerini.
Nina, non far la stupida by N. Malasomma.
Voglio vivere con Letizia by C. Mastrocinque.
1938 La casa del peccato by M. Neufeld.
1939 Batticuore by M. Camerini.
Grandi magazzini by M. Camerini.
Dora Nelson by M. Soldati.
1940 Centomila dollari by M. Camerini.
Una romantica avventura by M. Camerini.
1941 Con le donne non si scherza by G.C. Simonelli.
Luna di miele by G. Gentilomo.
1942 Un colpo di pistola by R. Castellani.
Margherita fra i tre by I. Perilli.
Una storia d'amore by M. Camerini.
1943 Le voyageur de la Touissaint by L. Daquin.
Le capitaine Fracasse by A. Gance.
Una piccola moglie by G. Bianchi.
Che distinta famiglia! by M. Bonnard.
1945 I dieci comandamenti (epis. Non rubare) di G.W. Chili.
1965 La Celestina P… R… by C. Lizzani.

PADOVANI LEA
1945 L'innocente Casimiro by C. Campogalliani.
1946 Outcry (Il sole sorge ancora) by A. Vergano.
1947 The White Devil (Il diavolo bianco) by N. Malasomma.
Call of the Blood (Il richiamo del sangue) by J. Clements and L. Vajda.
1948 Che tempi! by G. Bianchi.
I cavalieri dalle maschere nere by P. Mercanti.
Una lettera all'alba by G. Bianchi.
1949 Give Us This Day by E. Dmytryk.
1950 The Charge is Murder (Atto' di accusa) by G. Gentilomo.
1951 Fiamme sulla laguna by G.M. Scotese.
Honeymoon Deferred (Due mogli sono troppe) by M. Camerini.
La grande rinuncia / Suor Teresa by A. Vergano.
Three Steps North (Tre passi a Nord) by W. Lee Wilder.
I due derelitti by F. Calzavara.
1952 Totò e le donne by Steno [S. Vanzina] and M. Monicelli.
I figli non si vendono by M. Bonnard.
It Happened in Rome / Rome Eleven O'Clock (in G.B.) (Roma ore 11) by G. De Santis.
Don Lorenzo by C.L. Bragaglia.
1953 Papà, ti ricordo by M. Volpe.

Una di quelle by A. Fabrizi.
Cinema d'altri tempi by Steno [S. Vanzina].
1954 Forbidden Women (Donne proibite) by G. Amato.
La barriera della legge by P. Costa.
Amori di mezzo secolo (epis. Girandola 1910 by A. Pietrangeli).
Gran Varietà (epis. Il fine dicitore) (id.) by D. Paolella.
Anatomy of Love / A Slice of Life (in G.B.) (Tempi nostri epis. The Baby) by A. Blasetti.
Il seduttore by F. Rossi.
Guai ai vinti! by R. Matarazzo.
La Castiglione by G. Combret.
Napoli è sempre Napoli by A. Fizzarotti.
La tua donna by G. Paolucci.
1955 Divisione Folgore by D. Coletti.
Chéri Bibi il forzato della Guyana by M. Pagliero.
L'intrusa by R. Matarazzo.
La moglie è uguale per tutti by G.C. Simonelli.
Le dossier noir by A. Cayatte.
Scandal in Sorrento (Pane, amore e…) by D. Risi.
1957 Solo Dio mi fermerà by R. Polselli.
An Eye for an Euye (Oeil pour oeil) by A. Cayatte.
1958 Vive amore (Pane, amore e Andalusia) by X. Seto.
Modigliani of Montparnasse / The Lovers of Montparnasse (in G.B.)(Montparnasse 19) by J. Becker.
The Naked Maja (La Maja desnuda) by H. Koster and J.M. Russo.
1961 La princesse de Clèves by J. Delannoy.
1962 The Reluctant Saint by E. Dmytryk.
1963 The Empty Canvas (La noia) by D. Damiani.
1964 Germinal by Y. Allégret.
Frenesia dell'estate by L. Zampa.
1966 Our Men in Baghdad (Il gioco delle spie) by P. Bianchini.
Un uomo a metà by V. De Seta.
Gli altri, gli altri… e noi by M. Di Lorenzo [M. Arena].
1968 Candy (id.) by Ch. Marquand.
1970 Ciao, Gulliver by C. Tuzii.
1971 Equinozio by M. Ponzi.
1982 Ehrengard by E. Greco.
1989 Cuore di mamma by G. Benelli.
1990 The King's Whore (La putain du roi) by A. Corti.

PAMPANINI SILVANA
1947 L'Apocalisse by G.M. Scotese.
Il segreto di Don Giovanni by C. Mastrocinque.
1948 Arrivederci papà! by C. Mastrocinque.
Il barone Carlo Mazza by G. Brignone.
1949 I pompieri di Viggiù by M. Mattoli.
Anthony of Padua (Antonio di Padova) by P. Francisci.
Biancaneve e i sette ladri by G. Gentilomo.
Marechiaro by G. Ferroni.
1950 Lo sparviero del Nilo by G. Gentilomo.
La Bisarca by G.C. Simonelli.
È arrivato il cavaliere by Steno [S. Vanzina] and M. Monicelli.
47 morto che parla by C.L. Bragaglia.
Double Trouble (L'inafferrabile 12) by M. Mattoli.
1951 Io sono il Capataz by G.C. Simonelli.
La paura fa 90 by G.C. Simonelli.
Bellezze in bicicletta by C. Campogalliani.
Era lui… sì! sì! by V. Metz, M. Marchesi and M. Girolami.
Miracolo a Viggiù by L.M. Giachino.
Ha fatto 13 by C. Manzoni.
Una bruna indiavolata by C.L. Bragaglia.
O.K. Nero (O.K. Nerone) by M. Soldati.
1952 Il richiamo nella tempesta by O. Palella.
The Affair of Madame Pompadour (Le avventure di Mandrin) by M. Soldati.
Canzoni di mezzo secolo (epis. Sposi di guerra) by D. Paolella.
The Island Sinner (La peccatrice dell'isola) by S. Corbucci.
La donna che inventò l'amore by F. Cerio.
Frustrations (La tratta delle bianche)

by L. Comencini.
A Town on Trial (Processo alla città) by L. Zampa.
La presidentessa by P. Germi.
1953 Koenigsmark by S. Térac.
Dangerous Woman (Bufere) by G. Brignone.
Viva il cinema! by E. Trapani.
L'incantevole nemica by C. Gora.
Canzoni, canzoni, canzoni (epis. Signorina Grandi Firme) by D. Paolella.
Noi cannibali by A. Leonviola.
Vortice by R. Matarazzo.
A Husband for Anna (Un marito per Anna Zaccheo) by G. De Santis
1954 Amori di mezzo secolo (epis. Dopoguerra 1920 by Mario Chiari).
A Day in Court (Un giorno in pretura) by Steno [S. Vanzina].
Il matrimonio by A. Petrucci.
Allegro squadrone by P. Moffa.
Schiava del peccato by R. Matarazzo.
Orient Express (id.) by C.L. Bragaglia.
La principessa delle Canarie by P. Moffa.
1955 The Tower of Lust (La tour de Nesle) by A. Gance-
Canzoni di tutta Italia by D. Paolella.
La bella di Roma by L. Comencini.
Racconti romani by G. Franciolini.
1956 La loi des rues by R. Habib.
1957 Saranno uomini by S. Siano.
1958 La strada lunga un anno by G. De Santis.
1959 Sed de amor by A. Corona Blake.
1961 Mariti a congresso by L.F. D'Amico.
Guns of the Black Witch (Il terrore dei mari) by D. Paolella.
La spada dell'Islam by E. Bomba-
1064 Il gaucho by D. Risi.
1971 Mazzabubù… quante corna stanno quaggiù by M. Laurenti.
1983 Il tassinaro by A. Sordi.

PANARO ALESSANDRA
1954 Il barcaiolo di Amalfi by M. Roli [E. Pontiroli].
1955 Il campanile d'oro by G.C. Simonelli.
Gli innamorati by M. Bolognini.
Destinazione Piovarolo by D. Paolella.
1956 Cantando sotto le stelle by M. Girolami.
Mamma sconosciuta by C. Campogalliani.
Guardia, guardia scelta, brigadiere e maresciallo by M. Bolognini.
I miliardari by G. Malatesta.
Poor but Handsome (Poveri ma belli) by D. Risi.
1957 La trovatella di Pompei by G. Gentilomo.
Lazzarella by C.L. Bragaglia.
Amore e chiacchiere by A. Blasetti.
Irresistible (Belle ma povere) (id.) by D. Risi.
1958 Al servizio dell'imperatore by C. Canaille and E. Anton.
Totò, Peppino e le fanatiche by M. Mattoli.
L'ultima canzone by P. Mercanti.
1959 Avventura a Capri by G. Lipartiti.
I ragazzi dei Parioli by S. Corbucci.
Poveri milionari by D. Risi.
Cigarettes, whisky et p'tites pépées by M. Régamey.
Il raccomandato di ferro by M. Baldi.
Le notti dei teddy boys by L. Savona.
Cerasella by R. Matarazzo.
1960 Rocco and His Brothers (Rocco e i suoi fratelli) by L. Visconti.
1961 The Baccanthes (Le baccanti) by G. Ferroni.
Mariti a congresso by L.F. D'Amico.
1962 Ulysses Against Hercules (Ulisse contro Ercole) by M. Caiano.
Pecado de amor by L.C. Amadori.
The Son of Captain Blood (El hijo del capitan Blood) by T. Demicheli.
The Secret Mark of D'Artagnan (Il colpo segreto di D'Artagnan) by S. Marcellini.
1963 Blood of the Executioner (Il boia di Venezia) by L. Capuano.
Conquest of Mycene / Hercules Attacks (in G.B.) (Ercole contro Moloch) by G. Ferroni.
1964 Temple of the White Elephant (Sandok, il Maciste della giungla) by U. Lenzi.

219

1965 Schatz der Aztechen by R. Siodmak.
30 winchester per El Diablo by F.G. Carroll [G. Baldanello].
1966 Gli altri, gli altri… e noi by M. Arena.

PAOLA DRIA
1929 Sole by A. Blasetti.
1930 La canzone dell'amore by G. Righelli.
1931 Vele ammainate by A.G. Bragaglia.
Stella del cinema by M. Almirante.
Il medico per forza by C. Campogalliani.
Cortile by C. Campogalliani.
L'uomo dall'artiglio by N. Malasomma.
1932 Pergolesi by G. Brignone.
1933 Fanny by M. Almirante.
Il signore desidera? by G. Righelli.
1934 La fanciulla dell'altro mondo by G. Righelli.
The Blind Woman of Sorrento (La cieca di Sorrento) by N. Malasomma.
1935 Un colpo di vento by J. Dréville and C.F. Tavano.
Pensaci, Giacomino! by G. Righelli.
L'albero di Adamo by M. Bonnard.
1938 L'ultimo scugnizzo by G. Righelli.
Lotte nell'ombra by D.M. Gambino.
L'albergo degli assenti by R. Matarazzo.
1939 Il cavaliere di San Marco by G. Righelli.
Montevergine by C. Campogalliani.
Traversata nera by D.M. Gambino.
La mia canzone al vento by G. Brignone.
La notte delle beffe by C. Campogalliani.
1940 The Conquest of the Air (La conquista dell'aria) by A. Korda and R. Marcellini.
Cuori nella tormenta by C. Campogalliani.
1942 La pantera nera by D.M. Gambino

PARVO ELLI
1934 Loyalty of Love (Teresa Confalonieri) by G. Brignone.
1937 Il feroce Saladino by M. Bonnasrd.
Gatta ci cova by G. Righelli.
Lasciate ogni speranza by G. Righelli.
Voglio vivere con Letizia by C. Mastrocinque.
1938 Partire by A. Palermi.
Unsere kleine Frau by P. Verhoeven.
1939 Il marchese di Ruvolito by R. Matarazzo.
La notte delle beffe by C. Campogalliani.
1940 Arditi civili by D.M. Gambino.
La donna perduta by D.M. Gambino.
Miseria e nobiltà by C. D'Errico.
Il ponte dei sospiri by M. Bonnard.
1941 Ridi, pagliaccio! by C. Mastrocinque.
L'allegro fantasma by A. Palermi.
Beatrice Cenci by G. Brignone.
The King's Jester (Il re si diverte) by M. Bonnard.
1942 L'uomo venuto dal mare by R. De Ribon and B.L. Randone.
Sette anni di felicità by R.L. Savarese and E. Marischka.
Don Giovanni by D. Falconi.
M.A.S. by R. Marcellini.
I due Foscari by E. Fulchignoni.
Carmen (id.) by Christian-Jaque.
1943 Il fanciullo del West by G. Ferroni.
Desiderio by R. Rossellini and M. Pagliero.
1945 La porta del cielo by V. De Sica.
1946 A Yank in Rome (Un americano in vacanza) by L. Zampa.
Outcry (Il sole sorge ancora) by A. Vergano.
1947 I fratelli Karamazoff by G. Gentilomo.
1948 Legge di sangue by L. Capuano.
Il cavaliere misterioso by R. Freda.
1949 L'urlo by F. Cerio.
Vertigine d'amore by L. Capuano.
1950 Santo disonore by G. Brignone.
Tewlve Hours to Live (È più facile che un cammello) by L. Zampa.
1951 Totò terzo uomo by M. Mattoli.
1952 Rosalba, la fanciulla di Pompei by N. Montillo.
1953 Voto di marinaio by E. De Rosa.
1954 La Luciana by D.M. Gambino.
THe Loves of Three Women (The Face That Launched a Thousand Ships (in G.B.) (L'amante di Paride) by M. Allégret.

La campana di San Giusto by M. Amendola and R. Maccari.
1955 L'arte di arrangiarsi by L. Zampa.
Giuramento d'amore by R. Bianchi Montero.
L'ultimo amante by M. Mattoli.
1956 Mi permette, babbo by M. Bonnard.
1957 The Goddess of Love / Aphrodite, Goddess of Love (in G.B.) (La Venere di Cheronea) by G. Rivalta and V. Tourjanski.
1959 Il mondo dei miracoli by L. Capuano.
1960 Madri pericolose by D. Paolella.

PIERANGELI ANNA MARIA
1950 Tomorrow is Too Late (Domani è troppo tardi) by L. Moguy.
1951 Tomorrow is Another Day (Domani è un altro giorno) by L. Moguy.
Teresa by F. Zinnemann.
The Light Touch by R. Brooks.
1952 The Devil Makes Three by A. Marton.
1953 The Story of Three Lovers (epis. Trapeze by G. Reinhardt).
Sombrero by N. Foster.
1954 The Flame and the Flesh by R. Brooks.
Oh No, Masm'zelle (Mam'zelle Nitouche) by Y. Allégret.
1955 The Silver Chalice by V. Saville.
1956 Port Afrique by R. Maté.
Somebody Up There Likes Me by R. Wise.
1957 The Vintage by J. Hayden.
1958 Merry Andrew by M. Kidd.
1959 S.O.S. Pacific by G. Green.
1960 The Angry Silence by G. Green.
1961 White Slave Ship (L'ammutinamento) by S. Amadio.
1962 Sodom and Gomorrah by R. Aldrich.
Musketeers of the Sea (I moschettieri del mare) by Steno [S. Vanzina].
1964 Shadow of Evil (Banco à Bangkok pour OSS 117) by A. Hunebelle.
1965 Battle of the Bulge by K. Annakin.
Spy in Your Eye (Berlino, appuntamento per le spie) by V. Sala.
1966 MMM 83 – Missione Morte Molo 83 by S. Bergonzelli.
Per mille dollari al giorno by S. Amadio.
1967 King of Africa (Rey de Africa) by S. Howard and N. Scolaro.
1968 Red Roses for the Fuehrer (Rose rosse per il Führer) by F. Di Leo.
Every Bastard a King by U. Zohar.
1969 Love Me, Love My Wife (Addio, Alexandra!) by E. Battaglia.
1970 Mafia Mob (Viva América) by X. Seto.
In the Folds of the Flesh (Nelle pieghe della carne) by S. Bergonzelli.
Quell'amore particolare by C. Martinelli.
1971 Octaman by H. Essex.

PODESTÀ ROSSANA
1951 Tomorrow is Another Day (Domani è un altro giorno) by L. Moguy.
Strano appuntamento by D.A. Hanza.
I sette nani alla riscossa by P.W. Tamburella.
Cops and Robbers (Guardie e ladri) by Steno [S. Vanzina] and M. Monicelli.
1952 Il moschettiere fantasma by W. French [M. Calandri].
Gli angeli del quartiere by C. Borghesio.
Io, Amleto by G.C. Simonelli.
Don Lorenzo by C.L. Bragaglia.
1953 Luxury Girls (Fanciulle di lusso) by B. Vorhaus.
La voce del silenzio by G.W. Pabst.
Viva la rivista! (epis. Il gregario) by E. Trapani.
Addio, figlio mio! by G. Guarino.
Ulysses (Ulisse) by M. Camerini.
La red by E. Fernandez.
1954 Nosotros dos by E. Fernandez.
Le ragazze di San Frediano by V. Zurlini.
1955 Playa prohibida by F. Fuertos.
Helen of Troy by R. Wise.
Canzoni di tutta Italia by D. Paolella.
Non scherzare con le donne by G. Bennati.
1956 Santiago by G. Douglas.
1957 La Bigorne, caporal de France by R. Darène.
1958 La spada e la croce by C.L. Bragaglia.
Raw Wind in Eden by R. Wilson.
1959 Temptation Island (L'ile au bout du

monde) by E.T. Gréville.
Un vaso di whisky by J. Coll.
1960 Fury of the Pagans (La furia dei barbari) by G. Malatesta.
1961 La grande vallata by A. Dorigo.
Slaves of Rome / Blood of the Warriors (in G.B.) (La schiava di Roma) by S. Grieco.
1962 Sodom and Gomorrah by R. Aldrich.
Vengeance of the Gladiatirs (Solo contro Roma) by H. Wise [L. Ricci].
The Golden Arrow (L'arciere delle mille e una notte) by A. Margheriti.
Horror Castle / The Castle of Terror (La vergine di Norimberga) by A.M. Dawson [A. Margheriti].
1964 The Naked Hours (Le ore nude) by M. Vicario.
F.B.I. Operazione Baalbeck by M. Giannini and H. Fregonese.
1965 Sette uomini d'oro by M. Vicario.
1966 Il grande colpo dei sette uomini d'oro by M. Vicario.
1970 Il prete sposato by M. Vicario.
1971 Homo eroticus by M. Vicario.
1972 L'uccello migratore by Steno [S. Vanzina].
1973 Paolo il caldo by M. Vicario.
1975 Il gatto mammone by N. Cicero.
1976 Il letto in piazza by B. Gaburro.
1977 Pane, burro e marmellata by G. Capitani.
1979 Sette ragazze di classe by P. Lazaga.
1980 Tranquille donne di campagna by C. De Molinis [C. Giorgi].
Les seducteurs (epis. Le carnet d'Armando by D. Risi).
1983 Hercules (id.) by L. Coates [L. Cozzi].
1985 Segreti segreti by G. Bertolucci.

RALLI GIOVANNA
1943 The Children Are Watching (I bambini ci guardano) by V. De Sica.
1950 Lights of Variety (Luci del varietà) by A. Lattuada and F. Fellini.
1951 La famiglia Passaguai by A. Fabrizi.
1952 La famiglia Passaguai fa fortuna by A. Fabrizi.
Papà diventa mamma by A. Fabrizi.
1953 The Wolf / The Vixen (in G.B.) (La lupa) by A. Lattuada.
Amore in città (epis. Gli italiani si voltano by A. Lattuada).
Anni facili by L. Zampa.
Fermi tutti… arrivo io by S. Grieco.
Villa Borghese (id., epis. Incidente a Villa Borghese) by G. Franciolini.
1954 Prima di sera by P. Tellini.
I tre ladri by L. De Felice.
Le ragazze di San Frediano by V. Zurlini.
Madame du Barry (id.) by Christian-Jaque.
1955 Le signorine dello 04 by G. Franciolini.
Un eroe dei nostri tempi by M. Monicelli.
Racconti romani by G. Franciolini.
Les hussards by A. Joffé.
1956 Peccato di castità by G. Franciolini.
A Plea for Passion / The Bigamist (in G.B.) (Il bigamo) by L. Emmer.
Tempo di villeggiatura by A. Racioppi.
Una pelliccia di visone by G. Pellegrini.
1957 The Most Wonderful Moment (Il momemto più bello) by L. Emmer.
Le belle dell'aria by M. Costa.
1958 Come te movi, te fulmino! by M. Mattoli.
È permesso, maresciallo? by C.L. Bragaglia.
1959 Nel blu dipinto di blu by P. Tellini.
Le cameriere by C.L. Bragaglia.
Un uomo facile by P. Heusch.
Costa azzurra by V. Sala.
I ladri by L. Fulci.
General Della Rovere (Il Generale Della Rovere) by R. Rossellini.
My Wife's Enemy (Il nemico di mia moglie) by E. Puccini.
1960 Wait for the Dawn (Era notte a Roma by R. Rossellini.
1961 Pastasciutta nel deserto by C.L. Bragaglia.
Viva l'Italia by R. Rossellini.
Le goût de la violence by R. Hossein.
1962 Carmen di Trastevere by C. Gallone.
Warriors Fire (La guerra continua) by L. Savona.
La monaca di Monza by C. Gallone.

Horace '62 by A. Versini.
1964 La vita agra by C. Lizzani.
Liolà by A. Blasetti.
Let's Talk About Women (Se permettete parliamo di donne) by E. Scola.
La Fuga (id.) by P. Cavara.
1966 What Did You Do in the War, Daddy? by B. Edwards.
The Caper of the Golden Bulls / Carnival of Thieves (in G.B.) by R. Rouse.
1968 Deadfall by B. Forbes.
The Mercenary (Il mercenario) by S. Corbucci.
1969 La donna invisibile by P. Spinola.
1970 Una prostituta al servizio del pubblico e in regola con le leggi dello Stato by I. Zingarelli.
Cannon for Cordoba by P. Wendkos.
1971 Gli occhi freddi della paura by E.G. Castellari [E. Girolami].
1974 Per amare Ofelia by F. Mogherini.
We All Loved Each Other So Much (C'eravamo tanto amati) by E. Scola.
La polizia chiede aiuto by M. Dallamano.
1975 Di che segno sei? (epis. Terra) by S. Corbucci.
1976 Chi dice donna, dice donna (epis. La signorina X) by T. Cervi.
40 gradi all'ombra del lenzuolo (epis. L'attimo fuggente) by S. Martino.
Colpita da improvviso benessere by F. Giraldi.
Languidi baci, perfide carezze by A. Angeli.
1980 Arrivano i bersaglieri by L. Magni.
1981 Manolesta by P. Festa Campanile.
1990 Verso sera by F. Archibugi.
1992 Per non dimenticare by M. Martelli.
1994 Tutti gli anni, una volta l'anno di G. Lazotti.

ROSSI DRAGO ELEONORA
1949 The Pirates of Capri (I pirati di Capri) by E.G. Ulmer and G.M. Scotese.
1950 Due sorelle amano by J. Comin.
Altura by M. Sequi.
1951 Behind Closed Shutters (Persianen chiuse) by L. Comencini.
Verginità by L. De Mitri.
L'ultima sentenza by M. Bonnard.
1952 Enticement (Sensualità) by C. Fracassi.
Three Forbidden Stories (Tre storie proibite) by A. Genina.
Frustrations / Marked for Danger (in G.B.) (La tratta delle bianche(by L. Comencini.
Pride, Love and Suspicion (La fiammata) by A. Blasetti.
1953 Human Torpedos (I sette dell'Orsa Maggiore) by D. Coletti.
The Slave (L'esclave) by Y. Ciampi.
1954 Daughters of Destiny (epis. Elisabeth) / Love and the Frenchwoman (epis. Elisabeth) (Destini di donne – epis. La vittima della guerra by M. Pagliero).
Vestire gliignudi by M. Pagliero.
On Trial (L'affaire Maurizius) by J. Duvivier.
1955 Napoléon by S. Guitry.
The Girlfriends (Le amiche) by M. Antonioni.
1956 Done sole by V. Sala.
Il prezzo della gloria by A. Musu.
The Awakening / The Last Temptation (in G.B.) (Suor Letizia) by M. Camerini.
1957 Kean, genio e sregolatezza by V. Gassman.
Anyone Can Kill Me (Tous peuvent me tuer) by H. Decoin.
1958 La Tour, prends garde! by G. Lampin.
La strada lunga un anno by G. De Santis.
1959 Dagli Appennini alle Ande by F. Quilici.
La grana by M. Cloche.
The Facts of Murder / A Sordid Affair (in G.B.) (Un maledetto imbroglio) by P. Germi.
Estate violenta by V. Zurlini.
Vacanze d'inverno by C. Mastrocinque.
1960 David and Goliath (David e Golia) by F. Baldi and R. Pottier.
La garçonnière by G. De Santis.
L'impiegato by G. Puccini.
Die Rote Hand by K. Meisel.
Schlusskkord by W, Liebeneiner.
Under Ten Flags (Sotto dieci bandiere) by D. Coletti.

1961 Caccia all'uomo by R. Freda.
Tiro al piccione by G. Montaldo.
Sword of the Conqueror (Rosmunda e Alboino) by C. Campogalliani.
1962 I dongiovanni della Costa Azzurra by V. Sala.
Love at Twenty – epis. Rome (L'amour à vingt ans – epis. Rome by Renzo Rossellini jr.).
Anima nera by R. Rossellini.
Der Teppich des Grauens by H. Reinl.
Hypnosis / Dummy of Death (in G.B.) (Ipnosi) by E. Martin.
1963 The Shortest Day (Il giorno più corto) by S. Corbucci.
Tempesta su Ceylon by G. Oswald and G. Roccardi.
1964 L'amore facile (epis. Il vedovo bianco) by G. Puccini.
The Flying Saucer (Il disco volante) by T. Brass.
Love and Marriage – epis. The Last Card (L'idea fissa – epis. K'ultima carta by M. Guerrini).
Lets Talk About Women (Se permettete, parliamo di donne) by E. Scola.
Il treno del sabato by V. Sala.
1965 Assassinio made in Italy by S. Amadio.
El diablo también llora by J.A. Nieves Conde.
Io uccidi, tu uccidi (epis. Il plenilunio) by G. Puccini.
Su e giù (epis. Il colpo del leone) by M. Guerrini.
Uncle Tom's Cabin (Onkel Tom Hütte) by G. von Radványi.
1966 The Bible… in the Beginning (La Bibbia) by J. Huston.
1967 Mano di velluto by E. Fecchi.
1968 Love Problems (L'età del malessere) by G. Biagetti.
1969 Camille 2000 (id.) by R. Metzger.
1970 In the Folds of the Flesh (Nelle pieghe della carne) by S. Bergonzelli.

SANDRELLI STEFANIA
1961 Gioventù di notte by M. Sequi.
The Fascist (Il federale) by L. Salce.
Divorce, Italian Style (Divorzio all'italiana) by P. Germi.
1963 Les vierges by J.P. Mocky.
La bella di Lodi by M. Missiroli.
Il fornaretto di Venezia by D. Tessari.
L'ainé des Ferchaux by J.P. Melville.
1964 Seduced and Abandoned (Sedotta e abbandonata) by P. Germi.
La chance et l'amour (Les fiancés de la chance et E. Schlumberger).
1965 Io la conoscevo bene by A. Pietrangeli.
1966 Tender Scoundrel (Tendre voyou) by Jean Becker.
1967 The Climax (L'immorale) by P. Germi.
1968 Partner by B. Bertolucci.
1969 L'amante di Gramigna by C. Lizzani.
1970 Within and Without (Un'estate con sentimento) by R. Scarsella.
Brancaleone alle Crociate by M. Monicelli.
The Conformist (Il conformista) by B. Bertolucci.
1971 The Black Belly of Tarantula (La tarantola dal ventre nero) by P. Cavara.
1972 Il diavolo nel cervello by S. Sollima.
Alfredo, Alfredo (id.) by P. Germi.
1974 Delitto d'amore by L. Comencini.
We All Loved Each Other So Much (C'eravamo tanto amati) by E. Scola.
1975 Les magiciens by C. Chabrol.
1976 Le voyage de noces by N. Trintignant.
1900 (Novecento) by B. Bertolucci.
Police Python 357 by A. Corneau.
Quelle strane occasioni (epis. L'ascensore) by L. Comencini).
1978 Io sono mia by S. Scandurra,
Le maitre nageur by J.L. Trintignant.
Dove vai in vacanza? (epis. Sarò tutta per te by M. Bolognini).
1979 L'ingorgo by L. Comencini.
La verdad sobre el caso Savolta by A. Drove.
1980 La terrazza by L. Comencini.
Desire, the Interior Life (Desideria, la vita interiore) by G. Barcelloni.
1981 La disubbidienza by A. Lado.
1982 Bello mio bellezza mia by S. Corbucci.
Eccezzziunale… veramente by C. Vanzina.
1983 The Key (La chiave) by T. Brass.
Vacanze di Natale by C. Vanzina.

1984 Magic Moments by L. Odforisio.
Una donna allo specchio by F. Quaregna.
1985 Segreti segreti by G. Bertolucci.
Mi faccia causa by Steno [S. Vanzina].
L'attenzione by G. Soldati.
Mamma Ebe by C. Lizzani.
1986 Let's Hope It's a Girl (Speriamo che sia femmina) by M. Monicelli.
La sposa americana by G. Soldati.
1987 La sposa era bellissima by P. Gábor.
La famiglia by E. Scola.
D'Annunzio by S. Nasca.
Noyade interdite by P. Granier-Deferre.
Gli occhiali d'oro by G. Montaldo.
1988 Secondo Ponzio Pilato by L. Magni.
Stradivari by G. Battiato.
Il piccolo diavolo by R. Benigni.
Strana la vita by G. Bertolucci.
Mignon Has Left (Mignon è partita) by F. Archibugi.
1989 The Sleazy Uncle (Lo zio indegno) by F. Brusati.
1990 Il male oscuro by M. Minicelli.
Evelina e i suoi figli by L. Giampalmo.
L'africana by M. von Trotta.
Tracce di vita amorosa by P. Del Monte.
1991 Nottataccia by D. Camerini.
Non chiamarmi Omar by S. Staino.
Jamón, jamón by B. Luna.
1992 L'eil écarlate by S. Korber.
1993 Per amore solo per amore by G. Veronesi.
1995 Benvenuta Tatiana by S. San Miguel.
Con gli occhi chiusi by F. Archibugi.
Palermo-Milano solo andata by C. Fragasso.
Of Love and Shadows by B. Kaplan.
1996 Stealing Beauty (Io ballo da sola) by B. Bertolucci.

SANSON YVONNE
1946 Black Eagle (Aquila nera) by R. Freda.
1947 The Great Dawn (La grande aurora) by G.M. Scotese.
Flesh Will Surrender (Il delitto di Giovanni Episcopo) by A. Lattuada.
1948 Il cavaliere mistyeriosop by R. Freda.
1949 Children of Change (Campane a martello) by L. Zampa.
L'imperatore di Capri by L. Comencini.
Catene by R. Matarazzo.
1950 La cintura di castità by C. Mastrocinque.
Double Trouble (L'inafferrabile 12) by M. Mattoli.
Tormento by R. Matarazzo.
1951 Nobody's Child (I figli di nessuno) by R. Matarazzo.
1952 Wanda la peccatrice by D. Coletti.
Menzogna by U.M. Del Colle.
Nous sommes tous des assassins by A. Cayatte.
The Overcoat (Il cappotto) by A. Lattuada.
Chi è senza peccato by R. Matarazzo.
1953 Nerone e Messalina by P. Zeglio.
Noi peccatori by G. Brignone.
Quand tu liras cette lettre by J.P. Melville.
Les trois mousquetaires by A. Hunebelle.
1954 Star of India by A. Lubin and E. Anton.
Torna! by R. Matarazzo.
Frisky / Bread, Love and Jealousy (in G.B.) (Pane, amore e gelosia) by L. Comencini.
1955 La moglie è uguale per tutti by G.C. Simonelli.
L'angelo bianco by R. Matarazzo.
Il campanile d'oro by G.C. Simonelli.
The Miller's Wife (La bella mugnaia) by M. Camerini.
Il prigioniero della montagna by L. Trenker.
1957 L'ultima violenza by R. Matarazzo.
This Angry Age / The Sea Wall (in G.B.) (La diga sul Pacifico) by R. Clément.
1958 Malinconico autunno by R. Matarazzo.
1959 Il mondo dei miracoli by L. Capuano.
1961 I masnadieri by M. Bonnard.
Il re di Poggioreale by D. Coletti.
1962 Anima nera by R. Rossellini.

Lo smemoragto di Collegno by S. Corbucci.
1963 The Shortest Day (Il giorno più corto) by S. Corbucci.
1967 Days of Anger (I giorni dell'ira) by T. Valerii.
The Biggest Bundle of Them All by K. Annakin.
1968 The Prophet (Il profeta) by D. Risi.
1969 Il ragazzo che sorride by A. Grimaldi.

SCHIAFFINO ROSANNA
1956 Totò lascia o raddoppia by C. Mastrocinque.
Orlando e i paladini di Francia by P. Francisci.
1958 Un ettaro di cielo by A. Casadio.
La sfida by F. Rosi.
1959 Il vendicatore / Dubrowski by W. Dieterle.
La notte brava (id.) by M. Bolognini.
Ferdinando I re di napoli by G. Franciolini.
1960 Le bal des espions by M. Clément.
The Monotaur / Warlord of Crete (in G.B.) (Teseo contro il Minotauro) by S. Amadio.
1961 L'onorata società by R. Pazzaglia.
Seduction of the South (I briganti italiani) by M. Camerini.
Il ratto delle Sabine by R. Pottier.
Le miracle des loups by A. Hunebelle.
1962 Lafayette (La Fayette) by J. Dréville.
Crime Does Not Pay / The Gentle Art of Murder – epis. The Mask (Le crime ne paie pas – epis. Le masque) by G. Oury.
Two Weeks in Another Town by V. Minnelli.
Le livre de SAn Michele by G. Capitani and R. Jugert.
1963 Rogopag (epis. Illibatezza by R. Rossellini).
The Long Ships by J. Cardiff.
The Victors by C. Foreman.
La corruzione by M. Bolognini.
1964 The Cavern (Sette contro la morte) by P. Bianchini and E.G. Ulmer.
1965 Red Dragon (Das Geheimnis der drei Dschunken) by E. Hofbauer.
Mandragola / The Mandrake (in G.B.) (La mandragola) by A. Lattuada.
1966 El Greco (id.) by L. Salce.
Drop Dead, Darling by K. Hughes.
La strega in amore by D. Damiani.
1967 The Rover (L'avventuriero) by T. Young.
Encrucijada para una monja by J. Buchs.
1969 Simón Bolivar by A. Blasetti.
Scacco alla regina by P. Festa Campanile.
1971 Seven Times a Day by D. Heroux.
La Betìa, ovvero nell'amore per ogni gaudenzia ci vuole sofferanza by G. De Bosio.
Trastevere by F. Tozzi.
1972 Ettore lo fusto by E.G. Castellari [E. Girolami].
1973 The Heroes (Gli eroi) by D. Tessari.
The Man Called Moon (Un hombre llamado Noon) by P. Collinson.
Il magnate by G. Grimaldi.
1974 Commissariato di notturna by G. Leoni.
L'assassino ha riservato nove poltrone by G. Bennati.
Il testimone deve tacere by G. Rosati.
1975 Cagliostro (id.) by D. Pettinari.
La trastienda by J. Grau.
1976 La ragazza dalla pelle di corallo by O. Civirani.

SILVI LILIA
1935 Cantico della terra by S.F. Ramponi.
1937 Il signor Max by M. Camerini.
1938 Partire by A. Palermi.
1939 Assenza ingiustificata by M. Neufeld.
Il segreto di villa Paradiso by D.M. Gambino.
1940 Arditi civili by D.M. Gambino.
Giù il sipario by R. Matarazzo.
Dopo divorzieremo by N. Malasomma.
Scarpe grosse by D. Falconi.
1941 Barbablù by C.L. Bragaglia.
Scampolo by N. Malasomma.
1942 Violette nei capelli by C.L. Bragaglia.
La bisbetica domata by F.M. poggioli.

Happy Days (Giorni felici) by G. Franciolini.
1943 La vispa Teresa by M. Mattoli.
1944 Il diavolo va in collegio by J. Boyer.
1946 Biraghin by C. Gallone.
1951 Napoleone by C. Borghesio.

SPAAK CATHERINE
1960 The Hole (Le trou) by Jacques Becker.
Les Adolescentes (I dolci inganni) by A. Lattuada.
Il carro armato dell'8 settembre by G. Puccini.
1961 Three Truths in the Well (Le puits aux trois vérités) by F. Villiers.
1962 Crazy Desire / This Crazy Urge (in G.B.) (La voglia matta) by L. Salce.
Eighteen in the Sun (Diciottenni al sole) by C. Mastrocinque.
Sex Can Be Difficult – epis. The Women (L'amore difficile epis. Le donne by S. Sollima).
The Easy Life (Il sorpasso) by D. Risi.
1963 La parmigiana by A. Pietrangeli.
The Empty Canvas (La noia) by D. Damiani.
The Little Nuns (Le monachine) by L. Salce.
1964 La calda vita by F. Vancini.
Weekend at Dunkirk (Week-end à Zuydcoote) by H. Verneuil.
Tre notti d'amore by L. Comencini, R. Castellani and F. Rossi.
Circle of Love (La ronde) by R. Vadim.
1965 La bugiarda by L. Comencini.
Made in Italy (id., – epis. Cenerentola) by N. Loy.
Oggi, domani, dopodomani (epis. L'uomo dai cinque palloni by M. Ferreri).
1966 Madamigella di Maupin by M. Bolognini.
L'armata Brancaleone by M. Monicelli.
Non faccio la guerra, faccio l'amore by F. Rossi.
Adulterio all'italiana by P. Festa Campanile.
1967 Hotel by R. Quine.
La notte è fatta per… rubare by G. Capitani.
1968 Il marito è mio e l'ammazzo quando mi pare by P. Festa Campanile.
La matriarca by P. Festa Campanile.
1969 Una ragazza piuttosto complicata by D. Damiani.
Certain, Very Certain, As a Matter of Fact… Probable (Certo, certissimo, anzi… probabile) by M. Fondato.
If It's Tuesday, This Must Be Belgium by M. Stuart.
1970 Con quale amore, con quanto amore by P. Festa Campanile.
1971 Cat O'Nine Tails (Il gatto a nove code) by D. Argento.
1972 Causa di divorzio by M. Fondato.
Un uomo dalla pelle dura by F. Prosperi.
A Murder is a Murder… is a Murder (Un meurtre est un meurtre) by E. Périer.
1973 Cari genitori by E.M. Salerno.
Diary of a Cloistered Nun (Storia di una monaca di clausura) by D. Paolella.
La schiava io ce l'ho e tu no by G. Capitani.
1974 La via dei babbuini by L. Magni.
1975 Take a Hard Ride by A.M. Dawson [A. Margheriti].
1976 Los pajaros de Baden-Baden by M. Camus.
Bruciati da cocente passione by G. Capitani.
Febbre da cavallo by Steno [S. Vanzina].
1978 Per vivere meglio, divertitevi con noi (epis. Il teorema gregoriano) by F. Rossi.
1980 Rag. Arturo De Fanti bancario-precario by L. Salce.
Sunday Lovers – epis. Rome (Les séducteurs – epis. Le carnet d'Armando by D. Risi).
Io e Caterina by A. Sordi.
1981 Miele di donna by G. Angelucci.
1984 Claretta by P. Squitieri.
1989 E non se ne vogliono andare! by G. Capitani.
1990 E se poi se ne vanno? by G. Capitani.

221

Il segreto dell'uomo solitario by E. Guida.
Scandalo segreto by M. Vitti.

VALLI ALIDA

1936 I due sergenti by E. Guazzoni.
1937 Il feroce Saladino by M. Bonnard.
Sono stato io! by R. Matarazzo.
1938 L'ultima nemica by U. Barbaro.
L'ha fatto una signora by M. Mattoli.
L'amor mio non muore… by G. Amato.
La casa del peccato by M. Neufeld.
Mille lire al mese by M. Neufeld.
1939 Ball at the Castle (Ballo al castello) by M. Neufeld.
Assenza ingiustificata by M. Neufeld.
1940 Manon Lescaut by C. Gallone.
The Red Inn (Taverna rossa) by M. Neufeld.
La prima donna che passa by M. Neufeld.
Oltre l'amore by C. Gallone.
1941 Luce nelle tenebre by M. Mattoli.
Piccolo mondo antico by M. Soldati.
L'amante segreta by C. Gallone.
Schoolgirls Diary (Ore 9 lezione di chimica) by M. Mattoli.
1942 Catene invisibili by M. Mattoli.
We the Living (Noi vivi – Addio Kira!) by G. Alessandrini.
Le due orfanelle by C. Gallone.
Stasera niente di nuovo by M. Mattoli.
1943 Laugh Pagliacci (I pagliacci) by G. Fatigati.
T'amerò sempre by M. Camerini.
Apparizione by J. de Limur.
1944 Circo equestre Za-Bum (epis. Il postino; Gelosia) by M. Mattoli.
1945 La vita ricomincia by M. Mattoli.
Il canto della vita by C. Gallone.
1946 Eugenia Grandet by M. Soldati.
1947 The Paradine Case by A. Hitchcock.
1948 The Miracle of the Bells by I. Pichel.
1949 The Third Man by C. Reed.
1950 Walk Softly, Stranger by R. Stevenson.
The White Tower by T. Tetzlaff.
1951 Les miracles n'ont lieu qu'une fois by Y. Allégret.
Last Meeting (Ultimo incontro) by G. Franciolini.
1953 The World Condemns Them (Il mondo le condanna) by G. Franciolini.
The Lovers of Toledon (Les amants de Toledo) by H. Decoin and F. Palacios.
We, the Women – epis. Alida Valli (Siamo donne – epis. Alida Valli) by G. Franciolini.
1954 The Stranger's Hand (La mano delo straniero) by M. Soldati.
The Wanton Countess (Senso) by L. Visconti.
1957 The Cry (Il grido) by M. Antonioni.

La grande strada azzurra by G. Pontecorvo.
This Angry Age / The Sea Wall (in G.B.) (La diga sul Pacifico) by R. Clément.
1958 L'amore più bello / L'uomo dai calzoni corti by G. Pellegrini.
The Night Heaven Fell / Heaven Fell That Night (Les bijoutiers du clai de lune) by R. Vadim.
1959 Signé Arsène Lupin by Y. Robert.
1960 Il peccato degli anni verdi by L. Trieste.
The Horror Chamber of Dr. Faustus / Eyes Without a Face (in G.B.) (Les yeux sans visage) by C. Chabrol.
Le gigolo by J. Deray.
The Carmelites (Les dialogues des Carmélites) by Ph. Agostini and R.L. Bruckberger.
1961 The Happy Thieves by G. Marshall.
The Long Absence (Une aussi longue absence) by H. Colpi.
1962 Disorder (Il disordine) by F. Brusati.
Ophélia by C. Chabrol.
Al otro lado de la ciudad by A. Balcázar.
Four Women for One Hero (Homenaje a la hora de la siesta) by L. Torre-Nilsson.
La fille du torrent by H. Herwig.
The Castilian (El valle de lo espados) by X. Seto.
1963 The Getaway Face by B. Marshall.
El hombre de papel by I. Rodriguez.
1964 L'autre femme by F. Villiers.
1965 Umorismo in nero (epis. La cornacchia by G. Zagni).
1967 Oedipus Rex (Edipo re) by P.P. Pasolini.
1970 The Spider's Stratagem (La strategia del ragno) by B. Bertolucci.
Le champignon by M. Simenon.
1972 L'occhio nel labirinto by M. Caiano.
La prima notte di quiete by V. Zurlini.
Diary of an Italian (Diario di un italiano) by S. Capogna.
1973 It's Not Bad, It's Only a Game (No es nada Mama, solo un juego) by J.M. Forqué.
1974 The Tempter / The Antichrist (in G.B.) (L'Anticristo) by A. De Martino.
1975 La chair de l'orchidée by P. Chéreau.
Cher Victor (Ce cher Victor) by R. Davis.
Il caso Raoul by M. Ponzi.
Lisa and the Devil / House of Exorcism (in G.B.) (La casa dell'esorcismo) by M. Bava.
1976 1900 (Novecento) by B. Bertolucci.
Lejeu du solitaire by J.F. Adam.
1977 The Cassandra Crossing by G. Pan Cosmatos.
Suspiria by D. Argento.

Un cuore semplice by Giorgio Ferrara.
Berlinguer ti voglio bene by G. Bertolucci.
1978 Zoo/zéro by A. Fleisher.
Porco mondo by S. Bergonzelli.
Indagine su un delitto perfetto by A. Leviathan [G. Rosati].
1979 La Luna (id.) by B. Bertolucci.
Suor omicidi by G. Berruti.
Una casa en la fueras by E. Martin.
1980 Sezona mira a Pariju by P. Golubovic.
Inferno (id.) by D. Argento.
1981 La caduta degli angeli ribelli by M.T. Giordana.
Aspern Papers by E. De Gregorio.
1982 Sogni mostruosamente proibiti by N. Parenti.
1985 Segreti segreti by G. Bertolucci.
1986 Le jupon rouge by G. Lefèvre.
1987 A notre regrettable époux by S. Korber.
1991 La bocca by L. Verdone.
Zitti e mosca by A. Benvenuti.
1993 Il lungo silenzio by M. von Trotta.
1994 Bugie rosse by P.F. Campanella.
1995 A Month by the Lake by J. Irvin.

VITTI MONICA

1954 Ridere ridere ridere by E. Anton.
1955 Adriana Lecouvreur by G. Salvini.
1956 Una pelliccia di visone by G. Pellegrini.
1958 Smart Girls (Le dritte) by M. Amendola.
1960 The Adventure (L'avventura) by M. Antonioni.
1960 The Night (La Notte) by M. Antonioni.
1962 The Eclipse (L'eclisse) by M. Antonioni.
1963 The Three Fables of Love – epis. The Hare and the Turtle (Les quatre vérités – epis. La lièvre et la tortue) by A. Blasetti). Naughty, Nutty Chateau (Château en Suède) by R. Vadim.
Sweet and Sour (Dragées au poivre) by J. Baratier.
1964 Red Desert (Deserto rosso) by M. Antonioni.
High Infidelity – epis. The Victim (Alta infedeltà – epis. La sospirosa by L. Salce).
The Flying Saucer (Il disco volante) by T. Brass.
1965 Bambole! – epis. The Soup / Four Kinds of Love – epis. The Soup (in G.B.) (Le bambole – epis. La minestra by F. Rossi).
1966 Modesty Blaise by J. Losey.
Sex Quartet – epis. Fata Sabina (Le fate – epis. Fata Sabina by L. Salce).
1967 Fai in fretta ad uccidermi… ho freddo! by F. Maselli.
A Funny Thing Happened on the Way to the Crusades / The Chastity Belt (in

G.B.) (La cintura di castità) by P. Festa Campanile.
Ti ho sposato per allegria by L. Salce.
1968 La femme écarlate by J. Valère.
The Girl with a Pistol (La ragazza con la pistola) by M. Monicelli.
1969 Help Me, Darling (Amore mio, aiutami!) by A. Sordi.
1970 The Pizza Triangle / Jealousy, Italian Style (in G.B.) (Dramma della gelosia) by E. Scola.
Nini Tirabusciò, la donna che inventò la mossa by M. Fondato.
Le coppie (epis. 1° Il frigorifero by M. Monicelli; 3° epis. Il leone by E. De Sica).
1971 La pacifista by M. Jancsó.
La supertestimone by F. Giraldi.
Noi donne siamo fatte così by D. Risi.
1972 Gli ordini sono ordini by G. Giraldi.
1973 La Tosca by L. Magni.
Teresa la ladra by C. Di Palma.
Polvere di stelle by A. Sordi.
1974 The Phantom of Liberty (Le Fantôme de la liberté) by L. Buñuel.
1975 Midnight Pleasure (A mezzanotte va la ronda del piacere) by M. Fondato.
Lucky Girls (Qui comincia l'avventura) by C. Di Palma.
Duck in Orange Sauce (L'anatra alla'arancia) by L. Salce.
1976 Mimì Bluette… fiore del mio giardino by C. Di Palma.
Basta che non si sappia in giro (1° epis. Macchina d'amore by N. Loy – 3° epis. L'equivoco by L. Comencini).
L'altra metà del cielo by F. Rossi.
1977 La raisonn d'État by A. Cayatte.
1978 My Loves (Amori miei) by Steno [S. Vanzina].
Per vivere meglio, divertitevi con noi (1° epis. Un incontro molto ravvicinato) by F. Mogherini.
1979 An Almost Perfect Affair by M. Ritchie.
Four Tigers in Lipstick – 4° epis. A Mother; 6° epis. Beware of That Two People (Letti selvaggi – 4° epis. Una mamma; 6° epis. Attenzione a quei due) by L. Zampa.
1980 Non ti conosco più amore by S. Corbucci.
The Mystery of Oberwald (Il mistero di Oberwald) by M. Antonioni.
1981 Camera d'albergo by M. Monicelli.
Tango della gelosia by Steno [S. Vanzina].
1982 Io so che tu sai che io so by A. Sordi.
Scusa se è poco by M. Vicario.
1983 Flirt by R. Russo.
1986 Francesca è mia by R. Russo.
1990 Scandalo segreto by M. Vitti.

INDEX OF NAMES